The Time of Our Lives

Also by Peggy Noonan

What I Saw at the Revolution: A Political Life in the Reagan Era

Life, Liberty and the Pursuit of Happiness

*Simply Speaking: How to Communicate Your Ideas
with Style, Substance, and Clarity*

The Case against Hillary Clinton

When Character Was King: A Story of Ronald Reagan

A Heart, a Cross and a Flag

John Paul the Great: Remembering a Spiritual Father

Patriotic Grace: What It Is and Why We Need It Now

The Time
of Our
Lives

Politics, Passions, and Provocations

PEGGY NOONAN

TWELVE

New York   Boston

Twelve
Hachette Book Group
1290 Avenue of the Americas, New York, NY 10104
twelvebooks.com
twitter.com/twelvebooks

Originally published in hardcover and ebook by Twelve in November 2015
First Trade Paperback Edition: May 2017

Twelve is an imprint of Grand Central Publishing. The Twelve name
and logo are trademarks of Hachette Book Group, Inc.

The publisher is not responsible for websites (or their content)
that are not owned by the publisher.

The Hachette Speakers Bureau provides a wide range of authors for
speaking events. To find out more, go to www.hachettespeakersbureau.com
or call (866) 376-6591.

"What the Intrepid Said" (August 6, 1982); "The Royal Wedding"
(July 28, 1981); and "Tennessee Williams Died a Week Ago Today"
(March 4, 1983) reprinted with permission of CBS NEWS.

Library of Congress Cataloging-in-Publication Data has been applied for.

ISBNs: 978-1-4555-6313-5 (trade paperback)

Printed in the United States of America

LSC-C

10 9 8 7 6 5 4 3 2 1

In memory of Bill Safire, Bob Bartley, and Jane Jane

Contents

Preface

When this book was first published, I could see Donald Trump coming but didn't know he'd arrive. The 2016 primaries would not begin for twelve weeks. I took Donald Trump seriously and judged that he just might succeed if we could answer two questions. The first was, does he have the emotional temperament and psychological equipment to ultimately be seen by the American people as a possible president? The second concerned whether he could convince the American people he was in it for America, and not himself. If he did these things, I wrote, he could win, if not, not. He did win. But I'm not sure he ever quite proved he had the temperament and equipment for the office, and I'm not sure he was fully persuasive as to his motivation. And I'm not sure it mattered. I think many Trump supporters reached beyond the circle of traditional candidates because, with no illusions as to his essential nature, they wanted someone to make Washington work by breaking and refiguring it. They wanted him, a living blunt instrument, to get it back to its essential responsibilities. They were hiring a shock to the system. Looking back, one of the most memorable and revealing things I was told during the campaign came from a working man of about 40, black, who was delivering a chair to my apartment. I asked him as I asked everyone in 2016 if he had a sense of where he was going in terms of his choice for president, and if he had, would he tell me? He set down the chair and looked at me as if he were thinking, Is she going to give me a hard time if I give her the wrong answer? (You got a lot of that in 2016.) I think he decided no. In any case he finally replied, "The businessman. We need jobs."

You'll find a lot in here about the rise of Trump and the almost equally epochal rise, on the Democratic side, of Bernie Sanders.

If you are a columnist people ask your favorite columns, and they've asked what columns I found most memorable from this extraordinary cycle. They're in here. But when I think of what I'm proudest of in 2016, I think it is that I was one of those who kept their heads. Not everyone did. Things were polarized and passionate. Living in a time of dramatic history is living under daily pressure; this can have a bad impact on your judgment and limit your insight. But to be helpful you have to retain your journalistic and political composure. You can't let the turbulence of your times rob you of your peace, because then you'll be good for nothing. I thought the signal failure of some who were writing and thinking aloud in 2016 was a refusal or inability to take Trump supporters seriously—to understand how they see and experience America now, and its political system, to hear, ponder and respect their critiques. They couldn't do this because they lost their composure and let their anger eradicate their ability to listen.

I wanted to see clearly, I wanted to give a real-time, week-by-week report of what I was seeing, thinking, concluding. I didn't join a movement, neither NeverTrump nor YayTrump. I just tried to see and report.

The plan going forward: hope for the best, try to name what's working and what's not, and be loyal to what your eyes see—be loyal to your own observations, respect them, share them.

—Peggy Noonan, 2017

Introduction

The title of this book is derived from an observation of the writer Laurens van der Post: "We live not only our own lives but, whether we know it or not, also the life of our time." This is an orienting thought: We are part of the era in which we live, we must fully see this and pitch in. This is often on my mind. So these days is the instruction of Pope John XXIII: "Do not walk through time without leaving worthy evidence of your passage." I saw the quote on the bottom of a street pamphlet when I went to Rome in April 2014 to witness his canonization. I wrote it down on an envelope in my purse, and it's taped now to my office door.

I think that's what all writers are trying to do, leave worthy evidence of their passage. Anyway, these quotes sum up where I am in terms of my work and the attitudes I bring to it.

* * *

Here are some of the times of my life:

My professional life so far has consisted in three parts. I graduated college in 1974, having begun Fairleigh Dickinson University in Rutherford, New Jersey, as a night student and then attending during the day; I was 23 when I graduated. A few months later I began my career at a CBS-owned radio station in Boston, and in 1977 I joined CBS News in New York. In both jobs I functioned mostly as a news gatherer (reporter is too grand a term and was not in any case my title), editor and producer of network radio news broadcasts, and writer of editorials and essays.

In the second part, in the 1980s, I worked in the White House of Ronald Reagan, where I was a speechwriter for the president and, in the decade following, a writer of books and freelance op-ed pieces and essays. The third part began in 2000, when I became a columnist for the *Wall Street Journal*. The parts have some bleed—I have written books and essays during my time at the *Journal*—but hold in terms of general outline. In 2014 a friend with whom I often discuss our work urged me to gather together essays and columns I'd written the past 25 years and put the ones I like best in a collection. And so this book.

You will find in it a bit of walking the hallowed halls of the White House, the plainer but still august halls of CBS News when, as we felt, it was the greatest of the three American news networks, and the wounded streets of New York during 9/11 and after.

* * *

Putting this all together involved hauling from closets and warehouses big white storage boxes that contained what I'd written and rereading every piece. In time I had three huge piles—the yes pile, which was small, the no pile, which was larger, and the maybe pile, which was growing. My editor and friends and I sifted, winnowed and culled.

Rereading what you've written over the years is an interesting experience. You find things you got wrong (they're somehow never a surprise—you always remember what you got wrong), things you wish you could rethink and rewrite, mistakes of tone and tenor. You find things that seem as pertinent now as the day they were published, and things that bring tears to your eyes like the tears you had when you wrote them. You find things you'd forgotten that in retrospect were prescient: In a *Wall Street Journal* column I'd wondered if a man named Osama bin Laden would grimly pop up in the background as Bill Clinton gave his farewell speech in 2000. I was surprised there were only a few pieces I'd forgotten—I thought there would be more—and surprised I felt attached to so many. "That said exactly what I wanted to say," "God, the reaction," "I had a feeling of failure after that one."

As I sifted I discovered some preoccupations I didn't know I had—with British politics and culture, for instance. There's a steady theme of the importance of work itself in the shaping of the meaning of a life. There were more pieces on baseball than I would have guessed. I saw preoccupations of which I am aware: with America, with its culture and with the nature and importance of political leadership. There was a lot on the excitement of politics and the meaning of the greatness game.

Going through the boxes also gave me in a more acute way the sense of an arc. In the CBS boxes I saw scripts that reminded me I had been taught and mentored by the greatest broadcast news journalists of the 20th century. The boxes containing essays I had written in or about the White House reminded me in some new, fresh way of my good fortune in working for one of the greatest presidents of the 20th century, whom Republicans and conservatives see as the last unambiguously successful president of the modern era. Other boxes contained 15 years of work at one of the greatest daily newspapers on the planet, the *Wall Street Journal*.

Part of how I make my living is making speeches, and sometimes in introductions I am called a pioneer. This makes me uncomfortable for a number of reasons, including the fact that "pioneer" sounds pretty old. And yet in those boxes there was a sense of constantly being in pioneer territory—part of the first, great wave of women to enter modern broadcast journalism in the 1970s, among the first to enter politics and the White House in the 1980s, and to write about the experience. Then, in 2000, I joined a pioneer generation of Internet columnists writing not for paper but for screens.

* * *

Over some months I put aside the pieces I liked most, cut and cut again. The last cut is this book.

There are essays and op-ed pieces that appeared in various publications in the 1990s, a lecture given at Harvard, and columns I have written for the *Wall Street Journal*.

Because they predominate a word on how they came about.

In the spring of 2000, Bob Bartley, then and since 1972 the editorial page editor of the *Wall Street Journal*, called me at my home in New York. He said in his plain, spare way that there was this thing called the Internet and the *Journal* was going to have an online editorial page, and would I like to write a weekly column?

Sure, I said. Actually I probably paused a second so I'd seem deliberative but I didn't have to think.

He offered a monthly salary and I asked if we could add 10 percent so I'd be able to tell myself I'd negotiated toughly. He laughed and said sure. We shook hands over the phone, and later he would send me a letter of agreement. We were both sort of careless or lighthearted about it, but that phone call would change and add a great deal to my life.

I said yes so quickly because I had known Bartley for 10 years, had written op-ed pieces for his page and admired him. If he thought it was a good idea it probably was, if he thought I could do it I probably could. Also I knew something about him that I'm not sure he'd made generally known. He famously respected and was drawn to public policy and the political arena—his page was very much a center of the conservative political revival of the 1970s and '80s—but just as much he loved literature and writing. This suggested to me a spaciousness of approach on his part; it suggested it would be all right if I wrote a lot of non-column-like things. I had a sense that this would be important to me.

The first or second time I ever had a long conversation with Bob, about 1991, when we discussed my writing op-eds for the *Journal*, he brought along a paperback copy of a book, Mark Helprin's great novel *A Soldier of the Great War*. Bob had circled a long, descriptive paragraph. He held it toward me, tapped it with his finger, said nothing. But his eyes shined. He was saying: This is what I value, this is what I want. I took it as a charge: Write for our page but don't feel bound or constricted by thoughts of traditional form, approach, subject matter. Be yourself, like Mark.

The offer came at the right time for me personally. I had spent the previous 10 years working at home and bringing up a son on my own. He was now 13 and at school from 8 to 4 or later. I'd been offered columns when he was little by other papers and a syndicate, but I had the sense it would be too intense a professional life for me, too demanding in a daily sense when weighed along with being a mother. Better to be more low key and see if I could make a living writing books with long deadlines.

Now I could still work at home but I could go into the world more. In 1991 there was a book that made a particularly strong impression on me, in part because it told me something I knew I needed to hear. It was *American Cassandra* by Peter Kurth, a biography of the great midcentury newspaper columnist Dorothy Thompson. She was a real world-changer and had a big public life—traveling to the front, giving radio addresses, exhorting America to join the Second World War. She was a friend and headache to presidents. Her only child, a son with Sinclair Lewis, got lost in the shuffle. While saving the world she forgot to save him. In time this caused her great grief. My son was almost four. Message received. Get the children thing right, as Jackie Onassis once said, and everything else will fall into place. I set myself to doing that and things fell into place.

But also, and I should have said this earlier, Bob's offer sounded great, like the perfect and obvious next step, just one I hadn't thought to move toward until he called. But how wonderful to have a regular place and space into which to pour my thoughts. How wonderful to finally have a home base, and at one of the world's great newspapers. How wonderful to have a column at one of the few mainstream entities with an editorial page where conservative thoughts would not be received as obnoxious but welcome.

I would write only online, but that too had its advantages. It was low profile so if I failed, my failure would be a quiet one. If I didn't like it I could withdraw pretty much unnoticed.

*   *   *

A few weeks later Bob and I had another conversation in which we covered the particulars. How long, I asked, should each column be? Bob paused and said actually he didn't know. It was the Internet so there weren't any space limitations. "I guess as long as you want," he said. In time this would cause stress to the man who would become and continues as my editor, the writer James Taranto, for I took Bob at his word. From my first piece I proceeded as if 1,000 words just weren't enough for the *Journal*, it deserved more; less and I wasn't earning my way. This resulted in a lot of 3,000- and 5,000-word columns. But James was quick and thorough and made it work.

What was burdensome, he later told me, was my sense of deadlines. Bob had said each column would be posted online at 12:01 a.m. the day the column would run. What time, I had asked, should I file? Bob said, "I don't know. I guess before midnight, at some point." I'm afraid I took him literally there, too, and sometimes filed my 4,000-word pieces at 10 or 11 p.m. I'm amazed now James didn't kill me. It took me a while, a few years, to figure everything out and get the pieces shorter and the edit time longer.

I would start in the summer of 2000, during the national party conventions. What I remember was not my first piece going up but that I got an email from Bob a day or so after. He wrote one word: "Wow." From the taciturn Bob that was a lot. It was everything. I don't think he ever sent a reaction to one of my pieces again, ever, but that first was enough to propel me on happily for now 15 years.

*   *   *

Recently a friend, a fellow columnist, asked me if at the beginning I was afraid I wouldn't have a thought each week. I was startled and said no, that never occurred to me, I guess I figured there's always something going on. He asked if I set about to develop a "voice," a style. I was surprised again, and told him no, I hadn't given it a thought. Now he was surprised. He had worked hard to sound in his column exactly the way he sounded when he spoke, he said. I said it never occurred to me you could do it any other way. I had grown up reading Jimmy Breslin and Murray Kempton: They sounded exactly how they talked, which I would later find out in person, when meeting them, but somehow knew long before. After I had worked for Ronald Reagan I wondered if I would have trouble refinding my own sound, so used was I to working in his. But soon after I wrote my first book, and saw it was no struggle. You write as you, and sound like you, because you are: you.

Nor did I think about what kind of columnist I'd be, which is odd because there are a lot of different ways to be a columnist. I had a wonderful unconsciousness of various roles and approaches and didn't analyze or ponder them. A few months ago a highly regarded columnist announced to a luncheon group that when he sits down to write, he sort of tears open his shirt in his mind and puts on his

Superman cape and sets himself to playing the part of a passionate, crusading columnist. He had to make believe he was somebody else before he could write as himself. He realized he'd said something startling and turned to me. Don't you do that? he demanded. No. But writing, I agreed, is hard.

I admire columnists because they operate under constant stress—what's the topic, the story, the idea this week? Where's the data, the evidence, the quote? What's the insight? They're doing what they do in public and when they fail will fail publicly. They feel the necessity to be original, they're working essentially alone, and none of them can ever say "The muse didn't come," or "I'm blocked." There's no crying in baseball and no blockage in journalism: You have deadlines, you meet them.

As to the many ways to be a columnist, you can focus on one area—foreign affairs, local city politics—or train your eye on whatever's going by. You can limn the known facts of a question, list the pros and cons, note that only time will tell. There are great reporter-columnists who are out in America finding stories with national implications or out in the world seeing what cameras can't tell you. There are those who borrow from their lives for their material and those who are all outward, not inward. It was said once of the wife of a prominent Washington intellectual that she had one job, carrying his head around and getting it to the next symposium. Some columnists are like that, traveling heads. There is the pure information columnist—data from the campaign trail, the latest from a pollster, a quote from a political scientist—who presents his reporting and, at the end, asks questions that reflect a certain philosophical, intellectual or ideological bent. There are liberal columnists who see no enemies to the left, and conservatives with no enemies to the right. There are mischievous wits, philosopher kings, village explainers and great arguers for a cause.

I did what was natural, which is what I had already been doing in books and op-eds: *Here is what I think and why. Here is what I'm seeing, here's what I think is important.* I would give my judgments in real time, explain my reasoning, make a case. I would not limit my subject matter; whatever is interesting to me would probably be interesting to at least some readers. (I learned that at CBS; I'll tell you about it soon.) I would be direct, as clear as possible.

We're all experiencing history each day; why not name what you think you are seeing?

Some columnists don't declare their essential political persuasion. I already had in the Reagan years and my writing since, and would of course continue. My general view is that it's not polite to try to hide where you stand or shade what you're about. At the same time I understand and respect the desire not to be categorized and appreciate the fact that not everyone has a fully formed political philosophy, or wants one.

That I am politically conservative labels me, can be alienating for some readers and can allow my views to be dismissed—"That's what they think." It is complicated, too, in other ways. We live in an intensely polarized time. If you are conservative you are considered by other conservatives, rightly, to be part of a minority within the mainstream press. And you never let down your minority group, it's poor form. But what if you have an opinion that is heterodox, against the grain or surprising? Your readers may not like it. You let down the team, you're a coward and a cur.

But I can't do my job—I could never do my job!—unless I say what I really see and think. And sometimes what I see and think *is* against the grain or heterodox. You can't at that point bow to the feelings of the crowd, even when the crowd is full of people you like, and sometimes love. The minute you do that you're a hack, not in the good way of working scribe but in the bad way of slob. So you do it your way. And then duck.

Bob asked for a title. I thought for a few days and looked at the names of other columns, really wonderful ones—"Liberties" by Maureen Dowd, "Wonder Land" by Dan Henninger. Mine would be "Declarations."

* * *

I want to take a minute to talk about my view on writing. To me it is a full-body exercise: What you write comes from your brain, heart, spirit, soul and psyche, you hold nothing back, all parts are engaged. When you're writing you give the creative part of your brain full sway, you let it dominate, you don't let your critical side mug it or slow it down. Later, in editing, you bring your critical self to the fore, question the assertion, kill the aside. But the point is you give your writing everything you have at the moment you're doing it and rethink when the page has cooled.

I have always thought writing must somehow show great energy, the prime force of life. You are asking people for five minutes of their time to read you. They're busy. You have to show them from the top that you're engaged, that you mean it, that there's something you think is important that should be said. You don't "grab them by the collar"—I don't know how to do that and am never sure what it means since one person's collar-grabber is another person's snooze, and everyone in America is in any case tired of having their collar grabbed—but you do have to be clear, serious and not waste time huffing and puffing.

Nietzsche, in 1882, did "10 Rules for Writers," confining himself to the subject of style. I saw the list about a year ago when a friend sent it from a culture site and instantly recognized and responded to four points. His first rule: "Of prime necessity is life: a style should *live*." Yes, what you write must be alive. He said, "The richness of life reveals itself through a richness of gestures. One must learn to feel everything—the length and retardation of sentences...the choice of words, the pausing, the sequence of arguments—like gestures."

This, too, seems to me true though I never would have thought of it in precisely this way. I do something with what I write, always have, that I think is unusual. I read it from the top in my mind, with my voice though I'm not actually speaking. I do this over and over. If I stumble—if something stops me, if something makes me lose the thought I was trying to develop, if my mind wanders or jolts away—I go over it again to figure out what the problem is and how to refigure things to get it right.

Another: "Style ought to prove that one *believes* in an idea; not only that one thinks it but also *feels* it." Yes, exactly, completely true. It matters that it's not all dry and only cerebral, it matters that an idea is so real to you and so true to you that you feel it, and try also to communicate that feeling.

"Strategy on the part of the good writer of prose consists of choosing his means for stepping close to poetry but never stepping into it." Yes. I'm not even sure in a practical sense what this means but yes, I know what he means. Don't get too fancy, too show-offy, too obscure, too reaching for the exquisite or unusual. That just removes you from your purpose. It's a column, not a metaphysical exercise.

*   *   *

My editor said here that you want to see my writing. I don't think you do. Do you? I am writing all week in that I am thinking all week and making notes on thoughts, conversations, events, observations. By Wednesday I usually know my topic and have begun typing my notes into a file. Thursday all day I write the column, and file about 5 p.m.

It is my belief that deep down no writer knows precisely what he's doing and is simply thinking, thinking, thinking—testing a thought and writing it down as quickly as possible so it doesn't blot.

Wherever I have lived I've always had a desk (in the living room,

bedroom, TV room or now in a small home office). The desk is usually covered with pictures, drawings, mementos, quotes. The walls
are covered in pictures of friends and people I admire, quotes tacked
and taped up and some framed honorary doctorates to impress the
stupid, including me, and in a way to impress my ancestors: We did
OK.

I look at the blank screen, the antic blinking cursor, glance at
my notes, put my hands on the keyboard and go. I become good
at the point my interest in what I'm trying to say overwhelms
anxiety about how to say it. Desire to make a point defeats self-
consciousness and lets things begin. "The words flow" is not something that happens to me. They never flow. They come out, are not
right, are corrected. Or they come out right and are corrected into
something inferior, at which point I try to remember what I originally wrote.

While I work I listen to the news on TV or to movie music, the
scores of films. This has been my habit for a quarter century. Why
movie music? Because it is meant to help a story along and not be
the story itself. If you're listening to George Gershwin or Stephen
Sondheim or a show or opera or album you love it's too powerful,
you'd listen and stop writing. Movie music is moving but doesn't
take you away from your work. All my life I have been moved by
movie music—I mean from a young child watching endless repeats
of 1930's and 1940's movies on "Million Dollar Movie," broadcast
on a local New York television station.

*   *   *

People ask the difference between column writing, book writing
and speechwriting. In one sense they're not different: You're writing. You're laying pipe only the pipes are thoughts, as John Gregory
Dunne once said. But the best definition of writing I ever heard
came from the great historian David McCullough, who said, in

conversation, "To write is to think, and to write well is to think well." You think about what you want to say, you clarify it, question it, then say it.

A book demands a subject or theme that can be sustained over a few hundred pages. A book allows you to fully play out a thought, explain your ideas, establish a thesis, create a world the best you can. When I wrote *What I Saw at the Revolution*, my first book, I was trying to capture a whole world, what it was like to be in Washington, in the White House, at a dramatic time in history and see it truly but from the vantage point of an unimportant person, or an unknown one. It couldn't have been a column or an essay—a world takes time.

A book has a porous deadline. It's not due at 5 p.m. Thursday, it's due next April. This allows you to smooth out your work. Smoothing out for me means getting most quickly and directly to the point. A book is a more finished product but a less immediate one.

A column is more immediate but in terms of space more confined. You have a given number of words to introduce a subject or subjects and convey your views. Columns are more distinguished by what you leave out. Their immediacy is both a boon and a curse. You're in the fray, your thought is a provocation, maybe an addition, but you may get it wrong, and so wrong that two days later you're sitting there with your head in your hands, moaning. When you get it right and you think you've added to the conversation, even expanded it, that is satisfying in a way that is hard to explain. But you feel you made a difference.

A speech is a best-case case for somebody else, said as you think he or she would say it. What you bring as a writer and thinker is what you believe your principal agrees with and believes. You can take chances. If it's not what they think, they'll cut it. (There's a chapter here on the writing of the Challenger speech; it includes a story of taking a chance based on a hunch that turned out to be right.) If you are writing for a president or major political figure, the impact of your work will be broad and deep—the words will be remembered, because everything a president says is historically important and is heard.

But at the end of the day, it's all writing.

*   *   *

I want to go back to my early time writing a column on the Internet. As I said, I did not understand at the time that I was joining a pioneer generation of columnists, one whose readers read them only on screens, not in a paper. I was present at the creation of a new way of being a columnist. (At the same time, just after I began, a long-time syndicated columnist welcomed me to the ranks by noting I'd joined the last generation that would be able to make a living writing columns, because of the increasing number of voices freely available on a multiplying number of Web sites and platforms. So I'd be both a pioneer and one of the last of the Mohicans.)

For perhaps a century a newspaper column was usually 800 or 900 words long, and was subject to strictures and limitation in terms of space and to some degree subject matter. If the columnist pleased or angered readers he would get letters. A reader would sit down, write a letter, find out where to send it, make out the envelope, get a stamp, walk down the street, mail it. It would be a private communication between the reader and the columnist.

In the new world I could write as long as I liked about pretty much anything I liked, within the knowledge that this was going onto the site of the *Wall Street Journal,* which is not an antic publication and which, like the *Times* and other what-used-to-be-called broadsheets, has an appropriate sense of its own dignity.

But letters were now comments, and they were immediate. If the column went up at 12:01, the first comment was online at 12:04, and would be followed by many more. No one had to get the piece of paper, find the stamp. They just had to hit reply and send. And the comments were public, listed under a column one after another, on comment threads. And more often than not the commenters wrote under anonymous names.

I had been on the Web long enough to know this in the abstract, but when I first saw the comments under one of my columns all I could think was: Wow.

What I was looking at was a whole instant community. Hundreds and then thousands of people wrote in to agree or disagree, to say "great piece" and "stupid dumb article," to add experiences, insights, witticisms. And they didn't just disagree with me, they disagreed with each other and had flame wars. It was all kind of startling and wonderful.

I'd been online for a while so my personal email address was kind of out there, and people would write me personally after each column. There was a woman who, early on, wrote to say she hoped I would have a brain aneurysm as that's what people with views such as mine deserve. This was, in those early days, so surprising to me that I actually wrote back and told her it's not nice to write someone and say you wish them dead or disabled. She wrote back explaining why I deserved crippling. I actually wrote back, she responded. Fifteen years later we're still writing. I believe, though she's never quite said it, that she no longer wishes me dead, and I kind of love her. She's passionate and sincere—she's a good woman. She'll write and say she hopes I have a nice weekend and I'm wrong about Hillary and should be fired.

There is the man who'd write every few weeks, denouncing my views and vowing never to read me again. A month later I'd write something that got him mad—"I will never read you again." Months would pass, I'd write something enraging, he'd announce, clearly agitated, "I'm done reading you!" I finally wrote and said he's going to make himself sick if he keeps reading me, he's got to stop. He stopped writing. Then a few months later: "I'll never read you again!"

In time I would be the focus of email swarms arranged by political groups and encouraged by left- and right-wing Web sites— hundreds and thousands of comments would be launched my way, like arrows at Agincourt. I'd write something critical of George W. Bush and get swarmed with thousands of denunciations and insults; Hillary Clinton's people would do the same, and Sarah Palin's.

*   *   *

The new world allowed me to have better, more immediate knowledge than James Reston or Walter Lippmann were ever afforded that there are real human beings out there who are reading your thoughts, absorbing them and responding to them, and who through this come to have an actual relationship with you. It allowed me to have a relationship with them.

The Web is personal. It is not detached or distanced. It is immediate. You are a person talking to and hearing from other persons. You have a real and actual dialogue going, not some phony conversation in which a politician nods while staged supporters mouth pre-planned words but a real back-and-forth.

*   *   *

Some writers know who they're writing to, some don't. When my column was no longer only online but went into the newspaper, in 2006, I started hearing from a lot of couples who said, "We read you together in the morning." This made me happy. It also gave me a picture of who I'm writing to. It's Saturday morning, the *Weekend Journal* has hit the stoop. There's a couple and they're having coffee in the kitchen. It's only an accident that I don't know them, just a matter of circumstance that we're not friends. They're involved with life, have many responsibilities. They're starting the day with the papers, turn to the op-ed page, give me a minute. I tell them what I'm thinking. Sometimes I sort of imagine their disagreement or questioning, and try to address it. I almost want to start with the words "Hi, everyone." (My friend Kate O'Beirne once told me she'd like it if I began a paragraph with "As I was telling Kate..." I never managed that, but it is a chapter title of this book.)

* * *

I want to note a special challenge the Internet presents to both writers in general and women in particular.

Writers have to proceed through life with an attitude of openness. They have to be available to thoughts, views, sensations. You have to let the experience of life sort of wash over and through you to do your job. But if you are on the net and writing regularly—especially about politics and culture, but not only—you are operating in a highly dramatic, immediate, emotional, partisan and ideological environment. It's a sparky place full of attack and defend. And you can't as a writer be so open as you walk forward that the invective and dislike enter your head and heart and disfigure your thinking. You can't let your critics shape your conception of yourself. You have to try to not let it enter you...while still being open to what people are saying and life is doing. I think this is a big challenge for all writers now.

So is the fact—this is a stylistic challenge—that irony, the wry aside, and certain kinds of satire have become dangerous for writers. If Jonathan Swift were writing now he'd be pilloried coast to coast as the man who believes we should solve the problem of hunger by eating babies. I'm not sure an H. L. Mencken would survive the new environment of literalism, decontextualizing and cultural correctness.

I also believe—I have experienced—that the world of public

disputation is harder and more challenging for women. One reason is that our culture has become grosser, and so people feel freer to be gross. The other is the special excitement, the particular and odd sense of provocation with which people respond, still, to a woman who puts herself forward to speak her views. Both Hillary Clinton and Sarah Palin are absolutely correct when they speak of the different, higher bars women in public face. I think of it as almost primordial: When cavemen were sitting in a circle 'round the fire grunting over where to hunt antelopes tomorrow, they probably started waving their clubs in highest anger when a particularly outspoken cavewoman voiced her opinion.

What women inspire among their detractors on the Internet is often highly personal, intimate, and violative. Every woman in public life knows this. A few years ago there was a regular reader who had my email address and sometimes wrote. I saw after a while that his musings had turned dark: He'd begun obsessing about another columnist in a way that made me uneasy. I contacted her and forwarded the man's emails, thinking her paper might have some sort of security apparatus. She wrote back immediately. No, she said, her paper offers no protection. A stalker had one night a year before found her home, rung her doorbell and demanded conversation. He was the same stalker, she said, who'd harassed another woman columnist.

Women aren't better columnists than men, men aren't better than women, but when you judge their work it's not unfair to factor in that women are operating under a degree of difficulty and a host of challenges their male counterparts in general are not.

*   *   *

All columnists both are critics and have critics. My columns have come under criticism in two general areas. The first is that I do not tell people how to think about issues but tell them instead how I think. This is true, and I can only say that as an approach it is in line with my nature and I suppose temperament. When I tell you my view it puts the onus on me—here's my opinion, here's why I hold it. I would be embarrassed to feel that I was speaking from some supposed height, lecturing, or imitating a detachment I do not feel. The second criticism is that I tell people how I feel and even write of how *they* feel, or I believe they feel. There's truth in that, too, but here's how I see it. We come at politics and cultural issues, all of us, as full individuals—thinking, judging, weighing, feeling, taking it all in. It seems to me both limited and unrealistic to concentrate solely on the supposed data points and synthetically prepared statements regarding a case when in fact politics is a full-body exercise involving all parts of the human being—mind, soul, intellect, emotions.

I have been told there are some within my general profession who see my work as feminine and womanly. I hope by that they mean interesting and clear, but perhaps not. There are writers who believe their impenetrability and lack of liveliness is proof of their gravity. "I'm boring because I'm serious." No, you're boring because you're boring. If you were serious you'd be interesting. Here I take the opportunity to upbraid them. I think they should be more serious and work harder—hone it down, make it matter, take a chance—instead of typing whatever enters their little noggins and then swanning about as public personages at symposia. I hope that wasn't too emotional.

* * *

I think columnists—probably all writers but certainly columnists—are like baseball players in that they have good seasons and bad. They have hot streaks where they can't not hit the ball. They have cold streaks: *whiff, whiff, whiff.* But baseball players know they're in a streak when it's happening, because of the stats. Writers only know in retrospect. I could see this as I went through the boxes from the warehouse. Columnists have different seasons in another way, too. Sometimes for a time you're more soulful, sometimes more indignant or no-nonsense, sometimes fiery or amused. And you're not in control of any of this and it lasts as long as it lasts, and again it's only clear in retrospect.

* * *

I suppose the columnist who made the greatest impression on me is William Safire of the *New York Times*, who befriended me when I entered the Reagan White House. He had once been a speechwriter for Richard Nixon, so we had speechwriting in common. He urged me many times to be a columnist. He was more ambitious for me than I was.

His writing style didn't make a huge impression on me: It was his own, breezy, occasionally impassioned, more often marked by a light touch. He was sometimes unjust, sometimes scrupulously balanced. What really made an impression on me was Bill himself. He was funny, affectionate, practical about his work, not at all pretentious. He gave me the best advice I ever got as a writer, which is never to feel guilty about how much you read. Even though you're enjoying it doesn't mean you're just having fun—you're doing what you have to do to do what you do. When I worked for President Reagan and he was going to a battlefield I'd read 20 books about what happened there. People would come to my office, I'd be reading, they'd tap on the open door and say, "I'm glad you're not busy." Most of what I read wouldn't wind up in the speech, but I needed to know as much as possible to write with a feeling of some authority—and I needed to know what I was leaving out, and why. I had to leave it out with confidence, not out of ignorance. Anyway, Bill told me all that was good, and his advice has helped me every single day since 1984.

Safire had a good attitude toward his work. He loved to write, loved to mix it up, loved being part of the action. Once during the

Clinton administration, during one of its scandals, he called Hillary Clinton a "congenital liar." President Clinton said he'd like to punch him in the nose. Safire posed with a pair of boxing gloves. It was the talk of Washington. Bill loved every minute of it. I am less pugnacious than Bill—I like to write about things that are happening now so to a degree I like being in the thick of it, but I am not actually tickled by offending people. Sometimes I write tough criticisms. But deep in my heart I always hope I'm wrong, that it's not as bad as I say it is, that there are mitigating circumstances no one knows about, facts few can see, reasons for the bad decision that make it explicable.

* * *

Here I'd like to mention something connected to my writing that came to me forcefully while I was opening the big white boxes containing my work. One of them was full of scripts and news reports I had written at CBS in New York from 1977 through 1983. As I went through them I was conscious in a new way of what those years had been for me, what I had learned and been taught.

I was immensely fortunate to be at a CBS station and then the network in the 1970s. I was allowed to become part of something new and untried, but also to benefit from something old and hallowed. Through the first I got confidence, in the second some mastery of a craft.

At the station, WEEI in Boston, we were inventing news radio— local and national news on a 24-hour cycle seven days a week. It was brand-new. I was just out of college when I arrived, and felt lucky not only to have a job in the recession of the mid-1970s but to have it in more or less the field I wanted, which was writing.

For a long time I worked the overnight, from midnight to 8 a.m. I would write, from wire copy, a top-of-the-hour broadcast for an anchorman hunched over a microphone in a little studio down the hall from the newsroom. I also spent half my shift in another small studio on the phone, taping interviews with people in the news. Mostly that meant tracking down and interviewing by phone the person who witnessed the plane crash at a local airport, or the relative of a victim of a crime. Sometimes, early in the morning, it meant interviewing a congressman or city council member. My interviews were occasionally good but mostly serviceable. I did my homework, always tried to understand the pending legislation that might be voted on that day, but I rarely grilled them or forced them off course. I really admired those young journalists who did, who could. But I was always just grateful to get the interview, and let them make the case they wanted to make. I was also a little shy in interviews, and couldn't believe a congressman was talking to me. I was stronger as a writer, and eventually wrote the station's editorials.

But what I learned at WEEI is that you can really write something and it gets edited and goes on the air and others hear it and actually maybe it makes some kind of difference; you can interview someone and the sound of their answers goes on the air, and maybe their answers clear something up.

I didn't know I could do that. It was good, in my mid-20s, to learn I could.

When I went down to CBS News in New York, in 1977, my job for a long time was pretty much the same—interviews, writing morning broadcasts—but now on a network level. I was still on the overnight and still in a small space, Studio 5 at the Broadcast Center, but the interviews now were on national and international stories, and because CBS was a mighty network most of my calls were returned.

So I'm doing interviews at night and writing news shows early in the morning, and it was there, at CBS, that I really learned the essentials of what professional journalists do.

And here's the thing: I didn't fully understand this but I was being taught by masters.

At WEEI we'd all been young, recent college graduates. But at the network my colleagues, the radio editors and writers and anchors—were mostly veterans of the business. And some of them were great men. They taught me how to understand a story, how to tell it, how to do it clearly, in little space.

Here's an example of my education, a small one but one that provided an insight that has guided me since.

In 1980 the Mount St. Helens volcano in Washington State erupted. It really blew, with an eruption plume that was 15 miles high; it spread ash along a dozen states.

It was my job, over those days, to call everyone I could think of nearby or in surrounding towns to do audiotape interviews about what they had seen, experienced, and what was the latest. I'd record the interview and then cut the tape down to 10 or 20 seconds of someone describing a house sliding down a hill. Telephone operators still existed, and when I ran out of local police and fire departments, I'd actually dial an operator, ask to be connected to the Mount St. Helens area code, and then mention to that operator that I worked at CBS and could she help me figure out who to talk to on this big story. More often than not the operator would be sympathetic and helpful and say something like "My cousin works at City Hall a few towns over from the volcano, you could try him." Then she'd connect me.

One morning a week or so into the story I tracked down a guy who knew what was going on near the volcano. He didn't have that much to say and was dryly factual, which was fine. Then, as we chatted—I had learned to chat in interviews!—he told me actually the biggest problem right now is the long lines at the post office. Why's that, I said. Because, he said, everyone in town was picking up volcanic ash and putting it in envelopes and mailing it to their friends. The ash was slipping out of the envelopes and clogging the machines. I found this comic and lovely—how do we respond to

disasters? We get mementos!—but I thought it insufficiently serious
for inclusion in a sober network news broadcast so I didn't give it to
my editor to use.

Soon after, chatting in the newsroom, I mentioned it to our
morning anchor, a young man named Charles Osgood, who was
famous for writing the news with cleverness and wit. (He sometimes
turned news stories into poems. When Mao Tse Tung's wife was
arrested and anathematized during the Chinese Cultural Revolution, he reported it in a poem that began: "Old Chiang Ching / Is a
mean old thing."

The minute I told him about the post office, Charlie's ears perked
up. Put that on top, he said.

I was startled. I thought it was just a little story that would be
interesting to us. But Charles knew something interesting to us is
likely to be interesting to everyone. And though it was a small anecdote it said a lot about the mood around Mount St. Helens right
now: It tells us the emergency is over and human nature has kicked
in. Small details add up to big pictures. He explained all this, and
the lesson stayed with me.

There was something else, a great unplanned gift. In the CBS
newsroom in those days there were a bunch of old, semicurmud-
geonly correspondents and editors, and they taught me by reading,
editing and rewriting my hourly news broadcasts. When they had
time they would explain why this sentence was too long, that phrase
open to different interpretation. For many years I had been a writer
who wrote most comfortably for the eye. I had spent three years in
college writing features and editorials for the student newspaper, and
naturally wrote for readers. But the old men in the newsroom had
made their careers writing for listeners, for people absorbing information not through the eye but the ear. They knew how to write
words in the air, which is different from words on the page. More
than that, they communicated a deeply adult sense of excitement

about the gravity of news and the importance of reliable and trusted information: We can tell people what they need to know, we can actually help them understand the world better, see it clearer. They were thoughtful—this was a mission to them, a vocation—and had depth. "We have the ability to paint a big picture here—here's your paintbrush, paint well!"

And here's how they learned what they knew: They were the Murrow boys. They were the men who, with Edward R. Murrow, invented broadcast news. That was Eric Sevareid walking through the room checking out the wires, that was Charles Collingwood on his way to his office upstairs, that's Winston Burdett on the phone, that was Douglas Edwards in Studio 2. Richard C. Hottelet, Dallas Townsend. Some of them had literally been through the war with Murrow.

To me they were ancient—56! 64! Some were no longer considered at the top of their game, some hadn't succeeded at TV, some had never wanted to leave radio for TV. I was getting the last of them. They went over my copy, x-d out the mess of the second sentence, connected the first with the third, made it all mean something important. And in time, with their guidance and almost by osmosis, I learned a great craft.

In 1981 I became the writer of Dan Rather's daily radio commentary—which was, essentially, a daily five-minute column. And in 1984 I left CBS to go to Washington to work with Ronald Reagan. I was able to do both jobs in some part because of what I'd been taught by the men who helped invent broadcasting with Ed Murrow.

Did I know it at the time? Yes, to at least some degree. I told people of it, wrote of it. But I appreciate the luck of it more deeply now. (And I think, as I see my generation take the buyout, no, no, you must stay, you've got to teach the 27-year-olds what you know!)

Bonus anecdote:

I covered my first national political convention for CBS in 1980. I cannot remember where it was and I actually don't remember if it was the Democratic or Republican convention. I remember only this: I went early, before the convention opened. I walked out onto the huge, cavernous, empty convention floor, all my credentials around my neck, excited and nervous to be there. In the room were electricians and carpenters doing last-minute work. There was one reporter, standing by himself. It was Eric Sevareid. I had not until that moment met him. He looked my way, saw the credentials of our shop, nodded. I walked over and introduced myself. He asked if it was my first time covering a convention, I said yes. He said the first time he'd covered a convention for CBS was in 1948, and he too was so excited he went early, and there was no one there in the hall but one other reporter—H. L. Mencken. Eric had introduced himself. Mencken welcomed him and put out his hand.

"Welcome," Eric Sevareid said to me. And he put out his hand.

During the 2012 Republican convention I was on a *Face the Nation*, live from the floor the day before the convention started. I was navigated onto the set, over cables and past cameras, by a young producer. His name was Walt Cronkite IV. It was his first convention for CBS. I told him my story of Sevareid and Mencken.

"Welcome," I said, and put out my hand.

*   *   *

Well, we should get back to the book.

It is customary in introductions to collections to write of how, when and by what process one derived one's philosophical approach and views. I've written about those things over the years—you'll find some in this book—and don't suppose more is needed.

But I want to mention something I've never written of because it bears on some of the themes in this book, and animates one of them.

Regular readers know I speak often of my concerns about

modern America's culture, by which I mean the America we see all around us each day and experience as human beings. I grew up in what in my first book I called the old America, but in a relatively unprotected condition in that country. I survived to become myself because that old country was a more coherent place that, to a greater degree than now, knew what it was about.

So the story. I should say I was from a big, working-class family that was highly stressed and turbulent. We had moved when I was 5 years old from Brooklyn, New York, where I was born, to Massapequa, Long Island, and lived in that area until I was 16, when we moved to New Jersey.

Every summer when I was a child, from age 6 to age 13, I was sent, often for long stretches by myself, to stay at the home of two great-aunts in Selden, New York. Selden then, in the 1950s and early '60s, was almost unpopulated. It had woods and flat, barren fields. (It is now a Long Island suburb full of houses and people; then it was empty.)

It was very lonely. My two great-aunts, Etta and Jane Jane, were in their 70s, which in those days was ancient and certainly seemed so to me. Etta was a former cook in private homes in Manhattan and Jane Jane was a former lady's maid. Both were retired. Neither had had children. They were Irish immigrants, Etta a widow and Jane Jane never married.

Etta was a deeply distracted woman who didn't much like children. I remember her as almost completely silent. She would sit at her small, oilcloth-covered kitchen table and chain smoke without inhaling, with a faraway look in her eye. I remember her saying *whissshhtt* for "go away" and "bad cess" of those she didn't like; I remember her speaking often in Gaelic, the language she preferred for her sparse comments.

Jane Jane was equally distracted but also more ethereal—she recited poetry aloud—and viewed children kindly. She was kind to me and to the extent she could when nearby attempted to fill a parent's role. She would tell me things that had happened in history. There was a sense they were still happening in her imagination. She was religious and took me each Sunday to church.

Etta and Jane Jane didn't get along so there was a lot of silence in the house.

There was nothing to do in Selden. Every day was lonely and the nights were terrible. The little, two-bedroom house was on Sanitarium Road, which led to an old sanitarium for people with tuberculosis. It had been shut down and was now a hollow, spooky building that looked like a fortress. There was one family within walking distance, the Klines, less than a mile away, but they were not always available and they too had stresses.

I remember walking by myself in the woods and poking sticks at dead birds. I remember being fascinated by moss, and how mica shined in stones. I remember talking with Jane Jane and hearing about Woodrow Wilson, the *Lusitania*, and the Fourteen Points. She thought Wilson a great man who had saved Europe. At night I would get into bed with her in her little room with its little window and its bureau with pictures of the Sacred Heart. You would think sleep would be a relief after the empty days, but Jane Jane was a bit of a mystic and like most mystics had a great interest in the subject of death. To keep me company and talk me to sleep she would tell me of things like the Warning Signs of Death. She had no awareness that this might be frightening for a child; she meant only to be interesting and share what was on her mind.

She would tell me that when you are about to die a great warm mist suddenly comes over you like a dense cloud. This was Long Island in the 1950s, without air conditioning. It was 90 degrees at night. I'd listen and suddenly be bathed in sweat—the mist! My heart would race, rivulets of sweat running down my head—more mist! I couldn't take the blanket off because another warning sign of death is that a spirit touches your hand or foot, so I had to keep them covered. Another warning sign of death: Suddenly the ticking of a clock becomes very loud. I'd suddenly hear the clock on the bureau: It was ticking like a drum!

It was all fascinating and harrowing, and I promise she had no idea. In time she'd fall peacefully asleep. I would wait until she did, creep out of bed and go into the next room where I'd put the TV on low and watch it for hours—network dramas, old movies, Jack Paar. It was all jolly or thoughtful or hopeful, representative of future life, adult life. It was comforting.

But here is the thing. Etta and Jane Jane didn't have much, not a phone or a car, couldn't drive, were off in that lonely place in the house in a field. But Jane Jane understood a child needs at least something to look forward to. So once a week she would take me to the big stores in Riverhead, the Suffolk county seat, 25 miles away, or to Centereach, just five miles away.

She would announce the trip in the morning, put on her thin cotton housedress, put a black wool hat on her white-haired head, take her black purse and lead me out to Sanitarium Road. And we'd stand there. And when a car or truck came by we'd flag it down. Someone would stop and Jane Jane would explain in her Irish accent, with her reedy voice, that we needed to go to the stores and would you be going to Riverhead? They'd look at us, shake their heads, sort of shrug and say, "Sure. Come on in."

And they'd drive us, usually all the way. Jane Jane would entertain them with stories of the *Titanic* and World War I, both of which had captured her imagination when she was new to America. (Her arrival here, at the beginning of the second decade of the 20th century, coincided with the invention of mass media—radio, the movies, a million newspapers. Everything she absorbed then, everything blasted into her through the airwaves and the headlines, was on her mind for the rest of her life.)

We'd get to downtown Riverhead, or Centereach, and walk around in the air conditioning of the stores. We'd do almost every one of them—clothing stores, hardware store, candy store, five and ten (Heaven) and, at the end, the ice cream counter where we'd get a Coke. The air conditioning was so wonderful. The way everything smelled—the hardware store, the counter at the ice cream part of the store—was so wonderful. It was bliss. We didn't buy anything but you don't have to buy when you're a child, really, it's enough to look, touch, get excited by what you see. Some day you'll get it. There was a particular kindness I remember. There was a rack of magazines across from the counter in the five and ten, and they'd let you pick one up—*Look*, or *Life*, with pictures, or movie star magazines—read it while you had a Coke, and put it back when you were done. You didn't have to pay.

And when this was over, four or five hours later, we'd decide to go home.

Here is what we did. We'd stand outside a store—the dottie old lady in the soft flowered dress and the black wool hat, the fat, unkempt little girl—and we'd wait for someone to walk by, or drive by slow. And Jane Jane would call out, in the Irish accent with the reedy voice, "We are going home to Selden. Could you be taking us?" And they'd be surprised, and look at us, and fairly soon someone would feel amazement or pity or bemusement and say yes, sure, get in, and take us back to Sanitarium Road.

We did that for years, hitchhiking back and forth, the vulnerable old lady and the child.

I remember bouncing around in the back of pickup trucks watching the trees go by. I remember a big diesel truck that smelled like oil or gas and there was a big dog in the cab and we all squished in. I remember salesmen in short sleeves smoking with their arms out the window.

I never told people this story until the past year or so and when

I told my son, now a man, I said, at the end, wonderingly, "And nobody killed us."

My son reflected. "That should be the title of your next book," he said. This is my next book so I decided to put it in here.

The point of course is that while I was not quite protected as a child, the prevailing American culture itself at that point still functioned as a protective force. Things hadn't been let loose to such a degree. The messages, permissions, incitements and inducements of the culture were not rough, lowering, frightening.

Life then wasn't Arcadia, there was murder and mayhem because humans are humans, and "history is an abattoir"—but there was a greater feeling extant of safety on the street. Parents could say to their kids, essentially, "Go out and play in America," and know they'd come back OK that night. People don't feel that so much anymore, and it's a real loss. (It is right here to note that life would not have been so safe for a little girl and an old woman of color; the world might not have been so kind. But the larger point, that everyone was at least a little safer, I think maintains.) Sophisticated Europe, I learned years later, had looked at our culture—its blandness, its innocence, its babyish assumption that the good would triumph—and saw it a culture of children. We were more appropriately understood as a culture *for* children. And you know, that's not the worst thing.

Here is my concern. There are not fewer children living stressed, chaotic lives in America now, there are more. There will be more still, because among the things America no longer manufactures is stability. And the culture around them will not protect them, as the culture protected me. The culture around them will make their lives harder, more frightening, more dangerous. They are going to come up with nothing to believe in, their nerves essentially shot. And they're going to be—they are already—very angry.

So that is the story. When I speak of my concerns about the

cultural air all around us it is not abstract to me. I will always feel America's culture saved me when I was a child, preserved my optimism, allowed me to be hopeful for the future, allowed me to become myself.

*   *   *

A quick word on what's in this book. There are essays that appeared in various media outlets, all noted, and columns from the *Journal*. They are divided by subject matter. I've corrected a few mistakes in grammar and usage and removed some references that are now so obscure they puzzled me. I haven't changed any meaning or shaded any thought. I've changed a few titles because they were originally done in a rush and no longer seem right for the piece. All pieces are dated and can be found under their original title, with their original art, on the Internet.

CHAPTER 1

A Lecture

In the fall of 2009 I was a fellow at the Institute of Politics at the John F. Kennedy School of Government at Harvard University. I was asked by Professor Roger Porter, with whom I had worked in the Reagan White House, to speak to his class on "The American Presidency." Many of its members traditionally hope to enter government, and he asked that I speak to them about my experiences as a speechwriter. This is the lecture I gave.

There are many ways to view and approach political speechwriting. I think of speeches as the literature of politics. I always have. I did the day I walked into the White House in the spring of 1984. I think of speechwriting as...writing. It is not, to my mind and in my experience, "messaging," it is not "communications," it is not "media management"—it is not any of those things.

It is writing.

In a way it is an attempt to think, and to think aloud. In the thinking aloud you are attempting to persuade as to the validity of one's thoughts, views, philosophy, stands, decisions.

I always thought of speechwriting as a stream breaking off the big river of American literature. American literature is the Mississippi and there are many streams that flow from it—playwriting, novel writing, short story writing, the essay, poetry. Speechwriting to my mind, at its best, is one of them.

Why do presidents have speechwriters? (After all, they all rose in part by being able to speak on their own.) Because they cannot at the same time be president and write speeches. They have to do one or the other, they can't do both.

Presidents often speak four, five or six times a day—within the White House complex, in the Executive Office Building, in the Rose Garden, in an executive agency. They speak in venues that are heavily covered and those that are covered by no press at all.

They speak a lot. And everything they say counts. A president speaking sloppily and popping off about the economy can send the Dow Jones spiraling down a thousand points. Speaking offhandedly about foreign affairs, he can make an ally doubt the alliance. So it all counts.

Presidents cannot write all those speeches. They cannot take the time, they cannot get the solitude, and at the same time do everything else they have to do.

What is it to write for a president?

It's heaven. Your work matters, it's serious and you can take it seriously. You work with a president of the United States. As Bill Moyers said to me 25 years ago, how many in all American history have been lucky enough to do that? He guessed the number at that time was 20,000.

You should be young—maybe in your 20s or 30s, not past your early 40s. Arthur Schlesinger, speechwriter and aide for JFK, once told me, "No one should be a speechwriter after 40. For one thing, with writers the legs go first and you can't run through the halls anymore."

For another, over 40 you ought to be writing only your views, and in your voice, in your style—not Jack Kennedy's, not Harry Truman's or Ronald Reagan's. David Gergen, who introduced me today, writes as David, and I write as myself, and I think if we two were asked to write a speech for someone again we would be very poor speechwriters, because the person we were writing for would wind up sounding just like David Gergen or just like me, when they should be sounding just like them.

I want to jump to one experience I had as a speechwriter for Ronald Reagan.

There are many different sorts of speeches and addresses—the speech of ceremony and high state, the partisan speech, an inaugural address, an acceptance speech, "Rose Garden rubbish" as it's called, relatively unimportant speeches. Though in the modern media age, as I say, no presidential speech is ever unimportant.

All these speeches are different but the same. Because a president is giving them, and in the giving of them he is leading, he is speaking for and to the nation.

I want to speak quickly here of what might be called the speech of emergency. Something happened. It was unexpected. It has to be addressed—literally.

One speech of emergency is the Challenger speech. Do any of you remember it? January 28, 1986, 23 years ago.

In Washington it was a brilliantly sunny day. In the speechwriting department it was a slow day. No one expected much. In speechwriting, the big work had been done for that week, and that was the State of the Union speech that was to be given that night. It was a big day for the president, therefore, but not for the speechwriters, for whom the work had been done, the speech put to bed by two gifted speechwriters, Josh Gilder and Ben Elliott, the latter of whom ran Reagan's speechwriting office.

The president had already gone through the speech many times, made changes and edits. It had gone through staffing. The president probably had rehearsed it.

It's a pretty day, late morning, 11:30 or so. The president was meeting in the West Wing with a handful of the nation's television anchors, giving them a preview of what would be in that night's speech, an off-the-record conversation.

I was in my office catching up with stuff, talking on the phone. CNN was on the TV set to my left. The picture was on but the sound was off. Suddenly I see out of the corner of my eye something odd on the screen. It's showing a big blue sky, deep blue, brilliant, but cutting through the sky in the middle of the screen a deep, dense, discrete funnel of white cloud. And the funnel has been broken, as if the cloud itself had exploded and pieces of it shot crazily into the air. I thought: What the heck is that?

I hang up the phone. CNN had been covering the launch of the space shuttle Challenger from the Kennedy Space Center in Florida, and clearly something had happened.

I hit the volume, put up the sound. Nothing. Just the sound of static—spooky static. No one's saying anything. And then the CNN anchor for the launch, and Mission Control, are coming on, the anchor's saying "Something appears to have happened," and all you hear is the crackle of an empty line from Mission Control. Then you hear ground control saying things like "negative contact" and "loss of downline."

And then the CNN cameras cut to the people in the stands who'd been invited to come watch the launch. And the camera shows a woman, late middle age, and she is leaning against a man, maybe her husband, and she is looking up and she has started to cry.

And you know: a dreadful tragedy has occurred.

I watched, rapt. And so did everyone in America. (A study later said 85% of the people of the country knew what had happened within an hour—85%, an amazing percentage of people.)

Finally a statement came, I think from a press guy. There has been "a major malfunction," the vehicle has exploded.

Within the next hour it all became clearer. There had been a terrible accident, the Challenger blew up 73 seconds into its flight.

A seal on the solid rocket booster had failed, hot gas hit an external fuel tank, it all blew apart.

We all wanted to think there were survivors. It is funny, the power of human denial. We all hoped somehow there had been survivors, and we hoped this while we knew there were not, could not have been.

A search and recovery process began.

It was during that hour that a little girl walked into my office. She was the daughter of Ben Elliott who had for reasons I cannot recall taken his daughter to work that day. She was a child of 7 years, and my friend. She used to walk into my office and play on the floor.

She walked into my office and said, "The teacher was on the shuttle. Is the teacher all right?"

And it dawned on me: Every schoolchild in America was watching the launch of the Challenger because something unique had been done, there was a teacher on board, a civilian, not a professional astronaut but a public school teacher named Christa McAuliffe. And so schools throughout America had brought TV sets in so the kids could watch the teacher go into space with the astronauts.

And I knew Oh man, they are kids, they are not going to understand this.

And I knew too: The president is going to have to speak about this today. He is going to have to make a speech.

I started to write it. I called my boss, Ben, who was watching the coverage in shock like everyone else, and I said Ben I am writing the speech and he said Good, get going.

Now here I will tell you there is something Ronald Reagan's speechwriters had that a lot of other presidential speechwriters did not have, never had, and it is this: We knew what Ronald Reagan thought. We knew *how* he thought. We knew his views, his approach, we knew how he talked, we knew his philosophy. We knew *him*.

A speechwriter for Jimmy Carter once said to me, You guys were so lucky—we never knew how Carter was going to come down on any issue, we never knew where he'd stand, what he was gonna say.

But Reagan was vivid, he was clear, he had a philosophy that was well known to us.

So the writing. Where do you begin?

If you're Reagan you begin with the facts: Something terrible has happened. We all witnessed it. This is what we know so far.

Then . . . well, then what exactly?

At this point I was told the president was not able to speak to us—he was being briefed, he was talking to NASA, he was also talking to the anchors. He's meeting with aides, he's handling a crisis, they're trying to figure out what to do about the State of the Union that night.

But he trusts us. He knows his speechwriters know him.

At this point a woman runs into my office. Her name was Karna Small, an aide on the National Security Council. Karna had just been with the president in various meetings. She had taken notes on everything he'd said. Karna ran the notes in to me, knowing we'd be doing the speech.

The notes of what Reagan had just said to the anchors became the spine of the speech.

This is what he said:

He talked about the sacrifice of the families of the astronauts. He spoke of how this was a national tragedy with everyone in America saddened. He spoke of space as the last frontier. He said we've grown so used to dazzling success in space that this tragedy comes as a special shock. It was for him traumatic. And one of the anchors asked him about the schoolchildren watching. He said, "Pioneers have always given their lives on the frontier . . . but we have to make it clear to the children that life goes on, it continues." He said he couldn't put the teacher out of his mind, and her husband, and her children.

He would speak to the nation after the search and rescue efforts were suspended. That took two or three hours. In that time I worked on the speech and got it into a limited form of the staffing system.

So what did the president say in his five-minute address? And it had to be five minutes because . . . it was the old days. Ronald Reagan was going to speak, appropriately, and lead, and set a tone. But he wasn't going to horn in on your grief, or dominate the moment, or swan around or make it about him.

He had certain things he had to say at the top. He had to speak to the families of those we knew had died. He had to speak to the brokenhearted people of NASA, of the space program. He had to speak to the nation. He had to speak to the nation's kids, while saying to them what was appropriate to say to adults. The point being he had to speak to those who were 8 and those who were 80, in the same speech.

He said we are "pained to the core" by what happened. We have never had an event like this, and because of that we have forgotten the courage it takes to go into space. The seven in the crew overcame the dangers. They were daring, brave, saw the challenge and met it with joy.

Reagan said to the schoolchildren:

> And I want to say something to the children of America, who were watching the live coverage of the shuttle's takeoff. I know it's hard to understand but sometimes painful things like this happen. It's all part of the process of exploration and discovery. It's all part of taking a chance and expanding man's horizons. The future doesn't belong to the fainthearted—it belongs to the brave. The Challenger crew was pulling us into the future—and we'll continue to follow them.

Then to America and the world, a statement of resolution: "We'll continue our quest in space. There will be more shuttle flights and more shuttle crews and yes, more volunteers, more civilians, more teachers in space. Nothing ends here—our hopes and our journeys continue."

And then the ending of the speech.

While I had worked, over two hours or so, I had seen CNN using, over and over again, the last videotape of all the astronauts and crew walking that morning toward the space shuttle, in their space suits. And awkwardly, humorously, with heavy-gloved hands, they were waving goodbye.

I'm watching that over and over. I suddenly remembered a poem I learned in the seventh grade at McKenna Junior High in Massapequa, Long Island. It was a poem called "High Flight," by John Gillespie Magee, Jr. He had been a pilot who volunteered for the Canadian Air Force in 1939, an American who got in as the war began in Europe. In his poem, about the joy of flying—an unusual joy back then, for not many flew—in the poem he spoke of the sensation of breaking free from gravity, breaking "the surly bonds of earth," going upward so high he felt almost he could touch the face of God.

There was something transcending about the poem, not transcendent but transcending. It was a real attempt to define a particular kind of joy and make you know it.

And so I put it at the end of the speech.

Here's what I knew. Reagan was going to get the speech and change what he wanted, but if he said those words from the Magee poem, if I heard them on TV, it was going to be because Reagan knew that poem and it mattered to him. He wasn't going to say the words unless he knew the poem. And I just had a feeling he did, but only a feeling.

We got the speech through the editing process, there was no time for people to fuss too much with it, by which I mean to make not necessary changes but dithery and unnecessary ones. Sometimes people in a White House think a speech is a fondue pot and they all want to put in a fork.

The president gets it, reads it, makes his changes.

He comes on national TV, live from the Oval Office. He's sitting at the president's desk, which used to be the place presidents sat when they addressed the nation. They don't always do that now, it is unusual when they do. They stand and use a telegenic or dynamic background. But back then they didn't think so visually in terms of backdrops and such, they sat at the big desk.

Reagan gives the speech, gets to the end, and I hear him say of the Challenger crew "We will never forget them, nor the last time we saw them—this morning, as they prepared for their journey, and waved goodbye, and 'slipped the surly bonds of earth' to 'touch the face of God.'"

Now Reagan, during the speech, looked stricken. I could see it, he was upset.

And I found out later he thought, as he gave the speech, that it had not succeeded, it didn't somehow mysteriously do what needed doing. And that happens. And I picked up a little of that, I picked up his mood.

But the next morning something had shifted. I got a phone call from Tip O'Neill, the Democratic Speaker of the House of Representatives, a tough, burly pol from Cambridge, Mass. It probably goes without saying that Tip O'Neill didn't spend a lot of time calling Ronnie Reagan's speechwriters. But he did that day, he tracked me down and said, "I just want to tell you the president did a great job yesterday and thank you for your service." What a great moment, a gracious thing. Then a call from George Shultz, the secretary of state, then others.

And then a call from the president who, God bless him, was honest and told me he somehow hadn't thought the speech worked but then afterward knew it did. I asked how he knew it was OK and he said with a sort of self-teasing voice that he got a call from Frank Sinatra saying it was great, and Frank Sinatra didn't call after every speech!

He asked me how I knew he knew the poem "High Flight," and I said Mr. President, I didn't know, I just had a feeling.

It turned out he knew it because the poem was written on a plaque outside his daughter Patty's grade school, and when he'd drop her off in the morning sometimes he'd read it.

Later I was told but have never been able to confirm that the film actor Tyrone Power, who'd been a flier in World War II, had carried a copy of the poem in his wallet, and Reagan knew it in part because it was read at Power's grave site by Laurence Olivier, and Reagan was there...

So what do we learn?

Presidents lead in many ways, including with words.

Presidents are sometimes called to give context and meaning to the inexplicable. They are called to explain but also to stand for, to be. America felt wounded that day, and so did Ronald Reagan.

And sometimes presidents have to remind us we will get through this, it is painful right now but we'll all get through it, together. "And we will have more shuttle flights and more exploring and nothing stops here, we keep pushing on."

This is what presidents are called on to do sometimes: Face the tragedy, explain the tragedy, move on from the tragedy.

And for me, personally, I will tell you something about the professional lives you are about to have, about to begin.

Sometimes, and I'm not sure it happens more than half a dozen times in a professional life, you will have a day, or a week, or a moment, or a season, when you get to think to yourself, "This is why I'm here." This is why I'm in this office on this day. "This is why God put me here."

I had one of those days that day.

And when you have that day, that is a great day. You will never forget it.

I wish you many such days.

CHAPTER 2

People I Miss

When a great ship goes down, you want to point toward the horizon and mark where it was, what it looked like. You want to remember its beauty—its speed and route, and how it cut against the sky.

When Tim Russert died I wrote of what the world really values. "The world is a great liar. It shows you it worships and admires money, but at the end of the day it doesn't. It says it adores fame and celebrity, but it doesn't, not really. The world admires and wants to hold on to, and not lose, goodness. It admires virtue. At the end it gives its greatest tributes to generosity, honesty, courage, mercy, talents well used, talents that, brought into the world, make it better... That's what we talk about in eulogies, because that's what's important."

I have always been interested in trying to sum up or capture on deadline the meaning of the lives of people who have died. I'm not sure why. I think it's just that a life is a big thing and it bothers me to see someone leave without a full definition of, or tribute to, their achievements, their nature, their efforts.

I am interested in careers, in what all the commitment given to a job or a vocation in the end means.

I don't write about those I don't admire. I think inspiration is part of what we all need and part of what I myself am looking for. Most people, whatever their condition or place in life, are just trying every day to keep up their morale. Thinking about the lives of people who've moved us reminds us of what is possible, of how life can be adorned or made better.

All these appreciations are brief, limited in size to a column's or broadcast's length, or a magazine's available space. Some are about people I knew, some not. A few I had met, and carried from the encounter an impression. After some of these pieces I add some additional information or a thought I've had about the subject since I wrote about him or her.

* * *

A Life's Lesson

Tim Russert teaches us what the world really values.

The Wall Street Journal: June 20, 2008

When somebody dies, we tell his story and try to define and isolate what was special about it—what it was he brought to the party, how he enhanced life by showing up. In this way we educate ourselves about what really matters. Or, often, reeducate ourselves, for "man needs more to be reminded than instructed."

I understand why some think that the media coverage surrounding Tim Russert's death was excessive—truly, it was unprecedented—but it doesn't seem to me a persuasive indictment, if only because what was said was so valuable.

The beautiful thing about the coverage was that it offered extremely important information to those age 15 or 25 or 30 who may not have been told how to operate in the world beyond "Go succeed." I'm not sure why don't we tell the young as much as we ought, as clearly as we ought, what it is the world admires, and what it is they want to emulate.

In a way, the world is a great liar. It shows you it worships and admires money, but at the end of the day it doesn't. It says it adores fame and celebrity, but it doesn't, not really. The world admires, and wants to hold on to, and not lose, goodness. It admires virtue. At the end it gives its greatest tributes to generosity, honesty, courage, mercy, talents well used, talents that, brought into the world, make it better. That's what it really admires. That's what we talk about in eulogies, because that's what's important. We don't say "The thing about Joe was he was rich." We say, if we can, "The thing about Joe was he took care of people."

The young are told, "Be true to yourself." But so many of them have no idea, really, what that means. If they don't know who they are, what are they being true to? They're told, "The key is to hold firm to your ideals." But what if no one bothered, really, to teach them ideals?

After Tim's death, the entire television media for four days told you the keys to a life well lived, the things you actually need to live life well, and without which it won't be good. Among them: taking care of those you love and letting them know they're loved, which involves self-sacrifice; holding firm to God, to your religious faith, no matter how high you rise or low you fall. This involves guts, and self-discipline, and active attention to developing and refining a conscience to whose promptings you can respond. Honoring your calling or profession by trying to do within it honorable work, which takes hard effort, and a willingness to master the ethics of your field. And enjoying life. This can be hard in America, where sometimes people are rather grim in their determination to get and to have. "Enjoy life, it's ungrateful not to," said Ronald Reagan.

Tim had these virtues. They were great to see. By defining them and celebrating them the past few days, the media encouraged them. This was a public service, and also what you might call Tim's parting gift.

I'd add it's not only the young, but the older and the old, who were given a few things to think about. When Tim's friends started to come forward last Friday to speak on the air of his excellence, they were honestly grieving. They felt loss. So did people who'd never met him. Question: When you die, are people in your profession going to feel like this? Why not? What can you do better? When you leave, are your customers—in Tim's case it was five million every Sunday morning, in your case it may be the people who come into the shop, or into your office—going to react like this? Why not?

* * *

One of the greatest statements, the most piercing, was something Chuck Todd said when he talked on a panel on MSNBC. He was asked more or less why Tim stuck out from the pack, and he said, "He was normal!" In a city, Washington, in which many powerful people are deep down weird, or don't have a deep down, only a surface, Tim was normal. Like a normal man, he cared about his family and his profession and his faith. Pat Buchanan later said they're not making them now like they used to, Tim's normality is becoming the exception. The world of Russert—stability, Catholic school, loving parents, TV shows that attempted only to entertain you and not create a new moral universe in your head—that's over, that world is gone. Pat had a point, though it's not gone entirely of course, just not as big, or present, as it used to be.

Which got me thinking about one way in which Tim was lauded that, after a few days, was grating. And what's a column without a gripe? Tim, as all now know, was a working-class boy from upstate New York. But the amazement with which some of his colleagues talked of his background made them sound like Margaret Mead among the indigenous people of Borneo. An amazing rags-to-riches story—he was found among an amazing Celtic tribe that dragged its clubs across the tangled jungle floors of a land called "Buffalo," where they eat "wings" and worship a warrior caste known as "the Bills." Here he is, years later, in a suit.

This reflected a certain cultural insularity in our media, did it not? Tim came from a loving home, grew up in a house, in a suburb. He went to private Catholic schools. His father was a garbageman, which when I was growing up was known as a good municipal union job. Tim's life was as good as or better than 90% of his countrymen in his time. His background wasn't strange or surprising—it was normal.

Something not fully appreciated is the sense of particular sadness among conservatives, who felt Russert gave their views and philosophy equal time, an equality of approach. When Kate O'Beirne had a book out on the excesses of feminism a few years ago, the only network show on which she was asked to give the antiabortion argument was "Meet the Press." When I was on the book tour in 2000 for "The Case Against Hillary Clinton," Tim's was the only show that asked me to state my case at length, balancing it with an appearance of the same length by a Hillary supporter. I'm not sure network producers understand how grateful—embarrassing word, but true—conservatives are to be given time to say not only what they think but why they think it. Russert was big on why. He knew it was the heart of any political debate.

*   *   *

On the train coming back from his memorial on Wednesday, I talked to Tom Kean, a former governor of New Jersey and chairman of the 9/11 Commission. He told me of how a few years ago Tim, concerned about nuclear proliferation, invited Mr. Kean and Sam Nunn on "Meet the Press" to talk about it at length. No particular hook, he just wanted to gin up concern in Washington on an issue he knew was crucial. Mr. Kean said he had listened closely to all the journalists the past few days talking about how Tim prepared rigorously, was open-minded, civic minded, serious. He hoped they were listening to themselves, hoped they were reflecting on what they said. Emulation would be good there, too.

*   *   *

Joan Rivers: The Entertainer

The Wall Street Journal: September 5, 2014

There was nobody like her. Some people are knockoffs or imitations of other, stronger, more vivid figures, but there was never another Joan Rivers before her or while she lived. She was a seriously wonderful, self-invented woman.

She was completely open and immediately accessible. She had the warmth of a person who found others keenly and genuinely interesting. It was also the warmth of a person with no boundaries: She wanted to know everything about you and would tell you a great deal about herself, right away. She had no edit function, which in part allowed her gift. She would tell you what she thought. She loved to shock, not only an audience but a friend. I think from the beginning life startled her, and she enjoyed startling you. You only asked her advice or opinion if you wanted an honest reply.

Her intelligence was penetrating and original, her tastes refined. Her duplex apartment on the East Side of Manhattan was full of books in beautiful bindings, of elegant gold things on the table, lacquered boxes, antique furniture. She liked everything just so. She read a lot. She was a doctor's daughter.

We met and became friends in 1992, but the story I always remember when I think of her took place in June 2004. Ronald Reagan had just died, and his remains were being flown from California to Washington, where he would lay in state at the U.S. Capitol. A group of his friends were invited to the Capitol to take part in the formal receiving of his remains, and to say goodbye. Joan was there, as a great friend and supporter of the Reagans.

That afternoon, as we waited for the plane to land, while we were standing and talking in a ceremonial room on the Senate side, there was, suddenly, an alarm. Secret Service men and Capitol police burst into the room and instructed us to leave, quickly and immediately. An incoming plane headed for the Capitol was expected to hit within minutes. "Run for your lives," they commanded, and they meant it. Everyone in the Capitol ran toward the exits and down the great stairs. Joan was ahead of me, along with the television producer Tommy Corcoran, her best friend and boon companion of many years.

Down the long marble halls, down the long steps...At the bottom of the steps, in a grassy patch to the left, I saw Joan on the ground, breathless. Her high heel had broken, the wind knocked out of her. I'm not going any further, she said to Tommy. Keep going, she said. I should note that everyone really thought the Capitol was about to be attacked.

I stopped to ask if I could help, heard what Joan had said to Tommy and then heard Tommy's reply: "I'm staying with you."

"Run!" said Joan. She told him to save himself.

"No," said Tommy. "It wouldn't be as much fun without you." He said if anything happened they'd go together. And he sat down next to her and held her hand and they waited for the plane to hit.

Needless to say it didn't; some idiot flying an oblivious governor had drifted into restricted airspace. I don't know if they ever had any idea how close they'd come to being shot down.

But that was a very Joan moment, her caring about her friend and him saying life would be lesser without her.

*   *   *

I was lucky to have known her. I owe it to Steve Forbes, the publisher and former presidential hopeful who, with his family, owned a chateau in France near the Normandy coast. It was the family's custom once a year to invite friends and associates for a long weekend, and in the summer of 1992 I went, and met Joan. Talk about a life force.

We all stayed in beautiful rooms. Joan amused herself making believe she was stealing the furniture. It rained through the weekend, which Joan feared would make Steve and Sabina Forbes blue, so she organized a group of us to go into town to a costume-rental place so we could put on a show. All they had was French Revolution outfits, so we took them, got back to our rooms, and Joan and I wrote a play on what we announced were French Revolutionary themes. Walter Cronkite, another guest, was chosen by Joan as narrator. I think the play consisted mostly of members of Louis XIV's court doing Catskills stand-up. It was quite awful and a big success.

The highlight of the weekend was a balloon lift, a Forbes tradition—scores of huge balloons in brilliant colors and patterns would lift from the grounds of the chateau after dawn and travel over the countryside. It was so beautiful. I stood and watched, not meaning to participate, and was half pushed into a gondola. By luck Joan was there, full of good humor and information on what we were seeing below.

We held on hard as we experienced a hard and unplanned landing on a French farm. We were spilled out onto a field. As we scrambled and stood, an old farmer came out, spoke to us for a moment, ran into his farmhouse and came back with an old bottle of calvados. He then told us he hadn't seen Americans since D-Day, and toasted us for what America had done for his country. No one was more moved than Joan, who never forgot it.

*   *   *

I last saw her in July. A friend and I met her for lunch at a restaurant she'd chosen in Los Angeles. It was full of tourists. Everyone at the tables recognized her and called out. She felt she owed her fans everything and never ignored or patronized an admirer. She smiled through every picture with every stranger. She was *nice*—she asked about their families, where they were from, how they liked it here. They absolutely knew she would treat them well and she absolutely did.

The only people who didn't recognize Joan were the people who ran the restaurant, who said they didn't have her reservation and asked us to wait in the bar, where waiters bumped into us as they bustled by. Joan didn't like that, gave them 10 minutes to get their act together, and when they didn't she left. But she didn't just leave. She stood outside on the sidewalk, and as cars full of people went by with people calling out, "Joan! We love you!" she would yell back, "Thank you but don't go to this restaurant, they're rude! Boycott this restaurant!" My friend said, "Joan, stop it, you're going to wind up on TMZ."

"I don't care," she said. She felt she was doing a public service.

We went to a restaurant down the street, where when she walked in they almost bowed.

She wouldn't let a friend pay a bill, ever. She tipped like a woman who used to live on tips. She was hilarious that day on the subject of Barack and Michelle Obama, whom she did not like. (I almost didn't write that but decided if Joan were here she'd say, "Say I didn't like Obama!")

She was a Republican, always a surprising thing in show business, and in a New Yorker, but she was one because, as she would tell you, she worked hard, made her money with great effort and didn't feel her profits should be unduly taxed. She once said in an interview that if you have 19 children, she will pay for the first four but no more. Mostly she just couldn't tolerate cant and didn't respond well to political manipulation. She believed in a strong defense because she was a grown-up and understood the world to be a tough house.

She loved Margaret Thatcher, who said what Joan believed: The facts of life are conservative. She didn't do a lot of politics in her shows—politics divides an audience—but she thought a lot about it and talked about it. She was socially liberal in the sense she wanted everyone to find as many available paths to happiness as possible.

*   *   *

I am not sure she ever felt accepted by the showbiz elite, or any elite. She was too raw, didn't respect certain conventions, wasn't careful, didn't pretend to a false dignity. She took the celebrated and powerful down a peg. Her wit was broad and spoofing—she would play the fool—but it was also subversive and transgressive. People who weren't powerful or well-known saw and understood what she was doing.

She thought a lot about how things work and what they mean.

She once told me she figured a career was like a shark, either it is going forward or it is dying and sinking to the ocean floor. She worked like someone who believed that, doing shows in houses big and small all over the country, hundreds a year, along with her cable programs, interviews, and books. She supported a lot of people. Many members of her staff stayed for decades and were like family. Because of that, when I visited the hospital last week, I got to witness a show-business moment Joan would have liked. A relative was scrolling down on her iPhone. "Listen to this," she said, and read aloud something a young showbiz figure who had been lampooned by Joan had just tweeted. She said it was an honor to be made fun of by such a great lady. "Joan will be furious when she sees this," said the relative, shaking her head. "She won't be able to make fun of her in the act anymore."

It was Joan who explained to me 15 or 20 years ago a new dimension in modern fame—that it wasn't like the old days when you'd walk down a city street and people would recognize you. Fame had suddenly and in some new ways gone universal. Joan and a friend had just come back from a safari in Africa. One day they were walking along a path when they saw some local tribesmen. As the two groups passed, a tribesman exclaimed, "Joan Rivers, what are you doing here?!"

She couldn't believe it. This is Africa, she thought. And then she thought no, this is a world full of media that shows the world American culture. We talked about it, and I asked, beyond the idea of what might be called Western cultural imperialism, what else does the story mean to you? "It means there's no place to hide," she said. They can know you anywhere. At the time, the Internet age was just beginning.

Her eye was original. Twenty years ago, when everyone was talking about how wonderful it was that Vegas had been cleaned up and the mob had been thrown out, Joan said no, no, no, they are ruining the mystique. First of all, she said, those mobsters knew how to care for a lady, those guys with bent noses were respectful and gentlemen, except when they were killing you. Second, she said, organized crime is better than disorganized crime, which will replace it. Third, the mobsters had a patina of class, they dressed well and saw that everyone else did, so Vegas wasn't a slobocracy, which is what it is becoming with men in shorts playing the slots in the lobby of the hotel. The old Vegas had dignity. She hated the bluenoses who'd clean up what wasn't meant to be clean. No one wanted Sin City cleaned up, she said, they wanted to go there and visit sin and then go home.

* * *

Joan now is being celebrated, rightly and beautifully, by those who knew and loved her. They are defining her contributions (pioneer, unacknowledged feminist hero, gutsy broad) and lauding the quality of her craft.

But it is a great unkindness of life that no one says these things until you're gone.

Joan would have loved how much she is loved. I think she didn't quite know and yet in a way she must have: You don't have strangers light up at the sight of you without knowing you have *done* something.

But we should try to honor and celebrate the virtues and gifts of people while they're alive, and can see it.

She was an entertainer. She wanted to make you laugh. She succeeded so brilliantly.

* * *

America's First Lady

Few people get to symbolize a world, but Jacqueline Bouvier Kennedy Onassis did, and that world is receding, and we know it and mourn that, too.

Time Magazine: May 30, 1994

She was a last link to a certain kind of past, and that is part, but only part, of why we mourn so. Jackie Kennedy symbolized—she was a connection to a time, to an old America that was more dignified, more private, an America in which standards were higher and clearer and elegance meant something, a time when elegance was a kind of statement, a way of dressing up the world, and so a generous act. She had manners, the kind that remind us that manners spring from a certain moral view—that you do tribute to the world and the people in it by being kind and showing respect, by sending the note and the flowers, by being loyal and cheering a friend. She was a living reminder in the age of Oprah that personal dignity is always, still, an option, a choice that is open to you. She was, really, the last aristocrat. Few people get to symbolize a world, but she did, and that world is receding, and we know it and mourn that, too.

Those who knew her or watched her from afar groped for the words that could explain their feeling of loss. A friend of hers said, with a soft, sad voice, that what we're losing is what we long for: the old idea of being cultivated. "She had this complex, colorful mind, she loved a turn of phrase. She didn't grow up in front of the TV set, but reading the classics and thinking about them and having thoughts about history. Oh," he said, "we're losing her kind."

I echoed the sentiment to another of her friends, who cut me off. "She wasn't a kind, she was sui generis." And so she was.

America continues in its generational shift; the great ones of the '50s and '60s, big people of a big era, are going, and too often these days we're saying goodbye. But Jackie Kennedy's death is different. No ambivalence clouds her departure, and that leaves us feeling lonely. America this week is a lonelier place.

She was too young, deserved more time, and the fact that she didn't get it seems like a new level of unfairness. She never saw her husband grow old, and now she won't see her grandchildren grow up.

But just writing those words makes me want to break out of sadness and reach back in time and speak '60s-speak, or at least how the '60s spoke before they turned dark. So I guess I mean I want to speak Kennedyese. I want to say, Aw listen, kid, don't be glum. What a life she had.

She herself said something like this to a friend, in a conversation just months ago, when she first knew she was sick. She told him she was optimistic and hoped to live 20 more years. "But even if I have only five years, so what, I've had a great run."

They said it was a life of glamour, but it was really a life of splendor. I want to say, Listen, kid, buck up, don't be blue—the thing about this woman and her life is that she was a patriot, who all by herself one terrible weekend lifted and braced the heart of a nation.

That week in November '63, the weekend of the muffled drums, was the worst time for America in the last half of this century. We forget now the shame we felt as a nation at what had happened in Dallas. A president had been murdered, quite savagely, quite brutally, and the whole appalled world was looking and judging. And she redeemed it. She took away the shame by how she acted. She was young, only 34, and only a few days before she'd been covered in her husband's blood—but she came home to Washington and walked down those broad avenues dressed in black, her pale face cleansed and washed clean by trauma. She walked head up, back straight and proud, in a flowing black veil. There was the moment in the Capitol Rotunda, when she knelt with her daughter Caroline. It was the last moment of public farewell, and to say it she bent and kissed the flag that draped the coffin that contained her husband—and a whole nation, a whole world, was made silent at the sight of patriotism made tender. Her Irish husband had admired class. That weekend she showed it in abundance. What a parting gift.

A nation watched, and would never forget. The world watched, and found its final judgment summed up by a young woman, a British journalist who had come to witness the funeral, and filed home: "Jacqueline Kennedy has today given her country the one thing it has always lacked, and that is majesty."

To have done that for her country—to have lived through that weekend and done what she did from that Friday to that Monday—to have shown the world that the killing of the president was not America, the loving dignity of our saying goodbye was America—to have done that was an act of supreme patriotism.

And a lot of us thought that anything good or bad she did for the rest of her life, from that day on, didn't matter, for she'd earned her way, she deserved a free pass.

In a remarkable interview she gave Theodore White the following December, she revealed what a tough little romantic she was. "Once, the more I read of history the more bitter I got. For a while I thought history was something that bitter old men wrote. But then I realized history made Jack what he was. You must think of him as this little boy, sick so much of the time, reading in bed, reading history, reading the Knights of the Round Table, reading Marlborough. For Jack, history was full of heroes. And if it made him this way—if it made him see the heroes—maybe other little boys will see. Men are such a combination of good and bad. Jack had this hero idea of history, this idealistic view." And she spoke of Camelot and gave the world an image of her husband that is still, for all the revelations of the past three decades, alive. She provided an image of herself, too, perhaps more than she knew. The day before she died, a young schoolteacher in New York City who hadn't even been born when she spoke to Teddy White told me of his shock that she was leaving us. "I thought she would be like Guinevere," he said. "I thought she would ride off on a horse, in her beautiful silence, and never die."

Her friends saw a great poignance in her, and a great yearning. Behind her shyness there was an enormous receptivity to the sweetness of life and its grace. A few years ago, friends, a couple, gave a small dinner party for two friends who had just married, and Mrs. Onassis was among the guests. It was an elegant New York gathering, a handful of the renowned of show business and media and society, all gathered to dine on the top floor of a skyscraper. The evening was full of laughter and warm toasts, and the next day her hosts received from Mrs. Onassis a handwritten, hand-delivered letter. "How could there be an evening more magical than last night? Everyone is enhanced and touched by being with two people just discovering how much they love each other. I have known and adored [him] for so long, always wishing he would find happiness... Seeing him with [her] and getting to know her, I see he has at last—and she so exceptional, whom you describe so movingly, has too. I am so full of joy for both—I just kept thinking about it all day today. What wonderful soothing hosts you are—what a dazzling gathering of their friends—in that beautiful tower, with New York glittering below..."

With New York glittering below. The world, I am told, is full of those notes, always handwritten and lucid and spontaneous—and always correct. "The notes were the way she was intimate" with outsiders, said a friend. The only insiders, really, were her family.

There was always in her a sense of history and the sense that children are watching—children are watching and history will judge us, and the things that define our times are the great actions we take, all against the odds and with a private valor of which the world will little note nor long remember. But that's the big thing—the personal struggle, and the sense that our history day by day is forged from it. That was her intuition, and that intuition was a gift to us, for it helped produce the walk down the broad avenues of Washington that day when her heart was broken.

She was one sweet and austere tune. Her family arranged a private funeral, and that of course is what she'd want and that is what is fitting. But I know how I wish she would be buried.

I wish we could take her, in the city she loved or the capital she graced, and put a flag on her coffin and the coffin on a catafalque, and march it down a great avenue, with an honor guard and a horse that kicks, as Black Jack did, and muffled drums. I wish we could go and honor her, those of us who were children when she was in the White House, and our parents who wept that weekend long ago, and our children who have only a child's sense of who and what she was. I wish we could stand on the sidewalk as the caisson passes, and take off our hats, and explain to our sons and daughters, "That is a patriot passing by." I wish I could see someone's little boy, in a knee-length coat, lift his arm and salute.

"Tennessee Williams Died a Week Ago Today"

CBS News, "Dan Rather Reporting": March 4, 1983

Tennessee Williams died a week ago today and he'll be buried tomorrow. And I think there's one more thing to say about his life. It's not about writing or genius, not art or the theater. It's about work.

Up until the end, Tennessee Williams got up every morning and wrote. He was 72 and long past his prime, long past his great moments. But he got up every morning and sat at the typewriter and wrote.

That was his work. He wrote. And in the last 20 years of his life it couldn't have been easy for him because his great triumphs were behind him and he knew no one was going to applaud when he got up.

He knew what they'd say about his newest plays. They were going to say "Ah, his genius has abandoned him, he's lost it, he's not up to par." He knew the critics would say this because he'd written masterpieces, *Streetcar* and *Glass Menagerie*, and his name had grown so big and the expectation had grown so heavy. Every play had to be a masterpiece. And of course that was not possible because talent is finite; it is not endless. Even a genius gets only so much genius. And if you live a long life, as he did, you will probably use your genius up.

Other artists have reached this point and picked up a rifle, jumped off a ship or opened the oven door. Others have hung on to become talk-show intellectuals or sit in fat chairs and sell wine on TV. But Tennessee Williams never sold out, and he didn't check out early. He got up every morning and wrote.

For this alone you could call his life a triumph. But some people—a lot of people—played his life as a tragedy. You could see it in the papers—all that talk about his dark disturbed life, the booze and the drugs, the breakdowns and the whole sweaty morass of family fights and broken love. The most prestigious newspaper in New York found it necessary to say in his obituary that he'd grown "seedy and portly" in his later years. Which were tragic, remember, and full of failed talent.

Tragic my foot. That life was a triumph. And I will argue that it was most triumphant when his youth had left him and his audience had left him and his great gifts had dulled and he got up every morning and worked.

The other day I went to a service for a man named Jack Bolter, a modest quiet man who was a writer here. Jack loved words, and every day he'd show up at the desk in the newsroom and go through the wire copy and put together a brisk and informative news broadcast. It wasn't our biggest broadcast, not our most important one. Just a good solid report in the middle of the day. Jack showed up and put it together even when he was sick and even when he was tired. I think he knew what Tennessee Williams knew. That yes life is rich and wonderful and to be enjoyed, but one of the big things, one of the enduring things is the work you do and the work you leave behind you.

I just keep thinking of Jack and Tennessee Williams and of all the people who don't whine and don't cry and show up and do their work. Even when they're not in the best shape, even when it's not as good as they want, even when they know that no one will applaud when they get up. They're the best.

* * *

The wake for Tennessee Williams was held in the Frank E. Campbell funeral home, on Madison Avenue in the Upper East

Side of Manhattan. I had never known him but knew and admired his work, thought The Glass Menagerie *a masterpiece.* *"Blow out your candles, Laura..." So I decided to go to his wake, to be part of what I assumed would be a throng, which is what he deserved, to swell the crowd saying goodbye. And when I got to the funeral home, early, on a bright late-winter afternoon, I was shocked to see there was no crowd to swell. A few friends of his and some family members were standing in the room, ready to greet the crowd, and they had no one to greet but me. I shook everyone's hand, feeling embarrassed and sorry. They asked if I'd worked with him, been a friend. No, I said, "I'm just an admirer and feel he should be thanked for his work." I stayed a few minutes, until a few others came in, and left.*

Here is the odd part. Thirty years later I told that story to Terry Teachout, the theater critic of the Wall Street Journal. *Terry immediately asked, "Was the casket open?" It was a journalistic question, but it also had some theological significance. Williams had converted to Catholicism in the years before his death, and Catholics even to this day tend to have open caskets for viewing.*

But I couldn't remember. I just had no memory of it. Which was odd because that's exactly the kind of thing I would remember, and be able to describe.

A year or so after that conversation with Terry I was reading John Lahr's new biography of Williams. I was at the end of the book. Suddenly my mind presented to me a fully formed memory of how Tennessee Williams looked in his casket. His face seemed swollen, uniformly, like someone on medication. He was in a dark suit. His dark hair was combed back from his forehead almost severely. It was eerie how complete this picture came to me. But... what was it? Was it a recovered memory, or was it something that bubbled up from imagination? I didn't know.

Months later while going through papers for this book, I got from a warehouse the old journals and scripts from my CBS days, and found the tribute to Williams. And attached to it with a paper clip was a typed note I'd written when I filed away the script, after that day at Frank E. Campbell's. "The casket, in the middle of the room, was open. I looked down on a lonely genius I'd never seen in life."

Human memory, the odd way it works, is the damndest thing.

Britain Remembers a Great Briton

Mrs. Thatcher is with Wellington and Nelson now.

The Wall Street Journal: April 22, 2013

London

The funeral of Margaret Thatcher was beautiful, moving, just right. It had dignity and spirit, and in that respect was just like her. It also contained a surprise that shouldn't have been a surprise. It was a metaphor for where she stood in the pantheon of successful leaders of the 20th century.

The Right Honourable the Baroness Thatcher of Kesteven, LG, OM, FRS—so she was called on the front page of the service program—was a great lady, and the greatest peacetime prime minister of England in the 20th century. She unleashed her nation's economy, defeated selfish bullies who before her had always emerged victorious, and stood with the pope and the president against Soviet communism. The main project of her career was to advance the cause of human freedom and individual liberty. As David Cameron's education minister, Michael Gove, noted the other day, she saw economics not as a science but as one of the humanities. It wasn't about "immutable laws," it was about "the instincts and values" of human beings, their sense of justice and rightness. She was eloquent, stirring and had tons of guts. And of course she was a woman, the first British prime minister to be so. She made no special pleading in that area and did not claim to represent what we embarrassingly call women's issues. She was representing England and the issues British citizens faced. She did not ignore her sex and occasionally bopped political men on the head with small, bracing recognitions of their frailty. "The cocks will crow, but it's the hen that lays the eggs," she said. She noted that if you want anything said get a man, but if you want something done get a woman. All this she uttered in a proud but mock-stern tone. She was no victim. An oddity of her career is that she was routinely patronized by her inferiors. It seems to have steeled her.

A supporter told me in London of her frustrations with staff. She said once to her aides: "I don't need to be told *what*, I need to be told *how*." Meaning I have a vision, you have to tell me how we can implement it. That stayed in my mind. Politics now, in England as well as America, is dominated by politicians who are technicians. They always know how to do it. They just don't know what to do.

Thatcher's funeral was striking in that it was not, actually, about her. It was about what she thought it important for the mourners to know. The readings were about the fact of God, the gift of Christ, and the necessity of loving your country and working for its betterment. There were no long eulogies. In a friendly and relatively brief address, the bishop of London lauded her kindness and character. No funeral of an American leader would ever be like that: The dead American would be the star, with God in the position of yet another mourner who'd miss his leadership.

The pageantry, for an American, was most moving. The English as always do this brilliantly, but I wonder if they understand—they must, but it's not something they acknowledge—that when they bring out and put forward their splendor they are telling the world and themselves who they are and have been. Leading the procession into St. Paul's was the lord mayor of London, in velvet coat, breeches and buckled shoes. On his coat he wore Sir Thomas More's gold chain of office, taken from him before he was killed. Imagine a nation that puts such a man to death, contemplates it, concludes in the end it was wrong and now proudly displays the saint's chain at its greatest events. When I saw it I thought of a recent trip to the Vatican. Touring its archives, we were shown one of its proudest possessions: a letter from Galileo.

Things change. Time changes them. Great nations, and institutions, rethink. But only if they're great.

It mattered that the funeral was in August and splendid St. Paul's, mattered that Thatcher's coffin, placed under the great dome, stood directly over the tombs of Nelson and Wellington in the crypts below. (Marcus Binney in the *Times* said conservatives will note the above; happy to oblige.) This placing of Thatcher with the greats of the past, and the fact that the queen and Prince Philip came to her funeral, as they have for no prime minister since Churchill in 1965, served as an antidote to British television coverage surrounding her death.

It was terrible. They could not in any sustained way mark her achievements or even show any particular respect. All they could say was that she was "divisive and controversial," although sometimes they said "divisive and—well, really divisive." Anchors reported everything as if from a great distance, with no warmth; they all adopted the cool, analytical look they use when they mean to project distance. But as Tony Blair's aide Peter Mandelson, speaking at the think tank discussion at which Mr. Gove appeared, said, "to decide is to divide." He was quoting Mr. Blair.

And the more decisive, the more divisive.

In the past week left-wing political groups held death parties, all heavily reported, and threatened to demonstrate at the funeral. The head of the London police seemed to invite them to come. (Less important, but worth mentioning: The White House embarrassed itself by not sending a delegation of high-level current officeholders. Did the British notice? Oh yes. It's another way they think we're slipping.)

All this—the media, the left—had the effect of telling people: You'll look stupid if you speak in support of Thatcher, you'll look sentimental, old. And it may be dangerous to attend the funeral—there could be riots!

I wonder if certain people pushed this line so hard so that the day after the funeral they could report no one came.

So then, the surprise that was a metaphor.

At the end of the funeral they all marched down the aisle in great procession—the family, the queen, the military pallbearers carrying the casket bearing the Union Jack. The great doors flung open, the pallbearers marched forward and suddenly from the crowd a great roar. We looked at each other. Demonstrators? No. Listen. They were cheering. They were calling out three great hurrahs as the pallbearers went down the steps. Then long cheers and applause. It was electric.

England came. The people came. Later we would learn they'd stood 30 deep on the sidewalk, that quiet crowds had massed on the Strand and Fleet Street and Ludgate Hill. A man had held up a sign: "But We Loved Her."

"The end is where we start from." That is T. S. Eliot, whose "Little Gidding" she loved. When they died, Ronald Reagan, John Paul II, and Margaret Thatcher were old and long past their height of power. Everyone was surprised when Reagan died that crowds engulfed the Capitol; people slept on sidewalks to view him in state. When John Paul died the Vatican was astonished to see millions converge. "Santo Subito."

And now at the end some came for Thatcher, too.

What all three had in common: No one was with them but the people.

Margaret Hilda Thatcher, rest in peace.

* * *

A story I couldn't tell in the column:

When I went into St. Paul's Cathedral for Mrs. Thatcher's funeral, the ushers, looking at my ticket, kept gesturing me forward. This was surprising: I wasn't a member of an American delegation, part of an official party or a close friend. But the ushers in each section kept gesturing me forward, in the direction of the great church's altar. Finally I was directed to the ninth row, only eight behind Queen Elizabeth and Prince Philip. I felt mild dismay: They had put me in someone else's seat and that someone would come, and then we'd have to figure out where I was to be. But the minutes passed, the pews filled and no one came. Just before the service began I turned and looked at the pews behind me. My eyes met those of a middle-aged woman a few rows back. I did not know her. It was as if she read my mind and saw my confusion. "She loved you," she mouthed.

Later I found her in the crowd. She had worked with Mrs. Thatcher in the years after her prime ministership. "She always read your columns. She wanted you here. And there."

Columnists never know who's reading them, who's agreeing or shaking their head, who they have a relationship with, or an appointment with, when the column goes up or the paper comes out. I was very moved to find Mrs. Thatcher was a reader.

I had met her a number of times, talked with her. We had great talks about the world. She was eager in her retirement, which is when I knew her, to share her insights and experiences. When I think of those conversations what I remember first is a time we shared a weekend as house guests of a mutual friend on Long Island. We stayed up late two nights. On the last, she remembered being a child in wartime Britain and listening on the radio to Winston Churchill rally the nation. "Westward look, the land is bright..."

Thanks from a Grateful Country

For a man who changed the world, Ronald Reagan sure was modest.

The Wall Street Journal: June 7, 2004

He was dying for years and the day came and somehow it came as a blow. Not a loss but a blow. How could this be? Maybe we were all of us more loyal to him, and to the meaning of his life, than we quite meant to be.

And maybe it's more.

This was a life with size. It had heft, and meaning. I am thinking of what Stephen Vincent Benét, a writer whom he quoted, wrote on the death of his friend Scott Fitzgerald. "You can take off your hats now, gentlemen, and I think perhaps you'd better."

Ronald Reagan was not unappreciated at the end, far from it. But he was at the beginning.

* * *

His story was classically, movingly rags-to-riches; he was a nobody who became a somebody in the American way, utterly on his own and with the help of millions. He was just under 10 when the Roaring Twenties began, 16 when Lindbergh flew the ocean; he remembered as a little boy giving a coin to a doughboy leaning out a window of a troop train going east to the ships that would take them to the Marne and the Argonne Forest.

Ronald, nicknamed Dutch, read fiction. He liked stories of young men battling for the good and true. A story he wrote in

college had a hero arriving home from the war and first thing calling his girl. Someone else answered. Who is calling? "Tell her it's the
president," he said. He wrote that when he was 20 years old.

Many years later, in middle age, he was visited by a dream in
which he was looking for a house. He was taken to a mansion with
white walls and high sparkling windows. It was majestic. "This is a
house that is available at a price I can afford," he would think to himself. And then he'd come awake. From the day he entered the White
House for the first time as president, he never had the dream again.

His family didn't have much—no money, no local standing—
and they were often embarrassed. Jack Reagan was an alcoholic and
itinerant, a shoe salesman who drank when things were looking up.
They moved a lot. His mother was an Evangelical Christian who
was often out of the house helping others or taking in work at home.
(Like Margaret Thatcher's mother, and Pope John Paul's, too, Nell
Reagan worked as a seamstress at home, sewing clothes for money.)

Dutch and his brother, Moon, were often on their own. From
his father he learned storytelling and political views that were liberal
for the time and place. In old age he remembered with pride that
his father would smack him if he ever said anything as a child that
showed racial or religious bigotry. His mother gave him religious
faith, which helped him to trust life and allowed him to be an opti-
mist, which was his nature.

He wanted to be an artist, a cartoonist, a writer. Then he wanted
to be a sportscaster on radio, and talked his way in. Then he wanted
to be an actor. He went to Hollywood, became a star, did work that
he loved and married Jane Wyman, a more gifted actor than he.
They were mismatched, but she proved in her way to be as old-school
as he. In the decades after their divorce and long after he rose to
power, she never spoke publicly of him, not to get in the news when
her career was waning and not for money. She could have hurt him
and never did.

He volunteered for action in World War II, was turned away by doctors who told him with eyesight like his he'd probably shoot his own officer and miss. But they let him join behind the lines and he served at "Fort Roach" in Los Angeles, where he made training and information films. After the war, Ronald Reagan went on the local speaking circuit, talking of the needs of veterans and lauding the leadership of FDR and Truman. Once a woman wrote to him and noted that while he had movingly denounced Nazism, there was another terrible "ism," communism, and he ought to mention that, too. In his next speech, to industry people and others, he said that if communism ever proved itself the threat to decency that Nazism was, he'd denounce it, too. Normally he got applause in this part of the speech. Now he was met by silence.

In that silence he built his future, becoming a man who'd change the world.

The long education began. He studied communism, read Marx, read the Founders and the conservative philosophers from Burke to Burnham. He began to tug right. The Democratic Party and his industry continued to turn left. There was a parting.

A word on his intellectual reflexes. Ronald Reagan was not a cynic—he did not assume the worst about people. But he was a skeptic; he knew who we are. He did not think that people with great degrees or great success were necessarily smart, for instance. He had no interest in credentialism. He once told me an economist was a fellow with a Phi Beta Kappa key on one end of his chain and no watch on the other. That's why they never know what time it is. He didn't say this with asperity, but with mirth.

He did not dislike intellectuals—his heroes often were intellectuals, from the Founders straight through Milton Friedman and Hayek and Solzhenitsyn. But he did not favor the intellectuals of his own day, because he thought they were in general thick-headed. He thought that many of the 20th century's intellectuals were high-IQ dimwits. He had an instinctive agreement with Orwell's putdown that a particular idea was so stupid that only an intellectual would believe it.

He thought that intellectuals, like the great liberal academics of the latter half of the 20th century, tended to tie themselves in great webs of complexity, webs they'd often spun themselves—great complicated things that they'd get stuck in, and finally get out of, only to go and construct a new web for mankind to get caught in. The busy little spiders from Marx through Bloomsbury—some of whom, such as the Webbs, were truly the stupidest brilliant people who ever lived—through Harvard and Yale and the American left circa 1900 to 1990.

As president of the Screen Actors Guild he led the resistance to a growing communist presence in the unions and, with allies such as William Holden, outargued the boutique leftism of the Hollywood salons. But when a small army of congressional gasbags came to town, Ronald Reagan told the House Un-American Activities Committee that Hollywood could police itself, thank you. By the time it was over, even his harshest foes admitted he'd been fair. In the 1990s, an actress who'd been blacklisted, her career ruined, was invited by historians of Hollywood to criticize him. She said yes, she remembered him well. He was boring at parties. He was always talking about how great the New Deal was.

He wanted to be a great actor, but it never happened. He was a good actor. He married Nancy Davis, a young actress who'd gone to Smith. On their first date, she told me once, she was impressed. "He didn't talk, the way actors do, about their next part. He talked about the Civil War." They had children, made a life; she was his rock.

In 1962 he became a Republican; in 1966, with considerable initial reluctance, he ran for governor of California. The establishment of the day labeled him a right-wing movie star out of touch with California values; he beat the incumbent, Pat Brown, in a landslide.

He completed two successful terms in which he started with a huge budget deficit, left behind a modest surplus, cut taxes and got an ulcer. About the latter he was amazed. Even Jack Warner hadn't been able to give him an ulcer! But one day it went away. Prayer groups that did not know of his condition had been praying for him. He came to think their prayers healed him.

In his first serious bid for the presidency, in 1976, he challenged his own party's beleaguered incumbent, the hapless Gerald Ford. Ronald Reagan fought valiantly, state by state, almost unseated Mr. Ford, and returned from the convention having given one of the best speeches of his life. He told his weeping volunteers not to become cynical but to take the experience as inspiration. He promised he wouldn't go home and sit in a rocking chair. He quoted an old warrior: "I will lie me down and bleed awhile / And then I will rise and fight again." Four years later, he won the presidency from Jimmy Carter after a mean-spirited onslaught in which he was painted as racist, a man who knew nothing, a militarist. He won another landslide.

Once again he had nobody with him but the people.

*   *   *

In his presidency he did this: He outargued communism and refused to accept its claim of moral superiority; he rallied the West, rallied America and continued to make big gambles, including a defense-spending increase in a recession. He promised he'd place Pershings in Europe if the Soviets would not agree to arms reductions and told Soviet leaders that they'd never be able to beat us in defense, that we'd spend them into the ground. They were suddenly reasonable.

Ronald Reagan told the truth to a world made weary by lies. He believed truth was the only platform on which a better future could be built. He shocked the world when he called the Soviet Union "evil," because it was, and an "empire," because it was that, too. He never stopped bringing his message to the people of the world, to Europe and China and in the end the Soviet Union. And when it was over, the Berlin Wall had been turned into a million concrete souvenirs, and Soviet communism had fallen. But of course it didn't fall. It was pushed. By Mr. Know Nothing Cowboy Gunslinger Dimwit. All presidents should be so stupid.

He pushed down income taxes, too, from a high of 70% when he entered the White House to a new low of 28% when he left, igniting the long boom that, for all its ups and downs, is with us still. He believed, as JFK did, that a rising tide lifts all boats. He did much more, returning respect to our armed forces, changing 50-year-old assumptions about the place of government and the place of the citizen in the new America.

What an era his was. What a life he lived. He changed history for the better and was modest about it. He didn't bray about his accomplishments but saw them as the work of the American people. He did not see himself as entitled, never demanded respect, preferred talking to hotel doormen rather than State Department functionaries because he thought the doorman brighter and more interesting. When I pressed him once, a few years out of the presidency, to say what he thought the meaning of his presidency was, he answered, reluctantly, that it might be fairly said that he "advanced the boundaries of freedom in a world more at peace with itself." And so he did. And what could be bigger than that?

*   *   *

To be young and working in his White House at that time in human history was—well, we felt privileged to be there, with him. He made us feel not that we were born in a time of trouble but that we'd been born, luckily, at a time when we could end some trouble. We believed him. I'd think: This is a wonderful time to be alive. And when he died I thought: If I'd walked into the Oval Office 20 years ago to tell him that, he'd look up from whatever he was writing, smile, look away for a second and think, It's pretty much always a wonderful time.

And then he'd go back to his work.

And now he has left us. We will talk the next 10 days about who he was and what he did. It's not hard to imagine him now in a place where his powers have been returned to him and he's himself again—sweet-hearted, tough, funny, optimistic and very brave. You imagine him snapping one of those little salutes as he turns to say goodbye. Today I imagine saluting right back. Do you? We should do it the day he's buried, or when he lies in state in the Capitol Rotunda. We should say, "Good on you, Dutch." Thanks from a grateful country.

CHAPTER 3

As I Was Telling Kate...

I call this chapter As I Was Telling Kate because my friend Kate O'Beirne will like the title.

Its subject? History can move you. The people in history can move you. Valor can be found in surprising places.

* * *

Those Who Make Us Say "Oh!"

The Wall Street Journal: May 23, 2009

More than most nations, America has been, from its start, a hero-loving place. Maybe part of the reason is that at our founding we were a Protestant nation and not a Catholic one, and so we made "saints" of civil and political figures. George Washington was our first national hero, known everywhere, famous to children. When he died we had our first true national mourning, with cities and states reenacting his funeral. There was the genius-cluster that surrounded him, and invented us—Jefferson, Adams, Madison, Hamilton. Through much of the 20th century our famous heroes were in sports (Jack Dempsey, Joe Louis, the Babe, Joltin' Joe) the arts (Clark Gable, Robert Frost) business and philanthropy (from Andrew Carnegie to Bill Gates) and religion (Billy Graham). Nobody does fame like America, and they were famous.

The category of military hero—warrior—fell off a bit, in part because of the bad reputation of war. Some emerged of heroic size—Gens. Pershing and Patton, Eisenhower and Marshall. But somewhere in the 1960s I think we decided, or the makers of our culture decided, that to celebrate great warriors was to encourage war. And we always have too much of that. So they made a lot of movies depicting soldiers as victims and officers as brutish. This was especially true in the Vietnam era and the years that followed. Maybe a correction was in order: It's good to remember war is hell. But when we removed the warrior, we removed something intensely human, something ancestral and stirring, something celebrated naturally throughout the long history of man. Also it was ungrateful: Warriors put themselves in harm's way for us.

For Memorial Day, then, three warriors, two previously celebrated but not so known now by the young.

*   *   *

Alvin York was born in 1887 into a Tennessee farming family that didn't have much, but nobody else did so it wasn't so bad. He was the third of 11 children and had an average life for that time and place. Then World War I came. He experienced a crisis of conscience over whether to fight. His mother's Evangelical church tugged him toward more or less pacifist thinking, but he got a draft notice in 1917, joined the Army, went overseas, read and reread his Bible, and concluded that warfare was sometimes justified.

In the battle of the Argonne in October 1918, the Allies were attempting to break German lines when York and his men came upon well-hidden machine guns on high ground. As he later put it, "The Germans got us, and they got us right smart...and I'm telling you they were shooting straight." American soldiers "just went down like the long grass before the mowing machine at home."

But Cpl. York and his men went behind the German lines, overran a unit and captured the enemy. Suddenly there was new machine-gun fire from a ridge, and six Americans went down. York was in command, exposed but cool, and he began to shoot. "All I could do was touch the Germans off just as fast as I could. I was sharp shooting...All the time I kept yelling at them to come down. I didn't want to kill any more than I had to." A German officer tried to empty his gun into York while York fired. He failed but York succeeded, the Germans surrendered, and York and his small band marched 132 German prisoners back to the American lines.

His Medal of Honor citation called him fearless, daring and heroic. Warriors are funny people. They're often naturally peaceable, and often do great good when they return. York went home to Tennessee, married, founded an agricultural institute (it's still operating as an award-winning public high school) and a Bible school. They made a movie about him in 1941, the great Howard Hawks film "Sergeant York." If you are in Manhattan this week, you may walk down York Avenue on the Upper East Side. It was named for him. He died in Nashville in 1964 at 77.

*　*　*

Once, 25 years ago, my father (U.S. Army, replacement troops, Italy, 1945) visited Washington, a town he'd never been to. There was a lot to see: the White House, the Lincoln Memorial. But he just wanted to see one thing, Audie Murphy's grave.

Audie Leon Murphy was born in 1924 or 1926 (more on that in a moment) the sixth of 12 children of a Texas sharecropper. It was all hardscrabble for him: father left, mother died, no education, working in the fields from adolescence on. He was good with a hunting rifle: He said that when he wasn't, his family didn't eat, so yeah, he had to be good. He tried to join the Army after Pearl Harbor, was turned away as underage, came back the next year claiming to be 18 (he was probably 16) and went on to a busy war, seeing action as an infantryman in Sicily, Salerno and Anzio. Then came southern France, where the Germans made the mistake of shooting Audie Murphy's best friend, Lattie Tipton. Murphy wiped out the machine gun crew that did it.

On Jan. 26, 1945, Lt. Murphy was engaged in a battle in which his unit took heavy fire and he was wounded. He ordered his men back. From his Medal of Honor citation:

Behind him...one of our tank destroyers received a direct hit and began to burn. Its crew withdrew to the woods. 2d Lt. Murphy continued to direct artillery fire, which killed large numbers of the advancing enemy infantry. With the enemy tanks abreast of his position, 2d Lt. Murphy climbed on the burning tank destroyer, which was in danger of blowing up at any moment, and employed its .50 caliber machine gun against the enemy. He was alone and exposed to German fire from three sides, but his deadly fire killed dozens of Germans and caused their infantry attack to waver. The enemy tanks, losing infantry support, began to fall back.

Murphy returned to Texas a legend. He was also 5 foot 7, having grown two inches while away. He became an actor (44 films, mostly Westerns) and businessman. He died in a plane crash in 1971 and was buried with full honors at Arlington, but he did a warrior-like thing. He asked that the gold leaf normally put on the gravestone of a Medal of Honor recipient not be used. He wanted a plain GI headstone. Some worried this might make his grave harder to find. My father found it, and he was not alone. Audie Murphy's grave is the most visited site at Arlington with the exception of John F. Kennedy's eternal flame.

*   *   *

I thought of these two men the other night after I introduced at a dinner a retired Air Force general named Chuck Boyd. He runs Business Executives for National Security, a group whose members devote time and treasure to helping the government work through various 21st-century challenges. I mentioned that Chuck had been shot down over Vietnam on his 105th mission in April 1966 and was a POW for 2,488 days. He's the only former POW of the era to go on to become a four-star general.

When I said "2,488," a number of people in the audience went "Oh!" I heard it up on the podium. They didn't know because he doesn't talk about it, and when asked to, he treats it like nothing, a long night at a bad inn. Warriors always do that. They all deserve the "Oh!"

A Day at the Beach

How Ensign John Whitehead Helped Liberate Europe

The Wall Street Journal: July 5, 2008

It was May 1944, and 22-year-old John Whitehead of Montclair, N.J., an ensign on the USS Thomas Jefferson, was placed in charge of five of the landing craft for the invasion of Europe. Each would ferry 25 soldiers from the TJ, as they called it, onto the shore of France. John's landing site was to be a 50-yard stretch of shoreline dubbed Dog Red Beach. It fell near the middle of the sector called Omaha Beach, which in turn fell in the middle of the entire assault.

The TJ sailed to Portsmouth Harbor, which was jam-packed with ships. On June 1 the Army troops arrived, coming up the gangway one by one. "They were very quiet," John said this week. Word came on June 4 that they'd leave that night, but they were ordered back in a storm. The next morning, June 5, the rain was still coming down, but the seas were calmer. Around 8 that night, they cast off to cross the Channel. The skies were dark, rain lashed the deck, and the TJ rolled in the sea. At midnight they dropped anchor nine miles off the French coast. They ate a big breakfast of eggs and bacon. At 2 a.m. the crew began lowering the Higgins boats—"a kind of floating boxcar, rectangular, with high walls"—over the side by crane. The soldiers had to climb down big nets to get aboard. "They had practiced, but as Eisenhower always said, 'In wartime, plans are only good until the moment you try to execute them.'"

The Higgins boats pitched in the choppy sea. The soldiers, loaded down "like mountaineers" with rifles, flamethrowers, radio equipment, artillery parts, tarps, food, water, "70 pounds in all"—had trouble getting from the nets to the boats. "I saw a poor soul slip from the net into the water. He sank like a stone. He just disappeared in the depths of the sea. There was nothing we could do." So they boarded the boats on the deck and hoisted them down to the water.

It took John's five little boats four hours to cover the nine miles to the beach. "They were the worst hours of our lives. It was pitch black, cold, and the rain was coming down in sheets drenching us. The boats were being tossed in the waves, making all of us violently sick. We'd all been given the big breakfast. Hardly anyone could hold it down. Packed in like that, with the boat's high walls. A cry went up: 'For Christ's sake, do it in your helmet!'

"Around 4 a.m. the dawn broke and a pale light spread across the sea, and now we could see that we were in the middle of an armada—every kind of boat, destroyers, probably the greatest array of sea power ever gathered."

Now they heard the sound, the deep boom of the shells from the U.S. battleships farther out at sea, shelling the beach to clear a path. Above, barely visible through clouds, they saw the transport planes pushing through to drop paratroopers from the 82nd and 101st Airborne Divisions. "Those were brave men."

At 5 a.m. they were close enough to shore to see landmarks—a spit of land, a slight rise of a bluff. In front of them they saw some faster, sleeker British boats trying desperately to stay afloat in the choppy water. As the Americans watched, three of the boats flipped over and sank, drowning all the men. A British navigator went by in a different kind of boat. "He was standing up and he called out to my friend in a very jaunty British accent, 'I say, fellows, which way is it to Pointe du Hoc?' That was one of the landmarks, and the toughest beach of all. My friend yelled out that it was up to our right. 'Very good!' he cried out, and then went on by with a little wave of his hand."

Closer to shore, a furious din—"It was like a Fourth of July celebration multiplied by a thousand." By 6 a.m. they were 800 yards from shore. All five boats of the squadron had stayed together. The light had brightened enough that John could see his wristwatch. "At 6:20 I waved them in with a hard chop of my arm: Go!"

*   *   *

They faced a barrier, made a sharp left, ran parallel to the shore looking for an opening, got one, turned again toward the beach. They hit it, were in a foot or two of water. The impact jarred loose the landing ramps to release the soldiers as planned. But on John's boat, it didn't work. He scrambled to the bow, got a hammer, pounded the stuck bolt. The ramp crashed down and the soldiers lunged forth. Some were hit with shrapnel as they struggled through to the beach. Others made it to land only to be hit as they crossed it. The stuck ramp probably saved John's life. After he'd rushed forward to grab the hammer, he turned and saw the coxswain he'd been standing next to had been hit and killed by an incoming shell.

The troops of Omaha Beach took terrible fire. Half the soldiers from John's five boats were killed or wounded. "It was a horrible sight. But I had to concentrate on doing my job." To make room for the next wave of landings, they raised the ramp, backed out, turned around and sped back to the TJ. "I remember waving hello to the soldiers in the incoming boats, as if we were all on launches for a pleasure cruise. I remember thinking how odd that such gestures of civility would persist amid such horror."

Back at the TJ, he was told to take a second breakfast in the wardroom—white tablecloths, steward's mates asking if he'd like more. He thought it unreal: "from Dog Red Beach to the Ritz." He heard in the background the quiet boom of the liberation of Europe. Then back to a Higgins boat for another run at the beach. This time the ramp lowered, and he got off. Dog Red Beach was secure. The bodies of the dead and wounded had been carried up onto a rise below a bluff. He felt thankful he had survived. "Then I took a few breaths and felt elated, proud to have played a part in maybe the biggest battle in history."

* * *

John went on to landings in Marseilles, Iwo Jima and Okinawa. After he came home, he went on to chair Goldman Sachs, work in Ronald Reagan's State Department and head great organizations such as the International Rescue Committee. He is, in that beautiful old phrase, a public citizen.

But if you asked him today his greatest moment, he'd say that day on the beach, when he was alive and grateful for it. "At that moment, dead tired, soaked to the skin, I would not have wanted to be anywhere else in the world."

It is silly to think one generation is "better" than another. No one born in 1920 is, by virtue of that fact, better than someone born in 1960. But it is true that each era has a certain mood, certain assumptions—in John's era, sacrifice—and each generation distinguishes itself in time, or doesn't. John's did. He himself did. And what better day than today to say: Thanks, John.

How to Find Grace after Disgrace

The Wall Street Journal: July 12, 2013

What a scandal it was. It had everything—beautiful women, spies, a semi-dashing government minister married to a movie star, a society doctor who functioned, essentially, as a pimp. And the backdrop was an august English country estate where intrigue had occurred before.

Unlike modern political sex scandals, which are cold and strange, it was what a scandal should be: dark, glamorous. Human. No furtive pictures of privates sent to strangers, no haggling over the prostitute's bill.

President Kennedy loved hearing about the story, and when he was on the phone with his friend the British prime minister, as he often was, asking advice on Cuba or de Gaulle, he was as likely to be asking, sympathetically but pointedly as one who loves gossip would: *How's it going with Profumo? What's the latest?*

It was 50 years ago, the spring and summer of 1963. The prime minister was Harold Macmillan, the last Conservative giant before Margaret Thatcher but more broadly beloved, in part because he wasn't all that conservative. He was in tune with his times, until he wasn't. He'd been in government 11 years.

It came out that his secretary of state for war, John Profumo, 48, had become involved with a group of people who gathered at Cliveden, the country estate of the Astor family, about whom controversy had swirled since World War II. Years later Macmillan would write in his diary: "The old 'Cliveden' set was disastrous politically. The new 'Cliveden' set is said to be equally disastrous morally."

It was for Profumo. At a pool party hosted by the society doctor, he met a young woman, 19-year-old Christine Keeler, who was either a dancer or a prostitute depending on the day and claimant. They commenced an affair. But Miss Keeler was also, she later said, romantically involved with the Soviet naval attaché assigned to London. Yevgeny Ivanov was there the day Profumo met her. And as all but children would have known, a Soviet military attaché was a Soviet spy.

The affair lasted a few months and was over by 1962. But there was a letter. And there were rumors. They surfaced in Parliament, where the Labour Party smelled blood.

When Profumo was caught, he panicked—and lied. That's what did him in. And his lie was emphatic: He'd bring libel charges if the allegations were repeated outside the House.

Nearby, as he spoke, sat Harold Macmillan, glumly hoping or believing in his minister's innocence. When Profumo, on the urging of his wife, came clean, Macmillan was left looking like a doddering Tory fool, a co-conspirator in a cover-up, or at least a bungler of a major national-security question. Mortally wounded, he considered resigning. His government collapsed a year later.

Profumo—humiliated on every front page as an adulterer, a liar, a man of such poor judgment and irresponsibility that he mindlessly cavorted with enemy spies—was finished. Alistair Horne, in his biography of Macmillan, wrote of Profumo after the scandal as a "wretched" figure, "disgraced and stripped of all public dignities."

Everyone hoped he'd disappear. He did.

Then, three years later, he declared himself rehabilitated. In the midst of a classic Fleet Street scrum—"Do you still see whores?" demanded a hack from the Sun—Profumo announced he'd deepened and matured and was standing for Parliament "to serve the public." Of course, he said, "It all depends on the voters, whether they can be forgiving. It's all in their hands. I throw my candidacy on their mercy."

Well, people didn't want to think they were unmerciful. Profumo won in a landslide, worked his way up to party chief and 12 years later ran for prime minister, his past quite forgotten, expunged, by his mounting triumphs.

Wait—that's not what happened. Nothing like that happened! It's the opposite of what happened.

Because Profumo believed in remorse of conscience—because he actually had a conscience—he could absorb what happened and let it change him however it would. In a way what he believed in was *reality*. He'd done something he thought terrible—to his country, to his friends, to strangers who had to explain the headlines about him to their children.

He never knew political power again. He never asked for it. He did something altogether more confounding.

He did the hardest thing for a political figure. He really went away. He went to a place that helped the poor, a rundown settlement house called Toynbee Hall in the East End of London. There he did social work—actually the scut work of social work, washing dishes and cleaning toilets. He visited prisons for the criminally insane, helped with housing for the poor and worker education.

And it wasn't for show, wasn't a step on the way to political redemption. He worked at Toynbee for 40 years.

He didn't give interviews, never wrote a book, didn't go on TV. Alistair Horne: "Profumo...spent the rest of his life admirably dedicated to valuable good works, most loyally supported by his wife. At regular intervals, some journalist writing 'in the public interest' would rake up the old story to plague the ruined man and cause him renewed suffering. His haunted, unsmiling face was a living epitaph to the 'Swinging Sixties.'"

In November 2003, to mark the 40th anniversary of his work, Profumo gave an interview to an old friend. "Jack," said W. F. Deedes, "what have you learnt from this place?" After a pause for thought, Profumo said: "Humility."

He was president of Toynbee by then, respected, but nothing quite said what needed saying like what happened at Margaret Thatcher's 70th birthday party, in 1995. To show their countrymen what he'd done—and what they *thought* of what he'd done—they invited him, walked him through and put him in a particular place. They seated him next to the queen. People wonder about the purpose of establishments. That is the purpose of establishments.

When he died in 2006, at 91, the reliably ironic Daily Telegraph wore its heart on its sleeve. "No one in public life ever did more to atone for his sins; no one behaved with more silent dignity as his name was repeatedly dragged through the mud; and few ended their lives as loved and revered by those who knew him."

* * *

So what are we saying? You know.

We're saying the answer to the politician's question, "What is the optimum moment at which to come back from a big sex scandal, and how do I do it?" is this:

"You are asking the wrong question."

The right questions would go something like: "What can I do to stop being greedy for power, attention and adulation? How can I come to understand that the question is not the public's capacity to forgive but my own capacity to exercise sound judgment and regard for others?

"How can I stop being a manipulator of public emotions and become the kind of person who generates headlines that parents are relieved—grateful—to explain to their children?"

And of course the answer is: You can do what John Profumo did. You can go away. You can do something good. You can help women instead of degrading them, help your culture and your city instead of degrading them.

You can become a man.

"Oh Wow!"

The Wall Street Journal: December 24, 2011

The great words of the year? "Oh wow. Oh wow. Oh wow."

They are the last words of Steve Jobs, reported by his sister, the novelist Mona Simpson, who was at his bedside. In her eulogy, a version of which was published in the New York Times, she spoke of how he looked at his children "as if he couldn't unlock his gaze." He'd said goodbye to her, told her of his sorrow that they wouldn't be able to be old together, "that he was going to a better place." In his final hours his breathing was deep, uneven, as if he were climbing.

"Before embarking, he'd looked at his sister Patty, then for a long time at his children, then at his life's partner, Laurene, and then over their shoulders past them. Steve's final words were: 'OH WOW. OH WOW. OH WOW.' "

The caps are Simpson's, and if she meant to impart a sense of wonder and mystery she succeeded. "Oh wow" is not a bad way to express the bigness, power and force of life, and death. And of love, by which he was literally surrounded.

I wondered, too, after reading the eulogy, if I was right to infer that Jobs saw something, and if so, what did he see? What happened there that he looked away from his family and expressed what sounds like awe? I thought of a story told by a friend, whose grown son had died, at home, in hospice care. The family was ringed around his bed. As Robert breathed his last, an infant in the room let out a great baby laugh as if he saw something joyous, wonderful, and gestured toward the area above Robert's head. The infant's mother, startled, moved to shush him but my friend, her mother, said no, maybe he's just reacting to … something only babies see.

Anyway, I sent Ms. Simpson's eulogy to a number of people and spoke to some of them, and they all had two things in common in terms of their reaction. They'd get a faraway look, and think. And if they had a thought to share, they did it with modesty. No one said, "I think I can guess what he saw," "I know who he saw," or "Believe me, if he saw anything it was the product of the last, disordered sparks of misfiring neurons."

They were always modest, reflective. One just said, "Wow."

Modesty when contemplating death is a good thing.

When words leave people silent and thinking, they are powerful words. Steve Jobs' last words were the best thing said in 2011.

* * *

The unexpected cinematic gift of the year? "The Iron Lady," the movie about Margaret Thatcher, starring Meryl Streep, that's opening in this country on Dec. 30.

When words leave people yapping and not thinking they are often political words, but there isn't much that is, really, political about this film. Its makers don't seem that interested in the development of character, thought they had seized on a great one, and were right. It's a well-meaning and at times deeply moving meditation on old age and the enduring nature of love. It is good, not great, and contains within it a masterpiece.

"The Iron Lady" locates class as an important and largely ignored element of Mrs. Thatcher's struggle. The leftist intelligentsia of her day, which claimed loyalty to and identification with the poor and marginalized, was shot through with snobs and snobbery. Underneath their egalitarian chatter was (and to some degree still is) a hidden, hungry admiration for and desire to be associated with the well named and well connected. The top of the right, the Tories, who said they stood for tradition, the rights of the oppressed middle and the greatness of England, was heavily populated by a more familiar kind of snob, those who took more overt pleasure in their titles and pedigree, and wealth. They were not eager for change.

Both left and right looked down on women, especially styleless grinds and grocers' daughters who thought they were the equal of the boys. The movie suggests Mrs. Thatcher's defiance of the snobs while depicting her defeat of the snobs.

Mrs. Thatcher's political views are never granted any sympathetic legitimacy, though the movie subtly allows there may have been some legitimacy. Perhaps the great flaw is that it has too great a fear of exactly locating her greatness, and the meaning of her greatness. This is not so much a political as an aesthetic flaw: In the classic movies about Elizabeth I, for instance, you knew why you were watching the movie, why she was its subject and how she changed history.

And yes, the film descends at the end to a bit of the "Devil Wears Prada," as the prime minister berates her cabinet. I've actually seen her upbraid people. It was softer and sweeter and all the more cutting for that.

The masterpiece is Meryl Streep's portrayal of Mrs. Thatcher, which is not so much a portrayal as an inhabitation. It doesn't do justice to say Ms. Streep talks like her, looks like her, catches some of her spirit, though those things are true. It's something deeper than that, something better and more important. She tried to be Margaret Thatcher, and there's a real tribute in that.

* * *

The left in America has largely thrown in the towel on Ronald Reagan, but in Britain Thatcher-hatred remains fresh. Why?

Because she was a woman. Because women in politics are always by definition seen as presumptuous: They presume to lead men.

When they are as bright as the men they're disliked by the men, and when they're brighter and more serious they're hated. Mrs. Thatcher's very presence was an insult to the left because it undermined the left's insistence that only leftism and its protection of the weak and disadvantaged would allow women to rise. She rose without them while opposing what they stood for. On the other hand, some of the Tory men around her had been smacked on the head by her purse often enough to wish for revenge. What better revenge than to fail to fully stand up for her to posterity?

And so her difficult position. But one senses that is changing.

* * *

Final note. We are at a point in our culture when we actually have to pull for grown-up movies, when we must try to encourage them and laud them when they come by. David Lean wouldn't be allowed to make movies today, John Ford would be forced to turn John Wayne into a 30-something failure-to-launch hipster whose big moment is missing the toilet in the vomit scene in "Hangover Ten." Our movie culture has descended into immaturity, deep and inhuman violence, a pervasive and flattened sexuality. It is an embarrassment.

In Iraq this year I asked an Iraqi military officer doing joint training at an American base what was the big thing he'd come to believe about Americans in the years they'd been there. He thought. "You are a better people than your movies say." He had judged us by our exports. He had seen the low slag heap of our culture and assumed it was a true expression of who we are.

And so he'd assumed we were disgusting.

Credit, then, to those who make movies for grown-ups. I end with words I never expected to say: "Thank you, Harvey Weinstein. WELL DONE."

The Royal Wedding

CBS News: July 28, 1981

Reporting now from St. Paul's Cathedral—Christopher Wren's masterpiece in the heart of London. At the Royal Wedding tomorrow Prince Charles and Lady Diana will stand before the altar of this great church. But there's a story about what's *behind* the altar. It's the American War Memorial, a little place with a stained glass window that lets in the light. There's a little area where you can kneel and pray. And there is a book, a big book. It contains the names of the 28,000 American men and women who served in Britain and died in World War II. And each day in this cathedral, they turn a page.

An American in London is continually struck by the ties that bind. The ties of bloodlines (Lady Diana is said to have 200 American ancestors, including George Washington) and ties of blood (those names in the book at St. Paul's, where each day they turn a page). It is a romantic notion, but you could say that for centuries America and Britain have been giving each other some of their best. Winston Churchill's mother was Jennie Jerome of Brooklyn, U.S.A. And when John Kennedy made Churchill an honorary U.S. citizen, the old man was moved to tears. Kennedy's father, of course, was a U.S. Ambassador here. His son Joe died in World War II. And his name is in the book at St. Paul's, where each day they turn a page.

Our connections are not always sad, of course. You remember Lady Nancy Astor, the American who married a title and became a Member of Parliament. She's the one who married a title and became a Member of Parliament. She's the one who had that famous exchange with Churchill—"Sir, if you were my husband I'd put poison in your coffee!"—"Madame," said Churchill, "if you were my wife I would drink it!" Writers have been claiming that line as their own for years. England and America have been claiming each other's *writers* for years.

Take a walk through Poet's Corner in Westminster Abbey and you'll see a bust of Longfellow. Near him is T. S. Eliot, born and bred in Missouri, educated at Harvard. On his tombstone it says "The communication of the dead is tongued with fire beyond the language of the living." Down the aisle from Poet's Corner there's a memorial to the civilians who died in World War II, and dominating that little corner is a memorial to the 32nd President of the United States. It says "Franklin Delano Roosevelt, 1882–1945. A faithful friend of freedom and of Britain."

There is another friend of Britain we think of when we're in London. There is no statue to Ed Murrow here, no plaque in the West End, no little marker on a rooftop somewhere. But it was Murrow more than anyone else who brought the Battle of Britain home to the American people, and in a special way. When he wanted to show how the British could take it he didn't say they were brave; he put a microphone on the sidewalk during an air raid so you could hear the quiet pat of footsteps as Londoners walked calmly to the Underground...

You can't think of the things America and Britain gave each other without coming up against those clean and simple scripts that began "This is London." When you heard that, you knew something was coming, something was going to be *said*. It's a preface that lives in the language these two countries share, and in this profession. Which is why we think of it now and then, as each day we turn a page.

CHAPTER 4

America, America

I suppose America is the central intellectual subject of my life and I'm not wholly sure why beyond the obvious—if you know its history, with all its imperfections, why would you not love it and care about it? When I was a child I absorbed from my great-aunt, Jane Jane, a sense of love for this place she'd come to, that had rescued her from want and given her a job and many of the delights of life. When I was a young woman America was under siege and criticism—Vietnam, etc.—and I felt protective. That feeling of protectiveness accompanied me the rest of my life. This is a great project we're in.

* * *

"Is That Allowed?" "It Is Here."

The Wall Street Journal: July 7, 2012

There's something Haley Barbour reminded me of called the Gate Rule. The former Mississippi governor said it's the first thing you should think of when you think about immigration. People are either lined up at the gate trying to get out of a country, or lined up trying to get in.

It says something about the health of a nation when they're lined up to get in, as they are, still, with America. It says, of course, that compared with a lot of the rest of the world, America's economy isn't in such bad shape. But it says more than that. People don't want to come to a place when they know they'll be treated badly. They don't want to call your home their home unless they know you'll make room for them in more than economic ways.

And so this July 4, a small tribute to American friendliness, openness and lack of—what to call it? The old hatreds. They dissipate here. In Ireland, Catholics and Protestants could be at each other's throats for centuries, but the minute they moved here, they were in the Kiwanis Club together. The Mideast is a cauldron, but when its residents move here, they wind up on the same PTA committee. It sounds sentimental, but this is part of the magic of America, and the world still knows it even if we, in our arguments, especially about immigration, forget.

So, three stories of American friendliness, openness and lack of the old hatreds.

There was a teenager who came here with his parents and younger brother. They arrived in New York and got an apartment on 181st Street and Broadway. He spoke little English but went right into public school. The family needed money, so when he was 16, he transferred to night school and got a day job at a shaving-brush factory. He wore big, heavy rubber gloves and squeezed bleaching acid out of the bristles. Soon he went part-time to City College, and then he entered the U.S. Army.

This is a classic immigrant story. It could be about anyone. But the teenager went on to become an American secretary of state, and his name is Henry Kissinger. Here is another part of the story that is classic: how Americans treated him. The workers at the factory were older than he, mostly Italian American, some second generation. They wanted to help make him part of things, so they started taking him to baseball games. "It was the summer of 1939...I didn't know anything about baseball," he remembered this week. Now here he was in the roaring stands at Yankee Stadium.

About the people in the bleachers, he said, "The most striking thing was the enormous friendliness, the bantering." In Hitler's Germany, "I saw crowds, I'd go to the other side of the street." Here, no sense of looming threat. "That I would say was a very American part of my experience."

He was "enchanted" by the game—"the subtlety, the little nuances—you can watch what the strategy is and how they judge what the opponent is likely to do by the way the fielders position themselves...It is a game that combines leisure with highly dramatic moments!"

And there was the man called Joe DiMaggio. The factory workers would sort of say, "If you take a look at Joe DiMaggio," you will learn something about this country. DiMaggio was "infinitely graceful" as a fielder, "he would sort of lope towards the ball...nothing dramatic, he didn't tumble, he didn't strut, and he made it look effortless." He didn't "stand there wagging his bat...He would just stand there with his bat raised...He was all concentration."

Years later they met, and Mr. Kissinger, faced with his boyhood idol, that symbol of those early years, was awed. It was like being a kid and meeting a movie star: "I didn't know exactly what to say to him." They became friends. "He had a fierce kind of integrity."

So Henry Kissinger learned some things about Americans, and America, thanks to a bunch of Italian guys in a brush factory downtown. They were good to him. They were welcoming. Probably when they or their people were new here, someone was good to them.

That is American friendliness. Here is American openness— meaning if you are open to it, it will be open to you. Mary Dorian was an uneducated Irish farm girl with no family to speak of and no prospects. She came to America on her own, around 1920. She wrote to the one girl she knew, a distant cousin in Brooklyn, to ask that she meet her at the ship. Mary landed at Ellis Island, went to the agreed-upon spot, and the cousin wasn't there. She had forgotten. Mary, my grandmother, spent her first night in America alone on a park bench in lower Manhattan.

She went on to find Brooklyn and settle in. She joined an Irish club and a step-dancing club. They didn't have anything like that back home. We make a mistake when we worry that sometimes immigrants come here and burrow more into their old nationality than their new one. It's not a rejection of America, just a way of not being lonely, of still being connected to something. She met her husband in an Irish club, and she got a job hanging up coats in a restaurant. Then she became a bathroom attendant at Abraham & Straus on Fulton Street in downtown Brooklyn. When she died in 1960, a lot of black people came to the funeral. This, in a Brooklyn broken up into separate ethnic enclaves, was surprising, but it wouldn't have been to her. They were her coworkers from A&S, all the girls who worked in the ladies' room, and their families. They loved her.

When she died, Mary Dorian had a job, a family and friends.

She had come here with none of those things. She trusted America, and it came through.

As for the old hatreds:

There was a 7-year-old boy who came over from Germany on the SS Bremen. He was traveling with his younger brother—they, too, were fleeing the Nazis—and a steward. The Bremen anchored on Manhattan's West Side on May 4, 1939, and the children were joined by their father, who was already in New York. They stood on deck watching the bustle of disembarking, and then the boy saw something. "Across the street from where we were, and visible from the boat, was a delicatessen which had its name in neon with Hebrew letters," he remembered this week.

He was startled. Something with Hebrew letters—that was impossible back home. He asked his father, "Is that allowed?"

And his father said, "It is here."

It is here.

The little boy was Mike Nichols, the great film and stage director, who went on to do brilliant things with the freedom he was given here.

Sometimes we think our problems are so big we have to remake ourselves to meet them. But maybe we don't. Maybe we just have to remember who we are—open, friendly, welcoming and free.

Happy Fourth of July to this tender little country, to the great and fabled nation that is still, this day, the hope of the world.

On Letting Go

How we become American.

The Wall Street Journal: June 29, 2007

Happy Fourth of July. To mark this Wednesday's holiday, I share a small moment that happened a year ago in Bay Ridge, Brooklyn. I was at a wake for an old family friend named Anthony Coppola, a retired security guard who'd been my uncle Johnny's best friend from childhood. All the old neighborhood people were there from Clinton Avenue and from other streets in Brooklyn, and Anthony's sisters Tessie and Angie and Gloria invited a priest in to say some prayers. About a hundred of us sat in chairs in a little side chapel in the funeral home.

The priest, a jolly young man with a full face and thick black hair, said he was new in the parish, from South America. He made a humorous, offhand reference to the fact that he was talking to long-time Americans who'd been here for ages. This made the friends and family of Anthony Coppola look at each other and smile. We were Italian, Irish, everything else. Our parents had been the first Americans born here. We had all grown up with two things, a burly conviction that we were American and an inner knowledge that we were also something else. I think we experienced this as a plus, a double gift, though I don't remember anyone saying that. When Anthony's mother or her friend, my grandmother, talked about Italy or Ireland, they called it "the old country." Which suggested there was a new one, and that we were new in it.

But this young priest, this new immigrant, he looked at us and thought we were from the Mayflower. As far as he was concerned—as far as he could tell—we were old Yankee stock. We were the establishment. As the pitcher in "Bang the Drum Slowly" says, "This handed me a laugh."

This is the way it goes in America. You start as the Outsider and wind up the Insider, or at least being viewed as such by the newest Outsiders. We are a nation of still-startling social fluidity. Anyone can become "American," but they have to want to first.

It has had me thinking a lot about how people become American.

* * *

I don't know that when my grandfather Patrick Byrne and his sisters, Etta and Mary Jane, who had lived on a hardscrabble little farm in Donegal, on the west coast of Ireland, felt about America when they got here. I don't know if they were "loyal to America." I think they were loyal to their decision to come to America. In for a penny, in for a pound. They had made their decision. Now they had to prove to themselves it was the right one. I remember asking Etta what she'd heard about America before she got here. She said, "The streets were paved with gold." All the immigrants of the late 19th and early 20th century used that phrase.

When I was in college in the 1970s, I got a semester abroad my junior year, and I took a boat from England to Ireland and made my way back to Donegal. This was approximately 55 years after my grandfather and his sisters had left. There I met an old man who'd been my grandfather's boyhood friend. He lived by himself in a shack on a hill and was grateful the cousins I'd found had sent me to him. He told me he'd been there the day my grandfather, then a young man, left. He said the lorry came down the lane and stopped for my grandfather, and that his father, my great-grandfather, said goodbye. He said, "Go now, and never come back to hungry Ireland again."

My grandfather had his struggles here but never again went

home. He'd cast his lot. That's an important point in the immigrant experience, when you cast your lot, when you make your decision. It makes you let go of something. And it makes you hold on to something. The thing you hold on to is the new country. In succeeding generations of your family, the holding on becomes a habit and then a patriotism, a love. You realize America is more than the place where the streets were paved with gold. It has history, meaning, tradition. Suddenly that's what you treasure.

A problem with newer immigrants now is that for some it's no longer necessary to make The Decision. They don't always have to cast their lot. There are so many ways not to let go of the old country now, from choosing to believe that America is only about money, to technology that encourages you to stay in constant touch with the land you left, to TV stations that broadcast in the old language. If you're an immigrant now, you don't have to let go. Which means you don't have to fully join, to enmesh. Your psychic investment in America doesn't have to be full. It can be provisional, temporary. Or underdeveloped, or not developed at all.

And this may have implications down the road, and I suspect people whose families have been here a long time are concerned about it. It's one of the reasons so many Americans want a pause, a stopping of the flow, a time for the new ones to settle down and settle in. It's why they oppose the mischief of the Masters of the Universe in Washington, who make believe they cannot close our borders while they claim they can competently micromanage all other aspects of immigration.

* * *

It happens that I know how my grandfather's sister Mary Jane became an American. She left a paper trail. She kept a commonplace book, a sort of diary with clippings and mementos. She kept it throughout the 1920s, when she was still new here. I found it after she'd died. It's a big brown book with cardboard covers and delicate pages. In the front, in the first half, there are newspaper clippings about events in Ireland, and sentimental poems. "I am going back to Glenties…"

But about halfway through, the content changes. There is a newspaper clipping about something called "Thanksgiving." There are newspaper photos of parades down Fifth Avenue. And suddenly, near the end, there are patriotic poems. One had this refrain: "So it's home again and home again, America for me./ My heart is turning home again, and there I long to be./ In the land of youth and freedom beyond the ocean bars/ Where the air is full of sunlight, and the flag is full of stars."

Years later, when I worked for Ronald Reagan, those words found their way into one of his speeches, a nod from me to someone who'd made her decision, cast her lot and changed my life.

I think I remember the last time I told that story. I think it was to a young Mexican American woman who was a speechwriter for Bill Clinton. I think she completely understood.

God bless our beloved country on the 231st anniversary of its birth.

"To Old Times"

The Wall Street Journal: August 24, 2007

Once I went hot-air ballooning in Normandy. It was the summer of 1991. It was exciting to float over the beautiful French hills and the farms with crisp crops in the fields. It was dusk, and we amused ourselves calling out "Bonsoir!" to cows and people in little cars. We had been up for an hour or so when we had a problem and had to land. We looked for an open field, aimed toward it and came down a little hard. The gondola dragged, tipped and spilled us out. A half dozen of us emerged scrambling and laughing with relief.

Suddenly before us stood an old man with a cracked and weathered face. He was about 80, in rough work clothes. He was like a Life magazine photo from 1938: "French farmer hoes his field." He'd seen us coming from his farmhouse and stood before us with a look of astonishment as the huge bright balloon deflated and tumbled about.

One of us spoke French and explained our situation. The farmer said, or asked, "You are American." We nodded, and he made a gesture—I'll be back!—and ran to the house. He came back with an ancient bottle of calvados, the local brandy. It was literally covered in dust and dry dirt, as if someone had saved it a long time.

He told us—this will seem unlikely, and it amazed us—that he had not seen an American in many, many years, and we asked when. "The invasion," he said. The Normandy Invasion.

Then he poured the calvados and made a toast. I wish I had notes on what he said. Our French speaker translated it into something like "To old times." And we raised our glasses knowing we

were having a moment of unearned tenderness. Lucky Yanks, that a
wind had blown us to it.

That was 16 years ago, and I haven't seen some of the people
with me since that day, but I know every one of us remembers it and
keeps it in his good-memory hoard.

He didn't welcome us because he knew us. He didn't treat us
like royalty because we had done anything for him. He honored
us because we were related to, were the sons and daughters of, the
men of the Normandy Invasion. The men who had fought their way
through France hedgerow by hedgerow, who'd jumped from planes
in the dark and climbed the cliffs and given France back to the
French. He thought we were of their sort. And he knew they were
good. He'd seen them, when he was young.

*　　*　　*

I've been thinking of the old man because of Iraq and the coming
debate on our future there. Whatever we do or should do, there is
one fact that is going to be left on the ground there when we're gone.
That is the impression made by, and the future memories left by,
American troops in their dealings with the Iraqi people.

I don't mean the impression left by the power and strength of
our military. I mean the impression left by the character of our
troops—by their nature and generosity, by their kindness. By their
tradition of these things.

The American troops in Iraq, our men and women, are inspiring, and we all know it. But whenever you say it, you sound like a
greasy pol: "I support our valiant troops, though I oppose the war,"
or "If you oppose the war, you are ignoring the safety and imperiling
the sacrifice of our gallant troops."

I suspect that in their sophistication—and they are sophisticated—
our troops are grimly amused by this. Soldiers are used to being used.
They just do their job.

We know of the broad humanitarian aspects of the occupation—the hospitals being built, the schools restored, the services administered, the kids treated by armed forces doctors. But then there are all the stories that don't quite make it to the top of the heap and that in a way tell you more. The lieutenant in the First Cavalry who was concerned about Iraqi kids in the countryside who didn't have shoes, so he wrote home, started a drive, and got 3,000 pairs sent over. The lieutenant colonel from California who spent his off-hours emailing hospitals back home to get a wheelchair for a girl with cerebral palsy.

The Internet is littered with these stories. So is Iraq. I always notice the pictures from the wire services, pictures that have nothing to do with government propaganda. The Marine on patrol laughing with the local street kids; the nurse treating the sick mother.

A funny thing. We're so used to thinking of American troops as good guys that we forget: They're good guys! They have American class.

And it is not possible that the good people of Iraq are not noticing, and that in some way down the road the sum of these acts will not come to have some special meaning, some special weight of its own. The actor Gary Sinise helps run Operation Iraqi Children, which delivers school supplies with the help of U.S. forces. When he visits Baghdad grade schools, the kids yell, "Lieutenant Dan!"—his role in "Forrest Gump," the story of another good man.

*   *   *

Some say we're the Roman Empire, but I don't think the soldiers of Rome were known for their kindness, nor the people of Rome for their decency. Some speak of Abu Ghraib, but the humiliation of prisoners there was news because it was American troops acting in a way that was out of the order of things, and apart from tradition. It was weird. And they were busted by other American troops.

You could say soldiers of every country do some good in war

beyond fighting, and that is true enough. But this makes me think of the statue I saw once in Vienna, a heroic casting of a Red Army soldier. Quite stirring. The man who showed it to me pleasantly said it had a local nickname, "The Unknown Rapist." There are similar memorials in Estonia and Berlin; they all have the same nickname. My point is not to insult Russian soldiers, who had been born into a world of communism, atheism and Stalin's institutionalization of brutish ways of being. I only mean to note the stellar reputation of American troops in the same war at the same time. They were good guys.

They're still good.

We should ponder, some day when this is over, what it is we do to grow such men, and women, what exactly goes into the making of them.

Whatever is decided in Washington, I hope our soldiers know what we really think of them, and what millions in Iraq must, also. I hope some day they get some earned tenderness, and wind up over the hills of Iraq, and land, and an old guy comes out and says, "Are you an American?" And they say yes and he says, "A toast, to old times."

A Cold Man's Warm Words

Jefferson's tender lament didn't make it into the Declaration.

The Wall Street Journal: July 2, 2010

The tenderest words in American political history were cut from the document they were to have graced.

It was July 1, 2, 3, and 4, 1776, in the State House in Philadelphia. America was being born. The Continental Congress was reviewing and editing the language of the proposed Declaration of Independence and Thomas Jefferson, its primary author, was suffering the death of a thousand cuts.

The tensions over slavery had been wrenching, terrible, and were resolved by brute calculation: to damn or outlaw it now would break fragile consensus, halt all momentum and stop the creation of the United States. References to the slave trade were omitted, but the Founders were not stupid men, and surely they knew their young nation would have its date with destiny; surely they heard in their silence the guns of Fort Sumter.

Still, in the end, the Congress would not produce only an act of the most enormous human and political significance, the creation of America, it would provide history with one of the few instances in which a work of true literary genius was produced, in essence, by committee. (The writing of the King James Bible is another.)

The beginning of the Declaration had a calm stateliness that signaled, subtly, that something huge is happening:

"When in the Course of human events it becomes necessary for one people to dissolve the political bands which have connected them with another, and to assume among the powers of the earth, the separate and equal station to which the Laws of Nature and of Nature's God entitle them, a decent respect to the opinions of mankind requires that they should declare the causes which impel them to separate."

This gave a tone of moral modesty to an act, revolution, that is not a modest one. And it was an interesting modesty, expressing respect for the opinion of the world while assuming the whole world was watching. In time it would be. But that phrase, "a decent respect to the opinions of mankind," is still a marker, a reminder: We began with respect. America always gets in trouble when we forget that.

The second paragraph will, literally, live forever in the history of man. It still catches the throat:

"We hold these truths to be self-evident, that all men are created equal, that they are endowed by their Creator with certain unalienable Rights, that among these are Life, Liberty, and the pursuit of Happiness.—That to secure these rights, Governments are instituted among Men, deriving their just powers from the consent of the governed."

What followed was a list of grievances that made the case for separation from the mother country, and this part was fiery. Jefferson was a cold man who wrote with great feeling. He trained his eyes on the depredations of King George III: "He has plundered our seas, ravaged our coasts, burnt our towns... He is at this time transporting large Armies of foreign Mercenaries to complete the work of death, desolation and tyranny..."

Members of the Congress read and reread, and the cutting commenced. Sometimes they cooled Jefferson down. He wrote that the king "suffered the administration of justice totally to cease in some of these states." They made it simpler: "He has obstructed the Administration of Justice."

"For Thomas Jefferson it became a painful ordeal, as change after change was called for and approximately a quarter of what he had written was cut entirely." I quote from the historian David McCullough's "John Adams," as I did last year at this time, because everything's there.

Jefferson looked on in silence. Mr. McCullough notes that there is no record that he uttered a word in protest or in defense of what he'd written. Benjamin Franklin, sitting nearby, comforted him: Edits often reduce things to their essence, don't fret. It was similar to the wisdom Scott Fitzgerald shared with the promising young novelist Thomas Wolfe 150 years later: Writers bleed over every cut, but at the end they don't miss what was removed, don't worry.

"Of more than eighty changes in Jefferson's draft during the time Congress deliberated, most were minor and served to improve it," writes Mr. McCullough. But one cut near the end was substantial, and its removal wounded Jefferson, who was right to be wounded, for some of those words should have stayed.

Jefferson had, in his bill of particulars against the king, taken a moment to incriminate the English people themselves—"our British brethren"—for allowing their king and Parliament to send over to America not only "soldiers of our own blood" but "foreign Mercenaries to invade and destroy us." This, he said, was at the heart of the tragedy of separation. "These facts have given the last stab to agonizing affection, and manly spirit bids us renounce forever" our old friends and brothers. "We must endeavor to forget our former love for them."

Well. Talk of love was a little much for the delegates. Love was not on their mind. The entire section was removed.

And so were the words that came next. But they should not have been, for they are the tenderest words.

Poignantly, with a plaintive sound, Jefferson addresses and gives voice to the human pain of parting: "We might have been a free and great people together."

What loss there is in those words, what humanity and what realism, too.

"To write is to think, and to write well is to think well," David McCullough once said in conversation. Jefferson was thinking of the abrupt end of old ties, of self-defining ties and, I suspect, that the pain of this had to be acknowledged. It is one thing to declare the case for freedom and to make a fiery denunciation of abusive, autocratic and high-handed governance. But it is another thing, and an equally important one, to acknowledge the human implications of the break. These were our friends, our old relations; we were leaving them, ending the particular facts of our long relationship forever. We would feel it. Seventeen seventy-six was the beginning of a dream. But it was the end of one, too. "We might have been a free and great people together."

It hurt Thomas Jefferson to see these words removed from his great document. And we know something about how he viewed his life, his own essence and meaning, from the words he directed that would, a half century after 1776, be cut onto his tombstone. The first word after his name is "Author."

America and Britain did become great and free peoples together, and apart, bound by a special relationship our political leaders don't often speak of and should never let fade. You can't have enough old friends. There was the strange war of 1812, declared by America and waged here by England, which reinvaded, and burned our White House and Capitol. That was rude of them. But they got their heads handed to them in New Orleans and left, never to return as an army.

Even 1812 gave us something beautiful and tender. There was a bombardment at Fort McHenry. A young lawyer and writer was watching, Francis Scott Key. He knew his country was imperiled. He watched the long night in hopes the fort had not fallen. And he saw it—the rocket's red glare, the bombs bursting in air, gave proof through the night that our flag was still there.

And so to all writers (would-be, occasional and professional) and all editors, too, down through our history: Happy 234th Independence Day. And to our British cousins: Nice growing old with you.

America Is at Risk of Boiling Over

The Wall Street Journal: August 6, 2010

It is, obviously, self-referential to quote yourself, but I do it to make a point. I wrote the following on New Year's Day, 1994. America 16 years ago was a relatively content nation, though full of political sparks: 10 months later the Republicans would take the House for the first time in 40 years. But beneath all the action was, I thought, a coming unease. Something inside was telling us we were living through "not the placid dawn of a peaceful age but the illusory calm before stern storms."

The temperature in the world was very high. "At home certain trends—crime, cultural tension, some cultural Balkanization—will, we fear, continue; some will worsen. In my darker moments I have a bad hunch. The fraying of the bonds that keep us together, the strangeness and anomie of our popular culture, the increase in walled communities...the rising radicalism of the politically correct... the increased demand of all levels of government for the money of the people, the spotty success with which we are communicating to the young America's reason for being and founding beliefs, the growth of cities where English is becoming the second language... these things may well come together at some point in our lifetimes and produce something painful indeed. I can imagine, for instance, in the year 2020 or so, a movement in some states to break away from the union. Which would bring about, of course, a drama of Lincolnian darkness...You will know that things have reached a bad pass when Newsweek and Time, if they still exist 15 years from now, do cover stories on a surprising, and disturbing trend: aging baby boomers leaving America, taking what savings they have to live the rest of their lives in places like Africa and Ireland."

I thought of this again the other day when Drudge headlined increasing lines in London for Americans trading in their passports over tax issues, and the sale of Newsweek for $1.

Our problems as a nation have been growing on us for a long time. Their future growth, and the implications of that growth, could be predicted. But there is one thing that is both new since 1994 and huge. It took hold and settled in after the crash of 2008, but its causes were not limited to the crash.

The biggest political change in my lifetime is that Americans no longer assume that their children will have it better than they did. This is a huge break with the past, with assumptions and traditions that shaped us.

The country I was born into was a country that had existed steadily, for almost two centuries, as a nation in which everyone thought—wherever they were from, whatever their circumstances—that their children would have better lives than they did. That was what kept people pulling their boots on in the morning after the first weary pause: My kids will have it better. They'll be richer or more educated, they'll have a better job or a better house, they'll take a step up in terms of rank, class or status. America always claimed to be, and meant to be, a nation that made little of class. But America is human. "The richest family in town," they said, admiringly. Read Booth Tarkington on turn-of-the-last-century Indiana. It's all about trying to rise.

Parents now fear something has stopped. They think they lived through the great abundance, a time of historic growth in wealth and material enjoyment. They got it, and they enjoyed it, and their kids did, too: a lot of toys in that age, a lot of Xboxes and iPhones. (Who is the most self-punishing person in America right now? The person who didn't do well during the abundance.) But they look around, follow the political stories and debates, and deep down they think their children will live in a more limited country, that jobs won't be made at a great enough pace, that taxes—too many people in the cart, not enough pulling it—will dishearten them, that the effects of 30 years of a low, sad culture will leave the whole country messed up. And then there is the world: nuts with nukes, etc.

Optimists think that if we manage to turn a few things around, their kids may have it... almost as good. The country they inherit may be... almost as good. And it's kind of a shock to think like this; pessimism isn't in our DNA. But it isn't pessimism, really, it's a kind of tough knowingness, combined, in most cases, with a daily, personal commitment to keep plugging.

But do our political leaders have any sense of what people are feeling deep down? They don't act as if they do. I think their detachment from how normal people think is more dangerous and disturbing than it has been in the past. I started noticing in the 1980s the growing gulf between the country's thought leaders, as they're called—the political and media class, the universities—and those living what for lack of a better word we'll call normal lives on the ground in America. The two groups were agitated by different things, concerned about different things, had different focuses, different world views.

But I've never seen the gap wider than it is now. I think it is a chasm. In Washington they don't seem to be looking around and thinking, Hmmm, this nation is in trouble, it needs help. They're thinking something else. I'm not sure they understand the American Dream itself needs a boost, needs encouragement and protection. They don't seem to know or have a sense of the mood of the country.

And so they make their moves, manipulate this issue and that, and keep things at a high boil. And this at a time when people are already in about as much hot water as they can take.

To take just one example from the past 10 days, the federal government continues its standoff with the state of Arizona over how to handle illegal immigration. The point of view of our thought leaders is, in general, that borders that are essentially open are good, or not so bad. The point of view of those on the ground who are anxious about our nation's future, however, is different, more like: "We live in a welfare state and we've just expanded health care. Unemployment's up. Could we sort of calm down, stop illegal immigration and absorb what we've got?" No is, in essence, the answer.

An irony here is that if we stopped the illegal flow and removed the sense of emergency it generates, comprehensive reform would, in time, follow. Because we're not going to send the estimated 10 million to 15 million illegals already here back. We're not going to put sobbing children on a million buses. That would not be in our nature. (Do our leaders even know what's in our nature?) As years passed, those here would be absorbed, and everyone in the country would come to see the benefit of integrating them fully into the tax system. So it's ironic that our leaders don't do what in the end would get them what they say they want, which is comprehensive reform.

When the adults of a great nation feel long-term pessimism, it only makes matters worse when those in authority take actions that reveal their detachment from the concerns—even from the essential nature—of their fellow citizens. And it makes those citizens feel powerless.

Inner pessimism and powerlessness: That is a dangerous combination.

What the World Sees in America

It's not all something to be proud of.

The Wall Street Journal: April 21, 2011

I want to talk a little more this holiday week about what I suppose is a growing theme in this column, and that is an increased skepticism toward U.S. military intervention, including nation building. Our republic is not now in a historical adventure period—that is not what is needed. We are or should be in a self-strengthening one. Our focus should not be on outward involvement but inner repair. Bad people are gunning for us, it is true. We should find them, dispatch them and harden the target. (That would be, still and first, New York, though Washington, too.) We should not occupy their lands, run their governments or try to bribe them into bonhomie. We think in Afghanistan we're buying their love, but I have been there. We're not even renting it.

Our long wars have cost much in blood and treasure, and our military is overstretched. We're asking soldiers to be social workers, as Bing West notes in his book on Afghanistan, "The Wrong War."

I saw it last month, when I met in Afghanistan with a tough American general. How is the war going? I asked. "Great," he said. "We just opened a new hospital!" This was perhaps different from what George Patton would have said. He was allowed to be a warrior in a warrior army. His answer would have been more like "Great, we're putting more of them in the hospital!"

But there are other reasons for a new skepticism about America's just role and responsibilities in the world in 2011. One has to do with the burly, muscular, traditional but at this point not fully thought through American assumption that our culture not only is superior to most but is certainly better in all ways than the cultures of those we seek to conquer. We have always felt pride in our nation's ways, and pride isn't all bad. But conceit is, and it's possible we've grown as conceited as we've become culturally careless.

We are modern, they are not. We allow women freedom, they do not. We have the rule of law, they do not. We are technologically sophisticated, they are the Flintstones. We have religious tolerance. All these are sources of legitimate satisfaction and pride, especially the last. Our religious pluralism is, still, amazing.

I lately think of Charleston, S.C., that beautiful old-fashioned, new-fashioned city. On a walk there in October I went by one of the oldest Catholic churches in the South, St. Mary's, built in 1789. Across the street, equally distinguished and welcoming, was Kahal Kadosh Beth Elohim, a Jewish congregation founded in 1749. They've been across from each other peacefully and happily for a long time. I walked down Meeting Street to see the Hibernian Society, founded in 1801. My people wanted their presence known. In a brochure I saw how the society dealt with Ireland's old Catholic-Protestant split. They picked a Protestant president one year, a Catholic the next and so on. In Ireland they were killing each other. In America they were trading gavels. What a country! What a place. What a new world.

We have much to be proud of. And we know it.

But take a look around us. Don't we have some reasons for pause, for self-questioning? Don't we have a lot of cultural repair that needs doing?

*   *   *

Imagine for a moment that you are a foreign visitor to America. You are a 40-year-old businessman from Afghanistan. You teach a class at Kabul University. You are relatively sophisticated. You're in pursuit of a business deal. It's your first time here. There is an America in your mind; it was formed in your childhood by old John Ford movies and involves cowboy hats and gangsters in fedoras. You know this no longer applies—you're not a fool—but you're not sure what does. You land at JFK, walking past a TSA installation where they're patting the genital areas of various travelers. Americans sure have a funny way of saying hello!

You get to town, settle into a modest room at the Hilton on Sixth Avenue. You're jet-lagged. You put on the TV, not only because you're tired but because some part of you knows TV is where America happens, where America is, and you want to see it. Headline news first. The world didn't blow up today. Then:

Click. A person named Snooki totters down a boardwalk. She lives with young people who grunt and dance. They seem loud, profane, without values, without modesty, without kindness or sympathy. They seem proud to see each other as sexual objects.

Click. "Real Housewives." Adult women are pulling each other's hair. They are glamorous in a hard way, a plastic way. They insult each other.

Click. Local news has a riot in a McDonald's. People kick and punch each other. Click. A cable news story on a child left alone for a week. Click. A 5-year-old brings a gun to school, injures three. Click. A show called "Skins"—is this child pornography? Click. A Viagra commercial. Click. A man tried to blow up a mall. Click. Another Viagra commercial. Click. This appears to be set in ancient Sparta. It appears to involve an orgy.

You, the Kabul businessman, expected some raunch and strangeness but not this—this Victoria Falls of dirty water! You are not a philosopher of media, but you know that when a culture descends to the lowest common denominator, it does not reach the broad base at the bottom, it lowers the broad base at the bottom. This "Jersey

Shore" doesn't reach the Jersey Shore, it *creates* the Jersey Shore. It makes America the Jersey Shore.

You surf on, hoping for a cleansing wave of old gangster movies. Or cowboys. Anything old! But you don't find TMC. You look at a local paper. Headline: New York has a 41% abortion rate. Forty-four percent of births are to unmarried women and girls.

You think: Something's wrong in this place, something has become disordered.

The next morning you take Amtrak for your first meeting, in Washington. You pass through the utilitarian ugliness, the abjuration of all elegance that is Penn Station. On the trip south, past Philadelphia, you see the physical deterioration that echoes what you saw on the TV— broken neighborhoods, abandoned factories with shattered windows, graffiti-covered abutments. It looks like old films of the Depression!

By the time you reach Washington—at least Union Station is august and beautiful—you are amazed to find yourself thinking: "Good thing America is coming to save us. But it's funny she doesn't want to save herself!"

* * *

My small point: Remember during the riots of the 1960s when they said "the whole world is watching"? Well, now the whole world really is. Everyone is traveling everywhere. We're all on the move. Cultures can't keep their secrets.

The whole world is in the Hilton, channel-surfing. The whole world is on the train, in the airport, judging what it sees and likely, in some serious ways, finding us wanting.

And, being human, they may be judging us with a small, extra edge of harshness for judging them and looking down on them.

We have work to do at home, on our culture and in our country. A beautiful Easter to St. Mary's Church of Charleston and happy Passover to Kahal Kadosh Beth Elohim.

CHAPTER 5

Having Fun

Not all of life is serious. Some of it is fun, some of it sheer pleasure. Here are some moments of pleasure—in memory, in being in a new place and in being on a snowy day in Brooklyn.

*   *   *

American Diversity and the Wild West

The Wall Street Journal: August 28, 2014

Moran, Wyo.

Tenderfoot is in big sky country. On the drive from the airport to the ranch, the Tetons, a range of great splendor and dignity that Tenderfoot had thought were two mountains called Grand, are spread before her. It is dusk. To the left the Snake River curls softly against the road. To the right, open fields, working ranches, herds of buffalo. In the air the scent of sage. The sky is huge, a dome of softening blue. All this is expected—this is how the West *looks*—yet the real thing startles and overwhelms. You stare dumbly at the wonder of it.

"God's country," her host says, not as a brag but with awe still in his voice after more than 20 years here.

Tenderfoot's host, a friend of many years, a substantial and numeric man, tells her Wyoming facts. There are fewer people in this state than any other. ("They must be lonely," she thinks.)

Tenderfoot doesn't really like to be in a place where there aren't a lot of...witnesses. She's from the city and knows the canyons of downtown, the watering holes of the theater district. She knows her Brooklyn, her Long Island, her Jersey, is a walker in the city and a lost rube in the country. She is here because she loves her friends and will go far to see them. She does have a relationship with the American West and does in fact love it, but it is the West as mediated by John Ford, Cormac McCarthy and Larry McMurtry. She doesn't really know the real one.

"I'll fill you in on the bears," her host says. They've been coming in closer, charging hikers down hills and sauntering across property. Tenderfoot nods in a way she hopes looks offhand, like someone who knows the facts on the ground, the lay of the land, the curve of the bend. In that tone, she asks which are worse, the black bears or the brown ones, and, um, which have the claws. "The grizzlies can kill you," she is told. She receives this with equanimity. "I will never leave my room," she thinks.

The next day the conversation again turns to bears, and her host reminds everyone: "You go for a hike, just bring your bear spray."

"Um," says Tenderfoot, "do you spray it on yourself like bug spray? Or do you spray it on the bear?"

Another guest, sympathetically: "You spray it toward the bear. Like Mace."

"That's what I thought," Tenderfoot says.

She is game for riding and asks for a horse that is short, lame and stupid. They give her an Appaloosa named Grumpy. He is huge and gray and looks like something the conquistadors rode. Tenderfoot is ready to love him. She pats his thick neck and says sweet things like, "You and me, Grump." They go forward and it is beautiful—the stately lope, the soft, intelligent snorting—and she is barely offended when he tries to wipe her off on the side of a barn.

Later, loping slowly up a trail by a creek, past aspen and cottonwood, sage and pine trees, past spruce and willows and Indian paintbrush, she sees something on the ground.

She is now already speaking economically, like a Westerner.

"Big twig," she says.

"Actually that's a rattlesnake," says her guide. This happens in Tenderfoot's imagination but might as well be real.

Grumpy is in charge and knows his trails, barely stumbles. She likes the easy sway. It is mesmeric. "This is how the cowboys did it," she thinks, "this is how they put up with the boredom and peace."

She looks down at Grumpy's massive neck and thinks of…Cole Porter. "If Grumpy falls down here I'll shoot from the stirrups with a flick of the foot and tumble in the opposite direction." Being a writer, she knows she will write of the fall and need the names of things. "Is that a ravine or a valley?" she calls out to her friends. Silence. "It's a stream bed," somebody says.

In the coming days she would hike, mostly because she doesn't want her friends to call her Tenderfoot Lazybones. She will announce one night that she went on a 7.2-mile hike up a mountain and saw a blurry furry thing 10 feet tall and scared it away with a sound and a stick. It is perhaps closer to the truth that it was a half-mile amble on a hill and she saw a squirrel, but nobody presses her. And anyway that squirrel was big.

In between walking, staring at the stream and the sunflowers, walking through the tack room and staring at horses, Tenderfoot reads a wonderful book called "Wyoming Folklore," a collection of oral histories from old-timers who, in the 1930s, were asked for their memories of the wild Wyoming in which they'd grown up. Their stories were gathered by young writers working for the Federal Writers Project. It was a brilliant use of tax dollars because it was an act of real conservation: If these histories hadn't been written, they'd have been lost to us all forever.

The stories, told by nongarrulous people in old age, tell of a lost, brute, beautiful world and the tough, hardy, crazy people who lived in it: cowboys, miners, French peddlers, Irish railway men, German surveyors, desperadoes, drunken soldiers. Parents fleeing disappointment who couldn't settle down and dragged their hungry children through the wilderness looking for the perfect spot. Indian medicine men, mad prospectors, loggers, serial killers. The storms that bore down from nowhere and left 15 feet of snow. The Cheyenne on the warpath, the U.S. Army on the warpath, towns that rose up against soldiers and their rough ways. Cattle everywhere. Flash floods turning creeks into raging rivers. "It really rained in those days," said an old cowboy. Lightning made cattle panic and stampede over cliffs.

The legends of buried treasures, of lost mines, of gold nuggets large as wheat kernels. The sudden, raging wildfires. "Just as far as we could see east and west, just one inferno of flames," said one pioneer. A change in the wind was death to all. No firefighters; only a stream or a river could check a blaze.

The cold and privation, the sheer endurance it took to live in old Wyoming, in the wild, wild West.

At meals Tenderfoot tells stories of what she's read, but her friends already know them. Still, they are beautiful and powerful to her, and give rise to a thought she'd had before.

People say Americans are by nature isolationists, an odd thing to say of a people who came from everywhere on earth and stay in touch with everywhere. Maybe the truth is that America is so vast, so varied, contains so many different cultures and histories, which in turn give rise to different assumptions and even ways of being, that it has been the work of more than two centuries for America just to know itself. Europe is all bunched together, of course they know each other. We are spread out on a vast continent. It takes a while to take it all in. We're not uninterested in other countries, we just have so many nations right here.

Next Year Stay Home, America

The Wall Street Journal: November 29, 2013

I had a lot of jobs in a somewhat knockabout youth—waitress, clerk, temporary secretary, counter girl in a bakery (nice—no one's ever sad in a bakery) and in a flower shop (hard—for hours I removed the thorns from the tough, gnarly roses we sold, which left my hands nicked and bloodied). All the jobs of my teens and early 20s were wonderful in the sense that I was lucky to *have* a job. Unskilled baby boomers were crowding into an ailing economy; they took what they could and did their best from there. I could earn a salary to buy what I needed—clothes, food, money to go to college at night, then during the day. But the jobs were most wonderful in that they contributed to the experience hoard we all keep in our heads.

The best was waitressing. That's hard work, too, eight or 10 hours on your feet, but you get to know the customers. People will tell you their life stories over coffee. There's something personal, even intimate, in serving people food, and regulars would come in at 6 or 7 a.m. and in time you'd find you were appointments in each other's lives. At the Holiday Inn on Route 3 in New Jersey, long-haul truckers on their way to New York would stop for breakfast. They hadn't talked to anyone in hours. I'd pour coffee and they would start to talk about anything—the boss, the family, politics.

I learned from them what a TSA agent told me many years later: "Everyone's carrying the same things." I had asked the agent what she'd learned about people from years of opening their bags and seeing what was inside. She meant her answer literally: Everybody's carrying the same change of clothes, the same toiletries. But at the moment she said it we both understood that she was speaking metaphorically, too: Everyone's carrying the same burdens, the same woes one way or another. We have more in common than we know.

Once when I was 18 my friends and I ran away. We pooled our cash, bought a broken-down car for $200 and aimlessly drove south. We wound up in Miami Beach, in what was then a fallen-down, beat-up area and is now probably a millionaire's row. I worked at a restaurant whose name I remember as the Lincoln Lanes. Jackie Gleason did his TV show nearby, and the June Taylor dancers used to come in for lunch. They were so great—young and beautiful and full of tales about the show and about Jackie, who once drove by in his car. I thought of him when I first saw Chris Christie, years later. Mr. Christie on YouTube confronting an aggrieved constituent was sheer Gleason: "To the moon, Alice!"

The hardest job I had was working the floor at a women's clothing store on Park Avenue in Rutherford, N.J. It was part of a chain. It was boring when traffic was light—clocks go slow in retail when no one's there. There's no stool to sit on during your shift: You're working the floor so that's where they want you, walking around, folding sweaters, rearranging hangers. You don't have the same conversations with a harried woman trying on a skirt that you do with a tired trucker on his way to the city who decides to give you his philosophy of life.

One thing all these jobs had in common was something so common, so expected, that it was unremarked upon. You got holidays off. You were nonessential personnel. You worked at a place that didn't have to be open, so it wasn't. You got this gift, a day off, sometimes paid and sometimes not, but a break, an easement of responsibility.

I suppose the shops I worked at were unthinkingly following tradition. Thanksgiving, Christmas—these are days to be with friends and family and have a feast. Maybe if you pressed them they'd say something like: "This is what we do. We're Americans. Thanksgiving is a holiday. We're supposed to give thanks, together." They'd never trespass on a national day of commonality, solidarity and respect.

You know where we're going, because you've seen the news stories about the big retailers that decided to open on Thanksgiving evening, to cram a few extra hours in before the so-called Black Friday sales. About a million Wal-Mart workers had to be in by 5 p.m. for a 6 p.m. opening, so I guess they had to eat quickly with family, then bolt. Kmart opened on Thanksgiving, too, along with Target, Sears, Best Buy and Macy's, among others.

The conversation has tended to revolve around the question of whether it's good for Americans to leave their gatherings to go buy things on Thanksgiving. In a societal sense, no—honor the day best you can and shop tomorrow. But that's not even the question. At least shoppers were being given a choice. They could decide whether or not they wanted to leave and go somewhere else. But the workers who had to haul in to work the floor didn't have a choice. They had been scheduled. They had jobs they want to keep.

It's not right. The idea that Thanksgiving doesn't demand special honor marks another erosion of tradition, of ceremony, of a national sense. And this country doesn't really need more erosion in those areas, does it?

The rationale for the opening is that this year there are fewer shopping days between Thanksgiving and Christmas, and since big retailers make a lot of their profits during that time, something must be done. I suppose something should. But blowing up Thanksgiving isn't it.

There has been a nice backlash on the Internet, with petitions and Facebook posts. Some great retailers refused to be part of what this newspaper called Thanksgiving Madness. Nordstrom did not open on Thanksgiving, nor did T.J. Maxx, Costco or Dillard's. P.C. Richard & Son took out full-page ads protesting. The CEO was quoted last week saying Thanksgiving is "a truly American holiday" and "asking people to be running out to shop, we feel is disrespectful." Ace Hardware said, simply: "Some things are more important than money."

That is the sound of excellent Americans.

People deserve a day off if what they do is nonessential. Selling a toy, a jacket, even a rose is nonessential.

Black Friday—that creepy sales bacchanal in which the lost, the lonely, the stupid and the compulsive line up before midnight Friday to crash through the doors, trampling children and frightening clerks along the way—is bad enough, enough of a blight on the holiday.

But Thanksgiving itself? It is the day the Pilgrims invented to thank God to live in such a place as this, the day Abe Lincoln formally put aside as a national time of gratitude for the sheer fact of our continuance. It's more important than anyone's bottom line. That's a hopelessly corny thing to say, isn't it? Too bad. It's true.

Oh, I hope people didn't go. I hope when the numbers come in it was a big flop.

I hope America stayed home.

And happy Thanksgiving to our beloved country, the great and fabled nation that is still, this day, the hope of the world.

Snow Day

The Wall Street Journal: December 6, 2002

"Watch, he's gonna tax the snow." We turned toward the TV mounted on the wall. "Gonna pay for it now!" the counter clerk said, and people in line laughed as they paid for their papers. Mayor Mike Bloomberg had just come on to do a live news conference. They had the TV on in the candy store to get updates on the weather. Mr. Bloomberg announced this was "the first big test" of his administration. The guy next to me caught my eye; we smiled and thought: *Thanks for the context—we thought this was about the storm. We forgot it's about you!* It wasn't obnoxious, just comic, a pure moment of the inevitable solipsism of a modern mayor in the media age.

We were extroverting in the candy store yesterday afternoon on Montague Street in Brooklyn. Everyone was talking because it was snowing outside, heavily, with three inches on the ground and three or four more still in the sky. When I walked in, an old man pointed at me and said, "There is snow on your coat," in the manner of Sherlock Holmes making a discovery.

"They say it's snowing outside," I said in the manner of one sharing primo gossip.

"That explains it," he said.

Strangers smiled at each other as they trudged by on the street. Outside a church they were leaving noon mass, and a woman with an unplaceable accent said, "Nice day!" And we all smiled at that because we were in the middle of a storm but it was true. It *was* nice. It was beautiful. I came home to emails. One, from a friend in Maryland: "Got weather? We're under piles and piles of the stuff, predicting 10–12 inches. I love it. It's so quiet here, and wonderful soft monochromatic hues. This is the best." Another happy email from a friend who took his three-year-old to a hardware store, bought a cheap sled, and pulled his boy through Brooklyn. "Everyone we passed stopped to talk to us."

* * *

We are loving the snow in New York. Everyone is walking or looking out the windows or talking about how bad it's going to get. The storm began last night in the South, swept up through Washington, where it may leave eight inches; on through Baltimore and Philly, up to New York yesterday morning, heading later, they said, for Boston.

For every adult the first day of snow forever brings back memories of old snow days—the radio on and everyone listening, and the announcer saying "...and public and parochial schools on the South Shore have just announced they will not open." And from house to house you could almost hear the kids cheer. Freedom, a free day— what a gift from God.

This year, up here, the snow seemed more than ever an unexpected gift. At this point last year we were all still rocked by Sept. 11 and barely noticed the snow. (My unscientific telephone survey tells me no one in New York remembers any snow at all last year.) In fact we had very little, as if the heavens too were in shock.

But this one yesterday, this first snow—it was heavy, wet, coming down at a slant, it is building. It was a real snowfall. And it was beautiful.

The first snow always startles you. It makes everything look better. In the suburbs it gives a layer of cottony brightness to trees and fences and lawns; it covers the tricycle left in the driveway, turning its little aluminum frame into an abstract sculpture that says: *See how quickly yesterday turns into today.* In farm areas the snow is a blanket over cold corn and baby wheat. It heightens beauty, covers flaws, softens hard angles. It makes a row of trash cans a craggy white wall. It gives wholeness back to rusty fences and heightens the dignity of plain things like stoops and elegant things like steeples. It makes us see again what we'd been forgetting to notice.

* * *

But it isn't only the beauty. That's not the only thing a big snow brings.

"Yes, the newspapers were right: snow was general all over Ireland. It was falling on every part of the dark central plain, on the treeless hills, falling softly upon the Bog of Allen and, farther westward, softly falling into the dark mutinous Shannon waves." So wrote James Joyce at the end of his great short story "The Dead." They are famous words; it's a famous passage. Joyce's snow didn't fall over the house, or the city, or over his sensitive characters in a neighborhood in Dublin. Snow was falling all over Ireland, and touching everyone, as if they were together.

The biggest problem no one talks about in America, still, is loneliness. Maybe we don't hear about it much because most of the talkers about America—TV people, pundits of all sorts—are pretty well integrated into the world around them. And busy, so that if they're lonely they don't know it.

But a lot of people are lonely, encased in their thoughts about their own lives and experiences and memories and challenges. Encased in habit, too. And embarrassed to be alone in a technologically sophisticated place where a high value is put on our ability to reach out and touch someone.

But then something happens. Nature comes along and hands us something big—a storm or an earthquake—and the lonely come forward, if only by inches. We all find ourselves sharing the same preoccupation. This breaks down reserve and gets us thinking of and dealing with the same subject matter.

Bad weather, bad news makes you part of something: a community of catastrophe. You see your neighbor, and this time you don't just nod or keep walking. You call over, "Wow—you believe this?" And you laugh. You make phone calls. Weather makes you outward. It eases the lives of the lonely.

And then when the storm passes or the earthquake is old news, people retreat back into their aloneness with their own thoughts. They get quiet again. It will take another snowstorm or a hurricane before the ad hoc community of catastrophe springs up and makes them a member of something.

* * *

So that's what was in the air, too, yesterday: an easing of estrangement, a coming together, and people who didn't know each other talking.

I could see it all outside my window. I write in a room with a big window just beyond my computer. The window is seven feet tall and 40 inches wide. At this moment I am looking out the window at the church across the street. It is made of granite stone, is more than a century old, and its big brass doors were once the doors of the old ship the Normandie. To the right of the doors there is a little garden. In the middle of it is a statue of Mary of Fatima. She stands almost five feet high. Before her, two statues of kneeling children look up. There was a third but someone stole it. I have seen people stop and look at the statues at night. There is a lady in the neighborhood who every time she goes by stops and says something to Mary and nods; she sometimes gestures as if they are old friends catching up, and then walks on. You see wonderful things when you live across from statues.

The day of the storm, Mary and the children have snow on their heads and their cloaks. She is still looking down at the children, and they are looking up, their hands together in marble prayer. People are bustling by. The snow is coming at an angle against them as they walk by the church toward Montague Street, and they are leaning forward in the wind. A nanny and a child in a red jacket and a black cap just passed, holding hands. Now an old woman in a raincoat with an umbrella. Now a bunch of teenagers are running, throwing snowballs. A boy just literally slides by on the street as if his back were a sled. I want to applaud. There's laughter out there, great gaiety.

And now just outside the window I hear for the first time the authentic sound of winter in the north: a shovel scraping a sidewalk. It is an undistinguished and prosaic sound, and yet if I took a high-quality tape recorder and taped it and played it for a room full of 1,000 people and said, "What is this sound?" I'll bet 990 of them would know: That is someone shoveling snow. It is a distinctive sound. Soon I hope I hear the slap of tire chains on a blacktop road. I haven't heard that yet this year. I can't wait. I have no idea why.

* * *

It's dusk now, and it's still coming down. Snow is general all over the East. It is falling on every part of the crooked shore, on the tree-less hills, falling softly upon the Chesapeake Bay and, farther north, softly falling into the dark mutinous Montauk waves. It is falling, too, upon every part of the lovely churchyard across the way.

And this, to end. After snow gets you out of the house, and out of yourself, and into the world, it stops you in your tracks. Because it reminds you of something you know and forget to think about. It reminds you that there is a higher force at work, it is beyond and above, it governs all the heavens and "the snow falling faintly through the universe and faintly falling."

Thank you, James Joyce. I spent my snow day with you.

Nobody's Perfect, but They Were Good

The Wall Street Journal: June 4, 2010

We needed some happy news this week, and I think we got it. But first, a journey back in time.

It was Monday July 4, 1983, a painfully hot day, 94 degrees when the game began. We were at Yankee Stadium, and the Yanks were playing their ancestral foes, the Boston Red Sox. More than 40,000 people filled the stands. My friend George and I had seats in the upper decks, where people were waving programs against the heat, eating hot dogs, drinking beer and—oh, innocent days—smoking. In fact, it was the smoking that made me realize something was going on.

The Yankees' pitcher, Dave Righetti, who'd bounced from the majors to the minors and back again, was having a good game, striking out seven of the first nine hitters. The Yanks were scoring; the Red Sox were doing nothing. Suddenly, around the sixth or seventh inning, I realized the boisterous crowd had turned quieter. George was chain-smoking with a look of fierce intensity. "What's happening?" I asked him. "Don't say it," he replied. "If you say it, you jinx it." He said some other things, talking in a kind of code, and I realized: This may be a no-hitter. We may be witnessing history.

Now I'm watching not only the game but everyone around me. Fathers are with their kids, and you can tell they're starting to think: "I have given my son a great gift today." Just down from us was an old man, 75 or so, tall, slim and white-haired. I never saw him say a word to anyone, and throughout the game there was an empty seat beside him. I thought: He's got a wife in the hospital and she told him to take the afternoon off; he'd bought the tickets before she got sick, and he's by himself. He was so distracted and lonely looking but inning by inning the game started to capture him, and the last few innings he couldn't sit down.

Everyone else in New York was at the beach for the three-day weekend, but around us were regular people, working people who didn't have enough to be at the Jersey Shore or out on the island, but who had enough for a baseball game. Also there were diehard fans holding their game cards. Meaning everyone who was there deserved to be there, everyone who got the gift deserved it. It was one of those moments where life is just.

Twenty-five years later, on July 3, 2008, Anthony McCarron of New York's Daily News wrote of the final moments of the game. Righetti is facing the final batter, Wade Boggs, and is worried he'll tap the ball toward first and beat him to the bag. At the plate, Boggs is thinking, "If I get a hit here, with two out in the ninth inning, and break this thing up, I'm probably not getting out of here alive." As Mr. McCarron wrote, Righetti "snapped off a crisp slider, Boggs struck out swinging," and Righetti flung his arms out in joy.

The crowd exploded, they wouldn't stop jumping and cheering, and later they filled the bars around the stadium. It was raucous, joyful. Everyone acted as if they were related, because it is a beautiful thing when you witness history together. It's unifying.

Only later would it be noted that it wasn't only Independence Day, and a home game and the Red Sox, it was the anniversary of Lou Gehrig's 1939 farewell speech. So it was fitting everyone left feeling like the luckiest man on the face of the earth.

I bet you know where I'm going.

It was Wednesday night of this week, and it was a heartbreaker, and you have seen the videotape. Comerica Park in Detroit, the Tigers vs. the Cleveland Indians, and on the mound is Tigers pitcher

Armando Galarraga, 28. In his brief Major League career, he has not pitched a complete game, never mind a perfect one, but here he is. He's retired 26 straight batters. It's two out in the ninth with just one to go, one out between him and history. Indians shortstop Jason Donald is at the plate. Donald hits a grounder between first and second. Miguel Cabrera, the Tigers first baseman, fields it as Galarraga sprints to first. The pitcher takes the throw from Cabrera and steps on the base. Donald crosses it just a step later. Galarraga gets this look of joy. And the umpire blows it. He calls Donald safe. Everyone is shocked.

It's everything that follows that blunder that makes the story great.

When Galarraga hears the call, he looks puzzled, surprised. But he's composed and calm, and he smiles, as if accepting fate. Others run to the ump and begin to yell, but Galarraga just walks back to the mound to finish the job. Which he does, grounding out the next batter. The game is over.

The umpire, Jim Joyce, 54, left the field and watches the videotape. He saw that he'd made a mistake and took immediate responsibility. He went straight to the clubhouse where he personally apologized to Galarraga. Then he told the press, "I just cost the kid a perfect game." He said, "I thought [Donald] beat the throw. I was convinced he beat the throw until I saw the replay. It was the biggest call of my career."

Galarraga told reporters he felt worse for Joyce than he felt for himself. At first, reacting to the game in the clubhouse, he'd criticized Joyce. But after Joyce apologized, Galarraga said, "You don't see an umpire after the game come out and say, 'Hey, let me tell you I'm sorry.'" He said, "He felt really bad." He noted Joyce had come straight over as soon as he knew he'd made the wrong call.

What was sweet and surprising was that all the principals in the story comported themselves as fully formed adults, with patience, grace and dignity. And in doing so, Galarraga and Joyce showed kids How to Do It.

A lot of adults don't teach kids this now, because the adults themselves don't know how to do it. There's a mentoring gap, an instruction gap in our country. We don't put forward a template because we don't know the template. So everyone imitates TV, where victors dance in the end zone, where winners shoot their arms in the air and distort their face and yell "Whoooaahhh," and where victims of an injustice scream, cry, say bitter things and beat the ground with their fists. Everyone has come to believe this is authentic. It is authentically babyish. Everyone thinks it's honest. It's honestly undignified, self-indulgent, weak and embarrassing.

Galarraga and Joyce couldn't have known it when they went to work Wednesday, but they were going to show children in an unforgettable way that a victim of injustice can react with compassion, and a person who makes a mistake can admit and declare it. Joyce especially was a relief, not spinning or digging in his heels. I wish he hadn't sworn. Nobody's perfect.

Thursday afternoon the Tigers met the Indians again in Comerica Park. Armando Galarraga got a standing ovation. In a small masterpiece of public relations, Detroit's own General Motors gave him a brand-new red Corvette.

Galarraga brought out the lineup card and gave it to the umpire—Jim Joyce, who had been offered the day off but chose to work.

Fans came with signs that said "It was perfect."

It was.

Scenes from a Confirmation

My community.

The Wall Street Journal: June 15, 2001

As is fitting for a soft June afternoon with bright sun and a mild breeze, I have no thoughts today, only bits and pieces of thoughts. I continue to work on a book and find myself happy, tired and thinking about things that happened long ago when the world even then was not young. Also this has been a big week in my home, with my son having a birthday on Monday, being confirmed in the Catholic Church on Tuesday and taking part in closing exercises at school on Wednesday.

However (she said not at all defensively), it is not true that I have nothing to say. It is only true that I have nothing important to say. So go read Mickey Kaus or check Drudge or Romenesko's medianews, or cruise the papers or jump around this splendid site. All I'm going to do is something that a part of me has always wanted to do, and that is a gossip column with boldface names. Only the boldface names don't belong to the celebrated and famous. But they are very important in my neck of the woods, as we say on the Upper East Side of Manhattan.

* * *

St. Thomas More Church in Manhattan rocked Tuesday night with the strains of a small, well-trained choir singing into adulthood the eighth graders of the Narnia Class of 2001. Standing to the right of a statue of St. Joseph, in which the earthly father of

Jesus bears a striking resemblance to Douglas Fairbanks Jr., were
the confirmation candidates: Robert von Althann, Philippe Arman,
Timothy Barr, John Mason Coyne, Christine Culver, Michaela Cul-
ver, Henry Delouvrier, James Fouhey, John Gerard, Nicola John-
son, Christopher Latos, Skye Lehman, Nicholas Manice, Gregory
Marino, Diana Mellon, Christopher Mixon, Evan O'Brien, Patrick
Fionnbharr O'Halloran, Gregory Pasternack, Matt Petrillo, Rudi
Pica, Will Rahn, Brett Rehfeld, Jimmy Reinicke, Evan Richards,
Lily Salembier, Alexandra Schueler, Chris Skrela, Katrina Sullivan
and Giulia Theodoli.

They were confirmed in a ceremony that not only started on
time, it ended early because Bishop Patrick Sheridan likes both people and homilies to move at a brisk pace. Also there was a beautiful
young woman named Jennifer who was confirmed with the kids and
who walked proudly with them and didn't make them feel she was
any different. She did her part with great style.

When you are confirmed in the Roman Catholic Church, you
take as your own the name of a saint whose life you find moving or
inspiring. (Some take this very formally and internalize it; Bobby
Kennedy signed his name Robert Francis Xavier Kennedy into early
adulthood.) So many of the candidates this year chose unusual
names—Clement, Blaise, Augustine, Siobahn, Alejandro. One of
the girls took St. Michael the Archangel.

Will Rahn, son of a certain Wall Street Journal columnist, read
the intentions during mass—"for the poor of the world, that they
might find sustenance"—and Matt Petrillo did a Bible reading. The
boys were so tall and dignified in their red graduation-style gowns—
14-year-old boys are now often six feet tall—and they repeated with
deep voices the words, the prayer actually, said at baptism but voiced
at that time for the baby being baptized by his godparents. But Tuesday night they made the vows on their own, with their own voices.

"Do you renounce Satan and all his works?" they were asked.

"I do," they answered.

I wondered if those in the pews were struck by the starkness of those grave words, and I wondered, too, how many were thinking: This is like the end of "The Godfather," when Michael Corleone stands for Connie's baby at the baptism while his enemies are rubbed out. Francis Ford Coppola made great artistic use of the extraordinary dialogue of baptism but may have damaged the ceremony for an entire generation (no, for two) that would be relieved not to be thinking about gangster movies while taking part in the sacraments.

JoMarie Pica, mother of three and wife of Vin, had taught many of the boys in Christian doctrine classes and had readied them for confirmation. Three hours before the ceremony she was in an accident and the front of her SUV was smashed up. She went to the preconfirmation buffet at Natika and Victor von Althann's anyway, threw back two Advils and a glass of wine and walked into the church with the candidates holding her candle high.

I taught a small class of girls and got to walk in holding a candle, too. The writer Sim Johnston, who also lives in the neighborhood and also teaches one of the Christian doctrine classes, was there helping out the boys. My girls were beautiful and a little nervous, and a few of their sponsors were late—you have to have an adult Catholic who stands up with you, and for you, when you're confirmed—and Lily worried that her sponsor might not make it. I said don't worry, I'll stand in for her if she doesn't make it. And then I was so relieved for Lily and half disappointed for myself when her sponsor came to the altar with Lily and stood with her right hand on her shoulder as the bishop made the sign of the cross with holy oil on Lily's forehead.

Before the ceremony began the bishop stood with us in a little side room. He looked dignified and weighty, holding a tall staff shaped like a shepherd's crook and wearing a miter, the big pointy hat, or rather the liturgical headdress, that bishops and cardinals sometimes wear. He was in bright red robes. He had thick eyeglasses and gray hair and was in his 70s, and as the girls and the boys chirped and shoved and laughed he took a hard look at them and said "Quiet!" in a way that made me mildly ashamed of my inability to whip them into shape. They listened to him for at least eight seconds before becoming themselves again.

* * *

I love some of these children. Some of them have been my son's friends and in my house since preschool and I want to hug them when I see them. Some are so kindhearted that they bring tears to your eyes. Some of them are deep inside good and mean to do good in the world. A handful of them are brave, too, and have had a lot to put up with in their parents.

But some are victims of the self-esteem movement. They have a wholly unearned self-respect. No, an unearned admiration for themselves. And they've been given this high sense of themselves by parents and teachers who didn't and don't have time for them and who make it up to them by making them conceited. I'm not sure how this will play out as they hit adulthood. What will happen to them when the world stops telling them what they have been told every day for the first quarter century of their lives, which is: You are wonderful.

Maybe it will make for a supergeneration of strong and confident young adults who think outside the box and proceed through their lives with serenity and sureness. Maybe life will hit them upside the head when they're 24 and they get fired from their first job and suddenly they're destabilized by the shock of not being admired. Maybe it will send them reeling.

I always want to tell them: The only kind of self-respect that lasts is the kind you earn by honestly coming through and achieving. That's the only way you'll make a lasting good impression on yourself.

* * *

One of the best things about Tuesday night was that the church was almost full, and so many families with many generations were there, and it was a pretty night in June and everyone could have been somewhere else, and yet here they were, making their responses during the mass and making them with strong voices, as if they knew what comes next. Which in a mass is not always so easy. But here we all were, and it always seems a surprise to me, the acting out of such old beliefs in the heart of new-millennium Manhattan by sophisticated mommies and daddies and hip grandmas. It was moving. It was as if the Holy Spirit were saying "It's all right, there is a future here."

When it was over, families fanned out into neighborhood restaurants, and we went to an Italian place called Vico, where they had a vanilla cake for my son, who had taken his confirmation name from St. Jude. The cake had a cross and said "Hey Jude," and when the waiters brought it to him they sang happy birthday.

The restaurant—smallish, white-walled, with doors and windows open to the street—had some long tables with happy families. The Picas were across the room with an assortment of uncles and aunts, and with a handsome young man named Alex Mendik, who recently lost his well-loved father, Bernie, and whom everybody hugged with great affection. At our table was young Miles Pope, also an eighth grader, a young conservative intellectual who quotes Aristotle in an appropriate and unshowoffy manner, not an easy thing in a young man.

It was just a happy night. It was like the junior high school graduation scene in "A Tree Grows in Brooklyn" except we weren't in an ice-cream parlor and it cost roughly 200 times what egg creams for everyone cost Francie Nolan's mother. But the spirit of Mrs. Nolan, who made Francie so proud by knowing that on a night like this you should leave a tip, prevailed, and my son's father and my former husband, as flawed and messy modern Catholics say, was generous and charming and had a great debate with the boys about the nature of the modern European Union. My son's grandmother, Peggy Byrne, our Aunt Peggy, merrily made faces as the boys talked about continents and kings.

And then it was going on 11 p.m. and we all kissed goodbye and jumped in cabs or walked home. And I thought: I belong to a community. My son belongs to a community. This is it. It's a neighborhood community, and a community of faith, a school community and a community of old relationships that last forever.

You can forget that you are part of a community. You don't even notice it, and then one night you look around and realize that you're in the middle of it. It's a good feeling to be part of something so big and so important, and to realize that when we celebrate something like a confirmation, we're celebrating what we belong to and what we've just joined.

So I turned and told Jude.

Old Jersey Real

The greatness of The Sopranos.

***The Wall Street Journal*: June 8, 2007**

"The Sopranos" wasn't only a great show or even a classic. It was a masterpiece, and its end on Sunday night is an epochal event. With it goes an era, a time.

You know the story, and if you don't, you've absorbed enough along the way as you overheard people chat Monday morning around what we still call the water cooler and mean as the line at Starbucks. A New Jersey mobster with a family, a business and a therapist makes his way through life. It was a family drama that was a mob drama, but in some hard-to-put-your-finger-on way it was the great post-9/11 drama of our time.

"The Sopranos" first aired on HBO in 1999, but rewatching the first season, there's an air of preamble to it, as if something were coming. Something was, and the show really got its shape and mood from what followed in September 2001. Sometimes this was subtle—Tony goes to his old uncle's place upstate and suddenly thinks about going to live up there where it's safe, where the birds fly on the lake. Sometimes it wasn't—in the bar, he reads from a newspaper story about how unprotected the Port of Newark is. I remember this because at the time I'd begun to worry about the Port of Newark.

That kind of thing happened a lot with "The Sopranos." It was real, Old Jersey real (Satriale's butcher shop, not the mall) and primal. It was about big things, as all great drama is—the human hunger for dominance, for safety, for love; the desire to rise in the world;

the need to belong to something, to be a Jet or a Shark, a Crip or a Blood, and have mates, homies, esteemed colleagues or paisans; how we process the hypocrisy all around us, in our families and among our friends, as we grow up; how we process hypocrisy in ourselves.

Because it was primal, its dialogue was pared to the bone and entered the language. You disrespecting the Bing? You wanna get whacked? And other famous phrases, many of them obscene.

*   *   *

The drama of Tony, the great post-9/11 drama of him, is that he is trying to hold on in a world he thinks is breaking to pieces. He has a sense, even though he's only in his 40s, that the best times have passed, not only for the Italian mob but for everyone, for the country—that he'd missed out on something, and that even though he lives in a mansion, even though he is rich and comfortable and always had food in the refrigerator and Carm can go to Paris and the kids go to private school—for all of that, he fears he's part of some long downhill slide, a slide that he can't stop, that no one can, that no one will. Out there, he told his son and daughter, it is the year 2000, but in here it's 1950. His bluster, his desperate desire to re-create order with the rough tools of his disordered heart and brain, are comic, poignant, ridiculous, human.

Tony became a new and instantly recognizable icon, and his character adds to American myth, to America's understanding of itself. It's a big thing to create such a character, and not only one but a whole family of them—Uncle Junior, Christopher, Carmela. This is David Chase's great achievement, to have created characters that are instantly recognizable, utterly original, and that add to America's understanding of itself. And to have created, too, some of the most horrifying moments in all of television history, and one that I think is a contender for Most Horrifying Moment Ever. That would be Adriana desperately crawling—crawling!—through the leaves in the woods as she tries to flee her lovable old friend Silvio, who is about to brutally put her down.

* * *

Here is a question that touches on the mystery of creativity, and I'll probably put it badly because I can't define it better than what I'm going to say. David Chase is the famous and justly celebrated creator of "The Sopranos," the shaper of its stories. The psychological, spiritual and emotional energy needed to create a whole world, which is what he has done, is very great. It is a real expenditure, a kind of investment in life, a giving of yourself. You can't do what he does without something like love. Not sentimentality or softness or sweetness, but love. And yet in a way, if you go by "The Sopranos," Mr. Chase loves nothing. Human beings are appetite machines, and each day is devoted to meeting and appeasing those appetites. No one is good, there are no heroes, he sees through it all. The mental-health facility is a shakedown operation where they medicate your child into zombiehood and tell him to watch TV. Politicians are the real whores. The FBI is populated by smug careerists. In the penultimate show, a table full of psychotherapists top each other with erudite-seeming comments that show a ruthlessness as great as any gangster's. I guess I'm asking where the energy for creativity comes when you see with such cold eyes.

Not that they're unrealistic. They're not. One of the reasons the show was so popular—one of the reasons it resonated—is that it captured a widespread feeling that our institutions are failing, all of them, the church, the media, the law, the government, that there's no one to trust, that Mighty Mouse will not save the day.

In Mr. Chase's world, everyone's a gangster as long as he can find a gang. Those who don't are freelancers.

And what he seems to be telling us, as the final season ends, is that all your pity for Tony, all your regard for the fact that he, too, is caught, all your sympathy for him as a father, as a man trying to be a man, as a man whose mother literally tried to have him killed, is a mistake.

Because he is a bad man. He has passing discomfort but not conscience, he has passing sympathies but no compassion. When he kills the character who is, essentially, his son, Christopher, he does it spontaneously, coolly, and with no passion. It's all pragmatism. He's all appetite. Tony is a stone-cold gangster.

* * *

There have been shows on television that have been, simply, sublime. In drama there was "I, Claudius," a masterpiece of mood and menace—"Trust no one!"—from which writers and producers continue to steal (see HBO's "Rome") and PBS's "Upstairs Downstairs." A few others. "The Sopranos" is their equal, but also their superior: It is hard to capture the past but harder to capture the present, because everyone knows when you don't get it right. It takes guts to do today.

David Chase did, and he made a masterpiece. I'll be watching Sunday night, but I'll wake up that morning with blue moon in my eyes.

CHAPTER 6

Making Trouble

When you write a political column you find yourself making temporary friends and permanent enemies. This is in part a reflection of the old political adage, "Friends come and go but enemies accumulate." A column is a statement, and when you make critical statements in public about people, it's understandable that they don't forget.

What follows are some tough judgments.

* * *

"Dutch" Is Shocking Because It Is Simply Awful

The Wall Street Journal: October 1, 1999

New York's Central Park, 6:43 a.m. on a Thursday in late September, a morning dark, cool and rich with something latent. I walked along head down, lost in thought, trying to understand how a brilliant man could write, would write, such a base botch of a book. If only I were with him and could ask. Suddenly I stepped upon an acorn, and an electric shock tore through me. Suddenly, in an almost occult sense, I was there! In his office, in the townhouse on Capitol Hill. The rows of shelves groaning and gleaming with books, the long gray filing cabinet below and, within it, the famous yards of cards, the ones he showed so proudly on "60 Minutes," each marked in careful, spidery script with a Mont Blanc pen whose use signifies a commitment to calligraphy, a writer's love of sparkly things, or nothing much.

"Edmund," I said, "I'm writing like a nut because I'm imitating you! I agreed to review your book because I was sure you'd been unjustly criticized. I expected something of breadth, depth and sweep—something serious. Not this—high-dive belly-flop into the pools of Narcissus."

He looked at me—wire-rimmed glasses, soft bangs and beard. Why, he looks like Lytton Strachey! (Later, from my notes: "His unconscious homage to wiggy but groundbreaking Bloomsburian biographer?") At first he was dismissive—the criticism is the sort of thing that "always greets any kind of original idea." Then he was pleading. Fourteen years of expectation, 14 years of the elusive Reagan, and all the while as each year passed he got closer to... the battlefield. When his book on Teddy

Roosevelt came out in 1979 Teddy was long dead, the historical case long settled. But Ronald Reagan is alive, the argument rages, there is no settled opinion! The editors, reviewers and social figures with whom Mr. Morris dines—Mr. Reagan is, still, their full moon; they see him, they bay. And sometimes bite.

"Do you know how all this pressure left me?" he asked.

"Don't say barking mad."

"No—unnerved, in time enraged, at last quite desperate. So I got someone else to write the damn thing, a made-up character with a made-up life who has made-up interactions. I called him 'Edmund Morris.' If you don't like the book you can bloody well blame him."

* * *

I will.

But where to start.

Edmund Morris's "Dutch" (Random House, 874 pages, $35) is a shocking book, not a work of sustained scholarship but a mere entertainment, and not an entertaining one. It is at turns bilious and cold, corny and cynical, manic and flat. It is also almost heartbreaking in that it marks such a waste—of history's time, the Reagans' faith, the writer's talent.

The famous central literary device, as I think we all know, does not work; it confuses, frustrates, obscures what it was meant to illumine. The reader never quite understands who is talking and whether he is being given a fact, a joke, a serious opinion, a bit of speculation or a guess. The fictitious "Edmund Morris" is a bore, tedious and windy, and a distraction from the more compelling story, fitfully told, of Ronald Reagan.

From beginning to end a badly written meanness permeates. Mr. Reagan goes to "a hayseed school" where the girls have "ugly names" and wear "cheap perfume." His first radio broadcasts appeal to "Dust Bowl brats like little Hughie Sidey." His early California supporters are patriotic and honest but, tragically, lack "irony." They are "aesthetically blind, culturally retarded... they view all threats to the Constitution—their Constitution—with the utmost serious-ness." Silly them. At White House dinners Mr. Morris puts up with more tacky people, a boring female theologian and a Palm Beach socialite "stiff with jewels."

When he is not mean he is English, not necessarily the same thing. He has no feel for the Midwest, and when he gives his char-acters dialogue—"There was more 'nuff roasted chicken and corn as evening came on" and "Jay Russell got him a new Buick"—they sound like extras in "Show Boat."

His portrait of America in the '60s seems written by someone who wasn't there; clichés are not avoided but seized upon and held high. The free-speech battles at Berkeley get deservedly long attention, but the central characters are not Mr. Reagan and university president Clark Kerr but Mr. Morris and his fictitious son, "Gavin," who calls the Black Panthers "bad cats I dig in Oakland." You will, literally, wince.

The political perceptions and assertions are almost uniformly common wisdom. For all his references to dusty archives and the pains of research (one wonders why he makes so many), much of what Mr. Morris says about Reagan's presidency reads like clip-pings from Time magazine. A troika rules the White House, Edwin Meese has a messy briefcase, pragmatists and hardliners disagree, David Stockman is tense, supply-side economics silly. SDI, the mis-sile defense system Mr. Reagan fought to research and deploy, is presented, cheaply and cornily, as an idée fixe whose appeal to Mr. Reagan is its similarity to sci-fi novels and B movies. Mr. Morris does, however, allow others to make the case that holding to SDI at Reykjavik changed everything in the U.S.-Soviet relationship and was a key element in the Soviet collapse.

The book's judgments on Mr. Reagan are mixed but not balanced, and the language deployed seems an attempt to cloak the author's indecisiveness. The result is a striking inconsistency. Mr. Reagan is an apparent airhead. Mr. Reagan has a clean, orderly, serious mind. Mr. Reagan tells pointless stories. Mr. Reagan's stories have a serious allegorical purpose. Mr. Reagan is a yahoo. Mr. Reagan is a reader with a high enjoyment of style and a writer of crystalline clarity. Mr. Reagan lacks compassion and heart. Mr. Reagan's emotions well over when he speaks of about that which he deeply cares. Perhaps strangest of all, "Reagan was America, and he wasn't much else." What a sentence. You have to be very strange to think that isn't quite enough. The flaws of the book were reflected (and perhaps rehearsed) in Mr. Morris's "60 Minutes" interview last Sunday, in which he dismissed Mr. Reagan's character and gifts and then posed, weeping, as he read the president's last letter to the country.

"Dutch" has some moments. The reporting of the John Hinckley assassination attempt has the simple force and power of that old popular classic, Jim Bishop's "The Day Lincoln Was Shot." Mr. Morris's rendering of the blacklist era, almost thwarted by the insertion of fictional movie scripts and song-and-dance patter, is tugged along by the sheer force of Mr. Reagan's actions, which are presented as courageous and idealistic. The sections on the Reagan-Gorbachev summits are strong. All of the author's interruptions, conceits and bizarre devices cannot derail these few but solid narratives. Mr. Reagan's function in this book made me think of what was said of FDR: He is like the Staten Island ferry, big, unstoppable and bringing all the garbage along in its wake.

I am not sure what to make of the quality of the reporting and suspect we will be hearing more about it. It is simply not believable, as Mr. Morris contends, that Mr. Reagan "secretly despised" George Bush. He secretly despised no one, and you didn't have to know him well to know that. Mr. Morris's attribution of an "upstairs downstairs" social resentment between the Reagans and the Bushes seems similarly bizarre, and one can't help believe President Bush when he says it isn't true. A small anecdote in which I figure, expressing concern about Mr. Reagan before a speech, is weirdly hyped up but happened. I'm not sure other things did. The story that young Ronald Reagan wanted to join the Communist Party but was turned away because he wasn't bright enough (yes, Hollywood communists were famous for turning away rising stars who weren't bright) comes from the gossip of an aging left-wing Reagan foe and is confirmed by no one. Colin Powell is reported boasting to Mr. Morris, on the last morning of Mr. Reagan's presidency, that Mr. Reagan's filmed office goodbye was great: Once again he, Mr. Powell, and the senior staff "directed [Reagan] and scripted him and made him up and gave him his cues." It is hard to believe that Mr. Powell would talk like that, but if he did he is a conceited and ungrateful man, and quite stupid, too.

One senses this scene is in the book—that many stories are in it—not in an attempt to shed light, or make us understand, or explain Mr. Reagan, but merely to generate Bob Woodward–type headlines. This is unworthy of the author of "The Rise of Theodore Roosevelt."

There is one other scene, at the end of the book, that is striking. The author sees Nancy Reagan leave the North Portico for the last time as first lady. "I blew her a kiss, feeling absolutely no emotion," he writes. This actually is revealing, and for once you know exactly which Edmund that is.

A final note. I think this book's great purpose may be to demonstrate decisively, and perhaps finally, contemporary biography's obsession with the small. It is as if modern biographers cannot handle greatness and feel compelled to reduce it to petty and irrelevant things. This is puzzling and pointless. It is also tired and, because it so often seems driven only by rage and inadequacy, tiresome. You'd think it would fall out of style, if only for the reason that, as is demonstrated here, it does damage not to the subject but to the historian.

American Caligula

The Wall Street Journal: September 14, 1998

For seven months I have kept on my desk a picture from a tabloid. It is of two close friends of President Clinton, Linda Bloodworth-Thomason and the actress Markie Post. They are laughing and holding hands in joyous union as they jump up and down at where fate has put them. It had put them in the Lincoln Bedroom. They were jumping up and down on Lincoln's bed.

It seemed to me emblematic of the Clinton White House, a place where opponents' FBI files were read aloud over pizza and foreign contributors with cash invited in the back door. I thought: Something's wrong with these people, they lack thought and dignity. But most of all they seemed to lack respect, a sense of awe—not the awe that can cripple you with a false sense of your smallness but the awe that makes you bigger, that makes you reach higher as if in tribute to some unseen greatness around you.

That, it seemed to me last week, as the president spoke each day and the Starr Report was published, was Mr. Clinton's problem, his real sin—a fundamental lack of respect for his country, for its citizens, for his colleagues, for all of us. The pollsters have it wrong when, seeking to determine whether he can continue to govern, they ask, "Do you respect the president?" The real question is "Do you think he has any respect for us?"

I think he showed with a chilling finality last week that he does not. I believe he demonstrated that people and principles are, to him, objects to be manipulated. You can tell preachers you cherish scripture, tell Monica you cherish her, it doesn't matter. The object, as Dick Morris says the president told him, is to "win."

*   *   *

Never, in all of last week, did he explain why he put the country through eight terrible months of dissension and distraction, when he easily could have spared it the trauma (and spared his career, too). Never did he explain why he sent his media generals out every day to lie for him with conviction, and to slime his opponents. It was telling that when he spoke to the evangelicals he said some people needed apologizing to, and that first, and "most important," was his family. What followed was a litany of his friends and his staff. His country came in dead last in the litany, as it has in his actions.

In the report and in his comments, it was clear that the most important thing to Bill Clinton is, now and always, Bill Clinton. But what was amazing is that he seemed last week to think that we feel that way, too.

*   *   *

And so he spoke of the scandal as his "journey." He said it has helped him grow. He said it may make him stronger. He said it has been an exhausting week for him. He said this has been the most difficult time of his life. But then, as if to comfort us in our concern, he offered context: It may turn out to be the most valuable, too.

He noted that his drama may make American families stronger. He said it provides an opportunity for healing. He spoke moistly, glisteningly of the early days of his first presidential run "when nobody but my mother...thought I had a chance of being elected." He talked of a little boy who told him "he wanted to be a president just like me." The boy was "husky, like I was," the president said moistly, glisteningly.

He compared himself to Mark McGwire. Would you want

Mr. McGwire to give up now? he asked. But Mr. McGwire is a champion because he has shown himself the past 10 days to be what is now an amazing thing, a celebrity who is a good man. This is the exact opposite of what Mr. Clinton has shown. The weird solipsism, the over-the-top self-dramatizing continued in the Starr Report. There Mr. Clinton was not Mark McGwire but, as he told Sidney Blumenthal, a "character in a novel," a victim of a sinister force weaving a web of lies about Monica Lewinsky and him. He compared himself to the hero of "Darkness at Noon."

He told evangelical ministers at a prayer breakfast that he had reached "the rock bottom truth of where I am." He said he has "sinned." He bit his lip, lowered his moist eyes and said his "spirit is broken." He then went on to a raucous awards dinner where he laughed gaily, waved and announced, "Hillary and I have been… just lapping this up!"

For all he seemed to be, in Flannery O'Connor's phrase, a pious conniver. As he spoke to the evangelicals, I was reminded of his great learning experience in 1980, after he lost his reelection race for the governorship. Knowing the people of Arkansas had come to see him as different, as too liberal and too Yale, he immediately went out and joined the only local church choir that sang on TV every Sunday morning. People liked it. He manipulated them for gain, to win. And in 1982 he won.

The problem is not that he is an actor. As an actor he puts not only Ronald Reagan to shame, but Laurence Olivier. The problem is that he thinks people will believe anything, that if he says a thing it is true. He absorbs his lies, and becomes them. The country suffers for this.

Mr. Clinton seems—and this is an amazing thing to say about a president—to lack a sense of patriotism, a love of country, a protectiveness toward her. He dupes the secretary of state, who must be America's credible voice in the world, into lying for him to the public and press. He fears his phone is being tapped by foreign agents, opening him to international blackmail. But he does not discontinue phone sex. Instead he comes up with a cover story. He tells Ms. Lewinsky they can say they knew they were being bugged, and it was just a "put on." He sends the first lady to go on television, where she denies the Lewinsky charges and says, "This is a battle...some folks are going to have a lot to answer for."

It is similarly amazing to say of an American president that he is decadent—an Ozarks Caligula, as a placard he passed last week put it. While being sexually serviced he keeps the door ajar so his secretary can alert him to calls; while taking one from a congressman he unzips his pants and exposes himself so he can receive oral sex. He masturbates in front of his young lover in the bathroom near his study, and in a staff member's office. When Ms. Lewinsky asks him about rumors that he'd attempted to molest Kathleen Willey, he is indignant: He would never approach a woman with small breasts. When the Lewinsky story breaks, he asks a pollster, a man newly famous for letting a prostitute listen in while he advised the president on strategy, if he should tell the truth. The pollster tells him no. The president responds, "Well, we just have to win then."

* * *

It is interesting, by the way, that of the self-described hundreds and hundreds of women Bill Clinton has been involved with, it is Ms. Lewinsky who has done the most damage. The reason I think is that in picking her he made a crucial mistake: He chose someone much like himself. She describes herself as insecure as she makes demands. She learned to manipulate in this manner through the culture of therapy. Her wants are justified because she is, after all, burdened with fears, and can be comforted only by the meeting of her demands. He picked someone with as grand a sense of entitlement as his own. At the end of the affair she demands that he feel contrition; she also demands a job with these words: "I don't want to have to work for this position . . . I just want it to be given to me."

And he picked someone who is, like himself, an exhibitionist. It never occurred to Ms. Lewinsky to be discreet about their affair, not to tell a dozen friends and family about the cigar, the nicknames. But then discretion has never really occurred to him, either. That's how we know about so many of his affairs. He always leaves a trail, an open door. He wants us to know.

*   *   *

I once saw the president in one of those big Washington hotel dinners a few years ago shortly after he talked about his underwear on TV. He was in full self-deprecating mode, teasing himself for his mistake. But he went on a little too long; he talked too much about it, and the crowd seemed to be thinking what I was: Doesn't he know that as he stands up there going on and on about his shorts, we are starting to imagine him in his shorts? The poor man doesn't know. And then I thought: Yes he does! He wants us to imagine him like that. And he has lived out his presidency so we can.

Caligula made his horse a senator; Mr. Clinton made his whoring a centerpiece. Both did so because they lacked respect and concern for anything but themselves. Ancient times could tolerate its Caligula, but Mr. Clinton is, quaint phrase, the most powerful man in the world, the leader of the free world, the chief executive of the United States, commander of our armed forces, the man who one day may be forced by history to unleash a nuclear missile. It is not tolerable that such a person be in such a position, and have such power.

Jesse Jackson once said, "God isn't finished with me yet," and it was beautiful because it was true. God isn't finished with any of us. Maybe he will raise up Bill Clinton and make him a saint, a great one. Maybe he will make Bill Clinton's life an example of stunning redemption. But for now, and now is what we have, Bill Clinton is not wise enough, mature enough, stable enough—he is not good enough—to be the American president.

In the therapeutic language he favors, an intervention would seem to be in order. That would be impeachment, for the high crime and misdemeanor of having no respect for his office, for his country, and for its people.

Way Too Much God

Was the president's speech a case of "mission inebriation"?

The Wall Street Journal: January 21, 2005

It was an interesting Inauguration Day. Washington had warmed up, the swift storm of the previous day had passed, the sky was overcast but the air wasn't painful in a wind-chill way, and the capital was full of men in cowboy hats and women in long furs. In fact, the night of the inaugural balls became known this year as the Night of the Long Furs.

Laura Bush's beauty has grown more obvious; she was chic in shades of white, and smiled warmly. The Bush daughters looked exactly as they are, beautiful and young. A well-behaved city was on its best behavior, everyone from cops to doormen to journalists eager to help visitors in any way.

For me there was some unexpected merriness. In my hotel the night before the inauguration, all the guests were evacuated from their rooms at 1:45 in the morning. There were fire alarms and flashing lights on each floor, and a public address system instructed us to take the stairs, not the elevators. Hundreds of people wound up outside in the slush, eventually gathering inside the lobby, waiting to find out what next.

The staff—kindly, clucking—tried to figure out if the fire existed and, if so, where it was. Hundreds of inaugural revelers wound up observing each other. Over there on the couch was Warren Buffett in bright blue pajamas and a white hotel robe. James Baker was in trench coat and throat scarf. I had remembered my keys and eyeglasses but walked out of my room without my shoes. After a while the "all clear" came, and hundreds of us stood in line for elevators to return to our rooms. Later that morning, as I entered an elevator to go to an appointment, I said, "You all look happier than you did last night." A man said, "That was just a dream," and everyone laughed.

*   *   *

The inauguration itself was beautiful to see—pomp, panoply, parades, flags and cannonades. America does this well. And the most poignant moment was the manful William Rehnquist, unable to wear a tie but making his way down the long marble steps to swear in the president. The continuation of democracy is made possible by such personal gallantry.

There were some surprises, one of which was the thrill of a male voice singing "God Bless America," instead of the hyper-coloratura divas who plague our American civic life. But whoever picked the music for the inaugural ceremony itself—modern megachurch hymns, music that sounds like what they'd use for the quiet middle section of a Pixar animated film—was not successful. The downbeat orchestral arrangement that followed the president's speech was no doubt an attempt to avoid charges that the ceremony had a triumphalist air. But I wound up thinking: *This is America. We have a lot of good songs. And we watch inaugurals in part to hear them.*

Never be defensive in your choice of music.

*   *   *

The Inaugural Address itself was startling. It left me with a bad feeling, and reluctant dislike. Rhetorically, it veered from high-class boilerplate to strong and simple sentences, but it was not pedestrian. George W. Bush's second inaugural will no doubt prove historic because it carried a punch, asserting an agenda so sweeping that an observer quipped that by the end he would not have been surprised if the president had announced we were going to colonize Mars.

A short and self-conscious preamble led quickly to the meat

of the speech: the president's evolving thoughts on freedom in the world. Those thoughts seemed marked by deep moral seriousness and no moral modesty.

No one will remember what the president said about domestic policy, which was the subject of the last third of the text. This may prove to have been a miscalculation.

It was a foreign-policy speech. To the extent our foreign policy is marked by a division that has been (crudely but serviceably) defined as a division between moralists and realists—the moralists taken with a romantic longing to carry democracy and justice to foreign fields, the realists motivated by what might be called cynicism and an acknowledgment of the limits of governmental power—President Bush sided strongly with the moralists, which was not a surprise. But he did it in a way that left this Bush supporter yearning for something she does not normally yearn for, and that is: nuance.

The administration's approach to history is at odds with what has been described by a communications adviser to the president as the "reality-based community." A dumb phrase, but not a dumb thought: He meant that the administration sees history as dynamic and changeable, not static and impervious to redirection or improvement. That is the Bush administration way, and it happens to be realistic: History is dynamic and changeable. On the other hand, some things are constant, such as human imperfection, injustice, misery and bad government.

This world is not heaven.

The president's speech seemed rather heavenish. It was a God-drenched speech. This president, who has been accused of giving too much attention to religious imagery and religious thought, has not let the criticism enter him. God was invoked relentlessly. "The Author of Liberty." "God moves and chooses as He wills. We have confidence because freedom is the permanent hope of mankind... the longing of the soul."

It seemed a document produced by a White House on a mission. The United States, the speech said, has put the world on notice: Good governments that are just to their people are our friends, and those that are not are, essentially, not. We know the way: democracy. The president told every nondemocratic government in the world to shape up. "Success in our relations [with other governments] will require the decent treatment of their own people."

The speech did not deal with specifics—9/11, terrorism, particular alliances, Iraq. It was, instead, assertively abstract.

"We are led, by events and common sense, to one conclusion: The survival of liberty in our land increasingly depends on the success of liberty in other lands." "Across the generations we have proclaimed the imperative of self-government... Now it is the urgent requirement of our nation's security, and the calling of our time." "It is the policy of the United States to seek and support the growth of democratic movements and institutions in every nation and culture, with the ultimate goal of ending tyranny in our world."

Ending tyranny in the world? Well that's an ambition, and if you're going to have an ambition it might as well be a big one. But this declaration, which is not wrong by any means, seemed to me to land somewhere between dreamy and disturbing. Tyranny is a very bad thing and quite wicked, but one doesn't expect we're going to eradicate it any time soon. Again, this is not heaven, it's earth.

*   *   *

There were moments of eloquence: "America will not pretend that jailed dissidents prefer their chains, or that women welcome humiliation and servitude, or that any human being aspires to live at the mercy of bullies." "We do not accept the existence of permanent tyranny because we do not accept the possibility of permanent slavery." And, to the young people of our country, "You have seen that life is fragile, and evil is real, and courage triumphs." They have, since 9/11, seen exactly that.

And yet such promising moments were followed by this, the ending of the speech: "Renewed in our strength—tested, but not weary—we are ready for the greatest achievements in the history of freedom."

This is—how else to put it?—over the top. It is the kind of sentence that makes you wonder if this White House did not, in the preparation period, have a case of what I have called in the past "mission inebriation." A sense that there are few legitimate boundaries to the desires born in the goodness of their good hearts.

One wonders if they shouldn't ease up, calm down, breathe deep, get more securely grounded. The most moving speeches summon us to the cause of what is actually possible. Perfection in the life of man on earth is not.

Further Thoughts on the Passions of the Inaugural

The Wall Street Journal: January 27, 2005

I have been called old, jaded, a sourpuss. Far worse, I have been called French. A response is in order.

You know the dispute. Last week I slammed the president's Inaugural Address. I was not alone, but I came down hard, early and in one of the most highly read editorial pages in America. Bill Buckley and David Frum also had critical reactions. Bill Safire on the other hand called it one of the best second inaugurals ever, and commentators from right and left (Bill Kristol, E. J. Dionne) found much to praise and ponder. (To my mind the best response to the inaugural was the grave, passionate essay of Mark Helprin.) So herewith some questions and answers:

A week later, do I stand by my views?

Yes. If I wrote it today I wouldn't be softer, but harder.

Am I heartened by White House clarifications that the speech did not intend to announce the unveiling of a new policy?

Yes. My reaction is the exact opposite of Bill Bennett's and E. J. Dionne's, who were both disappointed. I am relieved.

Why don't I see the speech as so many others do, as a thematic and romantic statement of what we all hope for, world freedom? Don't we all want that?

Yes. But words have meaning. To declare that it is now the policy of the United States to eradicate tyranny in the world, that we are embarking on the greatest crusade in the history of freedom and that the survival of American liberty is dependent on the liberty of every other nation—seemed to me, and seems to me, rhetorical and emotional overreach of the most embarrassing sort.

What's wrong with a little overweening ambition? Shouldn't man's reach exceed his grasp?

True. But history is quite big enough right now. We've already been given a lot to grasp. The president will have real juice for the next 2½ years. If in the next 30 months he can stabilize and fortify Iraq, helping it to become a functioning democratic entity that doesn't encourage terrorism; further gird and undergird Afghanistan; keep the U.S. safe from attack; make our alliances closer; make permanent his tax cuts; and break through on Social Security, that will be huge. It will be historic. It will yield a presidency that even its severest critics will have to admit was enormously consequential, and its supporters will rightly claim as leaving a lasting legacy of courage and inspiration. We don't need more than that—it's quite enough. And it will be quite astonishing. Beyond that, don't overreach. Refrain from breast beating, and don't clobber the world over the head with your moral fabulousness.

What was the biggest mistake of the speech?

They forgot context. All speeches take place within a historical context, a time and place. A good speech acknowledges context, often without even mentioning it.

For a half century our country faced a terrible foe. Some feared conflagration. Many of us who did not were convinced it would not happen because the United States was not evil and the Soviet Union was not crazy. The Soviets didn't want war to achieve their ends, they wanted to achieve those ends without the expense and gamble of war. We rolled them back, bankrupted them, forced their collapse. And we did it in part through a change of policy in which Ronald Reagan declared: From here on in we tell the truth. He called the Soviet Union an evil empire because it was a) evil and b) an empire, and c) he judged a new and stark candor the way to begin progress. We'd already kissed Brezhnev; it didn't work. And it wasn't Reagan's way in any case.

Today is quite different. The context is different. Now we are up against not an organized state monolith but dozens, hundreds and thousands of state and nonstate actors—nuts with nukes, freelance bioterrorists, Islamofascists, independent but allied terror groups. The temperature of our world is very high. We face trouble that is already here. We don't have to summon more.

Healthy alliances are a coolant in this world. What this era demands is steely resolve and actions that remove those who want things at a full boil. In this world we must speak, yes, but softly, and carry many sticks, using them, when we must, terribly and swiftly. We must gather around us as many friends, allies and well-wishers as possible. And we must do nothing that provides our foes with ammunition with which they can accuse us of conceit, immaturity or impetuousness.

Here is an unhappy fact: Certain authoritarians and tyrants whose leadership is illegitimate and unjust have functioned in history as—ugly imagery coming—garbage-can lids on their societies. They keep freedom from entering, it is true. But when they are removed, the garbage—the freelance terrorists, the grievance merchants, the ethnic nationalists—pops out all over. Yes, freedom is good and to be strived for. But cleaning up the garbage is not pretty. And it sometimes leaves the neighborhood in an even bigger mess than it had been.

Am I saying we shouldn't support freedom then?

Hardly. But we should remember as we do it that history, while full of opportunity, is also a long tale of woe. And human vanity—not only that of others, but our own—only complicates our endeavors. Thomas Jefferson was a genius, a great man who loved liberty. But that love led him to headlong support of a French Revolution that proved more demonic than liberating. He was right to encourage the fire of liberty but wrong to lend his great name to Robespierre, Marat and the rest. So much of life is case by case, so many of our decisions must be discrete and particular and not "thematic." It is hard to do the right thing. That is why grown-ups often get headaches and children mostly don't.

Life is layered, complex, not always most needful of political action. For many people in the world the most important extra-familial relationship is not with the state but with God. Pope John Paul II helped free his beloved Poland from the Soviet yoke. But when he looked at Poland some years after its freedom was won, he wondered if many of his kinsmen had not chosen a kind of existential enslavement to Western materialism. He wondered if his people were not in some ways less free. It wasn't a stupid question. It was at the heart of life.

But isn't hard criticism of such an important speech at such a serious moment disloyal? You're a Bush supporter!

I am. I even took off from the Journal to work for his reelection. I did exciting and I hope helpful work at considerable financial loss. But loyalty consists of many things, including being truthful with our friends. As Reagan used to say, candor is a compliment. This White House can take it. Two years ago, after watching a series of rather too jocular and arguably too boastful news conferences from administration leaders on the coming war, I said that they seemed to be suffering from mission inebriation. I meant it. And meant it as a caution. The White House can be a hothouse. Emotions run high, tired minds run on adrenal fumes. When I said last week that they seemed again to be suffering from mission inebriation, I meant that, too.

As for criticizing Mr. Bush on something so big, that's why I did it: It's big. And so important. When you really disagree, you have to say so. In the end I found the president's thinking perplexing and disturbing. At any rate, in the end, as Jack Kennedy once said, "Sometimes party loyalty asks too much."

What do you think of David Frum's wondering if the fact that the system let this speech through doesn't suggest the system needs work?

I had a similar thought. I wonder if this White House, with its understandable but not always helpful Band of Brothers aspect, isn't different from previous White Houses in this. In other White Houses there were always too many people eager to show their worth by removing the meaning of the speech, or warning the president that such and such shouldn't be said. I get the impression no one in this White House wants to be the person in the speechwriter's memoir who tried to remove "Tear down this wall" or "evil empire." So often such people are defensive, anxious, unhelpful. They often lost the battle in the Reagan White House, to the benefit of history. But for this speech there seemed no one who wanted to think defensively and wield the editing stick. Which is bad, because such people are actually needed. They're like dead wood in a forest; they add to the ecology; they have their purpose.

Bill Buckley and David Gelernter suggest the speech was badly written. Isn't that really the essential problem?

No. It was badly thought. In any case most inaugural addresses are rather badly written, and I would know. We haven't had a truly great one since 1961, 44 years ago. In this case the document seems to me to bear hard the personal mark of the president, and not of writers. But it is not the plain-talking Bush we know so well. It is Bush trying to be fancy. It is a tough man who speaks the language of business, sports and politics trying to be high-toned and elegant.

You're being patronizing.

That's what jaded old French people are for.

We all have our different styles. The biggest style mistake you can make is to use someone else's style, or the moment's style if you will, and not your own.

Speaking of style, how did you like the headline on your piece last week?

I thought it was quite wicked and didn't capture the meaning of the piece. When I pointed this out to the editor he promised in the future to be more nuanced. But it was my fault. Advice to self: Don't go to cover a story before you've OK'd the headline on the previous one.

What are you looking forward to now?

I am hoping for a State of the Union address that is tough, clear, tethered, and in which the speaker takes his program seriously but himself rather more lightly. I am hoping the headline will be "Return to Planet Earth."

* * *

Two departures this week deserve note. A respectful and affectionate goodbye-from-columnating to Bill Safire of the New York Times, a great presence on that op-ed page for 30 years. He was a gutsy, witty wader into the fray. He has taken shots at me in the past, and in the spirit of comradely columnary aggression I wish I could take a goodbye shot back. (If he were sitting next to me now he'd say, "Don't be soft, I'm on top, start a pile-on!") But I can't. A classy and provocative pro from beginning to end. I'm going to miss his column a lot.

Johnny Carson's gift was that he seemed startled by sophistication. This was so American. It's why Americans loved him. When the starlet blurted the seamy detail, when someone said or did something too odd or too open to interpretation, Carson would give the audience the dry look. And east or west, north or south, we all got the joke. When we laughed together, in our separate houses, that was a kind of community. It was a good note on which to end the day. He was an American treasure. Rest in peace.

Time for an Intervention

The Wall Street Journal: September 18, 2012

What should Mitt Romney do now? He should peer deep into the abyss. He should look straight into the heart of darkness where lies a Republican defeat in a year the Republican presidential candidate almost couldn't lose. He should imagine what it will mean for the country, for a great political philosophy, conservatism, for his party and, last, for himself. He must look down unblinkingly.

And then he needs to snap out of it, and *move*.

He has got seven weeks. He's just had two big flubs. On the Mideast he seemed like a political opportunist, not big and wise but small and tinny. It mattered because the crisis was one of those moments when people look at you and imagine you as president.

Then his comments released last night and made months ago at the private fund-raiser in Boca Raton, Fla. Mr. Romney has relearned what four years ago Sen. Barack Obama learned: There's no such thing as private when you're a candidate with a mic. There's someone who doesn't like you in that audience. There's someone with a cellphone. Mr. Obama's clinger comments became famous in 2008 because when people heard what he'd said, they thought, "That's the real him, that's him when he's talking to his friends."

* * *

And so a quick denunciation of what Mr. Romney said, followed by some ideas.

The central problem revealed by the tape is Romney's theory of the 2012 election. It is that a high percentage of the electorate receives government checks and therefore won't vote for him, another high percentage is supplying the tax revenues and will vote for him, and almost half the people don't pay taxes and presumably won't vote for him.

My goodness, that's a lot of people who won't vote for you. You wonder how he gets up in the morning.

This is not how big leaders talk, it's how shallow campaign operatives talk: They slice and dice the electorate like that, they see everything as determined by this interest or that. They're usually young enough and dumb enough that nobody holds it against them, but they don't know anything. They don't know much about America.

We are a big, complicated nation. And we are human beings. We are people. We have souls. We are complex. We are not data points. Many things go into our decisions and our political affiliations.

You have to be sophisticated to know that. And if you're operating at the top of national politics, you're supposed to be sophisticated.

I wrote recently of an imagined rural Ohio woman sitting on her porch, watching the campaign go by. She's 60, she identifies as conservative, she likes guns, she thinks the culture has gone crazy. She doesn't like Obama. Romney looks OK. She's worried about the national debt and what it will mean to her children. But she's having a hard time, things are tight for her right now, she's on partial disability, and her husband is a vet and he gets help, and her mother receives Social Security.

She's worked hard and paid into the system for years. Her husband fought for his country.

And she's watching this whole election and *thinking*. You can win her vote if you give her faith in your fairness and wisdom. But not if you label her and dismiss her.

As for those workers who don't pay any income taxes, they pay payroll taxes—Social Security and Medicare. They want to rise in the world and make more money. They'd like to file a 1040 because that will mean they got a raise or a better job.

They too are potential Romney voters, because they're suffering under the no-growth economy.

So: Romney's theory of the case is all wrong. His understanding of the political topography is wrong.

And his tone is fatalistic. *I can't win these guys who will only vote their economic interests, but I can win these guys who will vote their economic interests, plus some guys in the middle, whoever they are.*

That's too small and pinched and narrow. That's not how Republicans emerge victorious—"I can't win these guys." You have to have more respect than that, and more affection, you don't write anyone off, you invite everyone in. Reagan in 1984 used to put out his hand: "Come too, come walk with me." Come join, come help, whatever is happening in your life.

You know what Romney sounded like? Like a kid new to politics who thinks he got the inside lowdown on how it works from some operative. But those old operatives, they never know how it works. They knew how it worked for one cycle back in the day.

They're jockeys who rode Seabiscuit and thought they won a race.

* * *

The big issue—how we view government, what we want from it, what we need, what it rightly asks of us, what it wrongly demands of us—is a good and big and right and serious subject. It has to be dealt with seriously, at some length. And it is in part a cultural conversation. There's a lot of grievance out there, and a sense of entitlement in many spheres. A lot of people don't feel confident enough or capable enough to be taking part in the big national drama of Work in America. Why? What's going on? That's a conversation worth having.

I think there is a broad and growing feeling now, among Republicans, that this thing is slipping out of Romney's hands. Today at a speech in New York with what seemed like many conservatives and Republicans in the audience, I said more or less the above. I wondered if anyone would say, in the Q&A, "I think you've got it wrong, you're too pessimistic." No one did. A woman asked me to talk about why in a year the Republicans couldn't lose, the Republican candidate seems to be losing.

I said pre-mortems won't help, if you want to help the more conservative candidate, it's a better use of your time to pitch in with ideas. There's seven weeks to go. This isn't over, it's possible to make things better.

Republicans are going to have to right this thing. They have to stabilize it.

It's time to admit the Romney campaign is an incompetent one. It's not big, it's not brave, it's not thoughtfully tackling great issues. It's always been too small for the moment. All the activists, party supporters and big donors should be pushing for change. People want to focus on who at the top is least constructive and most responsible. Fine, but Mitt Romney is no puppet: He chooses who to listen to. An intervention is in order. "Mitt, this isn't working."

Romney is known to be loyal. He sticks with you when you're going through a hard time, he rides it down with you. That's a real personal quality, a virtue. My old boss Reagan was a little colder. The night before he won the crucial 1980 New Hampshire primary—the night before he *won* it—he fired his campaign manager, John Sears. Reagan thought he wasn't cutting it, so he was gone. The economist Martin Anderson once called Reagan genially ruthless, and he was. But then it wasn't about John Sears's feelings or Ronald Reagan's feelings, it was about America. You can be pretty tough when it's about America.

Romney doesn't seem to be out there campaigning enough. He seems—in this he is exactly like the president—to always be disappearing into fund-raisers, and not having enough big public events.

But the logic of Romney's fund-raising has seemed, for some time, slightly crazy. He's raising money so he can pile it in at the end, with ads. But at the end will they make much difference? Obama is said to have used a lot of his money early on, to paint a portrait of

Romney as Thurston Howell III, as David Brooks put it. That was a gamble on Obama's part: Spend it now, pull ahead in the battle-grounds, once we pull ahead more money will come in because money follows winners, not losers.

If I'm seeing things right, that strategy is paying off.

Romney's staff used to brag they had a lower burn rate, they were saving it up. For what? For the moment when Americans would rather poke out their eyeballs and stomp on the goo than listen to another ad?

Also, Mr. Romney's ads are mostly boring. It's kind of an achievement to be boring at a moment in history like this, so credit where it's due: That musta taken effort!

*   *   *

When big, serious, thoughtful things must be said, then big, serious, thoughtful speeches must be given. Mr. Romney is not good at press conferences. Maybe because he doesn't give enough, and so hasn't grown used to them, and confident.

He should stick to speeches, and they have to be big—where America is now, what we must do, how we can do it. He needs to address the Mideast, too, because it isn't going to go away as an issue and is adding a new layer of unease to the entire election. Luckily, Romney has access to some of the best writers and thinkers in the business. I say it that way because to write is to think, and Romney needs fresh writing *and* fresh thinking.

Romney needs to get serious here. Or, he can keep typing out his stray thoughts with Stuart Stevens, who's sold himself as a kind of mad genius. I get the mad part.

Wake this election up. Wade into the crowd, wade into the fray, hold a hell of a rally in an American city—don't they count anymore? A big, dense city with skyscrapers like canyons, crowds and placards, and yell-ing. All of our campaigning now is in bland suburbs and tired hustings. How about: New York, New York, the city so nice they named it twice?

You say the state's not in play? It's New York. Our media lives here, they'll make it big. How about downtown Brooklyn, full of new Americans? Guys—make it look like there's an election going on. Because there is.

Be serious and fight.

If you're gonna lose, lose honorably. If you're gonna win, do it with meaning.

*   *   *

Romney always seems alone out there, a guy with a mic pacing an empty stage. All by himself, removed from the other humans. It's sad-looking. It's not working.

Time for the party to step up. Romney should go out there every day surrounded with the most persuasive, interesting and articulate members of his party, the old ones, and I say this with pain as they're my age, like Mitch Daniels and Jeb Bush, and the young ones, like Susana Martinez and Chris Christie and Marco Rubio—and even Paul Ryan. I don't mean one of them should travel with him next Thursday, I mean he should be surrounded by a posse of them every day. Their presence will say "This isn't about one man, this is about a whole world of meaning, this is about a conservative political philosophy that can turn things around and make our country better."

Some of them won't want to do it because they're starting to think Romney's a loser and they don't want to get loser on them. Too bad. They should be embarrassed if they don't go, and try, and work, and show support for the conservative candidate at a crucial moment. Do they stand for something or not? Is it bigger than them or not?

Party elders, to the extent you exist this is why you exist:

Right this ship.

*   *   *

So, these are some ideas. Others will have more, and they'll be better. But an intervention is needed.

The View from Gate 14

The Wall Street Journal: April 25, 2008

America is in line at the airport. America has its shoes off, is carrying a rubberized bin, is going through a magnetometer. America is worried there is fungus on the floor after a million stockinged feet have walked on it. But America knows not to ask. America is guilty until proved innocent, and no one wants to draw undue attention. America left its ticket and passport in the jacket in the bin in the X-ray machine, and is admonished. America is embarrassed to have put one one-ounce moisturizer too many in the see-through bag. America is irritated that the TSA agent removed its mascara, opened it, put it to her nose and smelled it. *Why don't you put it up your nose and see if it explodes?* America thinks.

And, as always: Why do we do this when you know I am not a terrorist, and you know I know you know I am not a terrorist? Why this costly and harassing kabuki when we both know the facts, and would agree that all this harassment is the government's way of showing "fairness," of showing that it will equally humiliate anyone in order to show its high-mindedness and sense of justice? Our politicians congratulate themselves on this as we stand in line.

All the frisking, beeping and patting down is demoralizing to our society. It breeds resentment, encourages a sense that the normal are not in control, that common sense is yesterday. Another thing: It reduces the status of that ancestral arbiter and leader of society, the middle-aged woman. In the new fairness, she is treated like everyone else, without respect, like the loud ruffian and the vulgar girl on the phone. The middle-aged woman is the one spread-eagled over there in the delicate shell beneath the removed jacket, praying nothing on her body goes beep and makes people look.

America makes it through security, gets to the gate, waits. The TV monitor is on. It is Wolf Blitzer. He is telling us with a voice of urgency of the Pennsylvania returns. But no one looks up. We are a nation of Willy Lomans, dragging our rollies through acres of airport, going through life with a suitcase and a slack jaw, trying to get home after a long day of meetings, of moving product.

No one in crowded gate 14 looks up to see what happened in Pennsylvania. No one. Wolf talks to the air. Gate 14 is small-town America, a mix, a group of people of all classes and races brought together and living in close proximity until the plane is called, and America knows what Samuel Johnson knew. "How small, of all that human hearts endure / That part which laws or kings can cause or cure."

Gate 14 doesn't think any one of the candidates is going to make their lives better. Gate 14 will vote anyway, because they know they are the grown-ups of America and must play the role and do the job.

*   *   *

So: Pennsylvania. As seen from the distance of West Texas, central California and Oklahoma, which is where I've been.

Main thought. Hillary Clinton is not Barack Obama's problem. America is Mr. Obama's problem. He has been tagged as a snooty lefty, as the glamorous, ambivalent candidate from Men's Vogue, the candidate who loves America because of the great progress it has made in terms of racial fairness. Fine, good. But has he ever gotten misty-eyed over...the Wright Brothers and what kind of country allowed them to go off on their own and change everything? How about D-Day, or George Washington, or Henry Ford, or the losers and brigands who flocked to Sutter's Mill, who pushed their way west because there was gold in them thar hills? There's gold in that history.

John McCain carries it in his bones. Mr. McCain learned it in school, in the Naval Academy and, literally, at grandpa's knee. Mrs. Clinton learned at least its importance in her long slog through Arkansas, circa 1977–92.

Mr. Obama? What does he think about all that history? Which is another way of saying: What does he think of America? That's why people talk about the flag pin absent from the lapel. They wonder if it means something. Not that the presence of the pin proves love of country—any cynic can wear a pin, and many cynics do. But what about Obama and America? Who would have taught him to love it, and what did he learn was lovable, and what does he think about it all?

Another challenge. Snooty lefties get angry when you ask them to talk about these things. They get resentful. *Who are you to question my patriotism?* But no one is questioning his patriotism, they're questioning its content, its fullness. Gate 14 has a right to hear this. They'd lean forward to hear.

This is an opportunity, for Mr. Obama needs an Act II. Act II is hard. Act II is where the promise of Act I is deepened, the plot thickens, and all is teed up for resolution and meaning. Mr. Obama's Act I was: I'm Obama. He enters the scene. Act III will be the convention and acceptance speech. After that a whole new drama begins. But for now he needs Act II. He should make his subject America.

*   *   *

Here's some comfort for him, for all Democrats. In Lubbock, Texas—Lubbock Comma Texas, the heart of Texas conservatism— they dislike President Bush. He has lost them. I was there and saw it. Confusion has been followed by frustration has turned into resentment, and this is huge. Everyone knows the president's poll numbers are at historic lows, but if he is over in Lubbock, there is no place in this country that likes him. I made a speech and moved around and I was tough on him and no one—not one—defended or disagreed. I did the same in North Carolina recently, and again no defenders. I did the same in Fresno, Calif., and no defenders, not one.

He has left on-the-ground conservatives—the local right-winger, the town intellectual reading Burke and Kirk, the old Reagan committeewoman—feeling undefended, unrepresented and alone.

This will have impact down the road.

I finally understand the party nostalgia for Reagan. Everyone speaks of him now, but it wasn't that way in 2000, or 1992, or 1996, or even '04.

I think it is a manifestation of dislike for and disappointment in Mr. Bush. It is a turning away that is a turning back. It is a looking back to conservatism when conservatism was clear, knew what it was, was grounded in the facts of the world.

The reasons for the quiet break with Mr. Bush: spending, they say first, growth in the power and size of government, Iraq. I imagine some of this: a fine and bitter conservative sense that he has never had to stand in his stockinged feet at the airport holding the bin, being harassed. He has never had to live in the world he helped make, the one where grandma's hip replacement is setting off the beeper here and the child is crying there. And of course as a former president, with the entourage and the private jets, he never will. I bet conservatives don't like it. I'm certain Gate 14 doesn't.

The Trigger-Happy Generation

If reading great literature traumatizes you, wait until you get a taste of life.

The Wall Street Journal: May 29, 2015

Readers know of the phenomenon at college campuses regarding charges of "microaggressions" and "triggers." It's been going on for a while and is part of a growing censorship movement in which professors, administrators and others are accused of racism, sexism, homophobia, classism, gender bias and ethnocentric thinking, among other things. Connected is the rejection or harassment of commencement and other campus speakers who are not politically correct. I hate that phrase, but it just won't stop being current.

Kirsten Powers goes into much of this in her book, "The Silencing." Anyway, quite a bunch of little Marats and Robespierres we're bringing up.

But I was taken aback by a piece a few weeks ago in the Spectator, the student newspaper of Columbia University. I can't shake it, though believe me I've tried. I won't name the four undergraduate authors, because 30 years from now their children will be on Google, and because everyone in their 20s has the right to be an idiot.

Yet theirs is a significant and growing form of idiocy that deserves greater response.

The authors describe a student in a class discussion of Ovid's epic poem "Metamorphoses." The class read the myths of Persephone and Daphne, which, as parts of a narrative that stretches from the dawn of time to the Rome of Caesar, include depictions of violence, chaos, sexual assault and rape. The student, the authors reported, is herself "a survivor of sexual assault" and said she was "triggered." She complained the professor focused "on the beauty of the language and the splendor of the imagery when lecturing on the text." He did not apparently notice her feelings, or their urgency. As a result, "the student completely disengaged from the class discussion as a means of self-preservation. She did not feel safe in the class."

Safe is the key word here. There's the suggestion that a work may be a masterpiece but if it makes anyone feel bad, it's out.

Later the student told the professor how she felt, and her concerns, she said, were ignored. The authors of the op-ed note that "Metamorphoses" is a fixture in the study of literature and humanities, "but like so many texts in the Western canon it contains triggering and offensive material that marginalizes student identities in the classroom." The Western canon, they continue, is full of "histories and narratives of exclusion and oppression" that can be "difficult to read and discuss as a survivor, a person of color, or a student from a low-income background."

That makes them feel unsafe: "Students need to feel safe in the classroom, and that requires a learning environment that recognizes the multiplicity of their identities." The authors suggest changing the core curriculum but concede it may not be easy. Another student, they report, suggested in her class that maybe instead they could read "a Toni Morrison text." A different student responded that "texts by authors of the African Diaspora are a staple in most high school English classes, and therefore they did not need to reread them." That remark, the authors assert, was not only "insensitive" but "revealing of larger ideological divides." The professor, they report, failed at this moment to "intervene."

The op-ed authors call for "a space to hold a safe and open dialogue" about classroom experiences that "traumatize and silence students," with the aim of creating environments that recognize "the multiplicity" of student "identities."

Well, here are some questions and a few thoughts for all those who have been declaring at all the universities, and on social media, that their feelings have been hurt in the world and that the world had just better straighten up.

Why are you so fixated on the idea of personal safety, by which you apparently mean not having uncomfortable or unhappy thoughts and feelings? Is there any chance this preoccupation is unworthy of you? Please say yes.

There is no such thing as safety. That is asking too much of life. You can't expect those around you to constantly accommodate your need for safety. That is asking too much of people.

Life gives you potentials for freedom, creativity, achievement, love, all sorts of beautiful things, but none of us are "safe." And you are especially not safe in an atmosphere of true freedom. People will say and do things that are wrong, stupid, unkind, meant to injure. They'll bring up subjects you find upsetting. It's uncomfortable. But isn't that the price we pay for freedom of speech?

You can ask for courtesy, sensitivity and dignity. You can show others those things, too, as a way of encouraging them. But if you constantly feel anxious and frightened by what you encounter in life, are we sure that means the world must reorder itself? Might it mean you need a lot of therapy?

Masterpieces, by their nature, pierce. They jar and unsettle. If something in a literary masterpiece upsets you, should the master-piece really be banished? What will you be left with when all of them are gone?

What in your upbringing told you that safety is the highest of values? What told you it is a realistic expectation? Who taught you that you are entitled to it every day? Was your life full of... unchecked privilege? Discuss.

Do you think Shakespeare, Frieda Kahlo, Virginia Woolf, Langston Hughes and Steve Jobs woke up every morning thinking

"My focus today is on looking for slights and telling people they're scaring me"? Or were their energies and commitments perhaps focused on other areas?

I notice lately that some members of your generation are being called, derisively, Snowflakes. Are you really a frail, special and delicate little thing that might melt when the heat is on?

Do you wish to be known as the first generation that comes with its own fainting couch? Did first- and second-wave feminists march to the barricades so their daughters and granddaughters could act like Victorians with the vapors?

Everyone in America gets triggered every day. Many of us experience the news as a daily microaggression. Who can we sue, silence or censor to feel better?

Finally, social justice warriors always portray themselves—and seem to experience themselves—as actively suffering victims who need protection. Is that perhaps an invalid self-image? Are you perhaps less needy than demanding? You seem to be demanding a safety no one else in the world gets. If you were so vulnerable, intimidated and weak, you wouldn't really be able to attack and criticize your professors, administrators and fellow students so ably and successfully, would you?

Are you a bunch of frail and sensitive little bullies? Is it possible you're not intimidated but intimidators?

Again, discuss.

By the way, I went back to the op-ed and read the online comments it engendered from the Columbia community. They were quite wonderful. One called, satirically, to ban all satire because it has too many "verbal triggers." Another: "These women are like a baby watching a movie and thinking the monster is going to come out of the screen and get them." Another: "These girls' parents need a refund."

The biggest slayer of pomposity and sanctimony in our time continues to be American wit.

The Wisdom of "Mr. Republican"

The Wall Street Journal: October 18, 2013

Are the Republicans in civil war or in the middle of an evolution? Sen. Robert A. Taft (1889–1953) says it need not be the former and can be the latter. Taft, known in his day (the 1930s through '50s) as "Mr. Republican," possessed a personal background strikingly pertinent to the current moment. He was establishment with a capital E—not just Yale and Harvard Law but a father who'd been president. And yet he became the star legislator and leader of the party's conservative coalition, which had a certain Main Street populist tinge. Taft contained peacefully within himself two cultural strains that now are seemingly at war.

In his personal style he was cerebral, courtly and spoke easily, if with limited eloquence. The secret of his greatness was that everyone knew his project was not "Robert Taft" but something larger, the actual well-being and continuance of America. His peers chose him as one of the five best U.S. senators in history, up there with Daniel Webster and Henry Clay. What would he say about today?

Senator?

"Nice talking with you even though I'm no longer with you. Out golfing with Ike one day and felt a pain in my hips. Thought it was arthritis, turned out to be cancer. It had gone pretty far, and I was gone soon after."

Why did they call you "Mr. Republican"?

"Well, I suppose in part because I never bolted the party, and, in spite of what were probably some provocations on my part, no one managed to throw me out, either. But I felt loyalty to the GOP as a great institution, one that historically stood for the dignity of the individual versus the massed forces of other spheres, such as government. I stayed, worked, fought it out."

What is the purpose of a party?

"A theater critic once said a critic is someone who knows where we want to go but can't drive the car. That can apply here. It is the conservatives of the party, in my view, who've known where we want to go, and often given the best directions. The party is the car. Its institutions, including its most experienced legislators and accomplished political figures, with the support of the people, are the driver. You want to keep the car looking good. It zooms by on a country road, you want people seeing a clean, powerful object. You want to go fast, but you don't want it crashing. You drive safely and try to get to your destination in one piece."

In the current dispute, he says, "both sides have something to admit. The GOP will not be a victorious national party in the future without the tea party. The tea party needs the infrastructure, tradition, capabilities—the car—in order to function as a fully coherent and effective national entity." He feels more sympathy toward the tea party than the establishment. "Their policy aims, while somewhat inchoate, seem on the right track. They need to be clearer about what they're for—intellectually more ordered. They can't lead with their hearts."

The establishment? "My goodness—lobbyists, consultants. I gather there's now something called hedge-fund billionaires." The establishment has a lot to answer for. "What they gave the people the past 10 years was two wars and a depression. That loosened faith in institutions and left people feeling had. They think, 'What will you give us next, cholera?'"

The tea party, in contrast, seems to him to be "trying to stand for a free citizenry in the age of Lois Lerner. They're against this professional class in government that thinks we're a nation of donkeys pulling their winged chariot.

"Their impatience with the status quo is right. Their sense of urgency is right. Their insight that the party in power has gone to the left of where America really is—right on that, too."

But the tea party has a lot to learn, and quickly. "It's not enough to feel, you need strategy. They need better leadership, not people interested in money, power and fame. Public service requires sacrifice. I see too many self-seekers there.

"The tea party should stop the insults—'RINO,' 'sellout,' 'surrender caucus.' It's undignified, and it's not worthy of a serious movement. When you claim to be the policy adults, you also have to be the characterological adults. Resentment alienates. An inability to work well with others does not inspire voters."

They should remove the chip from their shoulder. "Stop acting like Little Suzie with her nose pressed against the window watching the fancy people at the party. You've arrived and you know it. Forget the obsession with Georgetown cocktail parties. There hasn't been a good one since Allen Drury's wake." Taft paused: "You can Google him. He wrote a book."

Most important? "I don't like saying this but be less gullible. Many of your instincts are right but politics is drowning in money. A lot of it is spent trying to manipulate you, by people who claim to be sincere, who say they're the only honest guy in the room. Don't be the fool of radio stars who rev you up for a living. They're doing it for ratings. Stop being taken in by senators who fund-raise off your anger. It's good you're indignant, but they use consultants to keep picking at the scab, not to move the ball forward, sorry to mix metaphors. And know your neighbors: Are they going to elect a woman who has to explain she isn't a witch, or a guy who talks about 'legitimate rape'? You'll forgive politicians who are right in other areas, but your neighbors and the media will not. Get smart about this.

Don't let the media keep killing your guys in the field. Make it hard for them. Enter primaries soberly. When you have to take out an establishment man, do. But if you don't, stick with him but stiffen his spine."

What should the establishment do?

"Wake up and smell the Sanka! Listen, reason, talk. Advise in friendship. Be open to debate and get broader, ask yourself questions. Deep down, do you patronize those innocents on the farms, in the hinterlands? Or perhaps you understand yourself to be a fat, happy mosquito on the pond scum that is them? You had better get a mind adjustment on that, and soon. You're better than nobody. You had a good ride for 30 years. Now you're going to have to work for it."

How will a big merge happen?

"Day by day, policy by policy, vote by vote, race by race. On both sides they'll have to keep two things in mind. A little grace goes a long way, and 'A kind word turneth away wrath.'"

Ted Cruz? Here Taft paused. "That fellow is a little self-propelled." Another pause. "We had a saying, 'Give him time and space to fall on his face.'" Others with him on the Hill, however, are "good, smart, intend to make America better, and will be a big part of the future."

And don't forget, Taft says, "the first Mr. Republican. Abe Lincoln. First inaugural: 'We are not enemies but friends. We must not be enemies.' Members of the party should wake up every day saying those words."

CHAPTER 7

What I Told the Bishops

I have had an uneasy relationship with the Catholic Church the past 20 or so years. I am a believing Catholic, perhaps an ardent one. It is the core of my identity. But the sex scandals and other scandals put a distance between me and the church's leaders that I'd never before experienced. I felt that all Catholics have a responsibility to help right the Church, and my way of righting is writing. When I began to write about the sex scandals, some cardinals became angry. One accused me of disloyalty and another attempted to cause me professional embarrassments. The one who accused me of disloyalty was Cardinal Bernard Law, who presided over the Boston scandals, and barely escaped arrest. He told me, as you will see, that when the church is under pressure, it needs its friends to act as friends. I assured him I was a friend and was acting as one, and if the scandals didn't stop, he, the cardinal, would lose his mansion to trial lawyers. In fact, years later the mansion was lost, along with so much else. But what struck me was that that's the part of the conversation that really caught his attention, the part about real estate.

My church needs better leaders than it has.

* * *

What I Told the Bishops

The Wall Street Journal: September 15, 2003

A week ago today Cardinal Theodore McCarrick of Washington, Bishop Wilton Gregory, the head of the U.S. Catholic Bishops Council, and a handful of bishops met in Washington with a few dozen Catholic laymen to discuss the future of the church. The official name of the conference was "A Meeting in Support of the Church," but everyone knew the context.

Two months before, in July, Cardinal McCarrick and Bishop Gregory, both influential leaders in the church, held another meeting with laymen. That meeting, alas, was secret, and they had invited only those who might be characterized as church liberals. The story leaked, as stories do. Many, I among them, thought that holding a secret meeting to discuss a scandal borne of secrecy was ham-handed and tin-eared, at best. Why were only those who share one point of view asked to attend? Why was there no follow-up in terms of a statement from the participants on what was discussed, suggested, declared?

The cardinal and the bishop were said to be embarrassed when news of their meeting broke. Those often characterized as conservative asked for a similar meeting; the cardinal and the bishop obliged. And so last Monday's meeting, which thankfully was on the record, although participants were asked not to quote from the speeches they heard but rather to characterize them.

Last week several participants came forward to quote what they themselves had said at the meeting, and to give their general views.

I've been asked what I said, for I was one of the speakers. And so, here is what I said to the bishops.

* * *

First, I think in some small way the meeting was historic. The non-Catholic public would probably assume that bishops and cardinals frequently talk with conservatives in the church. The non-Catholic American public would probably assume bishops and cardinals *are* the conservatives in the church. But this is not so. Conservatives in the church often feel that they are regarded, and not completely unkindly, as sort of odd folk, who perhaps tend to have a third hand growing out of their foreheads and tinfoil hats on their heads. We say, "Please, we must speak more as a church about abortion," and church leaders say, "We may possibly do that after issuing the report on domestic employment policy." We ask the church to teach Catholic doctrine, and they point out that the press doesn't really like the church. We ask them to discuss the pressing issues of the moment, such as cloning—we're entering a world in which industrial fetal farms may grow replacement people for replacement parts—and instead they issue new directives on how it would be better if people sang songs during the mass after communion and hugged each other instead of shaking hands during the moment of peace.

So it was real news that Bishop Gregory and Cardinal McCarrick met with conservatives and heard them out for almost an entire day. And it was important that the conservatives assembled were so earnest (it was Princeton's Robert George who warned of a future that could include fetus farms) and so direct, too.

I had planned to address the teaching of Catholic doctrine, which is something the American Catholic Church doesn't really like to do in any depth, at least for the people in the pews. But it seemed to me that earlier speakers had so much to say on so many topics that are crucial and pending that the scandals were given short shrift. So I rearranged my speech as others spoke.

There were some central questions behind my remarks. *Do these men understand the extent and depth of the damage done by the scandal, and is still being done by it? Do they understand the church must move comprehensively to stop it?*

To speak of a problem so difficult and yet so delicate, and to do it in front of men who lead the wounded church, and who came up through a system that we now know to have been marked by institutional sickness, seemed to me—well, delicate is the best word I can come up with. And so I thought the only fair way to begin was to say that I meant to speak with candor, as one does among friends, that we all love the church and love Christ, and that candor demands candor about myself, too. I said that I speak from no great moral height, that I was certain I had "the least impressive personal biography in the room," that I am no moral exemplar, "far from it." I said I wanted to make this clear because "who we are both as individual people and as a church, who we really are, is at the heart of things."

Then I said my piece. I told them the scandal was in my view "the worst thing ever to happen in the history of the American church"; I told them they had to stop it now, deal with it fully; that if reports of abusive priests "continue to dribble out over the next two and four and six years, it will be terrible; it could kill the church." I spoke of how terrible it is that just the other day a priest in Maine was finally removed from his parish two years—two years!—after it was revealed that he was one of the priests who had set up the pornographic Web site "St. Sebastian's Angels." I said, "Two years after he was found to be doing what he was doing—and he's still in business!"

I attempted to paint a picture of a man in the suburbs of America, taking his kids to church. He stands in the back in his Gap khaki slacks and his plaid shirt ironed so freshly this morning that you can still smell the spray starch. He stands there holding his three-year-old child. He is still there every Sunday, he is loyal and faithful; but afterward—away from church, with his friends, at the barbecue and the lunch, he now feels free to say things about the church that only 10 years ago would have been shocking. "He thinks the church is largely populated by sexual predators, men whose job now is to look after their own." And then perhaps he says, "But not my priest." But maybe these days he doesn't say "but not my priest" anymore.

And so, I said, we must move. "We use buzzy phrases from the drug wars like zero tolerance" for sexual predators, but maybe we should use words that reflect who we are and where we stand—"defrocking" and "excommunication" being good words that speak of who we are as a church.

I told the bishops and the cardinal that we are a demoralized church, and—I told them this was hard to say—that they too must feel demoralized. "Imagine a leader of our church. He became a priest to help humanity, to bring it Christ. And he became a priest and did great work and rose to a position of leadership. And now he is in the meeting where the archdiocese lawyer muscles the single mother who brought suit against the local priest who molested her son after she took the boy to the priest so he could have a good male role model—and learn of the greatest male role model, Christ."

So, we are demoralized. But there is help. I spoke of the scene in Mel Gibson's movie, "The Passion," which I knew some in the audience had seen in screenings. Mr. Gibson had attempted, obviously, to base his film on the Gospels. But there are a few moments in which what might be called his art asserts itself, and he does it his way. There is one scene like this that for me was the great moving moment of the film. The broken and brutalized Christ falls under the weight of the cross. He is on his way to Golgotha. He's half dead. When he falls, his mother runs to help him, and he looks up at her, blood coming down his face, and he says, "See, Mother, I make all things new again."

I quoted this dialogue to the bishops and the cardinal. And when I said the words Christ spoke in the film my voice broke, and I couldn't continue speaking. I was embarrassed by this, but at the same time I thought, *Well, OK.*

What choked me was thinking of Jesus. And thinking of how we all want to be new again, and can be if we rely on him; but it's so hard, and deep in our hearts while we believe we do not believe, could not believe, or else we'd all be new again.

Anyway, I regained my voice and concluded my remarks with some hard advice. I said the leaders of the church should now— "tomorrow, first thing"—take the mansions they live in and turn them into schools for children who have nothing, and take the big black cars they ride in and turn them into school buses. I noted that we were meeting across the street from the Hilton, and that it would be good for them to find out where the cleaning women at the Hilton live and go live there, in a rent-stabilized apartment on the edge of town or in its suburbs. And take the subway to work like the other Americans, and talk to the people there. How moved those people would be to see a prince of the church on the subway. "They could talk to you about their problems of faith, they could tell you how hard it is to reconcile the world with their belief and faith, and you could say to them *Buddy, ain't it the truth.*"

I didn't know if this had hit its mark until the meeting was over, when an intelligent-looking and somewhat rotund bishop spoke to me as I waited for a cab. I was trying to rush to the airport and make the next shuttle home. He said, "I'd give you a ride but I don't have the limo!"

I laughed. Now I think perhaps I should have said, "You will."

I was asked privately after my speech if I meant to suggest the church should divest itself of its beautiful art and cathedrals and paintings and gold filigree. No way. We are neither Puritan nor Protestant; Catholicism is, among other things, a sensual faith, and it is our way to love and celebrate the beautiful. Moreover, regular people have as much access to this finery as the rich and powerful. But the princes of our church no longer need to live in mansions in the center of town. Those grand homes were bought and erected in part so the political leaders of our democracy would understand the Catholics have arrived. But they know it now. The point has been made.

* * *

Anyway, the response from the bishops and the cardinal was not clear to me. They did not refer to any of my points in their remarks afterward. When the meeting ended I tried to find Cardinal McCarrick to speak with him, but he was gone.

I don't imagine any of the laymen left the meeting with a feeling that great progress had been made in any area. I left with a feeling that some progress may have been made in some area, but I couldn't say what area or why.

I did not come away angry, as some have, or depressed. I came away satisfied that I'd said what I thought needed saying, and somewhat sad and perplexed. Why would this be happening? What does God want us to do? And how can flawed and ridiculous people like us help?

Someone at the meeting quoted the historian Paul Johnson saying some years back to a new Catholic, "Come on in, it's awful!" We all laughed, but you know I think it was the one thing everyone in the room agreed on.

Anyway, I've been asked what I said, and this was it. There has been no reporting of remarks from the meeting in July with the liberals of the church, and I hope there will be. It would be good if some of those who were there would report what they said, and how it was received by the bishops and cardinal. That might be helpful, as this old church finds its way.

How to Save the Catholic Church

The Wall Street Journal: April 16, 2010

The great second wave of church scandals appears this week to be settling down. In the Vatican they're likely thinking "the worst is over" and "we've weathered the storm." Is that good? Not to this Catholic. The more relaxed the institution, the less likely it will reform.

Let's look at the first wave. Eight years ago, on April 19, 2002, I wrote in these pages of the American church scandal, calling it calamitous, a threat to the standing and reputation of the entire church. Sexual abuse by priests "was the heart of the scandal, but at the same time only the start of the scandal": The rest was what might be called the racketeering dimension. Lawsuits had been brought charging that the church as an institution acted to cover up criminal behavior by misleading, lying and withholding facts. The most celebrated cases in 2002 were in Boston, where a judge had forced the release of 11,000 pages of church documents showing the abusive actions of priests and detailing then-Archbishop Bernard F. Law's attempts to hide the crimes. The Boston scandal generated hundreds of lawsuits, cost hundreds of millions of dollars in settlements and judgments, and included famous and blood-chilling cases—the repeat sexual abuser Father John Geoghan, who molested scores of boys and girls and was repeatedly transferred, was assigned to a parish in Waltham where he became too familiar with children in a public pool; Cardinal Law claimed he was probably "proselytizing."

In the piece I criticized Cardinal Theodore McCarrick, then archbishop of Washington, who had suggested to the Washington

Post that the scandal was media-driven, that journalists are having "a heyday." Then came the it-wasn't-so-bad defense: The bishop of Joliet, Ill., Joseph Imesch, said that while priests who sexually abuse children should lose their jobs, priests who sexually abuse adolescents and teenagers have a "quirk" and can be treated and continue as priests.

Really, he called it a quirk.

Does any of this, the finger-pointing and blame-gaming, sound familiar? Isn't it what we've been hearing the past few weeks?

At the end of the piece I called on the pope, John Paul II, to begin to show the seriousness of the church's efforts to admit, heal and repair by taking the miter from Cardinal Law's head and the ring from his finger and retiring him: "Send a message to those in the church who need to hear it, that covering up, going along, and paying off victims is over. That careerism is over, and Christianity is back."

The piece didn't go over well in the American church, or the Vatican. One interesting response came from Cardinal Law himself, whom I ran into a year later in Rome. "We don't need friends of the church turning on the church at such a difficult time," he said. "We need loyalty when the church is going through a tough time."

I'd suggested in the piece that the rarefied lives cardinals led had contributed to an inability to understand the struggles of others and the pain of those abused, and soon Cardinal Law and I were talking about his mansion outside Boston. He asked me how it would look if he'd refused to live there. I told him it would look good, but more to the point, the church was going to lose the cardinal's mansion to trial lawyers, and it should sell it first and put the money in schools.

Soon enough the mansion was gone, sold to pay the plaintiffs. Cardinal Law's successor, Archbishop Sean O'Malley, lives in an apartment in Boston's South End.

John Allen of the National Catholic Reporter once called Cardinal Law "the poster boy" of the American scandal. He has also become the poster boy for the church's problems in handling the scandal. And that has to do with its old-boy network, with the continued dominance of those who grew up in the old way.

In December 2002, Cardinal Law left Boston just hours before state troopers arrived with subpoenas seeking his grand jury testimony in what the state's attorney general, Thomas Reilly, called a massive cover-up of child abuse. The cardinal made his way to Rome, where he resigned, and where he stayed with Archbishop James Harvey, a close friend and, as head of the pontifical household, the most powerful American in the Vatican. Within a year Archbishop Harvey, too, was implicated in the scandal: The Dallas Morning News reported the Vatican had promoted a priest through its diplomatic corps even though it had received persistent, high-level warnings that he had sexually abused a young girl. The warnings had gone to Archbishop Harvey.

Cardinal Law received one of the best sinecures in Rome, as head of the Basilica of Saint Maria Maggiore and a member of the Vatican office tasked with appointing new bishops and correcting misconduct.

These stories are common in the church. Cardinal Angelo Sodano, a former Vatican secretary of state and now dean of the College of Cardinals, was a primary protector of the now-disgraced Father Marcial Maciel, founder of the Legion of Christ, described by a heroic uncoverer of the scandals, Jason Berry, in the National Catholic Reporter, as "a morphine addict who sexually abused at least twenty...seminarians."

I know this from having seen it: Many—not all, but many—of the men who staff the highest levels of the Vatican have been part of the very scandal they are now charged with repairing. They are defensive and they are angry, and they will not turn the church around on their own.

In a way, the Vatican lives outside time and space. The verities it speaks of and stands for are timeless and transcendent. For those who work there, bishops and cardinals, it can become its own reality. And when those inside fight for what they think is the life of the institution, they feel fully justified in fighting any way they please. They can do this because, as they rationalize it, they are not fighting only for themselves—it's not selfish, their fight—but to protect the greatest institution in the history of the world.

But in the past few decades, they not only fought persons—"If you were loyal you'd be silent"—they fought information.

What they don't fully understand right now—what they can't fully wrap their heads around—is that the information won.

The information came in through the cracks, it came in waves, in newspaper front pages, in books, in news beamed to every satellite dish in Europe and America. The information could not be controlled or stopped. The information was that something very sick was going on in the heart of the church.

Once, leaders of the Vatican felt that silence would protect the church. But now anyone who cares about it must come to understand that only speaking, revealing, admitting and changing will save the church.

The old Vatican needs new blood.

They need to let younger generations of priests and nuns rise to positions of authority within a new church. Most especially and most immediately, they need to elevate women. As a nun said to me this week, if a woman had been sitting beside a bishop transferring a priest with a history of abuse, she would have said: "Hey, wait a minute!"

If the media and the victims don't keep the pressure on, the old ways will continue. As for Cardinal Law, he should not be where he is, nor mitred nor ringed.

"Go and Repair My House"

The Wall Street Journal: March 15, 2013

I'll tell you how it looks: like one big unexpected gift for the church and the world.

Everything about Cardinal Jorge Mario Bergoglio's election was a surprise—his age, the name he took, his mien as he was presented to the world. He was plainly dressed, a simple white cassock, no regalia, no finery. He stood there on the balcony like a straight soft pillar and looked out at the crowd. There were no grand gestures, not even, at first, a smile. He looked tentative, even overwhelmed. I thought, as I watched, "My God—he's shy."

Then the telling moment about the prayer. Before he gave a blessing he asked for a blessing: He asked the crowd to pray for him. He bent his head down and the raucous, cheering square suddenly became silent, as everyone prayed. I thought, "My God—he's humble."

I wasn't sure what to make of it and said so to a friend, a member of another faith who wants the best for the church because to him that's like wanting the best for the world. He was already loving what he was seeing. He asked what was giving me pause. I said I don't know, the curia is full of tough fellows, the pope has to be strong.

"That is more than strength," he said of the man on the screen. "This is not cynical humanity. This is showing there is another way to be."

Yes. This is a kind of public leadership we are no longer used to—unassuming, self-effacing. Leaders of the world now are garish and brazen. You can think of half a dozen of their names in less than a minute. They're good at showbiz, they find the light and flash the smile.

But this man wasn't trying to act like anything else.

"He looks like he didn't want to be pope," my friend said. That's exactly what he looked like. He looked like Alec Guinness in the role of a quiet, humble man who late in life becomes pope. I mentioned that to another friend who said, "That would be the story of a hero."

And so, as they're saying in Europe, Francis the Humble. May he be a living antidote.

*　*　*

He is orthodox, traditional, his understanding of the faith in line with the teaching of John Paul II and Benedict XVI. He believes in, stands for, speaks for the culture of life.

He loves the poor and not in an abstract way. He gave the cardinal's palace in Buenos Aires to a missionary order with no money. He lives in an apartment, cooks his own food, rides the bus. He rejects pomposity. He does not feel superior. He is a fellow soul. He had booked a flight back to Argentina when the conclave ended.

But these two traits—his embrace of the church's doctrines and his characterological tenderness toward the poor—are very powerful together, and can create a powerful fusion. He could bridge the gap or close some of the distance between social justice Catholics and traditional, doctrinal Catholics. That would be a relief.

And he has suffered. Somehow you knew this as you looked at him Wednesday night. Much on this subject will come out.

The meaning of the name he chose should not be underestimated. Cardinal Bergoglio is a Jesuit, and the Jesuits were founded by St. Ignatius Loyola, who said he wanted to be like St. Francis of Assisi.

One of the most famous moments in St. Francis's life is the day he was passing by the church of St. Damiano. It was old and near collapse. From St. Bonaventure's "Life of Francis of Assisi": "Inspired by the Spirit, he went inside to pray. Kneeling before an image of the Crucified, he was filled with great fervor and consolation...While his tear-filled eyes were gazing at the Lord's cross, he heard with his bodily ears a voice coming from the cross, telling him three times: 'Francis, go and repair my house which, as you see, is falling into ruin.'" Francis was amazed "at the sound of this astonishing voice, since he was alone in the church." He set himself to obeying the command.

Go and repair my house, which is falling into ruin. Could the new pope's intentions be any clearer? The Catholic Church in 2013 is falling into ruin. It has been damaged by scandal and the scandals arose from arrogance, conceit, clubbiness and an assumption that the special can act in particular ways, that they may make mistakes but it's understandable, and if it causes problems the church will take care of it.

Pope Francis already seems, in small ways rich in symbolism, to be moving the Vatican away from arrogance. His actions in just his first 24 hours are suggestive.

He picks up his own luggage, pays his own hotel bill, shuns security, refuses a limousine, gets on a minibus with the cardinals. That doesn't sound like a prince, or a pope. He goes to visit a church in a modest car in rush-hour traffic. He pointedly refuses to sit on a throne after his election, it is reported, and meets his fellow cardinals standing, on equal footing. The night he was elected, according to New York's Cardinal Timothy Dolan, Vatican officials and staffers came forward to meet the new pope. He politely put them off: Not now, the people are waiting. Then he went to the balcony.

The church's grandeur is beautiful, but Francis seems to be saying he himself won't be grand. This will mean something in that old Vatican. It will mean something to the curia.

*   *   *

After the conclave, I'm grateful for two other things. First, after all the strains and scandals, they still came running. A pope was being picked. The smoke came out and the crowd was there in St. Peter's Square. They stood in the darkness, cold and damp, and they waited and cheered and the square filled up. As the cameras panned the crowd there was joy on their faces, and the joy felt like renewal.

People come for many reasons. To show love and loyalty, to be part of something, to see history. But maybe we don't fully know why they run, or why we turn when the first reports come of white smoke, and put on the TV or the computer. Maybe it comes down to this: "We want God." Which is what millions of people shouted when John Paul II first went home to Poland. This is something in the human heart, and no strains or scandals will prevail against it.

I viewed it all initially with hope, doubt and detachment. And then the white smoke, and the bells, and the people came running, and once again as many times before my eyes filled with tears, and my throat tightened. That in the end is how so many Catholics, whatever their level of engagement with the church, feel. "I was more loyal than I meant to be."

Much will unfold now, much will be seen. An ardent, loving 76-year-old cardinal in the middle of an acute church crisis is not going to sit around and do nothing. He's going to move. "Go and repair my house, which you see is falling into ruin."

Cardinal, Please Spare This Church

The Wall Street Journal: December 26, 2014

The Archdiocese of New York is threatening to close down my little church, a jewel in Catholicism's crown on 89th Street just off Madison, in Carnegie Hill, on the Upper East Side of Manhattan. This has caused great pain in our neighborhood this Christmas. St. Thomas More Church is where my son made his first holy communion, where he was confirmed. It is where at the presentation of the cross, on Good Friday, everyone in the parish who wants to—and that is everyone in the parish, poor people, crazy people, people just holding on, housekeepers, shopkeepers, billionaires—stands on line together, as equals, as brothers and sisters, to kiss the foot of the cross. It always makes me cry.

None of this is important except multiply it by 5,000, 10,000, a million people who've walked through our doors the past 75 years to marry, to bury, to worship.

There is context, of course, and context must always be respected. New York isn't the only place that is or will be closing churches, so the story may have some national application.

The Catholic Church, the greatest refuge of the poor in the history of the world, is always in need of money. The New York Archdiocese itself supports schools, hospitals, charities, churches, orders. It is in constant need. There is the refurbishment of mighty St. Patrick's Cathedral, which has been extremely expensive. There has been the cost, the past 20 years, of all the settlements and legal fees associated with the sex scandals. Compounding this is the constant bureau-cratic challenge to manage resources efficiently, professionally.

The church must save where it can. Churches have been closed. Most had particular stresses in common. Some had lost parishioners due to demographic change and a peeling off of the faithful. Some cannot support themselves financially and become a drain on the archdiocese. Some churches have fallen behind in repair and have become structurally dangerous. Some lost their place in the heart and life of their communities.

But the great mystery at the heart of the threatened closing of St. Thomas is more that none of these criteria apply to it. Not one.

St. Thomas More Church is not empty, it is vital, vibrant and alive. The other day at a special mass, the standing-room-only crowd spilled out onto the steps. People move into—and stay in—Carnegie Hill just for the church. Almost half the people at Sunday mass take long car and subway rides to worship there. (All this is from a list of facts about the church put together by its desperate parishioners.)

St. Thomas More not only supports itself financially, it gives money back to the archdiocese. It's not structurally unsound, it has just completed a major and costly refurbishment. It hasn't lost its school, it has a full, lively, respected preschool in the basement that families are desperate to get into. It is the sacramental home of all the Catholic schools in the area that don't have their own church or chapel. It is "a powerhouse of lay involvement in the spirit of Vatican II," says the parishioners' fact sheet, with a large parish council and four separate Catholic instruction programs for children. More can be said but at its heart it is a place for families, many of them old-style Catholics with four and five kids. Coffee hour after the 10 a.m. children's mass is jammed.

St. Thomas More functions too as a town hall for every secular group in the area. It is a meetinghouse for all of them. It is a citizen.

Our cardinal, my friend Timothy Dolan, being from Milwaukee, would not know, and the members of his many clusters and advisory boards would not know, that St. Thomas More is a mother root of the spiritual life of the Catholics on Manhattan's Upper East Side.

They're not talking about the closing of a church but the destroying of a world.

And for what? The archdiocese's arguments have been varied and lacking. They say there are other churches close by, that St. Thomas More can be relieved of its duties, blended and "merged" with the church of St. Ignatius. But St. Ignatius is near overwhelmed with its own schools and parish life, and could not absorb St. Thomas More's functions and programs.

The archdiocese then argues there is a shortage of priests. But St. Thomas More raises priests, three vocations born there the past 20 years. The cardinal's top media man, Joe Zwilling, last weekend pointed at St. Thomas More and asked, "What will you do in 20 years when there's no priest" to lead it? Well, over 20 years, in a church founded on miracles, we'll pray for vocations. More to the point, as one active friend of the archdiocese said to me, "In what way does closing a vital parish create more priests? Please share the logic."

Yes. Please.

The archdiocese appears to be scrambling for a respectable rationale. In the meantime parishioners wonder about the reasons for what they've come to call the second beheading of Thomas More.

Is it possible, they ask, the archdiocese is driven by what drove Henry VIII, politics and real estate?

That is an uncharitable thought. Let's explore it.

The archdiocese is defensive about closing churches in poor areas. What better way to comfort themselves, and avoid bad press, than closing one in an affluent area? Mr. Zwilling told this newspaper "it would be wrong and unjust" if only less affluent parishes were closed. To me, more sharply, Mr. Zwilling said just because St. Thomas More is in the black doesn't mean it is "protected."

The cardinal himself told one parishioner he sees it as a matter of fairness. "I can't just close poor parishes," the parishioner quoted him as saying. The parishioner responded, "Poor people are not helped because rich people are hurt."

All this seems in line with the de Blasio-ization of the times: Pick a target, move against it. Especially move on excellence, which can be painted as "elitist." If you can't help the poor you can at least afflict those you imagine to be rich.

Real estate? If St. Thomas More is closed, it can be sold. New York is experiencing a real-estate boom, Carnegie Hill is desirable. The church and its land could bring in $50 million, maybe $100 million. Any number of developers would jump at the chance. It's rumored—rumored—any number have.

*   *   *

In a true spirit of helpfulness, some members of St. Thomas More have searched for ways to keep their church alive, give even more money to the archdiocese and help it show greater, deeper affiliation with the needy. The cardinal could sell his grand private mansion in Midtown, just down the street from what has been assessed the most valuable piece of real estate in the city, Saks Fifth Avenue, judged to be worth almost $4 billion. Think of what the cardinal's mansion would sell or rent for! That would take care of everything. This is what Boston's Cardinal Sean O'Malley did: sell the cardinal's estate. He lives now in a small apartment in a modest part of town.

But that and other ideas can be explored in future columns. For now, Merry Christmas. May peace and love descend on all.

CHAPTER 8

Uneasy Pieces

These two pieces meant a lot to me at the time (1992 and 1998, respectively) and still do.

In the first I was trying to capture some of the current mood of members of my generation. In the second I tried to capture some things I was seeing in the country that, taken together, suggested to me: trouble ahead.

I poured my heart into each piece, working every day for months, wanting each to say something important. In both cases I received editorial reactions that I never forgot and that taught me something.

After I sent the editor of Forbes "You'd Cry Too If It Happened to You," we met for lunch to discuss it. He was the great Jim Michaels, and he warmly told me he liked the piece a lot. I was glad. I told him how hard I'd worked on it, meaning to communicate that I took the assignment seriously and had given it the best I had. He surprised me by saying "No you didn't." I think I said nothing. "Anything that reads this easy was easy," he said, and I realized that he meant it as a compliment. But I said no, you have to work hard to make it look easy. Jim was one great reporter and editor, a great person, too, but he stuck to his guns: It was easy.

I came after that conversation to think there was an odd thing with editors. If the draft you give them is lumpy, jagged or uneven but contains interesting thought, they'll see how hard you're trying and appreciate it. If you give it to them as realized and polished as you can make it, they're more likely not to see the effort. In time I came to wonder if when you give an editor an easy edit they experience it as ungenerous: They're part of the process, too. I never solved this quandary, to the extent it's a quandary. But I do wonder why I felt I had to tell him how hard I'd worked. You never really have to say that, and what does it matter, anyway, the finished work is the finished work. I think if I'd been a man, or an older woman, I would have teased him that actually I'd knocked it off on the subway the day before.

In the case of the second piece, the reaction I received was more startling, and more fundamental. Normally in those days you'd fax a piece into a magazine and a few days later you'd get a response. But days or a week passed and I hadn't heard anything, so I called the editor to make sure he'd received it, and see if he had any suggestions or problems. The editor was polite but his tone was somewhat distanced. Yes, yes, he said, we have it, it's fine. There was a pause. I couldn't get a handle on what was being said or not said, and I asked if anyone else there had seen it and perhaps had any thoughts. We all saw it, he said. He added, "It was upsetting." I didn't understand: The whole piece was upsetting?

The ending, he said.

Now I understood, and realized for the first time how surprising the last few pages might seem, how apart from the current thought curve, even how confounding.

Sometimes thoughts in your head seem to you so obvious that you assume that to one degree or another they're in everyone's head. But you know, they're not. At that moment in 1998 I came to see not everyone was seeing what I was seeing.

* * *

You'd Cry Too If It Happened to You

Forbes Magazine: September 14, 1992

In his lifetime he had seen America rise and rise and rise, some sort of golden legend to her own people, some sort of impossible fantasy to others... rise and rise and rise—and then... the golden legend crumbled, overnight the fall began, the heart went out of it, a too complacent and uncaring people awoke to find themselves naked with the winds of the world howling around their ears... A universal quilt enshrouded... all who participated in those times... Now there was a time of uneasiness... when all thinking men fretted and worried desperately about "how to catch up" and "how to get ahead"; and also, in the small hours of the night's cold terror, about what it would be like if America couldn't catch up, if history should have decided once and for all that America should never again be permitted to get ahead...

Well, so much for Camelot.

When Allen Drury wrote those words—they set the scene for his classic political novel, "Advise and Consent"—he was trying to capture the mood of America in 1959, as the peaceful and composed Eisenhower era receded, John Kennedy geared up for the presidency and the go-go '60s waited to be born. We remember those days as innocent and hopeful; Drury recorded them as anxious and depressed. Which demonstrates a small but not insignificant point:

It is writers—journalists, screenwriters, novelists, newswriters—we turn to more than anyone to tell us exactly how our country is doing, and they are precisely the last people who would accurately point out that in the long tape of history this is a pretty good few inches.

There are many reasons for this—catching and tagging whatever angst is floating around is their job—but the biggest is simple. Writers always see their time as marked by pain because it always is. Children die. People lose their homes. Life is sad. To declare the relative happiness of your era is to sound stupid and uncaring, as if you don't know people are suffering, when people always are.

I am inclined toward the long view. The life of people on earth is obviously better now than it has ever been—certainly much better than it was 500 years ago when people beat each other with cats. This may sound silly but now and then when I read old fairy tales and see an illustration of a hunchbacked hag with no teeth and bumps on her nose who lives by herself in the forest, I think: People looked like that once. They lived like that. There were no doctors, no phones, and people lived in the dark in a hole in a tree. It was terrible. It's much better now.

But we are not happier. I believe we are just cleaner, more attractive sad people than we used to be.

* * *

There are serious reasons members of my generation in particular are feeling a high level of anxiety and unhappiness these days, but first a word about how we "know" this: the polls.

I used to like polls because I like vox pop, and polls seemed a good way to get a broad sampling. But now I think the vox has popped—the voice has cracked from too many command performances. Polls are contributing to a strange new volatility in public opinion.

A year ago, at the conclusion of the Gulf war, George Bush's

approval ratings were at nearly 90%. As I write, they are 30%. This
is a huge drop, and in a way a meaningless one. President Bush didn't
deserve 90% support for having successfully executed a 100-hour
ground war; Abe Lincoln deserved a 90% for preserving the nation.
Bush didn't deserve 30% support because the economy is in recession; John Adams deserved a 30% for the Alien and Sedition laws. It
is all so exaggerated.

The dramatic rises and drops are fueled in part by mass media
and their famous steady drumbeat of what's not working, from
an increase in reported child abuse to a fall in savings. When this
tendency is not prompted by ideology it is legitimate: Good news
isn't news. But the volatility is also driven by the polls themselves.
People think they have to have an answer when they are questioned by pollsters, and they think it has to be "intelligent" and "not
naive." This has the effect of hardening opinions that haven't even
been formed yet. Poll questions do not invite subtlety of response.
This dispels ambiguity, when a lot of thoughts and opinions are
ambiguous.

And we are polled too often. We are constantly having our temperature taken, like a hypochondriac who is looking for the reassur-
ance that no man can have, i.e., that he will not die.

I once knew a man who was so neurotically fearful about his
physical well-being that in the middle of conversations he would
quietly put his hand to his wrist. He was taking his pulse. When I
was 7 or 8 years old, I became anxious that I would stop breathing
unless I remembered every few seconds to inhale. This mania was
exhausting. At night, on the verge of sleep, I would come awake in a
panic, gulping for air.

People who take their pulse too often are likely to make it race;
people obsessed with breathing are likely to stop. Nations that use
polls as daily temperature readings inevitably give inauthentic readings and wind up not reassured but demoralized.

*   *   *

There are reasons for our discontent. Each era has its distinguishing characteristics; each time a big barrel of malaise rolls down the hill there are specific and discrete facts rolling around inside. Here are some of ours:

Once in America if you lost your job—if you were laid off from the assembly line at Ford, for instance—you had reason to believe you'd be rehired. Business cycles, boom and bust—sooner or later they'd call you back. There was a certain security in the insecurity. Now it's different. Now if you're laid off from your job as the number two guy in public affairs at the main Jersey office of a phone company, you have reason to fear you'll never be hired back into that or any white-collar job, because employment now is connected less to boom and bust than to changing realities, often changing technologies, in the marketplace. The telephone company doesn't need you anymore.

You are a boomer, and obscurely oppressed.

But there is nothing obscure about your predicament. So many people are relying on you! You and your wife waited to have children, and now they're 8 and 10 and you're 48—too late to start over, to jeopardize the $75,000 a year you earn. And if you tried, you would lose your medical coverage.

Your mother and father are going to live longer than parents have ever lived and will depend on you to take care of them as they (as you, at night, imagine it) slide from mild senility to full dementia. Your children will have a longer adolescence, and expect you to put them through college just as mom and dad are entering a home.

Your biggest personal asset is your house, which has lost value. You have a hefty mortgage, your pension fund is underfunded, you don't think your Social Security benefits are secure and you do not trust the banks.

The last may be the most serious in terms of how people feel. In the years since the Depression we have been able to trust that the institutions we put our savings into would be there tomorrow and pay us interest. We don't know that anymore; most of us are afraid that all of a sudden a major bank, strained from its own feckless investments to middle-aged mall builders who make political contributions, will fold, taking the other banks with it.

We wonder, "in the small hours of the night's cold terror," if there is another depression and the banks fail, how will I and my family live? How will we buy food and gas and pay for electricity? We don't know how to grow things! What will we eat if it all collapses?

* * *

I think the essential daily predicament of modern, intelligent, early-middle-age Americans—the boomers, the basketball in the python—is this: There is no margin for error anymore. Everything has to continue as it is for us to continue with the comfort we have. And we do not believe that everything will continue as it is.

It is embarrassing to live in the most comfortable time in the history of man and not be happy. We all have so much!

Think of the set of "The Honeymooners."

What did Ralph and Alice have in 1955? A small rented apartment with a table, two chairs, a bureau, a picture on a faded wall. The set designer was spoofing the average.

Think of the set of "Family Ties": the couches, the lamps, the VCRs, the color TVs. There is art on the walls. The children had expensive orthodontia.

You will say, one show was about the working class, the other the middle class. But that's the point: The average couple was working class then and is middle class now.

We have so much more than mom and dad that we can't help but feel defensive about feeling so bad, and paying off our charge cards so late, and being found in the den surfing from channel to channel at 3 a.m., staring back at Brian Lamb's eyes.

And there's this: We know that we suffer—and we get no credit for it! Sometimes we feel the bitterness of the generation that fought World War I, but we cannot write our memoirs and say "goodbye to all that," cannot tell stories of how our boots rotted in the mud, cannot deflect the neighborhood praise and be modest as we lean against the bar. They don't know we're brave. They don't know we fight in trenches, too.

I find myself thinking of Auden's words about the average man in 1939, as darkness gathered over Europe—the "sensual man-in-the-street," barely aware of his emptiness, who promised that he will be "true to the wife," that some day he will be happy and good.

Auden called his era the "age of anxiety." I think what was at the heart of the dread in those days, just a few years into modern times, was that we could tell we were beginning to lose God—banishing him from the scene, from our consciousness, losing the assumption that he was part of the daily drama, or its maker. And it is a terrible thing when people lose God. Life is difficult and people are afraid, and to be without God is to lose man's great source of consolation and coherence. There is a phrase I once heard or made up that I think of when I think about what people with deep faith must get from God: the love that assuages all.

I don't think it is unconnected to the boomers' predicament that as a country we were losing God just as they were being born.

At the same time, a huge revolution in human expectation was beginning to shape our lives, the salient feature of which is the expectation of happiness.

* * *

It is 1956 in the suburbs in the summer. A man comes home from work, parks the car, slouches up the driveway. His white shirt clings softly to his back. He bends for the paper, surveys the lawn, waves to a neighbor. From the house comes his son, freckled, 10. He jumps on his father; they twirl on the lawn. Another day done. Now water the lawn, eat fish cakes, watch some TV, go to bed, do it all again tomorrow.

* * *

Is he happy? No. Why should he be? We weren't put here to be happy. But the knowledge of his unhappiness does not gnaw. Everyone is unhappy, or rather everyone has a boring job, a marriage that's turned to disinterest, a life that's turned to sameness. And because he does not expect to be happy, the knowledge of his unhappiness does not weigh on him. He looks perhaps to other, more eternal forms of comfort.

Somewhere in the '70s, or the '60s, we started expecting to be happy and changed our lives (left town, left families, switched jobs) if we were not. And society strained and cracked in the storm.

I think we have lost the old knowledge that happiness is overrated—that, in a way, life is overrated. We have lost, somehow, a sense of mystery—about us, our purpose, our meaning, our role. Our ancestors believed in two worlds, and understood this to be the solitary, poor, nasty, brutish and short one. We are the first generations of man that actually expected to find happiness here on earth, and our search for it has caused such unhappiness. The reason: If you do not believe in another, higher world, if you believe only in the flat material world around you, if you believe that this is your only chance at happiness—if that is what you believe, then you are not disappointed when the world does not give you a good measure of its riches, you are despairing.

In a Catholic childhood in America, you were once given, as the answer to the big questions: It is a mystery. As I grew older I was impatient with this answer. Now I am probably as old, intellectually, as I am going to get, and more and more I think: It is a mystery. I am more comfortable with this now; it seems the only rational and scientific answer.

My generation, faced as it grew with a choice between religious belief or existential despair, chose...marijuana. Now we are in our cabernet stage. (Jung wrote in a letter that he saw a connection between spirits and The Spirit; sometimes when I go into a church and see how modern Catholics sometimes close their eyes and put their hands out, palms up, as if to get more of God on them, it reminds me of how kids in college used to cup their hands delicately around the smoke of the pipe and help it waft toward them.) Is it possible that our next step is a deep turning to faith, and worship? Is it starting now with tentative, New Age steps?

It is a commonplace to note that we have little faith in our institutions, no faith in Congress, in the White House, little faith in what used to be called the establishment—big business, big media, the church. But there's a sort of schizoid quality in this. We have contempt for the media, but we have respect for newscasters and columnists. When we meet them we're impressed and admiring. We respect priests and rabbis and doctors. But we are cynical about what they're part of.

It's also famously true that we hate Congress and keep reelecting our congressmen. I don't know how to reconcile this. Sometimes I think there is a tinny, braying quality to our cynicism. We are like a city man in a Dreiser novel, quick with a wink that shows we know the real lowdown, the real dope. This kind of cynicism seems to me...a dodge. When you don't believe, you don't have to take part, invest, become part of. Skepticism is healthy, and an appropriate attitude toward those who wield power. But cynicism is corrosive and self-corrupting. Everyone at the top is a moral zero, I'll be a moral zero, too.

* * *

But our cynicism is also earned. Our establishments have failed us. I imagine an unspoken dialogue with a congressman in Washington:

Voter: "Do what is right!"

Politician: "But you'll kill me!"

Voter: "Maybe, but do it anyway! I hired you to go to Congress to make hard decisions to help our country. Take your term, do it and go home. Kill yourself!"

Politician: "But I have seniority and expertise and I'm up to speed on the issues. Replace me and it'll be six years before he knows what I know."

Voter: "Well, maybe we don't want him to know what you know. Maybe we want someone dumb enough not to know what's impossible and brave enough to want to do what's right."

Politician: "But I love this job."

Voter: "But we never intended Congress to be a career. We meant it to be a pain in the neck, like jury duty. And maybe I won't kill you. Maybe I'll respect you. Take a chance!"

* * *

The biggest scandal of the modern era, and the one that will prove to have most changed our politics, is the S&L scandal, in which certain members of both parties colluded to give their campaign contributors what they wanted at the expense of innocent taxpayers who will pay the bill, in billions, for generations.

Watergate pales, Teapot Dome pales. It is what was behind the rise of Perot. The voters think Washington is a whorehouse and every four years they get a chance to elect a new piano player. They would rather burn the whorehouse down. They figured Perot for an affable man with a torch. They looked at him and saw a hand grenade with a bad haircut.

Finally, another thing has changed in our lifetimes: People don't have faith in America's future anymore.

I don't know many people aged 35 to 50 who don't have a sense that they were born into a healthier country and that they have seen the culture deteriorate before their eyes.

We tell pollsters we are concerned about "leadership" and "America's prospects in a changing world," but a lot of this is a reflection of a boomer secret: We all know the imperfect America we were born into was a better country than the one we live in now, i.e., the one we are increasingly responsible for.

You don't have to look far for the fraying of the social fabric. Crime, the schools, the courts. Watch Channel 35 in New York and see your culture. See men and women, homo- and hetero-, dressed in black leather, masturbating each other and simulating sadomasochistic ritual. Realize this is pumped into everyone's living room, including your own, where your 8-year-old is flipping channels. Then talk to a pollster. You too will declare you are pessimistic about your country's future; you too will say we are on the wrong track.

Remember your boomer childhood in the towns and suburbs. You had physical security. You were safe. It is a cliché to say it, but it can't be said enough: We didn't lock the doors at night in the old America. We slept with the windows open! The cities were better. A man and woman falling in love could stroll the parks of a city at 2 a.m. Douglas Edwards, the venerable newscaster, once told me about what he called the best time. He sat back in the newsroom one afternoon in the late '70s, in the middle of the creation of the current world, and said, "New York in the '50s—there was nothing like it, it was clean and it was peaceful. You could walk the streets!" He stopped, and laughed at celebrating with such emotion what should be commonplace.

You know what else I bet he thought, though he didn't say it. It was a more human world in that it was a sexier world, because sex was still a story. Each high school senior class had exactly one girl who got pregnant and one guy who was the father, and it was the town's annual scandal. Either she went somewhere and had the baby and put it up for adoption, or she brought it home as a new baby sister, or the couple got married and the town topic changed. It was a stricter, tougher society, but its bruising sanctions came from ancient wisdom.

We have all had a moment when all of a sudden we looked around and thought: The world is changing, I am seeing it change. This is for me the moment when the new America began: I was at a graduation ceremony at a public high school in New Jersey. It was 1971 or 1972. One by one a stream of black-robed students walked across the stage and received their diplomas. And a pretty young girl with red hair, big under her graduation gown, walked up to receive hers. The auditorium stood up and applauded. I looked at my sister: "She's going to have a baby," she said.

The girl was eight months' pregnant and had had the courage to go through with her pregnancy and take her finals and finish school despite society's disapproval.

But: Society wasn't disapproving. It was applauding. Applause is a right and generous response for a young girl with grit and heart. And yet, in the sound of that applause I heard a wall falling, a 1,000-year wall, a wall of sanctions that said: We as a society do not approve of teenaged unwed motherhood because it is not good for the child, not good for the mother and not good for us.

The old America had a delicate sense of the difference between the general ("We disapprove") and the particular ("Let's go help her"). We had the moral self-confidence to sustain the paradox, to sustain the distance between "official" disapproval and "unofficial" succor. The old America would not have applauded the girl in the big graduation gown, but some of its individuals would have helped her not only materially but with some measure of emotional support. We don't so much anymore. For all our tolerance and talk, we don't show much love to what used to be called girls in trouble. As we've gotten more open-minded, we've gotten more closed-hearted.

Message to society: What you applaud, you encourage. And: Watch out what you celebrate.

(This section was written before Dan Quayle and "Murphy Brown," about which one might say he said a right thing in the wrong way and was the wrong man to say it. Quayle is not a stupid man, but his expressions reveal a certain tropism toward the banal. This is a problem with some Republican men. There is a kind of heavy-handed dorkishness in their approach that leaves them unable to persuasively address questions requiring delicacy; they always sound judgmental when they mean to show concern.)

Two final thoughts:

1. We might all feel better if we took personally the constitutional injunction to "preserve and protect."

Every parent in America knows that we're not doing a very good job of communicating to our children what America is and has been. When we talk about immigration, pro or con, there is, I think, an unspoken anxiety: We are not inculcating in America's new immigrants—as someone inculcated In our grandparents and great-grandparents—the facts of American history and why America deserves to be loved. And imperfect as it is, and as we are, we boomers love our country.

In our cities we teach not the principles that made our country great—the worth of the Founding Fathers, the moral force that led us to endure five years of horror to free the slaves, a space program that expanded the frontiers of human knowledge, the free market of ideas and commerce and expression that yielded miracles like a car in every garage and mass-produced housing. We are lucky in that the central fact of our country is both inspiring and true: America

192

PEGGY NOONAN

is the place formed of the institutionalization of miracles. Which made it something new in the history of man, something—better.

We do not teach this as a society and we teach it insufficiently in our schools. We are more inclined to teach that Columbus's encounter with the Americas produced, most significantly, the spreading of venereal disease to their innocent indigenous peoples.

We teach the culture of resentment, of grievance, of victimization. Our children are told by our media and our leaders that we are a racist nation in which minorities are and will be actively discriminated against.

If we are demoralized we have, at least in this, demoralized ourselves. We are certainly demoralizing our children, and giving them a darker sense of their future than is warranted.

*   *   *

2. It's odd to accuse boomers of reticence, but I think we have been reticent, at least in this:

When we talk about the difficulties of our lives and how our country has changed we become embarrassed and feel...dotty. Like someone's old aunt rocking on the porch and talking about the good old days. And so most of us keep quiet, raise our children as best we can, go to the cocktail party, eat our cake, go to work and take the vacation.

We have removed ourselves from leadership, we professional white-collar boomers. We have recused ourselves from a world we never made. We turn our attention to the arts, and entertainment, to watching and supporting them or contributing to them, because they are the only places we can imagine progress. And to money, hoping that it will keep us safe.

There Is No Time, There Will Be Time

Forbes ASAP: November 30, 1998

I suppose it is commonplace to say it, but it's true: There is no such thing as time. The past is gone and no longer exists, the future is an assumption that has not yet come, all you have is the moment—this one—but it too has passed... just now.

The moment we are having is an awfully good one, though. History has handed us one of the easiest rides in all the story of man. It has handed us a wave of wealth so broad and deep that it would be almost disorienting if we thought about it a lot, which we don't.

But: We know such comfort! We sleep on beds that are soft and supporting, eat food that is both good and plentiful. We touch small levers and heat our homes to exactly the degree we desire; the pores of our bare arms are open and relaxed as we read the Times in our T-shirts, while two feet away, on the other side of the plate glass window, a blizzard rages. We turn levers and get clean water, take short car trips to places where planes wait before whisking us across continents as we nap. It is all so fantastically fine.

Lately this leaves me uneasy. Does it you? Do you wonder how and why exactly we have it so different, so nice compared to thousands of years of peasants eating rocks? Is it possible that we, the people of the world, are being given a last great gift before everything changes? To me it feels like a gift. Only two generations ago, my family had to sweat in the sun to pull food from the ground.

Another thing. The marvels that are part of our everyday lives—computers, machines that can look into your body and see everything but your soul—are so astounding that most of us who use them don't really understand exactly what they're doing or how they do it. This too is strange. The day the wheel was invented, the crowd watching understood immediately what it was and how it worked. But I cannot explain with any true command how the MRI that finds a tumor works. Or how, for that matter, the fax works.

We could feel amazement, or even, again, a mild disorientation, if we were busy feeling and thinking long thoughts instead of doing—planning the next meeting, appointment, consultation, presentation, vacation. We are too busy doing these things to take time to see, feel, parse, and explain amazement.

Which gets me to time.

We have no time! Is it that way for you? Everyone seems so busy. Once, a few years ago, I sat on the Spanish Steps in Rome. Suddenly I realized that everyone, all the people going up and down the steps, was hurrying along on his or her way somewhere. I thought, *Everyone is doing something.* On the streets of Manhattan, they hurry along and I think, *Everyone is busy.* I don't think I've seen anyone amble, except at a summer place, in a long time. I am thinking here of a man I saw four years ago at a little pier in Martha's Vineyard. He had plaid shorts and white legs, and he was walking sort of stiffly, jerkily. Maybe he had mild Parkinson's, but I think: *Maybe he's just arrived and trying to get out of his sprint and into a stroll.*

All our splendor, our comfort, takes time to pay for. And affluence wants to increase; it carries within it an unspoken command: More! Affluence is like nature, which always moves toward new life. Nature does its job; affluence enlists *us* to do it. We hear the command for "More!" with immigrant ears that also hear "Do better!" or old American ears that hear "Sutter is rich, there's gold in them hills, onward to California!" We carry California within us; that is what it is to be human, and American.

So we work. The more you have, the more you need, the more

you work and plan. This is odd in part because of all the spare time we should have. We don't, after all, have to haul water from the crick. We don't have to kill an antelope for dinner. I can microwave a Lean Cuisine in four minutes and eat it in five. I should have a lot of extra time—more, say, than a cavewoman. And yet I do not. And I think: That cavewoman watching the antelope turn on the spit, she was probably happily daydreaming about how shadows played on the walls of her cave. She had time.

It's not just work. We all know the applications of Parkinson's Law, that work expands to fill the time allotted to complete it. This isn't new. But this is: So many of us feel we have no time to cook and serve a lovely three-course dinner, to write the long, thoughtful letter, to ever so patiently tutor the child. But other generations, not so long ago, did. And we have more time-saving devices than they did.

We invented new technologies so that work could be done efficiently, more quickly. We wished it done more quickly so we could have more leisure time. (Wasn't that the plan? Or was it to increase our productivity?)

But we have less leisure time, it seems, because these technologies encroach on our leisure time.

You can be beeped on safari! Be faxed while riding an elephant and receive email while being menaced by a tiger. And if you can be beeped on safari, you will be beeped on safari. This gives you less time to enjoy being away from the demands of time.

Twenty years ago when I was starting out at CBS on the radio desk, we would try each day to track down our roving foreign correspondents and get them to file on the phone for our morning news broadcasts. I would go to the daily log to see who was where. And not infrequently it would say that Smith, in Beirut, is "out of pocket," i.e., unreachable, unfindable for a few days. The official implication was that Smith was out in the field traveling with the guerrillas. But I thought it was code for "Smith is drunk," or "Smith is on deep background with a really cute source." I'd think, Oh, to be an out-of-pocket correspondent on the loose in Cairo, Jerusalem, Paris—what a thing.

But now there is no "out of pocket." Now everyone can be reached and found, anywhere, anytime. Now there is no hiding place. We are "in the pocket."

What are we in the pocket of? An illusion, perhaps, or rather many illusions: that we must know the latest, that we must have a say, that we are players, are needed, that the next score will change things, that through work we can quench our thirst, that, as they said in the sign over the entrance of Auschwitz, "Work Brings Freedom," that we must bow to "More!" and pay homage to California. I live a life of only average intensity, and yet by 9 p.m. I am quite stupid, struck dumb with stimuli fatigue. I am tired from 10 hours of the unconscious strain of planning, meeting, talking, thinking. If you clench your fist for 10 hours and then let go, your hand will jerk and tremble. My brain trembles.

I sit on the couch at night with my son. He watches TV as I read the National Enquirer and the Star. This is wicked of me, I know, but the Enquirer and the Star have almost more pictures than words; there are bright pictures of movie stars, of television anchors, of the woman who almost choked to death when, in a state of morning confusion, she accidentally put spermicidal jelly on her toast. These stories are just right for the mind that wants to be diverted by something that makes no demands.

I have time at 9. But I am so flat-lined that I find it very hard to make the heartening phone call to the nephew, to write the long letter. Often I feel guilty and treat myself with Häagen-Dazs therapy. I will join a gym if I get time.

When a man can work while at home, he will work while at home. When a man works at home, the wall between workplace and living place, between colleague and family, is lowered or removed.

Does family life spill over into work life? No. Work life spills over into family life. You do not wind up taking your son for a walk at work, you wind up teleconferencing during softball practice. This is not progress. It is not more time but less. Maybe our kids will remember us as there but not there, physically present but carrying the faces of men and women who are strategizing the sale.

I often think how much I'd like to have a horse. Not that I ride, but I often think I'd like to learn. But if I had a horse, I would be making room for the one hour a day in which I would ride. I would be losing hours seeing to Flicka's feeding and housing and cleaning and loving and overall well-being. This would cost money. I would have to work hard to get it. I would have less time.

Who could do this? The rich. The rich have time because they buy it. They buy the grooms and stable keepers and accountants and bill payers and negotiators for the price of oats. Do they enjoy it? Do they think, *It's great to be rich, I get to ride a horse?*

Oh, I hope so! If you can buy time, you should buy it. This year I am going to work very hard to get some.

* * *

During the summer, when you were a kid, your dad worked a few towns away and left at 8:30; Mom stayed home smoking and talking and ironing. You biked to the local school yard for summer activities—twirling, lanyard making, dodgeball—until afternoon. Then you'd go home and play in the street. At 5:30 Dad was home and at 6 there was dinner—meat loaf, mashed potatoes and canned corn. Then TV and lights out.

Now it's more like this: Dad goes to work at 6:15, to the city, where he is an executive; Mom goes to work at the bank where she's a vice president, but not before giving the sitter the keys and bundling the kids into the car to go to, respectively, soccer camp, arts camp, Chinese lessons, therapy, the swim meet, computer camp, a birthday party, a play date. Then home for an impromptu barbecue of turkey burgers and a salad with fresh Parmesan cheese followed by summer homework, Nintendo and TV—the kids lying splayed on the couch, dead eyed, like denizens of a Chinese opium den—followed by "Hi, Mom," "Hi, Dad" and bed.

Life is so much more interesting now! It's not boring, like 1957. There are things to do: The culture is broader, more sophisticated; there's more wit and creativity to be witnessed and enjoyed. Moms, kids and dads have more options, more possibilities. This is good. The bad news is that our options leave us exhausted when we pursue them and embarrassed when we don't.

Good news: Mothers do not become secret Valium addicts out of boredom and loneliness, as they did 30 and 40 years ago. And Dad's conversation is more interesting than his father's. He knows how Michael Jordan acted on the Nike shoot, and tells us. The other night Dad worked late and then they all went to a celebratory dinner at Rao's where they sat in a booth next to Warren Beatty, who was discussing with his publicist the media campaign for "Bulworth." Beatty looked great, had a certain watchful dignity, ordered the vodka penne.

Bad news: Mom hasn't noticed but she's half mad from stress. Her face is older than her mother's, less innocent, because she has burned through her facial subcutaneous fat and because she unconsciously holds her jaw muscles in a tense way. But it's OK because the collagen, the Botox, the Retin-A and alpha hydroxy, and a better diet than her mother's (Grandma lived on starch, it was the all-carb diet) leave her looking more...fit. She does not have her mother's soft, maternal weight. The kids do not feel a pillowy yielding when they hug her; they feel muscles and smell Chanel body moisturizer.

When Mother makes fund-raising calls for the school, she does not know it but she barks: "Yeah, this is Claire Marietta on the cookie drive we need your cookies tomorrow at 3 in the gym if you're late the office is open till 4 or you can write a check for $12 any questions call me." Click.

Mom never wanted to be Barbara Billingsley. Mom got her wish.

* * *

What will happen? How will the future play out?

Well, we're not going to get more time. But it's not pretty how it will happen, so if you're in a good mood, stop reading here and go hug the kids and relax and have a drink and a nice pointless conversation with your spouse.

Here goes: It has been said that when an idea's time has come, a lot of people are likely to get it at the same time. In the same way, when something begins to flicker out there in the cosmos, a number of people, a small group at first, begin to pick up the signals. They start to see what's coming.

Our entertainment industry, interestingly enough, has plucked something from the unconscious of a small collective. For about 30 years now, but accelerating quickly this decade, the industry has been telling us about The Big Terrible Thing. Space aliens come and scare us, nuts with nukes try to blow us up.

This is not new: In the '50s Michael Rennie came from space to tell us in "The Day the Earth Stood Still" that if we don't become more peaceful, our planet will be obliterated. But now in movies the monsters aren't coming close, they're hitting us directly. Meteors the size of Texas come down and take out the eastern seaboard, volcanoes swallow Los Angeles, Martians blow up the White House. The biggest grosser of all time was about the end of a world, the catastrophic sinking of an unsinkable entity.

Something's up. And deep down, where the body meets the soul, we are fearful. We fear, down so deep it hasn't even risen to the point of articulation, that with all our comforts and amusements, with all our toys and bells and whistles...we wonder if what we really have is...a first-class stateroom on the Titanic. Everything's wonderful, but a world is ending and we sense it.

I don't mean: "Uh-oh, there's a depression coming," I mean: We live in a world of three billion men and hundreds of thousands of nuclear bombs, missiles, warheads. It's a world of extraordinary germs that can be harnessed and used to kill whole populations, a world of extraordinary chemicals that can be harnessed and used to do the same.

Three billion men, and it takes only half a dozen bright and evil ones to harness and deploy.

What are the odds it will happen? Put it another way: What are the odds it will not? Low. Nonexistent, I think.

When you consider who is gifted and crazed with rage...when you think of the terrorist places and the terrorist countries...who do they hate most? The Great Satan, the United States. What is its most important place? Some would say Washington. I would say the great city of the United States is the great city of the world, the dense 10-mile-long island called Manhattan, where the economic and media power of the nation resides, the city that is the psychological center of our modernity, our hedonism, our creativity, our hard-shouldered hipness, our unthinking arrogance.

If someone does the big, terrible thing to New York or Washington, there will be a lot of chaos and a lot of lines going down, a lot of damage, and a lot of things won't be working so well anymore. And thus a lot more...time. Something tells me we won't be teleconferencing and faxing about the Ford account for a while.

The psychic blow—and that is what it will be as people absorb it, a blow, an insult that reorders and changes—will shift our perspective and priorities, dramatically, and for longer than a while. Something tells me more of us will be praying, and hard, one side benefit of which is that there is sometimes a quality of stopped time when you pray. You get outside time.

Maybe, of course, I'm wrong. But I think of the friend who lives on Park Avenue who turned to me once and said, out of nowhere, "If ever something bad is going to happen to the city, I pray each day that God will give me a sign. That He will let me see a rat stand up on the sidewalk. So I'll know to gather the kids and go." I absorbed this and, two years later, just a month ago, poured out my fears to a former high official of the United States government. His face turned grim. I apologized for being morbid. He said no, he thinks the same thing. He thinks it will happen in the next year and a half. I was surprised, and more surprised when he said that an acquaintance, a former arms expert for another country, thinks it will happen in a matter of months.

So now I have frightened you. But we must not sit around and be depressed. "Don't cry," Jimmy Cagney once said. "There's enough water in the goulash already."

We must take the time to do some things. We must press government officials to face the big, terrible thing. They know it could happen tomorrow; they just haven't focused on it because there's no Armageddon constituency. We should press for more from our foreign intelligence and our defense systems, and press local, state and federal leaders to become more serious about civil defense and emergency management.

The other thing we must do is the most important.

I once talked to a man who had a friend who'd done something that took his breath away. She was single, middle-aged and middle class, and wanted to find a child to love. She searched the orphanages of South America and took the child who was in the most trouble, sick and emotionally unwell. She took the little girl home and loved her hard, and in time the little girl grew and became strong, became in fact the kind of person who could and did help others.

Twelve years later, at the girl's high school graduation, she won the award for best all-around student. She played the piano for the recessional. Now she's at college.

The man's eyes grew moist. He had just been to the graduation. "These are the things that stay God's hand," he told me. I didn't know what that meant. He explained: These are the things that keep God from letting us kill us all.

So be good. Do good. Stay his hand. And pray. When the Virgin Mary makes her visitations—she's never made so many in all of recorded history as she has in this century—she says: Pray! Pray unceasingly!

I myself don't, but I think about it a lot and sometimes pray when I think. But you don't have to be Catholic to take this advice.

Pray. Unceasingly. Take the time.

CHAPTER 9

I Just Called to Say I Love You

You know what 9/11 was. It was the thing that changed our lives.

In the lecture to the Harvard government students a few chap-ters back, I spoke of those moments in a professional life when you can think. This is why I'm here. The topic that is engag-ing you is so all consuming to you, so important, so moves your mind and spirit, that your best pours out of you. You only get a few times in your life when that happens, and you usually don't know you had it until you look back.

I was acutely aware that in my town, New York, all of us in the days and months after were trying so hard to help, pitching in wherever we could. This was my pitching in. I was talking to the other wounded members of a wounded city. They wrote to me and told me of their experiences, troubles and efforts. Some of what they wrote wound up in my work. To me, in the year or so after 9/11, my work was a communal effort. You don't get to feel that way too often as a writer working alone. Just remem-bering it fills my eyes.

* * *

His Delicious, Mansard-Roofed World

Faith, effort and love will get us through this trying time.

The Wall Street Journal: October 26, 2001

I found the words on a yellow Post-it I'd stuck on the side of the bookcase in my office about a year ago. It had gotten covered up by phone numbers and pictures and doctors' appointment cards, and yesterday, looking for a number, I found it—a piece of yellow paper with the words "His delicious mansard-roofed world." It took me aback. And I remembered what it was.

That night I had been out with friends—it was last fall—and it was fun, and I got home thinking, simply, of something we all should think of more and I don't think of enough: how wonderful it is to be alive, the joy of it, the beauty. And as I thought it—this is the part I remember most sharply—a scene came into my mind of a little French town with cobblestone streets and sharply slanting roofs on 18th-century buildings. Which made me think, in turn, in a blink, of New York and its older architecture uptown and off the park, the old mansions off Fifth Avenue with sloping mansard roofs, and how this is the world we live in.

And I thought at that moment, with those pictures in my head: "His delicious, mansard-roofed world." He being God. I wrote down the words on a Post-it and put it on the bookcase, thinking some day I'd use them in writing about . . . something. Maybe joy. Maybe: us. Or maybe I'd just see them and think: That was a nice moment.

Anyway, the words captured for me a moment of thought.

And last night I found them and thought: *Oh—they speak of a moment in time.*

* * *

Yesterday afternoon, I was with a teenage friend, taking a cab down Park Avenue. It was a brilliant day, clear and sparkling, and as the cab turned left at 86th Street the sun hit the windows in one of those flashes of bright gold-yellow that can, on certain days or at certain times, pierce your heart. We had been quiet, not talking, on the way to see a friend, when I said, "Do you...find yourself thinking at all of the ways in which you might be feeling differently about the future if September 11th had never happened?"

"Oh yes," she said, softly. "Every day."

And she meant it. And neither of us said any more and neither of us had to.

* * *

There are a lot of quiet moments going on. Have you noticed? A lot of quiet transformations, a lot of quiet action and quiet conversations. People are realigning themselves. I know people who are undergoing religious conversions, and changes of faith. And people who are holding on in a new way, with a harder grip, to what they already have and believe in.

Some people have quietly come to terms with the most soul-chilling thoughts. A young man I know said to me last week, as we chatted in passing on the street, "I have been thinking about the end of the American empire." And I thought: *Oh, my boy, do you know the import, the weight, of the words you are saying?* And then I thought *Yes, he does. He's been thinking, quietly.*

Some people are quietly defining and redefining things. I am one of them. We are trying to define or paint or explain what the old world was, and what the new world is, and how the break between them—the exact spot where the stick broke, cracked, splintered—could possibly have been an hour in early September.

*   *   *

One thing that passes through our minds is what to call the Old World—"The Lost World," or "The Golden Age" or "Then." We don't have to know yet what to call the New World, and cannot anyway because it hasn't fully revealed itself, and so cannot be named.

But if we can name the Old World, we'll at least know exactly what it is we think we've lost. And this is a funny little problem, because if you go out onto your street right now, if you live anyplace but downtown Manhattan or Arlington, Va., the world outside looks exactly—exactly—like the one that existed a year ago. The pumpkins in the stores, the merry kids, the guy who owns the butcher shop outside smoking in his apron. Everything looks the same. Same people, same stores, same houses.

And yet we all feel everything has changed. And we're right.

People say things like "We have lost a sense of certainty," and I nod, for it is true. But on the other hand, I didn't feel so certain about the future last year. Did you?

People say we have lost the assumption that what we had would continue. Or, this being America, get better.

Certainly people who were carefree have lost their carefreeness. And with no irony I think: *That's a shame.* Carefreeness is good.

*   *   *

Lately when I think of the Old World I think of an insult that I mean as a tribute. It is the phrase *the narcissism of small differences*. In the world that has just passed, careless people—not carefree, care*less*—spent their time deconstructing the reality of the text, as opposed to reading the book. You could do that then. The world seemed so peaceful that you could actively look for new things to argue about just to keep things lively. You could be on a faculty and argue over where Jane Austen meant to put the comma, or how her landholding father's contextually objective assumptions regarding colonialism impacted her work. You could have real arguments about stupid things. Those were the days! It's great when life is so nice you have to invent arguments.

But the thing I remember as we approached the end of the Old World, the thing I had been thinking for years and marveled over and also felt mildly anxious about, was this: You could go out and order and eat anything in a restaurant. And I had a sense that this wouldn't last forever, and some day we'd look back on these days fondly.

I would actually think that. It actually seemed to me marvelous that we could order anything we wanted. Raspberries in February! Bookstores, shoe stores, computer stores, food stores. We could order anything. Www-dot-gimme-dot-com.

I think the general feeling was a lovely optimism, which was captured in a great '80s phrase: "The future's so bright, I gotta wear shades."

This was the thing: abundance. Not only of food but of potential, of hope, of the kid from the project's dream of being the next J. Lo, or West Point cadet or millionaire. Every middle-class kid in the suburbs thought it absolutely within his grasp to be the next Steven Spielberg or Russell Crowe, or to play Martin Sheen's assistant on "The West Wing," or to run the record industry or direct commercials.

Abundant dreams. There was peace—crime down for the first time in a generation, the world relatively quiet, and in the suburbs they were starting to sleep with the windows open again. And material goods, things from the factory and the farm. As Kevin Spacey says in the commercial for his new movie, "Your produce alone has been worth the trip!"

God, it was the age of abundance.

Or maybe just: The Abundance.

*   *   *

I know people who are feeling a sense of betrayal at the big change, as if they thought history were a waiter in a crisp white jacket and though they ordered two more of the same, instead—instead!—he brought them, on a pretty silver platter, something quite dreadful.

They feel betrayed because they thought what we have been living through the past four decades or so was "life." But it wasn't, it was "Superlife."

In the long ribbon of history life has been one long stained and tangled mess, full of famine, horror, war and disease. We must have thought we had it better because man had improved. But man doesn't really "improve," does he? Man is man. Human nature is human nature; the impulse to destroy coexists with the desire to build and create and make better. They've both been with us since the beginning. Man hasn't improved, the weapons have improved.

In the early 20th century the future was so bright they had to *invent* shades. They had everything—peace, prosperity, medical and scientific breakthroughs, political progress, fashion, glamour, harmless tasty scandals. The Gilded Age. And then all of a sudden they were hit by the most terrible war in all of European history, the most terrible plague in all of modern history (the Spanish flu) and on top of it all the most terrible political revolution in the history of man. And that was just the first 18 years.

*   *   *

People always think good news will continue. I guess it's in our nature to think that whatever is around us while we're here is what will continue until we're not.

And then things change, and you're surprised. I guess surprise is in our nature, too. And then after the surprise we burrow down into ourselves and pull out what we need to survive, and go on, and endure.

But there's something else, and I am thinking of it.

I knew for many years a handsome and intelligent woman of middle years who had everything anyone could dream of—home, children, good marriage, career, wealth. She was secure. And she and her husband had actually gotten these good things steadily, over 25 years of effort, and in that time they had suffered no serious reverses or illnesses, no tragedies or bankruptcies or dark stars. Each year was better than the previous.

It was wonderful to see. But as I came to know her I realized that she didn't think she had what she had because she was lucky, or blessed. She thought she had them because she was better. She had lived a responsible, effortful life; of course it had come together. She had what she had because she was good, and prudent.

She deserved it. She was better than the messy people down the block.

She forgot she was lucky and blessed.

You forget you're lucky when your luck is so consistent that it confounds the very idea of luck. You begin to think your good fortune couldn't be luck, it must have been... talent. Or effort. Or superiority.

The consistency of America's luck may have fooled many of us into forgetting we were lucky to be born here, lucky to be living now, lucky to have hospitals and operas and a film industry and a good electrical system. We were born into it. We were lucky. We were blessed.

We thought we were the heirs of John Adams, Ulysses S. Grant, Thomas Edison, Jonas Salk, Mr. Levitt of Levittown. And we are. But still, every generation ya gotta earn it. It doesn't mean you're better; it means you're lucky, and ya gotta earn it.

*   *   *

How did our luck turn bad, our blessings thin out?

Great books will be written about that. But maybe from this point on we should acknowledge what we quietly know inside: It was a catastrophic systems failure, a catastrophic top-to-bottom failure of the systems on which we rely for safety and peace.

Another way to say it: The people of the West were, the past 10 years or so, on an extended pleasure cruise, sailing blithely on smooth waters—but through an iceberg field. We thought those in charge of the ship, commanding it and steering it and seeing to its supplies, would—could—handle any problems. We paid our fare (that is, our taxes) and assumed the crew would keep us safe.

We thought our luck would hold, too.

The people—us, you and me, the sensuous man on the deck—spent a lot of time strolling along wondering *What shall I pursue today, gold or romance? Romance or gold? I shall ponder this over a good merlot.* We were not serious. We were not morally serious. We were not dark. We banished darkness.

The American people knew, or at least those paying attention knew, that something terrible might happen. But they knew the government had probably done what governments do to protect us. The people did not demand this; the government did not do it. Bad men were allowed in; bad men flourished here, fit right in, planned their deeds. They brought more bad men in after them. They are here among us now; they send anthrax through the mail and watch our reaction, predicating their next move perhaps upon our response.

Our intelligence system failed—but then for a quarter century we had been denying it resources, destroying its authority, dismantling its mystique. Our immigration system failed—but then in many ways it had been encouraged to fail. Our legal system failed.

One of our greatest institutions, American journalism, failed.

When the editors and publishers of our great magazines and networks want you to worry about something—child safety seats, the impact of air bags, drunk driving, insecticides on apples—they know how to make you worry. They know exactly how to capture your attention. Matthew Shepard and hate crimes, Rodney King and racism: The networks and great newspapers know how to hit Drive and go from zero to the American Consciousness in 60 seconds. And the networks can do it on free airwaves, a gift from our government.

Did the networks and great newspapers make us worry about what we know we should have worried about? No. Did they bang the drums? No. Did they hit this story like they know how to hit a story? No.

In January 2001 the Homeland Security report, which declared flatly that international terrorism would inevitably draw blood on American soil, was unveiled. They called a news conference in a huge Senate office building. Congressmen came, and a senator, Pat Roberts of Kansas. Only a half dozen reporters showed up, and one, from the greatest newspaper in the nation, walked out halfway through. It was boring.

Every magazine and newspaper had, over the past 10 years, a front-page story and a cover on the madmen in the world and the weapons they could seize and get and fashion. But they never beat the drum, never insisted that this become a cause.

Why? In part I think for the same reason our political figures didn't do anything. It would have been bad for ratings. *The people don't want serious things at 10 o'clock on a Tuesday night, they want Sela Ward falling in love.* I will never, ever forget the important Democrat who told me over lunch why Bill Clinton (president of the United States, January 1993 through January 2001) had never moved and would never move in a serious way to deal with the potential of nuclear and biological terrorism. Because it doesn't show up in the polls, he said. Because it doesn't show up in the focus groups.

* * *

It was a catastrophic systems failure, top to bottom. And we all share in it, some more than others.

Except.

Except those who did the remarkable things that day, Sept. 11, 2001—the firemen who charged like the Light Brigade, the businessmen who said "Let's roll." Which is, in part, why we keep talking about them. To remind ourselves who we are in the midst of the systems failure. They did the right thing just by being what they were, which gave us inspiration just when we needed it most.

And now we have to turn it all around.

Great books, as I said, will be written about these days, and the war on which we are embarked, on how it began and why America slept, and what America did when it awoke. Much awaits to be learned and told.

And what we must do now, in our anger and defensiveness, is support, assist and constructively criticize the systems that so catastrophically failed. For those systems still reign and we still need them. And they are trying to function now, and trying to protect us, with the same sense of loss we all share and the added burden of a mind-bending sense of remorse, frustration, anger and pain.

* * *

Where are we right now? We have reached the point in the story where the original trauma is wearing off (except in our dreams, where it's newly inflicted), where expressions of solidarity and patriotism are true but tired, and questions about exactly how well our institutions are handling this—not in the past but right now—are rising.

It all began 45 days ago. We know who did the bombings because they were on the planes, and they left receipts.

But we do not know who their confederates here were, do not

know who is spreading the anthrax that has hit Florida, New York and Washington, do not know the dimensions of the threat at home.

Authority figures are doubted. The letter carriers don't trust their superiors to take care of them, and how they feel is legitimate and understandable. The workers in the newsrooms, reassured by the boss that if they were going to get anthrax they would have had it by now, do not trust what they're being told, or the tellers. And that is legitimate and understandable.

We are reading anxious reports. Yesterday I read that the Nuclear Regulatory Commission had admitted it kept nuclear plant vulnerability studies out and about and available for any citizen to see in their libraries. (Q: What were they thinking? A: They weren't thinking; they were feeling, and what they were feeling was lucky.)

More and more one senses we're going to have to be taking as much responsibility for ourselves—and on ourselves—as we can. Doing our own research, taking our own actions, making our own decisions and acting on our guts.

A week after Sept. 11 I was on a TV show where I said I'd been thinking about "Mrs. Miniver," the 1942 movie with Greer Garson as the doughty British matron who saw her family—and thus her country—through the Blitz. I said that we were all going to have to be Mrs. Minivers now; we're going to have to keep the home front going.

I keep waiting for some talk show or news show to do the Mrs. Miniver segment, telling us what to do in case of real and terrible trouble.

And no one is doing it.

So we must all be doing it ourselves. I am researching and talking to experts. Next week I will talk about "How to Be Mr. and Mrs. Miniver"—from how much water to buy to where to put it and how to get everyone in your ambit together. I will share everything I'm told and hear. And let me tell you why I think, in all this mess, we must gather together and talk about how to get through it together, as citizens. *Because our systems are not fully working yet.*

It's a murky time. We're all feeling a little bit lonely, and all of us at one moment or another have the existential willies. Those who have 13 kids and 34 grandchildren are feeling as alone as those who are actually all alone.

We'd all best handle as much as we can ourselves, in and with our own little units.

It may become a terrifically tough time. But we are not alone, as you well know. God loves faith and effort, and he loves love. He will help us get through this, and to enjoy Paris and New York again, and to breathe deep of his delicious, mansard-roofed world.

Amen.

Miracle on Fulton Street

The el, the book party and the site of the Virgin.

The Wall Street Journal: December 14, 2001

My friends, this is the kind of column I used to do now and then before the world changed. I tell you what I've been doing and thinking and if you're interested you get a cup of coffee and sit down and read along, and if you're not you can go back to Opinion Journal's main page, or Drudge, or Salon, or Free Republic.

* * *

It is Christmas in New York. The weather as you know has been soft, nice and not freezing but often overcast. A friend who comes into New York each week from Chicago told me yesterday that on Michigan Avenue it's hustle and bustle and the world hasn't changed at all, it's Christmas, but on Madison Avenue it's dead. It happens that I often walk along Madison Avenue and hadn't noticed that, but there's some truth in what he said. Our great high-end commercial avenue doesn't have quite the cheery bustle of years past. But there's more love on it, more flags and more friendliness in the shops, and at a big expensive handmade furniture place in the 80s they still have the pictures of every fireman who died on Sept. 11, each face highlighted in the middle of a paper star, all the stars filling the store's main window. (In New York there has been a slight below-the-radar anti-fireman reaction to this kind of thing. Some people are tired of hearing the firemen praised, and they have a brother-in-law who's a fireman who's a worthless oaf who can't even pick up his shorts. The other day an Internet executive told me this.

I said: "Believe me, as soon as 343 Internet executives rush into a burning building and die so that strangers can live, I'm gonna drop the fireman like a rock and celebrate executives.")

* * *

I have had a Christmas party week, a very social week. I am not an especially social person but it's been a time for big gatherings, and I am grateful for it. In Brooklyn in my new neighborhood a house party in a grand brownstone mansion, thrown for the neighbors by a gentleman who in the '80s and '90s became rich. When I walked in I had the oddest sense of having been in this great home, or having been in a place very much like it, long ago. The huge rounded doorways, the height of the ceilings, the size of the rooms and placement of the windows.

I was born in Brooklyn half a century ago and not far from here, but in those days Brooklyn wasn't rich. It was still full of the families Betty Smith wrote about in "A Tree Grows in Brooklyn," only two generations older than Francie, the schoolgirl in the book, and not impoverished but working class. We lived in an Irish and Italian ghetto that was turning African American and Puerto Rican. Living with our family were old aunts who'd been maids and cooks in Manhattan, and an uncle who was a carpenter. My grandmother was the coat attendant at a dance hall in Brooklyn called the Lenruth Room when I was a little girl, and I remember being there with her when I was a child, and seeing people dance and touching the coats.

My grandparents lived in an apartment on Myrtle Avenue, in a walk-up on the fourth floor, and their bedroom faced the Myrtle Avenue el, which was about 10 feet outside their window. The whole apartment shook, literally shook, when the elevated trains came by.

When I was with my grandparents I would put my arms on the windowsill like the old ladies of the neighborhood and watch the trains go by.

I'll tell you who else did this, a generation or two before. The actor Tony Curtis, who a few years ago wrote a wonderful memoir of his years as New York street urchin and Hollywood hellion. He told this story. As a boy he would sit each morning at the window of his parents' apartment and watch the elevated trains. Every morning he'd see a man on the 8 a.m. train sitting in the same seat, wearing a brown hat and reading the Herald Tribune. The train would stop, young Tony would glance at the man and the man would glance at Tony. Then he'd go back to reading the paper and the train would roar off. One morning the train stops and the man isn't in his seat. Next day he's not there, next week. Then 10 days later he's back in his same seat with the paper and the brown hat. And he glances over at Tony and Tony glances at him. And for once they maintain their gaze. And the man lowers the paper and mouths, "I've been sick!" And the train roars off.

I love that story. It's a metaphor for how we know each other and don't know each other, how we have relationships we don't even remark upon and barely notice until they leave.

Did I have a relationship with the house of the rich man whose home I was in this week? I didn't see how I could, but I mentioned to the man's friend, standing in his great hallway, that I had the oddest feeling of knowing this place even though there had been no mansions in our lives when I was a kid. The man said, "Oh, this wasn't a mansion when you were a kid. He restored it to the way it was when it was first built. When you were a kid it was all broken up into 10 apartments. Regular people lived here."

So I could have been there before. And now I am here as an adult, as a person who writes of presidents, and the house is a mansion. Brooklyn is, has been, will ever be a place of miracles.

*   *   *

At a party in Manhattan, I spoke to a close aide to Rudy Giuliani, our king. He told me Rudy doesn't want to leave until the fire's out. Mr. Giuliani, of course, leaves as mayor in January, but his aide told me he is obsessed with putting out, as his final act, the infernal fires of Ground Zero, which still burn. Rudy wants the fires out by his last day as mayor. The city, the aide tells me, has been using satellite heat-finding imagery to pinpoint exactly where in the dead zone the fires are. "We find out where, we force foam in from one direction and the fire goes in another. We force foam in from the other direction and the fire goes up or down."

I asked him what, after three months, is still burning.

"Computers," he said.

"Computers?" I said.

He said the wires of computers, the innards and machinery of computers—they keep burning. "There isn't a piece of glass in the ruins, not a single piece," he said. The glass was melted and pulverized, turned to ash. There isn't a desk or chair in the ruins, either, he said—from two towers full of desks and chairs. Again, they were burned and pulverized by heat and force.

He mentioned another odd thing I'd noticed, we'd all noticed: Paper survived. Paper from offices of the Trade Center—merger agreements, divorce decrees, memos that Sandra in Accounting had a baby boy, custody petitions—the paper of the Towers shot into the air. When the Towers tumbled, it created a reverse vacuum and papers were sucked up into the gathering cloud and dispersed all over downtown, the rivers, Brooklyn and Queens. But the binders the papers were in—the legal binders, the metal rings inside them— they didn't survive.

What he told me made me think of a telephone repairman who wrote his memories of Sept. 11 and sent them to me after last week's column. He had been working on a telephone pole in Queens. He heard the explosions, the lines went down on him and everyone else. A piece of paper fluttered down and he caught it. It was a business card. A few days later he called the number on the card and asked for the name. A young woman answered. Yes, she said, she was alive, she had made it out of the building. No, she didn't know her business cards had made it to Queens. (Hollywood: Use this. In your version they fall in love.)

* * *

I went to a book party in downtown Manhattan, in the spacious condo of a man and woman who had been walking their children to the first day of school when the Towers were hit. They have three gorgeous kids, one of whom, aged about four, asked to stay up to see the guests this evening and then, overwhelmed by the smiles, crinkles, wrinkles, earrings and perfume of adults bending down to kiss, and frightened perhaps by the gooney look old people sometimes get when they look at childhood beauty, hid in her mother's skirt and then her father's arms. The guest of honor, a wonderful man of depth and charm, arrived late, from a television appearance. I hugged him, congratulated him, asked how he was. "My whole life is work," he said softly. Then he sucked in his abs, turned, shook hands with friends and worked the room.

We all feel that way so often: "My whole life is work." We all work so hard. But it is, as they say, a choice. We wouldn't have to work so hard if we would take everything we have and rent a $600-a-month apartment just outside a suburb of Tulsa, and join a local church and get a job in a hardware store and be peaceful and kind and take the elderly neighbor to the hospital every other week for chemo.

But it is not the American dream to want to live outside a suburb of Tulsa in a $600-a-month apartment. It is the American dream to, among other things, be at the book party celebrating your friend's bestseller surrounded by brilliant, accomplished and interesting Americans who take part in the world, who are immersed in it and try to turn it this way and that.

We work so hard to find happiness. But more and more I think of what a friend told me on the phone 10 years ago after I had written an essay on the subject. He called and said: "This is a famous quote from someone, I forget who, and this is what you mean. 'Happiness is a cat. Chase it and it will elude you, it will hide. But sit and peacefully do your work, live your life and show your love and it will silently come to you and curl itself upon your feet.'"

*   *   *

After the book party, I went to a dinner party in upper Manhattan, at the home of a writer and thinker and his smart, bubbly wife. It was the three-month anniversary of Sept. 11, and naturally the talk was: 9/11. Normally these conversations end in something like resolve and laughter, with someone saying something upbeat. But not this night, and I was glad of it. I spoke to a man, a dynamic businessman and a good person who was, to my surprise, utterly changed. I hadn't seen him in more than a year. I found out that until recently he had been at Ground Zero every day since Sept. 11. He had lost his office, scores of friends and coworkers, had rushed to the site and worked there for months as a helper and organizer.

Now he is a changed man. He used to carry success on his shoulders like a well-padded suit, and now in his eyes there is grief, grief, a deep well of grief. "I had to go to the doctor because I couldn't stop smelling the smell," he tells me. It is the olfactory disorder of Ground Zero: Work there long enough and you can't lose the acrid burning smell, your nose absorbs it as if it were memory and won't let go. You wake up 30 miles away at home in your bed and it's 4 a.m. and you smell it and you think you're going mad.

He told me how Sept. 11 had changed his life. "I am more religious," he said. He looked like he wasn't sure what that meant and was surprised to find it happening to him, didn't fully understand it but knew it was true: He's more religious. And, he said, what he wants to do now is not make money but help people, serve the public, do good.

And he meant it. It wasn't post-traumatic virtue disorder, it was: A life in change.

* * *

I find myself drawn to and heartened by people who can't get over Sept. 11. Because I can't, either, and I never will. But then I talk to them and realize: They're here, and I'm here, and we're at the party, so we'll get over it.

* * *

On the way home and for no particular reason I remembered something I was told a few weeks ago by a friend who had in another time and for other reasons become a changed person.

I have known him for years but had not known the story he told me. He had been a roaring alcoholic, a man who'd lived to drink and gamble. But something was changing in him, and one night he was at home drinking by himself when he saw something on TV— something someone said, something that moved him deeply. And suddenly he knew his life must change. He picked up the phone and called the 24-hour hotline at a local rehab hospital. And he said, slurring, "I want to spick to a dahkter, I think I'm an alcaholic."

"Is that you, Billy?" said the woman who answered the phone.

He was shocked. Someone must have reported him! They must keep the numbers of known local alcoholics!

"How did you know my name?" he demanded.

"Because you call every night at 2 a.m. How's your daughter?"

For two weeks he'd been getting drunk every night and calling the rehab line and having long conversations with whoever answered. And it was news to him. The next day he entered rehab, and for many years he has been a changed man.

People change. It's not true that they don't. It is true that it is more unusual than it is usual.

*   *   *

At the dinner party a friend told me of his son, a Marine at Camp Lejeune. My friend and his wife may or may not see their boy for Christmas, it depends on his orders. The mother, a beautiful lady, frankly admitted her fear for her son. The father was proud and wistful. I mentioned an acquaintance of ours who has a handsome young son in ROTC and who will join the armed forces when he graduates in June. I bumped into her and she told me that this is where parenthood makes hypocrites of us all—you know our country needs men like this, you know we must fight, but not my boy, not my son.

The father and mother I was talking to smiled and nodded. It's the same for them. "Let me tell you what my son said to me when I told him how worried I was about him," the father said. "Dad, I am fully capable, fully trained and armed to defend myself, and I am not the target. You are not armed and trained and you are the target. Worry about you."

*   *   *

I worry about all of us, and so no doubt do you. But Wednesday I had a wonderful, heartening experience online that I will share with you because it may help you, too. I like to go to Christian Web sites such as www.redeemer.com, where you can find the Rev. Tim Keller's inspiring and informative sermons. I go to Catholic Web sites, too, and Wednesday I marked a great feast day of the church at one.

* * *

It was the feast of Our Lady of Guadeloupe, a celebration of the event 500 years ago in which the Mother of Christ appeared before an earnest and loving Mexican peasant named Juan Diego. The appearance and the miracles that followed sparked what was probably the biggest mass religious conversion in the history of the Americas. And indeed Our Lady of Guadeloupe is considered by Catholics to be our country's patroness.

As America becomes more Latin and Hispanic, the feast has become bigger, grander. It was marked in Washington with a mass at the Shrine of the Immaculate Conception, and there were masses and festivities in Albuquerque, N.M., Houston and Phoenix and Tucson, Ariz. But according to an article on a Catholic Web site the biggest celebration in the U.S. took place in Los Angeles. "Following a procession through the city's streets, Cardinal Roger Mahoney celebrated a mass for nearly 20,000 who gathered on the football field in the Cal State Los Angeles Stadium." Twenty thousand.

And, most delightfully to me of all, yesterday in Rome, at the end of a general audience, Pope John Paul II for the first time ever activated a Web page. They brought him a laptop and he hit a key with his Parkinson-pained finger and suddenly www.virgende guadalupe.org.mx was born.

At another site I found that people were writing prayers of gratitude and petition to mark the feast, and I read them. They were so moving and beautiful.

There is so much going on in America, in churches and on Internet sites, that no one in normal media, elite media or any media really seems to touch. But I continually discover and rediscover that there is a whole world of people who exist apart from the New York Times, the Washington Post and our beloved Wall Street Journal, who exist as part of a real and strong and authentic American community and indeed a world community.

At the site I visited the prayers and petitions to Our Lady were in English, Spanish and French.

They asked for consolation for those who died or lost loved ones in the Trade Center attacks, they asked for protection for our country and peace for the world. "I pray for the people and kids in Afghanistan," said one.

Most were in one way or another personal: "Dear Blessed Lady, intercede for me and pray for me that with your help I can get the money to save my home. Ask your divine son to show his infinite mercy."

"Dear Lady, please . . . pray for dj's, entertainers, artists, performers and media and writers."

"Mama Mary . . . please pray for . . . all the teachers, everyone serving in the armed forces, President Bush, all the leaders especially of the Philippines, all the terrorists, bin Laden, all the priests and religious and our Holy Father."

"Dear Lady of Guadeloupe, please let all my friends forgive me for all that I have done."

"*Pour les enfants abandonnes.*"

"*Senora, en tu dia te recuerdo y te amo. Gracias madre por todos tus bienes.*"

"*Je taime et mercies de rester avec moi et ma petite famille je taime tres fort dis bonjour a Padre Pio pour moi.*"

"Happy Feast Day, my Lady Mother. You seem so close today, telling me to let the desire of my heart be that of your Son's, and to let his desire be mine . . . bring me back to my monastic community, my Lady, though I have failed and fallen so many times."

"Jesus, Son of Mary, our Mother—forgive me and help me to know and love her more. I desire to be just like her . . . Mama Mary, help me to let go of covetousness, vanity, lust for the flesh and food... and all the vices and weaknesses that separate me from your son... (help) all my students, especially John."

"Blessed Mother on this, your feast day, please free [my loved one] from the bondage of drug addiction."

"I beg for my estranged husband and for the purity and sanctity of my children... Please, my Mama, obtain a miracle for my family."

"Dearest Lady Thank you for all the trials I have received these past few years for in them I have found a new love of God."

There were men praying to be better husbands, wives to be better wives, prayers to be freed of alcoholism and healed after infidelity, for runaway children and broken families.

All were marked by humility and gratitude, many by pain and anxiety. They prayed so hard for our country, and there was a sense that they knew that they were praying at a time of heightened alert, and during Ramadan and in a time of extraordinary need.

I found it all so moving. So now I go there and pray along with them, and feel enlivened by their community. It's as good as, better than, a wonderful dinner party.

*　*　*

I will leave you with a happy thought. The other day into my imagination popped a scene that I dearly hope will happen. I imagined that I was walking along Fulton Street in Brooklyn. It was a pretty afternoon, just pre-dusk, and the street was full of shoppers. And suddenly a woman came running from the Wiz, and she shouted to no one, to everyone, "They found Osama! They caught bin Laden!" And the street stopped stock still and then someone cheered and then we all cheered, and we went into the Wiz and watched the reporters telling the story on all the big TV monitors, row after row of them. And strangers talked to strangers and people who hadn't wept since Sept. 11 found themselves with tears in their eyes, and it was an unforgettable moment in American history.

Actually, I shared this scene with my table at the dinner party earlier in the week.

"Dead or alive?" someone asked. I shook my head. "The way you imagined it, is Osama dead or alive?"

I said I didn't know and didn't care. A man said I should care, it's bad if he's alive, that means crazy hostage things and suicide bomber nuts. Someone else said, "I feel sure that when they get him if they get him it will be an unknown CIA agent who gets him, and we'll never know his name." He will be invited to the White House and shake the president's hand and be assigned somewhere far away, and it will be one of the great secrets of all time. He will be The Man Who Got Osama. And we won't even know his name.

I thought, "Oh no, we must know his name and dedicate things to him like mountains and libraries." I said we have to know and she said no, if he is known he will be in danger, and so will his family: "The *Jihad* never forgets."

Well, we'll see how it goes.

We'll see how it ends.

For me today more prayer sites, and a visit to the pained and peaceful people of faith. And then on to Fulton Street, where there's a big Macy's and a Wiz and television and appliance stores. On to the great bustle of Brooklyn in 2001, where miracles still happen, and have.

Courage under Fire

The 21st century's first war heroes.

The Wall Street Journal: October 5, 2001

Forgive me. I'm going to return to a story that has been well documented the past few weeks, and I ask your indulgence. So much has been happening, there are so many things to say, and yet my mind will not leave one thing: the firemen, and what they did.

Although their heroism has been widely celebrated, I don't think we have gotten its meaning, or fully apprehended its dimensions. But what they did that day, on Sept. 11—what the firemen who took those stairs and entered those buildings did—was to enter American history, and Western history. They gave us the kind of story you tell your grandchildren about. I don't think I'll ever get over it, and I don't think my city will, either.

What they did is not a part of the story but the heart of the story.

* * *

Here in my neighborhood in the East 90s many of us now know the names of our firemen and the location of our firehouse. We know how many men we lost (eight). We bring food and gifts and checks and books to the firehouse, we sign big Valentines of love, and yet of course none of it is enough or will ever be enough.

Every day our two great tabloids list the memorials and wakes and funeral services. They do reports: Yesterday at a fireman's funeral they played "Stairway to Heaven." These were the funerals for yesterday:

- Captain Terence Hatton, of Rescue 1—the elite unit that was among the first at the Towers—at 10 a.m. at St. Patrick's Cathedral on Fifth Avenue.
- Lt. Timothy Higgins of Special Operations at St. Elizabeth Ann Seton Church, on Portion Road in Lake Ronkonkoma, out in Long Island.
- Firefighter Ruben Correa of Engine 74 at Holy Trinity Catholic Church on West 82nd Street, in Manhattan.
- Firefighter Douglas Miller of Rescue 5, at St. Joseph's Church on Avenue F in Matamoras, Pa.
- Firefighter Mark Whitford of Engine 23, at St. Mary's Church on Goshen Avenue in Washingtonville, N.Y.
- Firefighter Neil Leavy of Engine 217 at Our Lady Queen of Peace, on New Dorp Lane in Staten Island.
- Firefighter John Heffernan of Ladder 11 at Saint Camillus Church in Rockaway, Queens.

And every day our tabloids run wallet-size pictures of the firemen, with little capsule bios. Firefighter Stephen Siller of Squad 1, for instance, is survived by wife, Sarah, daughters Katherine, Olivia and Genevieve and sons Jake and Stephen, and by brothers Russell, George and Frank, and sisters Mary, Janice and Virginia.

What the papers are doing—showing you that the fireman had a name and the name had a face and the face had a life—is good. But of course it is not enough, it can never be enough.

* * *

We all of course know the central fact: There were two big buildings and there were 5,000-plus people and it was 8:48 in the morning on a brilliant blue day. And then 45 minutes later the people and the buildings were gone. They just went away. As I write this almost three weeks later, I actually think: That couldn't be true. But it's true. That is pretty much where New Yorkers are in the grieving process: "That couldn't be true. It's true." Five thousand dead! "That couldn't be true. It's true." And more than 300 firemen dead.

Three hundred firemen. This is the part that reorders your mind when you think of it. For most of the 5,000 dead were there—they just happened to *be* there, in the buildings, at their desks or selling coffee or returning email. But the 300 didn't happen to be there, they *went* there. In the now-famous phrase, they ran into the burning building and not out of the burning building. They ran up the stairs, not down, they went into it and not out of it. They didn't flee, they charged. It was just before 9 a.m. and the shift was changing, but the outgoing shift raced to the Towers and the incoming shift raced with them. That's one reason so many were there so quickly, and the losses were so heavy. Because no one went home. They all came.

And one after another they slapped on their gear and ran up the stairs. They did this to save lives. Of all the numbers we've learned since Sept. 11, we don't know and will probably never know how many people that day were saved from the flames and collapse. But the number that has been bandied about is 20,000—20,000 who lived because they thought quickly or were lucky or prayed hard or met up with (were carried by, comforted by, dragged by) a fireman.

I say fireman and not "firefighter." We're all supposed to say firefighter, but they were all men, great men, and *fireman* is a good word. Firemen put out fires and save people, they take people who can't walk and sling them over their shoulders like a sack of potatoes and take them to safety. That's what they do for a living. You think to yourself: Do we pay them enough? You realize: We couldn't possibly pay them enough. And in any case a career like that is not about money.

*　*　*

I'm still not getting to the thing I want to say.

It's that what the New York Fire Department did—what those

men did on that brilliant blue day in September—was like D-Day. It was daring and brilliant and brave, and the fact of it—the fact that they did it, charging into harm's way—changed the world we live in. They brought love into a story about hate—for only love will make you enter fire. Talk about your Greatest Generation—the greatest generation is the greatest pieces of any generation, and right now that is: them.

So it was like D-Day, but it was also like the charge of the Light Brigade. *Into the tower of death strode the three hundred.* And though we continue to need reporters to tell us all the facts, to find out the stories of what the firemen did in those Towers, and though reporters have done a wonderful, profoundly appreciative job of that, what we need most now is different.

We need a poet. We need a writer of ballads and song to capture what happened there as the big men in big black rubber coats and big boots and hard peaked hats lugged 50 and 100 pounds of gear up into the horror and heat, charging upward, going up so sure, calm and fast—so humorously, some of them, cracking mild jokes—that some of the people on the stairwell next to them, going down, try-ing to escape, couldn't help but stop and turn and say "Thank you," and "Be careful, son," and some of them took pictures. I have one. On the day after the horror, when the first photos of what happened inside the Towers were posted on the Internet, I went to them. And one was so eloquent—a black-and-white picture that was almost a blur: a big, black-clad back heading upward in the dark, and on his back, in shaky double-vision letters because the person taking the picture was shaking, it said "Byrne."

Just Byrne. But it suggested to me a world. An Irish kid from Brooklyn, where a lot of the Byrnes settled when they arrived in America. Now he lives maybe on Long Island, in Massapequa or Huntington. Maybe third-generation American, maybe in his 30s, grew up in the '70s when America was getting crazy, but became what his father might have been, maybe was: a fireman. I printed copies of the picture, and my brother found the fireman's face and first name in the paper. His name was Patrick Byrne. He was among the missing. Patrick Byrne was my grandfather's name, and is my cousin's name. I showed it to my son and said, "Never forget this—ever."

* * *

The Light Brigade had Tennyson. It was the middle of the Crimean War, and the best of the British light cavalry charged on open terrain in the Battle of Balaclava. Of the 600 men who went in, almost half were killed or wounded, and when England's poet laureate, Alfred, Lord Tennyson, learned of it, he turned it into one of the most famous poems of a day when poems were famous:

> *Theirs not to make reply,*
> *Theirs not to reason why,*
> *Theirs but to do and die:*
> *Into the valley of Death*
> *Rode the six hundred.*
>
> *Cannon to right of them,*
> *Cannon to left of them,*
> *Cannon in front of them*
> *Volley'd and thunder'd:*
> *Stormed at with shot and shell,*
> *Boldly they rode and well,*
> *Into the jaws of Death,*
> *Into the mouth of Hell*
> *Rode the six hundred.*

I don't think young people are taught that poem anymore; it's martial and patriarchal, and even if it weren't it's cornball. But then, if a Hollywood screenwriter five weeks ago wrote a story in which buildings came down and 300 firemen sacrificed their lives to save others, the men at the studios would say: *Nah, too cornball. That couldn't be true.* But it's true.

Brave men do brave things. After Sept. 11, a friend of mine said something that startled me with its simple truth. He said, "Everyone died as the person they were." I shook my head. He said, "Everyone died who they *were*. A guy who ran down quicker than everyone and didn't help anyone—that was him. The guy who ran to get the old lady and was hit by debris—that's who he was. They all died who they were."

*   *   *

Who were the firemen? The Christian scholar and author Os Guinness said the other night in Manhattan that horror and tragedy crack open the human heart and force the beauty out. It is in terrible times that people with great goodness inside become most themselves. "The real mystery," he added, "is not the mystery of evil but the mystery of goodness." Maybe it's because of that mystery that firemen themselves usually can't tell you why they do what they do. "It's the job," they say, and it is, and it is more than that.

So: The firemen were rough repositories of grace. They were the goodness that comes out when society is cracked open. They were *responsible*. They took responsibility under conditions of chaos. They did their job under heavy fire, stood their ground, claimed new ground, moved forward like soldiers against the enemy. They charged.

There is another great poet and another great charge, Pickett's charge, at Gettysburg. The poet, playwright and historian Stephen Vincent Benét wrote of Pickett and his men in his great poetic epic of the Civil War, "John Brown's Body":

There was a death-torn mile of broken ground to cross,
And a low stone wall at the end, and behind it the Second Corps,
And behind that force another, fresh men who had not fought.
They started to cross that ground. The guns began to tear them.

From the hills they say that it seemed more like a sea than a wave,
A sea continually torn by stones flung out of the sky,
And yet, as it came, still closing, closing and rolling on,
As the moving sea closes over the flaws and rips of the tide.

But the men would not stop:

You could mark the path that they took by the dead that they left
   behind,
. . . . .
And yet they came on unceasing, the fifteen thousand no more,
And the blue Virginia flag did not fall, did not fall, did not fall.

The center line held to the end, he wrote, and didn't break until it wasn't there anymore.

The firemen were like that. And like the soldiers of old, from Pickett's men through D-Day, they gave us a moment in history that has left us speechless with gratitude and amazement, and maybe relief, too. *We still make men like that. We're still making their kind. Then that must be who we are.*

We are entering an epic struggle, and the firemen gave us a great gift when they gave us this knowledge that day. They changed a great deal by being who they were.

They deserve a poet, and a poem. At the very least a monument. I enjoy the talk about building it bigger, higher, better, and maybe we'll do that. But I'm one of those who thinks: Make it a memory.

The pieces of the Towers that are left, that still stand, look like pieces of a cathedral. Keep some of it. Make it part of a memorial. And at the center of it—not a part of it but at the heart of it—bronze statues of firemen looking up with awe and resolution at what they faced. And have them grabbing their helmets and gear as if they were running toward it, as if they are running in.

Welcome Back, Duke

From the ashes of September 11 arise the manly virtues.

The Wall Street Journal: October 12, 2001

A few weeks ago I wrote a column called "God Is Back," about how, within a day of the events of Sept. 11, my city was awash in religious imagery—prayer cards, statues of saints. It all culminated, in a way, in the discovery of the steel-girder cross that emerged last week from the wreckage—unbent, unbroken, unmelted, perfectly proportioned and duly blessed by a Catholic friar on the request of the rescue workers, who seemed to see meaning in the cross's existence. So do I.

My son, a teenager, finds this hilarious, as does one of my best friends. They have teased me, to my delight, but I have told them, "Boys, this whole story is about good and evil, about the clash of good and evil." If you are of a certain cast of mind, it is of course meaningful that the face of the Evil One seemed to emerge with a roar from the furnace that was Tower One. You have seen the Associated Press photo, and the photos that followed: The evil face roared out of the building with an ugly howl—and then in a snap of the fingers it lost form and force and disappeared. If you are of a certain cast of mind, it is of course meaningful that the cross, which to those of its faith is imperishable, did not disappear. It was not crushed by the millions of tons of concrete that crashed down upon it, did not melt in the furnace. It rose from the rubble, still there, intact.

For the ignorant, the superstitious and me (and maybe you), the face of the Evil One was revealed, and died; for the ignorant, the superstitious and me (and maybe you), the cross survived. This is how

God speaks to us. He is saying "I am." He is saying "I am here." He is saying "And the force of all the evil of all the world will not bury me."

I believe this quite literally. But then I am experiencing Sept. 11 not as a political event but as a spiritual event.

And, of course, a cultural one, which gets me to my topic.

It is not only that God is back, but that men are back. A certain style of manliness is once again being honored and celebrated in our country since Sept. 11. You might say it suddenly emerged from the rubble of the past quarter century, and emerged when a certain kind of man came forth to get our great country out of the fix it was in.

I am speaking of masculine men, men who push things and pull things and haul things and build things, men who charge up the stairs in 100 pounds of gear and tell everyone else where to go to be safe. Men who are welders, who do construction, men who are cops and firemen. They are all of them, one way or another, the men who put the fire out, the men who are digging the rubble out and the men who will build whatever takes its place.

And their style is back in style. We are experiencing a new respect for their old-fashioned masculinity, a new respect for physical courage, for strength and for the willingness to use both for the good of others.

You didn't have to be a fireman to be one of the manly men of Sept. 11. Those businessmen on Flight 93, which was supposed to hit Washington, the businessmen who didn't live by their hands or their backs but who found out what was happening to their country, said goodbye to the people they loved, snapped the cellphones shut and said, "Let's roll." Those were tough men, the ones who forced that plane down in Pennsylvania. They were tough, brave guys.

*   *   *

Let me tell you when I first realized what I'm saying. On Friday, Sept. 14, I went with friends down to the staging area on the West Side

Highway where all the trucks filled with guys coming off a 12-hour shift at Ground Zero would pass by. They were tough, rough men, the grunts of the city—construction workers and electrical workers and cops and emergency medical workers and firemen.

I joined a group that was just standing there as the truck convoys went by. And all we did was cheer. We all wanted to do some kind of volunteer work but there was nothing left to do, so we stood and cheered those who were doing. The trucks would go by and we'd cheer and wave and shout "God bless you!" and "We love you!" We waved flags and signs, clapped and threw kisses, and we meant it: *We loved these men.* And as the workers would go by—they would wave to us from their trucks and buses, and smile and nod—I realized that a lot of them were men who hadn't been applauded since the day they danced to their song with their bride at the wedding.

And suddenly I looked around me at all of us who were cheering. And saw who we were. Investment bankers! Orthodontists! Magazine editors! In my group, a lawyer, a columnist and a writer. We had been the kings and queens of the city, respected professionals in a city that respects its professional class. And this night we were nobody. We were so useless, all we could do was applaud the somebodies, the workers who, unlike us, had not been applauded much in their lives.

And now they were saving our city.

I turned to my friend and said, "I have seen the grunts of New York become kings and queens of the city." I was so moved and, oddly I guess, grateful. Because they'd always been the people who ran the place, who kept it going, they'd just never been given their due. But now—"And the last shall be first"—we were making up for it.

* * *

It may seem that I am really talking about class—the professional classes have a new appreciation for the working class men of Lodi,

N.J., or Astoria, Queens. But what I'm attempting to talk about is actual manliness, which often seems tied up with class issues, as they say, but isn't always by any means the same thing.

Here's what I'm trying to say: Once about 10 years ago there was a story—you might have read it in your local tabloid, or a supermarket tabloid like the National Enquirer—about an American man and woman who were on their honeymoon in Australia or New Zealand. They were swimming in the ocean, the water chest high. From nowhere came a shark. The shark went straight for the woman, opened its jaws. Do you know what the man did? He punched the shark in the head. He punched it and punched it again. He did not do brilliant commentary on the shark, he did not share his sensitive feelings about the shark, he did not make wry observations about the shark, he punched the shark in the head. So the shark let go of his wife and went straight for him. And it killed him. The wife survived to tell the story of what her husband had done. He had tried to deck the shark. I told my friends: That's what a wonderful man is, a man who will try to deck the shark.

I don't know what the guy did for a living, but he had a very old-fashioned sense of what it is to be a man, and I think that sense is coming back into style because of who saved us on Sept. 11, and that is very good for our country.

Why? Well, manliness wins wars. Strength and guts plus brains and spirit wins wars. But also, you know what follows manliness? The gentleman. The return of manliness will bring a return of gentlemanliness, for a simple reason: Masculine men are almost by definition gentlemen. Example: If you're a woman and you go to a faculty meeting at an Ivy League university, you'll have to fight with a male intellectual for a chair, but I assure you that if you go to a Knights of Columbus Hall, the men inside (cops, firemen, insurance agents) will rise to offer you a seat. Because they are manly men, and gentlemen.

It is hard to be a man. I am certain of it; to be a man in this world is not easy. I know you are thinking *But it's not easy to be a woman*, and you are so right. But women get to complain and make others feel bad about their plight. Men have to suck it up. Good men suck it up and remain good-natured, constructive and helpful; less-good men become the kind of men who are spoofed on "The Man Show"—babe-watching, dope-smoking nihilists. (Nihilism is not manly, it is the last refuge of sissies.)

* * *

I should discuss how manliness and its brother, gentlemanliness, went out of style. I know, because I was there. In fact, I may have done it. I remember exactly when: It was in the mid-'70s, and I was in my mid-20s, and a big, nice, middle-aged man got up from his seat to help me haul a big piece of luggage into the overhead luggage space on a plane. I was a feminist, and knew our rules and rants. "I can do it myself," I snapped.

It was important that he know women are strong. It was even more important, it turns out, that I know I was a jackass, but I didn't. I embarrassed a nice man who was attempting to help a lady. I wasn't lady enough to let him. I bet he never offered to help a lady again. I bet he became an intellectual, or a writer, and not a good man like a fireman or a businessman who says "Let's roll."

But perhaps it wasn't just me. I was there in America, as a child, when John Wayne was a hero, and a symbol of American manliness. He was strong, and silent. And I was there in America when they killed John Wayne by a thousand cuts. A lot of people killed him— not only feminists but peaceniks, leftists, intellectuals, others. You could even say it was Woody Allen who did it, through laughter and an endearing admission of his own nervousness and fear. He made nervousness and fearfulness the admired style. He made not being able to deck the shark, but doing the funniest commentary on not decking the shark, seem . . . cool.

But when we killed John Wayne, you know who we were left with. We were left with John Wayne's friendly-antagonist sidekick in the old John Ford movies, Barry Fitzgerald. The small, nervous, gossiping neighborhood commentator Barry Fitzgerald, who wanted to talk about everything and do nothing.

This was not progress. It was not improvement.

I missed John Wayne.

But now I think...he's back. I think he returned on Sept. 11. I think he ran up the stairs, threw the kid over his back like a sack of potatoes, came back down and shoveled rubble. I think he's in Afghanistan now, saying, with his slow swagger and simmering silence, "Yer in a whole lotta trouble now, Osama-boy."

I think he's back in style. And none too soon.

Welcome back, Duke.

And once again: Thank you, men of Sept. 11.

Time to Put the Emotions Aside

Tomorrow begins the post-9/11-trauma era.

The Wall Street Journal: **September 11, 2002**

Rudy Giuliani said the other day that he wasn't absolutely sure the next morning, on Sept. 12 that the sun would actually come up. When it did, he was grateful. And so we are today, as we mark the anniversary of the day that changed our lives.

We are all busy remembering. A friend in Washington emails in the middle of the night yesterday: She cannot sleep because jets are roaring overhead, and because this is the anniversary of the last time she talked to Barbara Olson. Another email, from an acquaintance: "Last year this time we were comforting each other in instant messages." Most everyone is getting and sending these messages.

I thought it would be flatter, this formal time of remembering, and not so authentic. Days that are supposed to be rich in meaning often aren't. But people seem to be vividly re-feeling what they experienced a year ago, and being caught unaware, mugged by a memory. Last week a friend was telling me where he was, and in the middle of the telling a sob rose from nowhere and cut off his words. Yesterday on CNN Rosalynn Carter seemed taken aback by welling tears when she was asked how she had explained terrible events to her children when they were young. She told them, she said, that bad times didn't mean God wasn't there. Bad times meant God was weeping, too.

Washington is marking this day with patriotism and a certain martial dignity. New York is approaching the anniversary with solemnity and respect. We are immersing ourselves in the trauma to free ourselves of the preoccupation. The great words of great presidents will be read, and some schoolchildren will hear the Gettysburg Address and the Preamble to the Constitution for the first time.

A company of bagpipers will cross the Brooklyn Bridge, retracing the route of the hardy firemen of Brooklyn who roared across the bridge toward Manhattan a year ago this morning. Sirens blaring, they craned their necks to see the smoking ruins of the place where they would make their stand. For six months after that day, bagpipes were the sound of New York in mourning. They were played at all the funerals. None of us in New York will ever hear their rich and lonely wail in the same way again.

*   *   *

What we are doing is taking a last hard and heartbreaking look at what happened last year. In time we will put the memories away, pack them away in a box with a pair of old gloves, and a citation and a badge, and some clippings and pictures. This is what Emily Dickinson called "the sweeping up the heart." She said it was "solemnest of industries enacted upon earth."

But before we put it all away, there is a story to remember. There was a glittering city, the greatest in the history of man, a place of wild creativity, of getting, grabbing and selling, of bustle and yearning and greed. It was brutally attacked by a band of primitives. The city reeled. We knew what to expect: The selfish, heartless city-dwellers would trample children in their path as they raced for safety, they'd fight for the lifeboats like the wealthy on the Titanic.

It didn't happen. It wasn't that way at all. They were better than they knew! They saved each other—they ran to each other's aid, they died comforting strangers.

Then the capital city was attacked, and there too goodness broke out. And sleeping boomers on planes came awake and charged the cockpit to keep the plane from hitting the home of the American president.

And then the mighty nation hit back at the primitives, and hit again.

This is, truly, some story. This is not a terrible thing to have to tell our children. It is a warm story. But now a certain coldness is in order.

* * *

The sun rises tomorrow on the new era, the post-9/11-trauma era. We will make our way through the next year without the wild emotional force of 9/11 pushing us forward. We can be cool now, and deadly if need be.

This can be the year when we find Osama bin Laden. This, the next 12 months, can be when we deal the death blow to the Taliban, for this drama will not even begin to end until we have laid Osama and Osama-ism low. This is one case in which justice and vengeance are intertwined.

This is the year when the president and his advisers will or will not make the case, as they say, on Iraq. The president thinks a key part of the war on terror will be moving against Saddam Hussein and liberating Iraq from his heavy hand. But if Mr. Bush is to make the case it will not be with emotional rhetoric, with singing phrases, with high oratory. It will not, in this coming cooler time, be made with references to evil ones. All of that was good, excellent and Bushian the past passionate year. But now Mr. Bush should think in terms of Sgt. Joe Friday, "Just the facts, ma'am."

"Saddam is evil" is not enough. A number of people are evil, and some are even our friends. "Saddam has weapons of mass destruction" is not enough. A number of countries do. What the people need now is hard data that demonstrate conclusively that Saddam has weapons of mass destruction which he is readying to use on the people of the U.S. or the people of the West.

If Mr. Bush has a good case, he will make it and the people will back him. If he does not, he will not convince the American people that blood and treasure must go to this endeavor. The people must believe, as Mr. Bush does, that their children are endangered. There was a time—I think it was Sept. 10, 2001—that Americans may not have been able to accept such an assertion. That time has passed.

* * *

There's another area where coldness is called for. The folly of what is happening to our airline industry is due to a wet and weepy conception of what is fair. People are afraid to fly because they see what a politically correct joke our airline security is. Searching for every last toenail clipper, forcing 85-year-old people with walkers to stand spread-eagled as some oafish wand-wielder in a blue jacket humiliates them—this is absurd and cowardly. Let's get coldly serious: Arm the pilots, fortify cockpits, man flights with marshals and profile passengers. We don't have a transportation secretary who is willing to do these things. Someday when something terrible happens we'll wish we did. Why not coldly remove Norman Mineta now?

Warm tears, honest remembrances, passionate tributes, giving credit where it's due, absorbing 9/11, teaching our children what it meant and means: These are good things. And a little coldness starting at sunrise tomorrow: That will be good, too.

The Nightmare and the Dreams

How has September 11 affected our national unconscious?

The Wall Street Journal: July 19, 2002

It is hot in New York. It is so hot that once when I had a fever a friend called and asked me how I felt and I said, "You know how dry and hot paper feels when it's been faxed? That's how I feel." And how I felt all day yesterday. We feel as if we've been faxed.

I found myself fully awake at 5 a.m. yesterday and went for a walk on the Brooklyn Bridge. Now more than ever the bridge, with its silver-corded cables and dense stone casements, seems like a great gift to my city. It *spans*. In the changed landscape of downtown it is our undisturbed beauty, grown ever more stately each year. People seem to love it more now, or at least mention it more or notice it more. So do I. It's always full of tourists but always full of New Yorkers, too.

I am struck, as I always am when I'm on it, that I am walking on one of the engineering wonders of the world. And I was struck yesterday that I was looking at one of the greatest views in the history of man's creation: Manhattan at sunrise. The casements were like medieval arches; the businessmen with umbrellas like knights without horses, storming the city walls; and the walls were silver, blue and marble in the light.

And all of it was free. A billionaire would pay billions to own this bridge and keep this view, but I and my jogging, biking and hiking confreres have it for nothing. We inherited it.

The sun rose in haze, its edges indistinct, but even at 6:30 a.m. you could feel it heavy on your arms and shoulders. When I looked at it I thought of what Robert Bolt called the desert sun in his screenplay of David Lean's "Lawrence of Arabia." He called it the Anvil.

*   *   *

As I rounded the entrance to the bridge on the Brooklyn side, a small moment added to my happiness. It was dawn, traffic was light, I passed a black van with smoked windows. In the driver's seat with the window down was a black man of 30 or so, a cap low on his brow, wearing thick black sunglasses. I was on the walkway that leads to the bridge; he was less than two feet away; we were the only people there. We made eye contact. "Good morning!" he said. "Good morning to you," I answered, and for no reason at all we started to laugh, and moved on into the day. Nothing significant in it except it may or may not have happened that way 30 or 40 years ago. I'm not sure the full charge of friendliness would have been assumed or answered.

It made me think of something I saw Monday night on local TV and thought to point out somewhere along the way. They were showing the 1967 movie "Guess Who's Coming to Dinner" with Katharine Hepburn, Sidney Poitier and Spencer Tracy, the slightly creaking old drama—It was slightly creaking when it first came out—about a young white woman and a young black man who fall in love, hope to marry and must contend with disapproving parents on both sides. It's held up well. Parts of it seemed moving in a way I didn't remember, and pertinent. Sidney Poitier, who has always brought his own natural stature to whatever part he's playing, had a lovely kind of sweet intelligence, and everyone in the movie was physically beautiful, in the way of the old productions of the old Hollywood.

There was a bit of dialogue that packed a wallop. Spencer Tracy as the father of the would-be bride is pressing Mr. Poitier on whether he has considered the sufferings their mixed-race children might have to endure in America. Has he thought about this? Has his fiancée? "She is optimistic," says Mr. Poitier. "She thinks every one of them will grow up to become president of the United States. I on the other hand would settle for secretary of state." Those words, written 35 years ago by the screenwriter William Rose, may have seemed dreamy then. But in its audience when the movie came out would likely have been a young, film-loving Army lieutenant named Colin Powell who, that year, was preparing for a second tour of duty in Vietnam. And now he is secretary of state. This is the land dreams are made of.

*   *   *

Late Tuesday, on a subway ride from Brooklyn to the north of Manhattan, I resaw something I'd noticed and forgotten about. It is that more and more, on the streets and on the train, I see people wearing ID tags. We all wear IDs now. We didn't use to. They hang from thick cotton string or an aluminum chain; they're encased in a plastic sleeve or laminated; they're worn one at a time or three at a time, but they're there.

I ponder the existential implications. What does it mean that we wear IDs? What are we saying, or do we think we're saying? I mean aside from the obvious.

I imagined yesterday the row of people across from me on the train, looking up all of a sudden from their newspaper, their paperback, their crossword puzzle book and answering one after another:

"It means I know who I am," says the man in blue shirt and suspenders.

"It means I can get into the building," says the woman in gray.

"It means I am a solid citizen with a job."

"I am known to others in my workplace."

"I'm not just blowing through life, I'm integrated into it. I belong to something. I receive a regular paycheck."

"I have had a background check done by security and have been found to be a Safe Person. Have you?"

I wonder if unemployed people on the train look at the tags around the other people's necks and think, *Soon I hope I'll have one, too.* I wonder if kids just getting their first job at 17 will ever know that in America we didn't all used to be ID'd. Used to be only for people who worked in nuclear power plants or great halls of government. Otherwise you could be pretty obscure. Which isn't a bad way to be.

I work at home on my own and do not have an ID. But I am considering issuing myself one and having it laminated at the local Hallmark shop. It will have a nice picture and a title—President, CEO & CFO. I will wear it on the subway and when I get home I will hold it up in front of my doorbell, which I'll rig so when I swipe the tag my front door pops open. Then I'll turn to the friends I'm with and wink. "I know people here. I can get you in."

*   *   *

A month ago there were news reports of a post-Sept. 11 baby boom. Everyone was so rocked by news of their mortality that they realized there will never be a perfect time to have kids but we're here now so let's have a family. I believed the baby-boom story and waited for the babies.

Then came the stories saying: Nah, there is no baby boom, it's all anecdotal, there's no statistical evidence to back it up. And I believed that, too. But I've been noticing something for weeks now. In my neighborhood there is a baby boom. There are babies all over in Brooklyn. It is full of newborns, of pink soft-limbed infants in cotton carriers on daddy's chest. It is full of strollers, not only regular strollers but the kind that carry two children—double-wides. And triple-wides. In the stores and on the streets there are babies cooing, dribbling, staring, sleeping. I see them and feel a rush of tenderness. I want to kiss their feet, I want to make them laugh. Kids are always looking for someone to make them laugh. The sight of any dog can do it. The sight of another baby can do it. The sight of an idiotic adult covering her eyes with her hands and moving her hands away quickly can do it. I would know.

I don't care what anyone says, there have got to be data that back up what I'm seeing: that after Sept. 11, there was at least a Brooklyn baby boom.

* * *

A dream boom, too. The other day I spoke with a friend I hadn't seen since the world changed. He was two blocks away when the Towers fell, and he saw everything. We have all seen the extraordinary footage of that day, seen it over and over, but few of us have seen what my friend described: how in the office buildings near the World Trade Center they stood at the windows and suddenly darkness enveloped them as the Towers collapsed and the demonic cloud swept through. "It was total darkness," he told me. But the lights were on. They stood in his office wearing wet surgical masks. They couldn't go out, but inside their building the smoke worked its way into the air conditioning. So they turned it off and stood there sweating and watching on TV what was happening two blocks away.

Did you see those forced to jump? I asked.

"Yes," he said, and looked away. No descriptions forthcoming.

Have you had bad dreams?

"Yes," he said, and looked away. No descriptions forthcoming.

I thought about this for a few days. My friend is brilliant and by nature a describer of things felt and seen. But not this time. I spoke to a friend who is a therapist. Are your patients getting extraordinary dreams? I asked.

"Always," he laughs.

Sept. 11 related?

"Yes," he says, mostly among adolescents.

I asked if he was saving them, writing them down. He shook his head no.

So: The Sept. 11 Dream Project. We should begin it. I want to, though I'm not sure why. I think maybe down the road I will try to write about them. Maybe not. I am certain, however, that dreams can be an expression of a nation's unconscious, if there can be said to be such a thing, and deserve respect. (Carl Jung thought so.)

To respect is to record. There is a response function at the end of this column, and you can use it to send in your Sept. 11–related dream—recurring, unusual, striking, whatever. (If you are a psychiatrist, send as many as you like—without identifying your patients, of course.) I will read them, and appreciate them and possibly weave them into a piece on what Sept. 11 has done to our dream lives and to our imaginations, when our imaginations are operating on their own, unfettered, unstopped, spanning.

I Just Called to Say I Love You

The sounds of 9/11, beyond the metallic roar.

The Wall Street Journal: September 8, 2006

Everyone remembers the pictures, but I think more and more about the sounds. I always ask people what they heard that day in New York. We've all seen the film and videotape, but the sound equipment of television crews didn't always catch what people have described as the deep metallic roar.

The other night on TV there was a documentary on the Iron Workers of New York's Local 40, whose members ran to the site when the Towers fell. They pitched in on rescue, then stayed for eight months to deconstruct a skyscraper some of them had helped build 35 years before. An ironworker named Jim Gaffney said, "My partner kept telling me the buildings are coming down and I'm saying 'no way.' Then we heard that noise that I will never forget. It was like a creaking and then the next thing you felt the ground rumbling."

Rudy Giuliani said it was like an earthquake. The actor Jim Caviezel saw the second plane hit the Towers on television and what he heard shook him: "A weird, guttural, discordant sound," he called it, a sound exactly like lightning. He knew because earlier that year he'd been hit. My son, then a teenager in a high school across the river from the Towers, heard the first plane go in at 8:45 a.m. It sounded, he said, like a heavy truck going hard over a big street grate.

* * *

I think, too, about the sounds that came from within the buildings and within the planes—the phone calls and messages left on
answering machines, all the last things said to whoever was home
and picked up the phone. They awe me, those messages.

Something terrible had happened. Life was reduced to its essentials. Time was short. People said what counted, what mattered. It
has been noted that there is no record of anyone calling to say "I
never liked you," or "You hurt my feelings." No one negotiated past
grievances or said "Vote for Smith." Amazingly—or not—there is
no record of anyone damning the terrorists or saying "I hate them."

No one said anything unneeded, extraneous or small. Crisis is a
great editor. When you read the transcripts that have been released
over the years, it's all so clear.

Flight 93 flight attendant Ceecee Lyles, 33 years old, in an
answering-machine message to her husband: "Please tell my children
that I love them very much. I'm sorry, baby. I wish I could see your
face again."

Thirty-one-year-old Melissa Harrington, a California-based trade
consultant at a meeting in the Towers, called her father to say
she loved him. Minutes later she left a message on the answering
machine as her new husband slept in their San Francisco home.
"Sean, it's me," she said. "I just wanted to let you know I love you."

Capt. Walter Hynes of the New York Fire Department's Ladder 13 dialed home that morning as his rig left the firehouse at 85th
Street and Lexington Avenue. He was on his way downtown, he said
in his message, and things were bad. "I don't know if we'll make it
out. I want to tell you that I love you and I love the kids."

Firemen don't become firemen because they're pessimists. Imagine being a guy who feels in his gut he's going to his death, and he

calls on the way to say goodbye and make things clear. His widow later told the Associated Press she'd played his message hundreds of times and made copies for their kids. "He was thinking about us in those final moments."

Elizabeth Rivas saw it that way, too. When her husband left for the World Trade Center that morning, she went to a Laundromat, where she heard the news. She couldn't reach him by cell and rushed home. He'd called at 9:02 and reached her daughter. The child reported, "He say, mommy, he say he love you no matter what happens, he loves you." He never called again. Mrs. Rivas later said, "He tried to call me. He called me."

There was the amazing acceptance. I spoke this week with a medical doctor who told me she'd seen many people die, and many "with grace and acceptance." The people on the planes didn't have time to accept, to reflect, to think through; and yet so many showed the kind of grace you see in a hospice.

Peter Hanson, a passenger on United Airlines Flight 175, called his father. "I think they intend to go to Chicago or someplace and fly into a building," he said. "Don't worry, Dad—if it happens, it will be very fast." On the same flight, Brian Sweeney called his wife, got the answering machine and told her they'd been hijacked. "Hopefully I'll talk to you again, but if not, have a good life. I know I'll see you again some day."

There was Tom Burnett's famous call from United Flight 93. "We're all going to die, but three of us are going to do something," he told his wife, Deena. "I love you, honey."

These were people saying, essentially, *In spite of my imminent death, my thoughts are on you, and on love.* I asked a psychiatrist the other day for his thoughts, and he said the people on the planes and in the Towers were "accepting the inevitable" and taking care of "unfinished business." "At death's door people pass on a responsibility—'Tell Billy I never stopped loving him and forgave him long ago.' 'Take care of Mom.' 'Pray for me, Father. Pray for me, I haven't been very good.'" They address what needs doing.

This reminded me of that moment when Todd Beamer of United 93 wound up praying on the phone with a woman he'd never met before, a Verizon Airfone supervisor named Lisa Jefferson. She said later that his tone was calm. It seemed as if they were "old friends," she later wrote. They said the Lord's Prayer together. Then he said, "Let's roll."

*   *   *

This is what I get from the last messages. People are often stronger than they know, bigger, more gallant than they'd guess. And this: We're all lucky to be here today and able to say what deserves saying, and if you say it a lot it won't make it common and so unheard, but known and absorbed.

I think the sound of the last messages, of what was said, will live as long in human history, and contain within it as much of human history, as any old metallic roar.

Eleven/9/11

The Wall Street Journal: September 11, 2012

It was a beautiful day, that's what everyone remembers. So clear, so crisp, so bright. It sparkled as I walked my 14-year-old son out to go to the subway that would take him to his new high school, in Brooklyn. He was now a commuter: a walk to the 86th Street subway station and then the 4 or 5 train downtown near the Towers and over the river. That was about 7:30 in the morning. It was beautiful at noon when I went to mass at St. Thomas More church on 89th Street. And between those two events, his departure and the mass, the world had changed, changed utterly. After mass, at the rise of 86th Street, the day was so clear you could see all the way downtown to the towering debris cloud.

But it was beautiful. That was one of the heartbreaking elements.

* * *

The things I will never forget. Looking up at a silent TV screen as I returned email at my computer. Seeing a long-distance shot of the World Trade Center with smoke coming out of the side. Putting up the sound. Hearing a food cart vendor with a heavy accent saying to a reporter on the scene: "That was no small plane, that was a big jet, a jumbo jet." Knowing it was true. Hearing the TV chatter that a pilot might have accidentally hit the Tower. Knowing it was not true. Grabbing the phone to call my son's school to make sure he had arrived, that he'd gotten there safe, that he hadn't tarried or gotten off downtown to walk around because it was a beautiful day. Busy signal. Again. Busy. Calling a friend whose husband often worked downtown. No, she said, he's in London. Talking with her as we watched the screen together and then the second plane went in, right before our eyes, and there was no denying what it was. Calling school. Busy. And then the phones went down.

And then the buildings fell. That was the thing, they heaved up and groaned to the ground and brought a world with them. We could have taken it if the buildings didn't fall. That's why the day was so uniquely a New York trauma, for all that happened in Washington and Pennsylvania: The buildings went down and we saw it. My friends saw the jumpers, who fled the flames. To this day they don't talk about it. My friend saw the faces of the passengers on the first plane, so low did they fly by his building. He saw their faces in the passenger windows. He never told anyone about that, including his wife, until two years ago.

Hearing that 20,000 or 30,000 people might have been in the buildings. Hearing something about the firemen—a lot of them died, a lot of them tried to charge up the stairs to the fire. The man standing on line in Murphy's Market after mass. He was covered in Pompeii ash. He had walked uptown. He was standing there in shock with a bottle of water and a banana. The bad boys who hung out near a local school and were said to sell drugs: They took their big boom box and put in on the steps so people walking by could sit down and hear what was happening. I sat down and listened and when I left I said, "Thank you, gentlemen," and they nodded because they knew: They'd been gentlemen.

And, funnily, such a blur of images so vivid that years later you think you actually saw them when you didn't. A few days after the attack, I read of someone seeing a transit worker or policeman in a car downtown, parked and motionless, and he had on the radio and it was blaring "Heroes," and he was crying. I remembered it a few years later and found the Peter Gabriel version. "I can remember /

Standing by the wall…And we kissed as if nothing could fall…We can be heroes…just for one day." It still makes me weep, and when I hear it I see the transit worker or cop again, even though I never saw him.

* * *

Worried sick about my son and no way to reach him. And then miraculously the dead phone rang, at 3 p.m. My 14-year-old on the line at the phone at the school that was working that moment, other students crowded behind him. I am fine, he said, but we still don't know everything that happened, tell me what you know. "It was Arab terrorists," I said. And he muffled the phone and I heard him announce to the kids, "It was terrorism, an Arab group."

"It appears to be over," I said.

"The attack is over, it appears to be all over," he said. On it went as I filled him in and he filled them in. He told them the Towers and the Pentagon were hit but not the State Department, that was a rumor. He was calm, collected, in the middle of history.

He told me he would not get home tonight, all the bridges closed and public transportation stopped, he'd stay over, with some Manhattanite students, at a teacher's house, he'd be home some time tomorrow, he'll be fine, don't worry.

He made it home the next day about noon. And he told me what he'd seen. The subway from Brooklyn to the city curved up over the East River, and everyone on it always turned to look at sparkling, majestic downtown Manhattan. And this day they all turned and they saw the dead cloud, the lost empty buildings, and they all went Oh. A long soft sigh: *Oooohhhhh*.

There is an unwritten story in how brave our children were that day, and have been since, and what that day was to them. But those who were adolescents or early teenagers on 9/11: They never talk about it. They took it all in but they never talk about it.

*   *   *

As for me, I notice that in the early years after 9/11, when they did their replays of the event on the news, I always used to watch with some kind of pain that was being worked out while it was being reexperienced. But now I can't watch. Because it causes some kind of pain that is not going to be worked out, and that has to do more with what followed that day than the day itself.

But I want to end with the beauty of that day, and a parallel. I have been reading Paul Fussell's "The Great War and Modern Memory." He notes that those who were there remembered the summer of 1914, the months just before the start of World War I, as the most beautiful of their lives. Bright, clear, stormless—no sign of the harrowing trenches just around the corner, of the 7,000 a day who would be wounded or killed on the Somme alone, among British troops alone. "All agree that the prewar summer was the most idyllic for many years. It was warm and sunny, eminently pastoral." For the great writers who would fight the war, it was carefree, innocent. Siegfried Sassoon "was busy fox hunting," Robert Graves climbing mountains in Wales, Wilfred Owen tutoring French boys in English near Bordeaux. "For the modern imagination that last summer has assumed the status of a permanent symbol for anything innocently but irrecoverably lost."

Like that beautiful September day, like dawn on September 11, 2001.

*   *   *

So that was my 9/11. The boy who returned, the world that was ended, the pictures that will never leave your mind. Like this one: A few weeks later I was pouring coffee for construction workers at St. Paul's church downtown and a guy came in and introduced himself. He was a member of the Iron Workers Local 40. They were dismantling the bottom of the Towers. He read my columns online, he said. He took his coffee and came back later and in his hand was a paper bag and in the bag were a heavy little heart and a heavy little cross, just cut from the North Tower. "I want you to have these," he said. As I write they are on my desk, in front of me, burnt and bent, but there.

A Masterpiece of a Museum

The Wall Street Journal: May 23, 2014

New York's new 9/11 museum is a masterpiece. It is the first big thing built to mark that day that is fully worthy of it.

It also struck me as a departure from a growing style among those who create and tend historic sites. That style involves the banishment of meaning—of the particular, of the real and tangible, even of the human. The plaques on landmarked buildings often tell us of the architectural school under which the edifice was created but little of the great man or woman born there. A few weeks ago, during a visit to the occasional residence of a former American president, a museum official noted with pride the lack of furniture—no chair the president sat in, or bureau he used. Such personal artifacts, she said, would only distract visitors from pondering the sublime greatness of the president's achievements. Absence creates a space in which the past can be fully contemplated.

Actually *presence* is likelier to prompt contemplation. Meaning matters; things that are real and tangible are moving. A single bullet dug from the ground of Gettysburg can tell you as much about what that battle was, the sheer bloody horror of it, as a chapter of a book. People know this naturally, which is why Gettysburg years ago had to stop people from digging around. They were tearing the place apart.

Physical reality is crucial in understanding history. The bullet says the battle was real.

The physicality of things is why people collect autographs: "His hand touched this, his eye considered this document." It's why Catholics keep relics of saints, why people collect mementos of all sorts. It's why it was so thrilling when they found the Titanic in 1985. "It was real, it all happened, there it is. There's the door of the grand salon."

The street-level World Trade Center memorial site—the gleaming buildings and reflective pools—seems to me part of the modern trend. There are no heroic statues, nothing to tell us what the firemen did. In the imagination of curators and historical custodians, the Higher Blankness gives us space in which to contemplate meaning. Instead we see emptiness and it feels... empty, bled of import.

But belowground the new museum is a masterpiece of particularity. Everything in it says the real and physical *does* matter, and what happened on that day—the facts of it, the meaning of it, who did what and how, who survived and died—matters.

It is a true history of the day and its aftermath. You see the ruined fire truck from Ladder Company 3. The helmet of a fireman. The red bandanna that Welles Crowther, a young equities trader, wore when he lost his life saving others in the South Tower. There are things picked from the debris like bullets from the field at Gettysburg: a woman's purse, her eyeglasses, the shoes a man wore as he fled the collapse. The early reports on TV, the "missing" posters, mass cards. The cross at Ground Zero, the votive candles, the tridents, the slurry wall, the survivors' staircase, which people in the buildings walked down to safety. And the posters and poems and banners and flags and funeral cards that were suddenly all over the city as New York, in the days and weeks after, began to come back.

What a relief to see history treated as something with meaning.

After I went a friend made a face and asked if it was sad. Amazingly enough, it was not. It was moving, stirring and at moments painful, but not sad. Because you are moved by it, you wind up with a mild case of what Tom Wolfe called information compulsion. You see something—a collection of papers that fluttered from the Towers as they burned—and it evokes a world of memory, and you find yourself saying aloud, "I remember," and, "That day I saw a man covered in ashes waiting patiently on line at my grocery uptown in the 90s—he'd made it all the way up and was standing there in ashes waiting to pay for a bottle of water."

Because the museum does not dodge reality but shows you what really happened, you wind up reflective. Contemplative in a way that blankness does not engender.

All of it is presented coherently, sensitively, intelligently—nothing vulgar or sentimental, nothing exploitative. The space itself is massive, which underscores the brute massiveness of the event. The lighting is intensely targeted but not harsh, just bright where it needs to be. Someone did beautiful sound design—turn this corner and you hear the EMT operators trying to deal with a flood of unbelievable data, turn that corner and it's the wailing bagpipes at a fireman's funeral.

It is all just so real, and done with such exquisite respect for the human beings who were there and wound up that day enmeshed in history.

The memorial and museum cost about $700 million combined. A press officer notes the nonprofit foundation that oversees both does not receive city, state or federal funding.

The admission price is high, $24 for adults. I mentioned this to a press representative who later noted that family members of those who died, and the families of rescue and recovery workers, are admitted free, and there are free hours for the public Tuesdays from 5 to 8 p.m.

There has been a controversy about the gift shop, which is said to be cheesy, and undignified. The criticism was led by local politicians who didn't like the T-shirts and jewelry, the NYPD dog vests and little bronze earrings.

I always sit up and listen when New York City pols call something crass, because they'd know, right?

But is the criticism fair? The Oklahoma City Memorial Museum, the Holocaust Museum, Gettysburg and other sites also have gift shops that sell trinkets and books. All are meant to support maintenance and operations, which at the 9/11 site will cost an estimated $60 million a year.

Gift shops also exist because people want something to remind them of the day and what they saw. When they buy something with "9/11" on it, they are remembering it, and asking you to remember, too. And cheesiness is in the eye of the beholder. When I was 10 or so I went to a historical museum and the gift shop sold cheap renderings of the Declaration of Independence and the Emancipation Proclamation. I bought them and taped them all over my room. I'd have bought Independence Hall earrings too if I could.

Kids like things that remind them of something important. So do grown-ups. Although I suppose we're all supposed to think big abstract thoughts and never indulge our need for the tangible, for something you can hold in your hand.

I'm sorry, but stop. You're in the middle of a masterpiece. The shop helps pay the bills. Leave it alone.

We're all so used to being disappointed at 9/11-related memorials that we think criticism must be the only legitimate response. At this point it's a reflex.

But the creators of the 9/11 museum should be deeply proud. Finally someone has created something worthy of the day.

Bravo.

CHAPTER 10

War

What the Intrepid Said

CBS News: August 6, 1982

(In the summer of 1982 the USS Intrepid came to the piers of the West Side of Manhattan as a museum. We wanted to do a "Dan Rather Reporting" on it. We aimed it at the children who would visit.)

* * *

The aircraft carrier the USS Intrepid—home from the sea, home from history. Docked now on the West Side of Manhattan and serving as a museum.

A reporter walked its decks, put his hand upon the turrets and saw the big guns. He listened to the lap-lap-lap of still water and in that sound he heard—oh, a trick of the imagination, a fancy—but in the lap-lap-lap of still water he thought he heard the ship. He thought, "I think it talks to me."

It says:

I am the Intrepid who stands in the moonlight grave and still. I am the Intrepid, fast carrier, Essex class.

Thirty years I sailed the sea. I knew the greatest battle in naval history. History lived within me. It lives within me still.

The Philippines, Formosa, Okinawa. Do you know those names? My planes covered the boys who held the beachheads. Some of them hold them still. I was hit by so many torpedoes, so many kamikazes, that they called me "The Unlucky I."

Now I am a monument.

Children run across my decks and squeal; I am like a strong old man. Children look at me and stare and ask "Oh what was it like?" What was it like...

Listen a moment. They commissioned me in '43 and sent me off with 3,000 boys. Farmboys and drugstore clerks now fliers and sailors. Boys don't have majesty but my boys did. It was the times. Across the world bad men did bad things and my boys went to sea to stop them.

They stopped them at the Battle of Leyte Gulf, the biggest battle in naval history. The Japanese sent three naval attack forces after us but we pounded away and pounded back and that was the beginning of the end of the Japanese.

Then that terrible day: 25 November '44. The day after Thanksgiving.

A rumble in the sky and the sound for general quarters and the men looked up and said O sweet Jesus and a kamikaze crashes into my flight deck and a kamikaze plows into the hangar and—My boys are down there, they're down there and the hangar explodes and it's an inferno and my boys die of smoke and fire.

All my lost boys!

I think sometimes I feel their presence.

Late at night when the moon is dull and the clouds are high—I hear their laughter, I feel their presence! There is movement within me. The shadows move.

And you there, child of '82, standing on my deck in your brand-new sneakers. A boy fell there. He was manning a five-inch gun and he was shooting and he fell, he fell where your shadow is! Walk softly there, boy: walk softly...

I am the Intrepid. I survived.

I cover a beachhead called memory, and tell you of my times.

I am the Intrepid.

History lived within me.

It lives within me still.

A Time for Grace

The Wall Street Journal: August 31, 2007

What will be needed this autumn is a new bipartisan forbearance, a kind of patriotic grace. This is a great deal to hope for. The president should ask for it, and show it.

Gen. David Petraeus, the commander of U.S. forces in Iraq, will report to Congress on Sept. 11. From the latest metrics, it's clear the surge has gained some ground. It is generally supposed that Gen. Petraeus will paint a picture of recent decreases in violent incidents and increases in safety. In another world, that might be decisive: It's working, hang on.

At the same time, it's clear that what we call Iraq does not wholly share U.S. objectives. We speak of it as a unitary country, but the Kurds are understandably thinking about Kurdistan, the Sunnis see an Iraq they once controlled but that no longer exists, and the Shia—who knows? An Iraq they theocratically and governmentally control, an Iraq given over to Iran? This division is reflected in what we call Iraq's government in Baghdad. Seen in this way, the non-latest-metrics way, the situation is bleak.

Capitol Hill doesn't want to talk about it, let alone vote on it. Lawmakers not only can't figure a good way out, they can't figure a good way through.

But we're going to have to achieve some rough consensus, because we're a great nation in an urgent endeavor. The process will begin with Gen. Petraeus's statement.

Particular atmospherics and personal dynamics are the backdrop to the debate. People are imperfect, and people in politics tend to be worse: "Politics is not an ennobling profession," as Bill Buckley once said. You'd better be pretty good going in, because it's not going to make you better. Politicians are individuals with a thirst for power, honors, and fame. When you think about that you want to say, "Oh dear." But of course "democracy is the worst form of government, except for all the others."

* * *

All sides in the Iraq debate need to step up, in a new way, to the characterological plate. From the pro-war forces, the surge supporters and those who supported the Iraq invasion from the beginning, what is needed is a new modesty of approach, a willingness to admit it hasn't quite gone according to plan. A moral humility. Not meekness—great powers aren't helped by meekness—but maturity, a shown respect for the convictions of others.

What we often see instead, lately, is the last refuge of the adolescent: defiance. An attitude of *Oh yeah? We're Lincoln, you're McClellan. We care about the troops and you don't. We care about the good Iraqis who cast their lot with us. You'd just as soon they hang from the skids of the last helicopter off the embassy roof.* They have been called thuggish. Is this wholly unfair?

The antiwar forces, the surge opponents, the "I was against it from the beginning" people are, some of them, indulging in grim, and mindless, triumphalism. They show a smirk of pleasure at bad news that has been brought by the other team. Some have a terrible, quaking fear that something good might happen in Iraq, that the situation might be at least to some degree redeemed. Their great interest is that Bushism be laid low and the president humiliated. They make lists of those who supported Iraq and who must be read out of polite society. Might these attitudes be called thuggish also?

Do you ever get the feeling that at this point Washington is run by two rival gangs that have a great deal in common with each other, including an essential lack of interest in the well-being of the turf on which they fight?

*   *   *

Not only hearts and minds are invested in a particular stand. Careers are, too. Candidates are invested in a position they took; people are dug in, caught. Every member of Congress is constrained by campaign promises: "We'll fight" or "We'll leave." The same for every opinion spouter—every pundit, columnist, talk show host, editorialist—all of whom have a base, all of whom pay a price for deviating from the party line, whatever the party, and whatever the line. All this freezes things. It makes immobile what should be fluid. It keeps people from *thinking*.

What is needed is simple maturity, a vow to look to—to care about—America's interests in the long term, a commitment to look at the facts as they are and try to come to conclusions. This may require in some cases a certain throwing off of preconceptions, previous statements and former stands. It would certainly require the mature ability to come to agreement with those you otherwise hate, and the guts to summon the help of, and admit you need the help of, the other side.

Without this, we remain divided, and our division does nothing to help Iraq, or ourselves.

It would be good to see the president calming the waters. Instead he ups the ante. Tuesday, speaking to the American Legion, he heightened his language. Withdrawing U.S. forces will leave the Middle East overrun by "forces of radicalism and extremism"; the region would be "dramatically transformed" in a way that could "imperil" both "the civilized world" and American security.

Forgive me, but Americans who oppose the war do not here understand the president to be saying: *Precipitous withdrawal will create a vacuum that will be filled by killing that will tip the world to darkness.* That's not what they hear. I think they understand him to be saying, *I got you into this, I reaped the early rewards, I rubbed your noses in it, and now you have to save the situation.*

His foes feel a tight-jawed bitterness. They believe it was his job *not* to put America in a position in which its security is imperiled; they resent his invitation to share responsibility for outcomes of decisions they opposed. And they resent it especially because he grants them nothing—no previous wisdom, no good intent—beyond a few stray words here and there.

And here's the problem. The president's warnings are realistic. He's right. At the end of the day we can't just up and leave Iraq. That would only make it worse. And it is not in the interests of America or the world that it be allowed to get worse.

* * *

Would it help if the president were graceful, humble, and asked for help? Why, yes. Would it help if he credited those who opposed him with not only good motives but actual wisdom? Yes. And if he tried it, it would make news. It would really, as his press aides say, break through the clutter.

I don't see how the president's supporters can summon grace from others when they so rarely show it themselves. And I don't see how anyone can think grace and generosity of spirit wouldn't help. They would. They always do in big debates. And they would provide the kind of backdrop Gen. Petraeus deserves, the kind in which his words can be heard.

The World the Great War Swept Away

The Wall Street Journal: August 8, 2014

In this centennial year of the Great War some things have not been said, or at least I haven't heard them. Among them:

All the smart people knew the war would never come. The continent to which war came was on such an upward trajectory in terms of prosperity, inventiveness and political culture that it could have become—it arguably already was—a jewel of civilization. And the common man who should have wept at the war's commencement instead cheered.

John Keegan went into these points in his classic history "The First World War," published in 1998.

His first sentence is beautiful in its simplicity: "I grew up with men who had fought in the First World War and with women who had waited at home for news of them." His father and uncles saw combat, his aunt was "one of the army of spinsters" the war produced.

His overall assessment is blunt: "The First World War was a tragic and unnecessary conflict." Leaders who lacked "prudence" and "good will" failed one after another to stop an eminently stoppable train of events that produced a conflagration. That was tragic not only in terms of loss of life, and psychological, physical, emotional and even spiritual injury to survivors, but because the war destroyed a rising, bettering world: "the benevolent and optimistic culture of the European continent." It of course also left "a legacy of political rancor and racial hatred so intense" that it guaranteed the world war that would follow 20 years later, which by Keegan's calculation was five times as destructive of human life. Auschwitz and the other extermination camps "were as much relics of the First as the Second world war." "They have their antecedents...in the fields where the trenches ran."

World War I didn't do nearly as much material damage as World War II. No big European city was destroyed in World War I, and the Eastern and Western fronts ran mostly through forests and farmlands, which were quickly returned to use at the war's end. "Yet it damaged civilization, the rational and liberal civilization of the European enlightenment, permanently for the worse and, through the damage done, world civilization also."

Prewar European governments, imperial ones included, paid formal and often practical respect "to the principles of constitutionalism, the rule of law and representative government." Confidence in those principles all but collapsed after the war: "Within fifteen years of the war's end, totalitarianism, a new word for a system that rejected the liberalism and constitutionalism which had inspired European politics since the eclipse of monarchy in 1789, was almost everywhere on the rise." To Russia came communism, to Germany Nazism, to Italy fascism and Spain Francoism. All these infections spread from a common wound: the dislocation and death of the Great War.

The world swept away had been a rising and increasingly constructive one, where total war was unimaginable: "Europe in the summer of 1914 enjoyed a peaceful productivity so dependent on international exchange and cooperation that a belief in the impossibility of general war seemed the most conventional of wisdoms."

Informed opinion had it that the disruption of international credit that would follow war "would either deter its outbreak or bring it speedily to an end." And the business of Europe was business. Industrial output was expanding; there were new goods and manufacturing opportunities, such as the production and sale of internal combustion machines. There were new profit centers, new sources of raw materials, including precious metals. Populations were increasing. Steamships and railways were revolutionizing transport. Capital was circulating. "Belgium, one of the smallest countries in Europe, had in 1914 the sixth largest economy in the world," thanks to early industrialization, new banking and trading methods, and industrial innovators.

Europe was increasingly international—independent nations were dealing and trading with each other. "Common Christianity—and Europe was overwhelmingly Christian by profession in 1914 and strongly Christian in observance also"—found frequent expression in philosophical and political pursuits, including the well-being of labor. Movements to restrict working hours and forbid the employment of children were going forward. European governments were spurred by self-protectiveness: Liberalized labor laws were a way to respond to and attempt to contain the power and appeal of Marxism.

"Europe's educated classes held much of its culture in common." They knew Mozart and Beethoven and grand opera. "Tolstoy was a European figure," as were Victor Hugo, Balzac, Zola, Dickens, Shakespeare, Goethe and Dante. High-school students in England were taught French, and French students German. Study of the classics remained universal, scholars from all the countries of Europe knew Homer, Thucydides, Caesar and Livy. All shared the foundational classics of philosophy, Aristotle and Plato.

Europe as a cultural entity was coherent and becoming more so. By the beginning of the 20th century tourism "had become a middle-class pleasure" because of railways and the hotel industry that followed.

But Europe was also heavily armed. All countries had armed forces, some large and costly ones led by influential, respected figures. What do armies in peacetime do? Make plans to kill each other just in case. Keegan: "[A] new era in military planning had begun; that of the making of war plans in the abstract, plans conceived at leisure...and pulled out when eventuality becomes actuality." What do soldiers who've made brilliant plans do? Itch to use them. Europe's armies came to see their jobs as "how to assure military advantage in an international crisis, not how to resolve it."

Soon enough they had their chance.

As you read of the war and its aftermath, you are always stopped by this fact: There is no recorded instance of masses of people gathering together to weep the day it was declared. They should have. The beautiful world they were day by day constructing was in jeopardy and ultimately would be consumed. Yet when people heard the news they threw their hats in the air, parading and waving flags in every capital. In Berlin "crowds thronged the streets shouting, cheering and singing patriotic songs." In London the same. In St. Petersburg thousands waved banners and icons. In Paris, as the city's regiments pushed off, "an immense clamour arose as the Marseillaise burst from a thousand throats."

Western Europe hadn't had a big and costly ground war since 1871. Maybe they forgot what war was. Surely some would have liked the drama and excitement—the interruption in normality, the break in the boring dailiness of life. Or the air of possibility war brings—of valor, for instance, and shown courage. Camaraderie, too, and a sense of romantic engagement with history. A sense of something to live for—victory.

Once a few years ago a reporter who had covered wars talked about this with a brilliant, accomplished, famously leftist editor in New York. At the end of a conversation on a recent conflict the reporter said, quizzically: "Why is there so much war? Why do we do that?"

"Because something's wrong with us," the editor replied.

I told him it was the best definition of original sin I'd ever heard.

A New Kind of "Credibility" Gap

The Wall Street Journal: September 20, 2013

Washington

An accomplished American diplomat once said that there are two templates of American foreign policy thinking. The first is Munich and the second is Vietnam.

When America does not move militarily as some people wish it to, they say, "This is another Munich"—appeasement that in the end will summon greater violence and broader war. When America moves militarily as some people do not wish it to, they say, "This is Vietnam"—jumping in where we do not belong and cannot win.

This is serviceable as a rough expression of where our foreign policy debates tend to go. But I suspect the past 12 years' experience in the Mideast has left us with a new template: "It's Chinatown," from the classic movie. This is where you try to make it better and somehow make it worse, in spite of your best efforts. This is a place where the biggest consequences are always unintended.

Surely this is part of the reason for the clear and quick public opposition to a U.S. strike in Syria, and it echoed in the attention paid to former Defense Secretary Robert Gates's statement this week that such a move "would be throwing gasoline on a very complex fire in the Middle East."

This week I spoke to a few U.S. senators about the meaning of the Syria drama. They were a mix—some had given supportive soundings early on; all had been taken aback by the public reaction, the wave of calls and emails. There was gossip. Apparently some White House staffers have a new nickname for the president: "Obam-me," because it's all about him and his big thoughts. I guess the second-term team is not quite as adoring as the first.

Two senators spoke of their worry about what the Syria mess—the threat, the climb down, the lunge at a lifeline, the face-saving interviews—signaled to the world about U.S. credibility. If an American president says there's a red line and the red line is crossed, there can be no question: America must act. No one said this but I think I correctly inferred a suggestion that the American people may not be willing right now to appreciate the fact that in a world full of bad guys the indispensable nation must show it is serious.

It seems to me U.S. credibility *is* a key issue in the Syria drama, but the problem is not that the U.S. public is newly unconcerned with it. The problem is that the public now sees the issue of U.S. credibility very differently from the way many lawmakers understand it.

For weeks I've been going back in my mind to a talk I had with a deeply accomplished, America-loving foreign policy expert. He, too, felt credibility was at issue. He said the other leaders of the world are no longer certain we are a great military power. I started to answer but someone joined us and the conversation turned. But I wanted to say no, the world thinks we are a great military power. They know all about the missiles and tanks and satellites, they've seen our soldiers. They know our might. The world is no longer certain we are a great *nation*, which is a different problem.

The world knows a lot about us, and in ways removed from specific military actions. Their elites come here, and increasingly their middle class. They know our unemployment problem—it's not a secret. They take the train from New York to Washington and see the abandoned factories. They know about our budget problems, they know who holds our bonds. They read about the kids who are bored so they killed the visiting Australian baseball player, and the kids so bored they killed a World War II veteran. They read about the state legislator who became a hero for defending late-term abortions—they see the fawning interviews. They go home with the story of the guy who spent his time watching violent videos and then, amazingly, acted out his visions of violence at the Washington Navy Yard. They notice our mass killings are no more than two-day stories.

And of course it isn't only "the world" that sees this—Americans see it. And they are worried about their country. Deep down they, too, wonder if we are still a great nation or will be able to remain one. They think our economy is in a shambles and our government incapable, at the moment, of creating the conditions that will allow it to come back. They fear our culture is rotting our children's heads.

And so, asked to support a strike that could spark a response that could start a real war, they say no, not now and not in Chinatown. But this is not a turning inward, it is not about fortress America. They do not think they are protecting an unsullied beacon of light from the machinations and manipulations of the cynical Old World. They have fewer illusions than their policy makers do!

They are not "armchair isolationists." If you've ever taken a walk in one of our cities or suburbs—if you've ever taken a walk in America—you know we have all the people in the world here. You can barely get them off the phone back home with Islamabad, Galway and Lagos. Longtime Americans deal every day, in the office and the neighborhood, with immigrants and others from every culture and country. And so many of the new Americans are trying desperately to adhere to America, to find reasons to adhere. They are not unaware of the larger world. They came from the larger world. They're trying to love where they are.

They know this place is in need of help and attention. They care about it. That impulse should be encouraged and lauded, not denigrated as narrow-minded or backward. They're trying to be practical. They're Americans trying to take stock in their nation and concluding: "We have got to get ourselves in order, we have got to turn our attention to getting stronger. Then we will be fully credible in the world."

What I am saying is that the old, Washington definition of credibility, which involves the projection of force in pursuit of ends it thinks necessary, and the American people's definition of credibility, which is to become stronger and allow the world, and the young, to understand you are getting stronger, are at variance. And that will have implications down the road.

The public's sense of U.S. credibility, and how it is best secured and projected, probably began to vary more broadly from Washington's when the Great Recession hit home, five years ago this week.

Political leaders have got to start twigging on to this. It's not as if it just happened. They can argue for any foreign military action they think necessary, but the American people will not be of a mind to support it until they think someone is really trying to clean up America.

A diplomat might say, "But the world will not go on vacation while America gets its act together!" True enough, and that fact will demand real shrewdness from America's leaders, who in the past few weeks got quite a lesson in how Americans on the ground view American priorities.

On Setting an Example

The Wall Street Journal: November 16, 2007

I thought I'd say a word for the Beaconists.

This election year we will, sooner or later, be asked to think about, and concentrate on, what American foreign policy should be in the future. We will have to consider, or reconsider, what challenges we face, what the world really is now after the Cold War and after 9/11, what is needed from America, and for her.

In some rough and perhaps tentative way we will have to decide what philosophical understanding of our national purpose rightly guides us.

Part of the debate will be shaped by the tugging back and forth of two schools of thought. There are those whose impulses are essentially interventionist—we live in the world and must take part in the world, sometimes, perhaps even often, militarily. We are the great activist nation, the spreader of political liberty, the superpower whose meaning is made clear in action.

The other school holds profound reservations about all this. It is more modest in its ambitions, more cool-eyed about human nature. It feels more bound by the old advice attributed to one of the Founding Generation, that we be the friend of liberty everywhere but the guarantor only of our own.

Much has changed in the more than two centuries since he said that: many wars fought, treaties made, alliances forged. And yet as simple human wisdom, it packs a wallop still.

Those who feel tugged toward the old Founding wisdom often

use the word "beacon." It is our place in the scheme of things, it is our fate and duty, to be a beacon of liberty. To stand tall and hold high the light. To be an example, to be an inspiration, to encourage. We do not invent constitutions and impose them on other countries; instead they, in their restlessness, in their human desire to achieve a greater portion of freedom, will rise up in time and create their own constitution. And because they created it, and because it reflects their conception of justice, they will hold it more dearly.

So we are best, in the world as it is now, the beacon, not the bringer, of freedom. We are its friend, not its enforcer.

As a foreign policy this sounds, or has been made to sound, unduly passive. *We'll sit around being a good example and the rest of them can take a hike.* But if you want to be a beacon, it's actually a hard job. It involves activism. You can't be a beacon unless as a nation you're in pretty good shape. You can't be a beacon unless you send forth real light. You can't be a beacon unless you really do inspire.

Do we always? No. We're not always a good example for the world. And so, for the coming holiday, a few baseline areas, some only stylistic, in which we could make our light glow brighter in— and for—the world.

* * *

It would be good to have the most visible symbols of our country, the president and the Congress, be clean. So often they seem not to be. They are scandal-ridden, or an embarrassment, or seem in the eyes of the world to be bought and paid for by special interests or unions or industries or professions. Whether you are liberal or conservative, you agree it is important that the world be impressed by America's leaders, by their high-mindedness and integrity. Leaders who are not dragged through the mud because they actually don't bring much mud with them. There is room for improvement here.

To be a beacon is to speak softly to the world, with dignity, with elegance if you can manage it, or simple good-natured courtesy if you can't. A superpower should never shout, never bray "We're No. 1!" If you're No. 1, you don't have to.

To be a beacon is to have a democracy in which issues of actual import are regularly debated. Instead our political coverage consists of daily disquisitions on "targeted ads," "narratives," "positioning" and "talking points." We really do make politicians crazy. If a politician cares only about his ads and his rehearsed answers, the pundits call him inauthentic. But if a politician ignores these things to speak of great issues, we say he lacks "fire in the belly" and is incompetent. So many criticisms of politicians boil down to: He's not manipulating us well enough! We need more actual adults who are actually serious about the business of the nation.

To be a beacon is to keep the economic dream alive. We're still good at this. The downside is the rise in piggishness that tends to accompany prosperity. It is not good to embarrass your nation with your greed. It disheartens those who are doing their best but are limited, or unlucky, or just haven't made it work yet. It is good when you have it not to keep it all but to help the limited, and unlucky, and those who just haven't made it work yet. Keep it going, Porky.

To be a beacon is to continue another thing we're good at, making the kind of citizens who go into the world and help it: the doctors, the scientists, the nurses. They choose to go and help. The world notices, and says, "These are some kind of people, these Americans."

To be a beacon is to support the creation of a culture that is not dark, or sulfurous, or obviously unwell. We introduce our culture to our new immigrants each day through television. Just for a moment, imagine you are a young person from Africa or South America, a new American. You come here and put on the TV, for even the most innocent know that TV is America and America is TV, and you want to learn quickly. What you see is an obvious and embarrassing obsession with sex, with violence, with sexual dysfunction. You see the routine debasement of women parading as the liberation of women.

*   *   *

Conservatives have wrung their hands over this for a generation. But really, if you are a new immigrant to our country, full of hope, animated in part by some sense of mystery about this country that has lived in your imagination for 20 years, you have got to think: *This is it? This ad for erectile dysfunction? Oh, I have joined something that is not healthy.*

Sad to think this. They want to have joined a healthy and vibrant and well-balanced nation, not a sick circus.

I haven't even touched upon poverty, the material kind and the spiritual kind. I haven't touched on a lot. But if we were to try harder to be better, if we were to try harder to be and seem as great as we are, we wouldn't have to bray so much about the superiority of our system. It would be obvious to all, as obvious as a big light in the darkness.

To be a brighter beacon is not to choose passivity, or follow a path of selfishness. It would take energy and commitment and thought. We've always had a lot of that.

A happy Thanksgiving to all who love the great and fabled nation that is still, this day, the hope of the world.

Can the Republican Party Recover from Iraq?

The war almost killed the GOP. Whether it can come back is yet to be seen.

The Wall Street Journal: March 21, 2013

The air has been full of 10th-anniversary Iraq war retrospectives. One that caught my eye was a smart piece by Tom Curry, national affairs writer for NBC News, who wrote of one element of the story, the war's impact on the Republican Party: "The conflict not only transformed" the GOP, "but all of American politics."

It has, but it's an unfinished transformation.

Did the Iraq war hurt the GOP? Yes. The war, and the crash of '08, half killed it. It's still digging out, and whether it can succeed is an open question.

Here, offered in a spirit of open debate, is what the war did to the GOP:

- *It ruined the party's hard-earned reputation for foreign affairs probity.* They started a war and didn't win it. It was longer and costlier by every measure than the Bush administration said it would be. Before Iraq, the GOP's primary calling card was that it was the party you could trust in foreign affairs. For half a century, throughout the Cold War, they were serious about the Soviet Union, its moves, feints and threats. Republicans were not ambivalent about the need for and uses of American power, as the Democrats were in the 1970s and 1980s,

but neither were they wild. After Iraq, it was the Republicans
who seemed at best the party of historical romantics or, alter-
natively, the worst kind of cynic, which is an incompetent
one. Iraq marked a departure in mood and tone from past
conservatism.

- *It muddied up the meaning of conservatism and bloodied up its
  reputation.* No Burkean prudence or respect for reality was
  evident. Ronald Reagan hated the Soviet occupation of the
  Warsaw Pact countries—really, hated the oppression and violence. He said it, named it and forced the Soviets to defend
  it. He did not, however, invade Eastern Europe to liberate it.
  He used military power sparingly. He didn't think the right
  or lucky thing would necessarily happen. His big dream was a
  nuclear-free world, which he pursued daringly but peacefully.

- *It ended the Republican political ascendance that had begun in
  1980.* This has had untold consequences, and not only in foreign affairs. And that ascendance was hard-earned. By 2006
  Republicans had lost the House, by 2008 the presidency. Mr.
  Curry quotes National Review's Ramesh Ponnuru at a recent
  debate at the American Enterprise Institute: "You could make
  the argument that the beginning of the end of Republican
  dominance in Washington was the Iraq War, at least a stage
  of the Iraq War, 2005–06." In 2008 a solid majority of voters said they disapproved of the war. Three-quarters of them
  voted for Barack Obama.

- *It undermined respect for Republican economic stewardship.* War
  is costly. No one quite knows or will probably ever know the
  exact financial cost of Iraq and Afghanistan, which is interesting in itself. Some estimates put it at $1 trillion, some $2
  trillion. Mr. Curry cites a Congressional Budget Office report
  saying the Iraq operation had cost $767 billion as of Janu-
  ary 2012. Whatever the number, it added to deficits and debt

and, along with the Bush administration's domestic spending, helped erode the Republican Party's reputation for sobriety in fiscal affairs.

- *It quashed debate within the Republican Party.* Political parties are political; politics is about a fight. The fight takes place at the polls and in debate. But the high stakes and high drama of the wars—and the sense within the Bush White House that it was fighting for our very life after 9/11—stoked an atmosphere in which doubters and critics were dismissed as weak, unpatriotic, disloyal. The GOP—from top, the Washington establishment, to bottom, the base—was left festering, confused and, as the years passed, lashing out. A conservative movement that had prided itself, in the 1970s and 1980s, on its intellectualism—"Of a sudden, the Republican Party is the party of ideas," marveled New York's Democratic Sen. Pat Moynihan in 1979—seemed no longer capable of an honest argument. Free of internal criticism, national candidates looked daffy and reflexively aggressive—John McCain sang "Bomb, Bomb Iran"—and left the party looking that way, too.
- *It killed what remained of the Washington Republican establishment.* This was not entirely a loss, to say the least. But establishments exist for a reason: They're supposed to function as the Elders, and sometimes they're actually wise. During Iraq they dummied up—criticizing might be bad for the lobbying firm. It removed what credibility the establishment had. And they know it.

* 　 * 　 *

All this of course is apart from the central tragedy, which is the human one—the lost lives, the wounded, the families that will now not be formed, or that have been left smaller, and damaged.

Iraq and Afghanistan have ended badly for the Republicans, and the party won't really right itself until it has candidates for national office who can present a new definition of what a realistic and well-grounded Republican foreign policy is, means and seeks to do. That will take debate. The party is now stuck more or less in domestic issues. As for foreign policy, they oppose Obama. In the future more will be needed.

Many writers this week bragged about their opposition to the war, or defended their support of it. I'm not sure what good that does, but since I'm calling for debate, here we go.

I had questions about an invasion until Colin Powell testified before the U.N. in February 2003. In a column soon after: "From the early days of the debate I listened to the secretary of state closely and with respect. I was glad to see a relative dove in the administration. It needed a dove. Mr. Powell's war-hawk foes seemed to me both bullying and unrealistic. Why not go slowly to war? A great nation should show a proper respect for the opinion of mankind, it should go to the world with evidence and argument, it should attempt to win allies. A lot of people tracked Mr. Powell's journey, and in a way took it with him. Looking back I think I did, too."

Mr. Powell told the U.N. Saddam Hussein must be stopped and asserted that Iraq had developed and was developing weapons of mass destruction. That turned out not to be true.

But I believed it, supported the war and cheered the troops. My break came in 2005, with two columns that questioned Mr. Bush's thinking, his core premises and assumptions, as presented in his second Inaugural Address. That questioning in time became sharp criticism, accompanied by a feeling of estrangement. In the future I would feel a deeper skepticism toward both parties.

So that was my Iraq, wronger than some at the start, righter than some at the end, and not shocked by the darkening picture I saw when I went there in 2011.

Henry Kissinger said recently that he had in his lifetime seen America enthusiastically enter four wars and struggle in the end to end each of them.

Maybe great nations do not learn lessons, they relearn them.

I called for a serious Republican debate on its foreign policy, but the Democrats need one, too. What's their overarching vision? Do they have a strategy, or only sentiments?

There's a lot of Republican self-criticism and self-examination going on. What about the Democrats'?

What America Thinks about Iraq

The Wall Street Journal: June 20, 2014

"The past is never dead. It's not even past."

We are back to 2003 (the invasion), 2007 (the surge) and 2011 (the withdrawal).

How does the American public view what is going on in Iraq now—the burgeoning war, the fall to ISIS of cities we fought for and held, the possible fall of Baghdad and collapse of the country? What attitude and approach will the public support in response?

Here is my sense of it:

They believe going in was a disaster.

They believe getting out is producing a disaster.

They believe the leadership in Washington failed in both cases, in the going in and the getting out.

They think George W. Bush made the wrong call and followed with the wrong execution. As for those around him, they had no realistic plan for what would happen after they toppled Saddam Hussein and seem to have thought George Washington would spring from the rubble and take it from there. There was no sophisticated and realistic game plan. American officials did not seem to know there was a difference between a Sunni and a Shia. They were frequently taken aback by events that were predictable. They assumed good luck, a terrible, ignorant thing to assume in a war.

The American people believe Barack Obama viewed Iraq as a personal political problem. He won the presidency being antiwar, so he had to anti-the-war before his reelection. He did it without appropriate care and commitment, which probably guaranteed we'd wind up where we are. He is out of his depth. Amazingly, he radiates a sense that he isn't all that invested, that he doesn't drag himself to the golf course to get a break and maintain balance, but plays golf because at the end of the day Iraq, like other problems, challenges and scandals, isn't making him bleed inside.

And the people don't like any of this. Americans hate incompetence, but most of all and in a separate class they hate *bloody* incompetence. They've seen it now from two administrations.

The bright spot: the earnest professionalism of our troops, still unsurpassed.

But the loss of life, the financial cost, the loss of prestige, the sense that somehow after 9/11 we squandered the sympathy and support of the world, the danger to the world when America gets beat or looks beat, the inspiration that is to evil-minded men—these things the American people would hate.

They do not believe the architects of Iraq told them the full truth in the past or are candid and forthcoming even now, more than 11 years after the invasion. The architects do not speak of what they got wrong and exactly how, when and why. Their blame-laying sounds less like strength than spin. They are like what Talleyrand is said to have observed of the Bourbons, that they have learned nothing and forgotten nothing. Because of this they are not fully credible when they critique the current president and not fully believable when they offer new strategies.

When you have been catastrophically wrong, you have to bring a certain humility to the table.

The American people do not want to go back into Iraq. They will be skeptical of all plans, strategies and decisions because they lack faith in their leaders. If they hear "We are sending 300 military advisers," they will think: *It won't end there.*

They don't think the U.S. can solve Iraq. They think only Iraq can do that.

They think Iraq's leader, Nouri al-Maliki, is a loser who lives in Loserville. Get rid of him? Tell him to resign? Sure, but who will replace him, the loser next door? Should he reform his government, making it more respectful, tolerant and accountable? Sure. But do the ISIS forces look like men who'll respond, "Wow, he's being a better leader, let's lay down our arms!"? No, actually, they don't.

Americans are worried about the country's standing in the world. They want to be the most powerful and respected nation in the world, because we are Americans and that's how we roll.

They have the feeling that what America has to do now, the missing part of the terrible puzzle, is to rebuild here, refind our strength, be rich again, pump out jobs, unleash our energy—let it bound out of the ground and help turn our economy around. We have to reset our relationship with *ourselves*. We have to become strong again—that is the key not only to our confidence but to the world's respect.

Here's a terrible thing, though: They don't really have any faith that this remedial work will get done, that the economy will be reignited, that corrupt governance and crony capitalism will be stopped. They don't have any particular faith that it will happen with the generation of losers we have now in Washington.

They do not think the bad guys will wait and pause while America says, "Excuse me, I need time to get my act together. Could you present your existential challenge later?"

They think the fighting in Iraq will likely continue and spread. They think a lot of violent extremists will kill a lot of violent extremists, and many good and innocent people, too. It always happens. It's one of the reasons war is terrible.

They know something is wrong with their thinking, that it's not fully satisfying but instead marked by caveats and questions.

If the oil we need is truly endangered, and this tips us into a new recession...

If daily we see shootings and beheadings of people who bravely and kindly stood with us during the war...

All that will have a grinding, embittering effect on the public mood. And if some mad group of jihadists, when their bloody work in Iraq is finished, decide to bring their efforts once again to an American city—well then, obviously, all bets will be off.

But the old American emotionalism, the assumption that the people of Iraq want what we want, freedom and democracy, is over. Ten years ago if you announced you had reservations about what the people of Iraq really want, and maybe it isn't freedom and democracy first, such reservations were called ethnocentric, belittling, bigoted. That's over, too. We are hard-eyed now.

In the long term, the U.S. experience in Iraq will probably contribute to the resentment, the sheer ungodly distance and lack of trust and faith between the people who are governed in America and those who govern them, between the continent and the city called Washington. Also between the people and the two great political parties, both of which blundered.

Pundits and pollsters have been talking about a quickening of the populist spirit, and the possibility of a populist rise, for at least a quarter century. But they're doing it more often now.

There is a growing disconnect between the American people and their government, a freshened resentment. We are not only talking about Iraq when we talk about Iraq, we are also talking about ourselves. We are not only talking about the past, we are talking about the future.

The architects of the Iraq invasion always said the decision to invade was crucial, consequential, a real world-changer. They had no idea.

CHAPTER 11

What I Saw at the Evacuation

Is there more to be said about Ronald Reagan? Yes, always, and history won't stop talking about him any more than it has any other big president. Here are some looks at the meaning of his life and reactions to his death.

* * *

Russia, the Big Picture

The Wall Street Journal: April 2, 2014

People sometimes ask "What would Reagan think?" and "What would Reagan do?" I don't understand this and tend not to play. How would I know, how would you? He was a man of his time and place who responded to the great questions of his day. He could be surprising—actually he was both constant and surprising. The famous cold warrior who spiked defense spending worried fairly constantly about nuclear weapons and was willing to gamble all to get rid of them at Reykjavik.

Also he was human, and you can never calculate with complete certainty what a human would do.

Mostly I steer clear because the question is both frivolous and, around the edges, sad. "What would FDR do?" "What would JFK do?" "Only Lincoln's wisdom will suffice." Boo hoo. This is nostalgia as an evasive tool. You're alive, what would *you* do?

But the past few weeks I've been witness to many discussions of Russia at gatherings of American diplomats, journalists and historians, and taken part in interviews with experts and foreign policy thinkers. I am coming to conclude that almost everyone is missing the headline and focusing instead on a factoid in the seventh or tenth graf. Journalists pound diplomats with questions about U.S. sanctions, as if they believe the right one will do the trick and solve the problem. Diplomats dilate on the last Kerry-Lavrov meeting, or the next, or the credibility and potential impact of the Kiev government's most recent accusation.

One sophisticated observer will muse aloud about the Russian government for the first time really starting to clamp down on the Internet, while another will mention offhandedly the high state of Russian nationalist feeling—and anti-U.S. feeling—among politicians and the press in Moscow. But they don't seem to understand the implications of their observations.

The American leadership class has taken on a certain ship-of-fools aspect when it comes to Russia. They are missing the essential story.

So the other night I was walking from a gathering when a writer and academic, a smart, nice man, turned to me and said, softly, "How do you think Reagan would view what is going on? How do you think he'd see all this?" And I surprised myself by answering.

*   *   *

I said that what people don't understand about Reagan is that his self-concept in the first 40 years of his life, meaning the years in which you really become yourself, was as an artist. Not a political leader or an economist, not a geostrategist, but an artist. I saw this when I went through his papers at the Reagan Library. As a boy and young man he was a short story writer, a drawer of pictures, then an actor. He acted in college, went into broadcasting and then went on to act professionally. He paid close attention to script, character, the shape of the story. He came to maturity and middle age in Hollywood, which was full of craftsmen and artists, and he respected them and was one of them.

He cared about politics and came to see himself as a leader when he was immersed in Screen Actors Guild politics, and later led that union.

But he, to himself, was an artist.

And the thing about artists is they try to see the picture whole. They try to get the big shape of things. They're creative, intuitive. Someone once said a great leader has more in common with an artist than an economist, and it's true. An artist has imagination, tries to apprehend the full sweep of what's happening. An actor understands what moment you're in in the drama.

And so with that as context, I said, this is how I think Reagan would view the moment we're in:

The Soviet Union fell almost a quarter century ago. It was great news, a victory for civilization. That fall was followed by something: a series of Russian governments trying to maintain stability and pick up the pieces, turning toward democracy, toward modernity, really going for a non-state-dominated economy. Russian leaders were to some significant degree accommodating to the West, which had vanquished them. They engaged in reconstruction on many fronts, reinvention, too. They moved in varying degrees toward Western values.

Again, it lasted almost a quarter century.

Now it is over.

That history has ended and something new has begun. Now we are in an era so new we don't even have a name for it. Maybe we'll call it "Putinism," maybe "Cold War II," who knows—but it's brand new and it's different from the past not only in tone but in nature, character and, presumably, intent.

Vladimir Putin is in control. The state is increasingly entwined with him. We don't know how much autonomy he has, as Richard Haass of the Council on Foreign Relations noted the other day. But we have to assume it is significant. We know he is not only in charge but popular, and the tougher he is, the more popular he appears to be. (A real question: Will Russian democracy itself survive this new era? We will find out in the next few years.) A spirit of nationalism is rising, and that nationalism may contribute in time to a feeling of blood in the air. The Russian government is clamping down on the press, on free speech.

The Russian government isn't trying to please us or work with us anymore. Mr. Putin has formally set himself as our antagonist.

Something big got broken here. It will have worldwide implications, and be a major foreign policy challenge for the United States in the coming years.

But we are in a new time and will have to plan anew and think anew.

That is how I think the artist formerly known as Reagan would judge what's happening. He'd see it clear and figure it from there. He wouldn't think it was about sanctions and tweeted insults.

*   *   *

I would add that to create a new strategy we will not only have to see Mr. Putin clearly. We will have to consider—honestly—what steps and missteps, what assumptions and attitudes, led to this moment not only there, but here. We will have to figure out how the new moment can be nonviolently countered. This in turn will require being honest about ourselves—who we are, what we need and what we want—and our allies, and their particular character and imperatives. It would be good to remember it is not 1950. That, truly, was another world.

It is my opinion that Reagan wouldn't be alarmist because there's no use in alarm. At the same time he'd be serious as a heart attack about what has happened and what it implies. Being serious would not involve putting down Russia as a merely regional power, as President Obama recently did. No nuclear power is merely regional. If Putin were merely regional, he wouldn't have been able to save Obama's bacon in Syria.

I do think Reagan would be startled—that isn't quite the word, because it doesn't encompass a sense of horror—that it clearly won't be the American president leading the West through the start of the new era, but a German chancellor.

That, actually, would have taken him aback.

Why We Talk about Reagan

The Wall Street Journal: February 8, 2002

A small band of former aides and friends of Ronald Reagan were all over TV this week talking about the former president on his 91st birthday. Our memories and reflections were treated with thoughtfulness and respect by the media. It wasn't always this way but I'm glad it is now, and I think there are reasons for it.

Journalists feel an honest compassion for Mr. Reagan's condition—everyone is saddened by the thought that this great man who was once so much a part of our lives no longer knows he was great, no longer remembers us. It's big enough to be called tragic: this towering figure so reduced by illness. Part of it, too, is a growing appreciation of Nancy Reagan, who is doing now what she did for 50 years, protecting him, protecting his memory and his privacy. Only now she does it 24-7 at the age of 78, and without the help and comfort of the best friend of her life: him. She told me some months ago how to this day she'll think of something and want to say "Honey, remember the time..." Or something will happen and she'll want to ask him what he thinks. And of course she can't.

* * *

It is also true—I am sorry to be cynical, but I have worked in media, have enjoyed and even shared its cynicism—that the hungry maw of every network and cable news show is hoping, on the day the former president leaves us, to get the Get. To get Mrs. Reagan on the air, or the former president's children, or his associates in history. The more

sympathetic they are now, the better the chance they'll get the Big
Get. And this is understandable. It's what news people want to do:
Get the story.

Whatever the reasons, it's good to see Mr. Reagan's memory
held high by those who admire and understand him, and have the
arguments for his greatness heard with respect in the media.

But let me tell you why we make those arguments as often as
we can. When I talk about Mr. Reagan, media people often preface
my remarks, or close them, with words like this: "You adore him."
Or, "You of course have great affection for him and so it's your view
that…"

These are not unfriendly words, but they're a warning to the
viewer: Take what you hear with a grain of salt. Needless to say the
grain-of-salt warning doesn't come when the subject is, say, JFK or
FDR or Martin Luther King, all of whom had friends, supporters
and biographers who have spent decades advancing their causes with
affection and respect.

And that's why those of us who talk about Mr. Reagan talk
about Mr. Reagan, why we stick to the subject. After he leaves us
the media may well conclude that they have no particular reason to
listen politely when we speak of him. So we do it now.

And we do it because history is watching. Because young people
are coming up. Because new generations rise and look at the past
and think: Who was great, who was worthy of emulation, who can I
learn from? Children whose parents have not for whatever reason led
them or nurtured them sufficiently sometimes feel a particular need
to look at the historical past and think: Who can I learn from there
as I try to put together a good life?

Who indeed. There is something the past few days I've found
difficult to communicate on TV, in part because it sounds pretentious in the chatty atmosphere of the newsnook, but it's at the heart
of what I'm trying to say. Laurens van der Post, in a memoir of his

relationship with Carl Jung, said that we all forget the obvious: "We live not only our own lives but, whether we know it or not, also the life of our time." We add to that larger life or detract; we give or withhold, we lead or shrink back, we put ourselves on the line for the truth or we ignore the summons, we meet the great challenge of our age or we retreat to our gardens. It is not bad to tend your garden, and is in fact necessary; you can find wholeness, solace and truth there, too. But to tend it and also step forward into history, to step into the life of your age, to step onto history's stage and seek to take part constructively, to try to make your era better—that is a very great thing. And that is what Mr. Reagan did, and successfully. He helped his world.

* * *

Ronald Reagan's old foes, the political and ideological left, retain a certain control of the words and ways by which stories are told. They run the academy, the media; they control many of the means by which the young—that nice, strong 20-year-old boy walking down the street, that thoughtful girl making some money by yanking the levers of the coffee machine at Starbucks—will receive and understand history.

But the academy and the media may not in time tell Mr. Reagan's story straight; and if they do not tell the truth it will be for the simple reason that they cannot see it. They have been trained in a point of view. It's hard to break out of your training.

Those of us who lived in and feel we understood the age of Ronald Reagan have a great responsibility: to explain and tell and communicate who he was and what he did and how he did it and why. Where he came from and what it meant that he came from there. What it meant, for instance, that he came from the political left, was trained in it and then left it—for serious reasons, reasons as serious as life gets. And: what it cost him to stand where he stood. That is always one of the great questions of history, of the story of a political or cultural figure—"What did it cost him to stand where he stood?" You learn a lot when you learn the cost.

If we don't tell the young they'll never know.

That is why we don't let the subject pass. It's too rich with meaning. To speak of Mr. Reagan honestly, to speak of his fabled life and his flaws, is to make a contribution to the young, who 10 and 20 and 40 years from now will be running history and who will need lives on which to pattern their own, lives from which to draw strength.

The young could do worse. The young often have.

What I Saw at the Evacuation

Reagan's Funeral, Part 3
The Wall Street Journal: June 24, 2004

June 9, 2004, approximately 5 p.m., U.S. Capitol

What I was thinking was: Everyone here brought their souls. We are all these physical repositories of ourselves, of our characters and personalities and ambitions. But everybody is a soul, has a soul, and all these people gathered for the funeral of the great man of their lives, and they brought their souls.

I tell you this because it somehow has to do with what followed.

Many, not all, were aging or old. They had run the country 20 and 30 years ago. They had lived lives of import and meaning. But they were not this afternoon their official selves, their old formal selves, but something else.

* * *

We were in the Mansfield Room, just off the Capitol Rotunda, a big tall gold-trimmed room ringed with old oil portraits of great men—Jefferson, Adams. The ones who made their country. As I stood near the entrance looking out at them, I had a visual memory of a book party long ago, in 1990 I think, in the sizable outdoor yard of William Safire's house in suburban Maryland. It was late springtime or early summer. A sudden breeze came up, strong and out of nowhere, and hundreds, thousands, of small petals and pieces of pollen filled the air and fell upon our heads. Like a benediction. It seemed barely noticed by the busy talkers, who laughed and shook their heads and continued talking. But it was beautiful. God is here.

At the Capitol, there were 100 or so of us in the room, friends and colleagues and coworkers of Ronald Reagan. Air Force One would soon bring back to Washington his flag-draped coffin. From Andrews Air Force Base a cortege would take him to the Capitol. The senators and congressmen were already massing in the Rotunda, where they would receive him. There would be a ceremony, and speeches. Then the politicians would leave, and the friends and colleagues of Ronald Reagan would depart the Mansfield Room to enter the Rotunda and say goodbye to the old man we loved, and loved in a way, some of us, that we didn't even understand until we saw the coffin.

In that room, the Mansfield Room, there was a lot of laughing and remembering. "Remember the time...?" "Were you here when they put Jack Kennedy to rest?" Over here Jack and Joanne Kemp, leaders of the 1970s revolution that became part of the '80s revolution. Richard Allen, Reagan's first national security adviser. Judge William Clark, his second. Ed and Ursula Meese, who were there from the early days, in California. Paul and Carol Laxalt—Paul was a senator from Nevada, part of the Western rebellion that lit the country in the 1970s, Carol bubbly as champagne. Jim Miller, Reagan's budget director, still a big serious man in a big serious suit, and his wife. Bill Bennett, Reagan's education secretary, and his wife, Elayne.

Jeane Kirkpatrick, dignified, gutsy, with great cheekbones and still-saucy or potentially saucy eyes. Somewhere along the way, I have always felt, she made a decision. She chose to follow the academic and analytical part of her nature—"There is a difference between totalitarian governments and authoritarian governments and we must acknowledge it"—and not perhaps other parts of her inner self, parts perhaps less definitive and constructive and perhaps more merry. But that kind of decision was true of a lot of people there, and always is when leaders are gathered. The pope felt the promptings of an artist, and followed another call. Life is options up to a point, and then it's decisions made.

Ann Dore McLaughlin, Reagan's labor secretary, and her husband, Tom Korologos, just back from Iraq for George W. Bush. They stood together looking beautiful. A late marriage; they glowed. Al Haig and his wife. I am fascinated by Mr. Haig. Portrayed as rather too intense in Oliver Stone's cinematically dazzling and historically demented "Nixon," Mr. Haig did in fact help run the government as the Nixon administration ended, and helped talk him into resigning when that was the right thing to do for the country. He earned his pride. By the time he was Ronald Reagan's secretary of state it was clear he did not enjoy what might be called creative chaos in foreign affairs, and his pride at that point was such that he regularly threatened to resign. Reagan was patient, for a while. And then Mr. Haig was gone, and George Shultz, standing right over there, took his place.

Tricia Nixon Cox, her husband, Ed, and their son, grown taller now than his father, were there. I said hello. She is a New Yorker, as were many in the group. Her father was the last president before Reagan to die. He did not have a state funeral. He was buried instead in relative quiet, in his beloved California. He had been the first and only president to resign from office, and thought putting the country through a state funeral was the wrong thing to do. In 1960 he had refused to contest an eminently contestable presidential election because he didn't want to put the country through it, he felt it was the wrong thing to do. Richard Nixon, even when portrayed compassionately, is shown bathed in sweat and resentment. But he had a class—a patriotism—that has not been appreciated and understood. I said to Tricia that I would never forget the last time I saw her father, in a news clip on television, sobbing great racking sobs at the funeral of his wife, Patricia. I had been taken aback by his heartbreak. "Thank you," Tricia said. "It's really not known—no one knows how much he loved her, and what a good marriage they had. He adored my mother." It is a wonderful thing to know that about your parents.

Dan and Marilyn Quayle were sitting over there—he grayer and she unaged, with short, chic hair. Their son studied in China and married a Chinese girl. Everyone talks about globalization and immigration, and these are fine abstractions, but the Quayle family is now part Chinese and the Bush family is part Mexican, and maybe you think that means nothing but it means plenty. Over here in a corner Sen. Pete Domenici watched the TV monitors waiting for Air Force One to land with the Reagans at Andrews. He had tears in his eyes. They were the only unexpected tears I saw that day.

Over here the great Hugh Sidey, historian of presidents, tall and gray. And Gahl Burt, former social secretary for Nancy Reagan and former wife of Richard Burt, of the famous-in-the-'80s two Richards. Richard Burt was at State (squishy! soft! an establishment-loving undersecretary for George Shultz), and Richard Perle was at Defense (hard-liner! prince of darkness! right-wing nut!). I watched them both in those days. They had quite a bureaucratic war. And you know what? They were a good team. Maybe they fought each other, but they were a good team, as pragmatist Jim Baker and conservative Ed Meese were a good team, and conservative William Clark and pragmatist Mike Deaver. You know why? Because it all worked. Life is a mess and nothing is perfect and there were zigs that should have zagged, and no one got everything he wanted, but it all worked, and the country profited. You need 20 years of looking back to figure this out.

It was such a coming together.

*   *   *

I was standing looking out the big entranceway toward an arched and high-ceilinged hall. There a beautiful young man in a white jacket was giving my son a ginger ale from a small bar just beyond the doorway. My son—6 feet tall, in his first suit, with a sober tie and cuff links, also his first—was taking the plastic cup of ginger ale in his hand and talking to a very beautiful woman, Blaine Trump, down from New York with her husband, Robert. I saw them say hello, saw my son take the ginger ale, when a rude man rushed by and knocked the glass from his hand.

Only he wasn't a rude man. He was a frightened man, and he was trying to save our lives.

The man walked quickly and heavily and placed himself in the huge doorway of the Mansfield Room. He had on a brown wool sports jacket.

"Excuse me! Excuse me!" he barked. The old lions in that room looked at him and turned away. They thought him a functionary sent to tell us the body would soon land in Andrews. They continued talking.

"Quiet! Quiet!" He was ordering us now. I was standing just to his left, and when he said "Quiet" the second time I looked at him. His voice was under control and his face was inexpressive, but his carotid artery, just above his collar, was pounding. As this thought registered—something is wrong—he said, "We are evacuating the Capitol! Now! This is not an exercise! We are evacuating. Leave the Capitol. Now."

My eyes met my son's and I gave him the chin up-deadeye look that parents give children to say: I'm coming.

I walked through the doorway and took his arm. In the halls there was running and shouting, scores of people rushing by. Someone in a uniform called out, "Incoming unidentified aircraft, 60 seconds out."

We were moving now, down the hall and toward an exit onto the great Capitol steps. There someone called, "Aircraft incoming." George and Charlotte Shultz were behind me, Joan Rivers was over there with Tommy Corcoran. You never know who you'll die with.

As we moved down the Capitol steps a guard yelled "Run for your lives! Ladies, take off your shoes, run for your lives! Go north. North!"

Ed Meese ran with two new knees—he'd just had replacement surgery. Oatsie Charles, a great Washington social figure, a friend to all for a long time, was in a wheelchair pushed by her grandson Nick, who is at the Georgetown School of Foreign Service. When they got to the Capitol steps two cops stood at each side of the wheelchair, picked her up and carried her down the long steps.

I said to my son, "Hold my hand and don't let go, we can't get separated." About halfway down the steps I suddenly wanted to share some thoughts on history. I slowed a little. I was very angry to be driven from our Capitol by terror scum. My son was, too, and said of them words boys don't normally say in front of their mothers. I wanted to speak to him about the vagaries of history, how it is a wonderful and exciting thing but there are moments when it gives you agita. I literally said "agita," a word I don't use much, a word from my childhood listening to the Italians next door. I had slowed my descent, and people were rushing past. This is when a generational transfer of power occurred within my family.

My son turned to me and in a tone both soft and commanding he said, "Mom: Move it."

And I realized: Yes, son, of course, this is no time for a disquisition. We ran to the bottom of the steps and toward the street. By now I was thinking that perhaps 60 seconds had passed. I was also thinking: These things are not exactly precise. I thought: *I did not expect when I put on my shoes this morning that I might die in them today. I thought: Medium-sized plane, an imperfect hit—our guys are scrambling up there now. Above the Dome—we will get it, and it will come down. But if a medium-sized plane hits the Capitol grounds, exactly what happens? That is, how wide the conflagration? How wide the fireball? Would we be safe in the park over there? Where?*

A Capitol Hill cop was yelling, "This way, this way!" Another yelled, "Run for your lives!" A Capitol Hill worker, a young heavyset woman in what I think was a cafeteria uniform, broke down in sobs. I wanted to go to her. A friend ran to her and put her arms around her and walked with her. My son and I holding hands and moving fast as we could. I thought of the scene in "Empire of the Sun"—I did not want to lose my son in the melee, and if it came to it I didn't want him to die alone. People were running and yelling and sometimes screaming.

We wound up in a group—Oatsie and Nick, Robert and Blaine Trump. We met up after a few blocks and surveyed the options. If the plane was going to hit and the plane was carrying bad stuff, nukes or chems or bios, we'd want to be in a big solid place. Union Station, three blocks away. Run for it. Inside is coolness and marble and communications and TVs in a nice cool bar. We all thought: *They might bomb the station. I thought: If they're gonna take out the Capitol with nukes, they won't bother with the station today.*

So we ran there. I heard reports later of pushing and shoving and people falling as the evacuation from the Capitol began. I saw none of this. I saw people running. And I saw Capitol Police standing their ground, directing people toward what they thought was the safe area, and I saw them running toward the Capitol to help people who needed them. I saw nothing but excellence. If these people had been at Pearl Harbor, they would have manned the guns. I'll tell you who else stood their ground: the photographers for the news services and newspapers. Those crazy bastards took pictures of us running and then moved closer to where we were running from to get more dramatic pictures of the last to leave. Shooters, they are something.

* * *

We got to the station, got Oatsie and Nick up the right ramps, got into some tall cool bar. We were dripping with sweat, which soaked through our shirts. I forgot to tell you it was 92 degrees at 3 p.m. We were heaving from running and catching our breath. We asked that they put the big Jumbotron TV on. When Oatsie was rolled in she was asked by a waiter what she would like. She said, "I would like a cool, dry chardonnay." I said that sounded just about right. My son wanted a Japanese beer. He had earned it.

We settled in. I asked Oatsie Charles who was the first president she'd ever seen with her eyes. She said, "Franklin D. Roosevelt." She told us of him, and of her friend JFK. "He had natural charisma—just natural charm."

We listened to her stories of history as the drums beat for Ronald Reagan on the jumbo TV. And at that moment on a Sony Jumbo-tron in a little table in a railroad station bar, we watched the body of Ronald Reagan arrive at Andrews and be met by a car. There were other people there in the bar and they were young office workers, commuters talking on cellphones and flirting and laughing. I got up and went to the bar, I introduced myself and told them we'd been evacuated and now we were watching our friend who we'd loved come home to us from California and I asked if they'd like to join us. They were so wonderful—kind and sweet, and they nodded and lowered their voices. And a few came and turned their seats to join our small group and watch our friend come home.

And so we mourned Ronald Reagan, in a room full of strangers who for once were not strangers, in Union Station, as Oatsie Charles told us about FDR and JFK and what it was like to know history. We were all together. And let me tell you: Our souls were there.

CHAPTER 12

My Beautiful Election

The 2008 presidential election was one of the most unforgettable of my lifetime. Somebody took down a political machine that couldn't be taken down. Someone came from nowhere and triumphed. A great party collapsed in confusion but had as its standard bearer a true hero. What a story. I watched it all, loving its barbaric yawp.

* * *

Sex and the Presidency

The Wall Street Journal: October 19, 2007

Where do things stand now with Hillary Clinton? What is her trajectory almost a year since it became clear she was running for the presidency?

Some time back I said she doesn't have to prove she is a man, she has to prove she is a woman. Her problem is not her sex, as she and her campaign pretend. That she is a woman is a boon to her, a source of latent power. But to make it work, she has to seem like a woman.

No one doubts Mrs. Clinton's ability to make war. No close or longtime observer has ever been quoted as saying that she may be too soft for the job. Instead one worries about what has always seemed her characterological bellicosity. She invented the War Room, listened in on the wiretaps, brought into the White House the man who got the private FBI files of the Clintons' perceived enemies.

This is not a woman who has to prove she's tough enough and mean enough; she is more like a bulldozer who has to prove she won't always be in high gear and ready to flatten you. In private, her friends say—and I have seen it to be true—that she is humorous, bright, interested in the lives of others. But as a matter of political temperament and habit of mind, she is neither patient, high minded nor forbearing. Those who know Mrs. Clinton well, and my world is thick with them, have qualms about her toughness, not doubts.

But she is making progress. She is trying every day to change her image, and I suspect it's working. One senses not that she has become more authentic, but that she has gone beyond her own discomfort at her lack of authenticity. I am not saying she has learned to be herself. I think after a year on the trail she's learned how to not be herself, how to comfortably adopt a skin and play a part.

Her real self is a person who wants to run things, to assert authority, to create systems and have people conform to them. She is not a natural at the outsized warmth politics demands. But she is moving beyond—forgive me—the vacant eyes of the power zombie, like the Tilda Swinton character in "Michael Clayton." The Boston Globe, dateline Manchester, N.H.: "Clinton is increasingly portraying herself more as motherly and traditional than as trailblazing and feminist." In a week of "Women Changing America" events Mrs. Clinton has shared tales of Chelsea's childhood and made teasing references to those who are preoccupied by her hairstyles and fashion choices. On "The View" she joked of her male rivals, "Well, look how much longer it takes me to get ready." This was a steal from JFK's joke about Jackie when she was late for an appearance: "It takes her longer to get ready, but then she looks so much better."

Her fund-raising emails have subject lines like "Wow!" and "Let's make some popcorn!" Her grin is broad and fixed. She is the smile on the Halloween pumpkin that knows the harvest is coming. She's even putting a light inside.

In New York this week she told a women's lunch that "we face a new question—a lot of people are asking whether America is ready to elect a woman to the highest office in our land." She suggested her campaign will "prove that America is indeed ready." She also quoted Eleanor Roosevelt: "Women are like tea bags—you never know how strong they are until they get in hot water."

*   *   *

Mrs. Clinton is the tea bag that brings the boiling water with her. It's always high drama with her, always a cauldron—secret Web sites put up by unnamed operatives smearing Barack Obama in the tones of Tokyo Rose, Chinese businessmen having breakdowns on trains after the campaign cash is traced back, secret deals. It's always flying monkeys. One always wants to ask: Why? What is this?

The question, actually, is not whether America is "ready" for a woman. It's whether it's ready for Hillary. And surely as savvy a campaign vet as Mrs. Clinton knows this.

Who, of all the powerful women in American politics right now, has inspired the unease, dismay and frank dislike that she has? Condi Rice, Nancy Pelosi, Dianne Feinstein? These are serious women who are making crucial decisions about our national life every day. They inspire agreement and disagreement; they fight and are fought with. But they do not inspire repugnance. Nobody hates Barbara Mikulski, Elizabeth Dole or Kay Bailey Hutchison; everyone respects Ms. Rice and Ms. Feinstein.

Hillary's problem is not that she's a woman; it's that unlike these women—all of whom have come under intense scrutiny, each of whom has real partisan foes—she has a history that lends itself to the kind of doubts that end in fearfulness. It is an unease and dismay based not on gender stereotypes but on personal history.

* * *

But here's why I mentioned earlier the latent power inherent in the fact that Hillary is a woman.

It is true that 54% of the electorate is composed of women and that what feminist sympathies they have may be especially enlivened this year by a strong appeal. It is not true that women in general vote in anything like a bloc, but it is probably true—I think it is true— that they share in a general way some rough and broad sympathies.

One has to do with what it is to be a woman in the world. To be active on any level in the life of the nation is to be immersed in controversy. If you are a woman, the to and fro, the fights you're in, will to some extent be sharpened or shaped by what used to be called sexism. There isn't a woman in America who hasn't been patronized—or worse—for being a woman, at least to some degree, and I mean all women, from the nun patronized by the bullying bishop to the congresswoman not taken seriously by the policy intellectual to the school teacher browbeaten by the school board chairman to the fare collector corrected by the huffy businessman. It happens to every woman.

Conservative women tend not to talk about it except to each other, and those conversations are voluble and pointed. They don't go public with their complaints because they're afraid it will encourage liberals to pass a law, and if you wanted more laws, or thought laws could reform human nature and make us all nice, you wouldn't be a conservative. Their problem is sharpened by the fact that some conservative men are boorish and ungentlemanly to show how liberated they are. But I digress.

Or rather I don't. The point is there are many women who will on some level be inclined to view Mrs. Clinton's candidacy through the lens of their experience as women, and there is real latent sympathy there if she could tap it, which is what she's trying to do.

But first, or more important, she will have to credibly and persuasively address what it is in her history—in her—that inspires such visceral opposition. That would be quite something if she did, or even tried.

Over the Top

The Wall Street Journal: March 7, 2008

An overview:

From the first voting in Iowa on Jan. 3 she had to prove that Clintons Are Magic. She wound up losing 11 in a row. Meaning Clintons aren't magic. He had to take her out in New Hampshire, on Super Tuesday or Junior Tuesday. He didn't. Meaning Obama isn't magic.

Two nonmagical beings are left.

What the Democrats lost this week was the chance to paint the '08 campaign as a brilliant Napoleonic twinning of strategy and tactics that left history awed. What they have instead is a ticket to Verdun. Trench warfare, and the daily, wearying life of the soldier under siege. The mud, the cold, the dank water rotting the boots, all of it punctuated by mad cries of "Over the top," bayonets fixed.

Do I understate? Not according to the bitter officers debating doomed strategy back in HQ. More on that in a minute.

This is slightly good for John McCain. Hillary Clinton and Barack Obama hemorrhage money, exhaust themselves, bloody each other. He holds barbecues for the press and gets rid of a White House appearance in which the incumbent offers his dread embrace. *Do it now, they'll forget by the summer.* The president does not understand how unpopular he is and after a year on the trail with the faithful neither does Mr. McCain. Mr. Bush confided to a friend a few months ago, as he predicted a Giuliani win, that he'll eventually come out and campaign for the nominee big time. Talk about throwing the drowning man an anvil.

But it is not good for Mr. McCain that when he officially won this week it barely made page three. The lightning is on the Democratic side. Everything else seems old, like something that happened a year ago that you forgot to notice.

How did Hillary come back? Her own staff doesn't know. They fight over it because if they don't know how she carried Ohio and Texas they can't repeat the strategy.

So they figure backward. She won on Tuesday and did the following things in the weeks before, so ... it was the kitchen-sink strategy. Or Hispanic outreach. Or the 3 a.m. ad. (The amazing thing was not that they lifted the concept from Walter Mondale's 1984 run, but that the answer to the question "Who are you safer with?" was The Woman. Not that people really view Hillary as a woman, but still: That would not have been the answer even 20 years ago.)

Did she come back because Mr. Obama's speech got a little boring? Was he coasting and playing it safe? Or was it that he didn't hit her hard enough? "He hasn't been able to find a way to be tough with a woman opponent," they say on TV. But that's not it, or is only half the truth. The other half is that it has long been agreed in the Democratic Party that one must not, one cannot, ever, refer to the long caravan of scandals that have followed the Clintons for 15 years. *"We don't speak of the Clintons that way."*

But why not? Everyone else does. Yes, the Obama sages will respond, that's the point: Everyone knows about cattle futures, etc. Everyone knows that if you Yahoo "Clintons" and "scandals" you get 4,430,000 hits.

But what if they do need to be reminded? What if they need to be told exactly what Mr. Obama means when he speaks of the tired old ways of Washington?

But voicing the facts would violate party politesse. So he loses the No. 1 case against her. But by losing the No. 1 case, he loses the No. 2 case: that she is the most divisive figure in the country, and that this is true because people have reason to view her as dark, dissembling, thuggish.

* * *

One Obama supporter on TheRoot.com apparently didn't get the memo. That is the great threat to the Clintons, the number of young and independent Democrats who haven't received the memo about how Democrats speak of the Clintons. Writer Mark Q. Sawyer: "If Obama won't hit back, I will. Why aren't we talking about impeachment, Whitewater and Osama?"

What do I think is the biggest reason Mrs. Clinton came back? She kept her own spirits up to the point of denial and worked it, hard, every day. She is hardy, resilient, tough. She is a train on a track, an Iron Horse. But we must not become carried away with generosity. The very qualities that impress us are the qualities that will make her a painful president. She does not care what you think, she will have what she wants, she will not do the feints, pivots and backoffs that presidents must. She is neither nimble nor agile, and she knows best. She will wear a great nation down.

In any case the Clinton campaign, which has always been more vicious than clever, this week did a very clever thing. They preempted any criticism of past scandals by pushing a Democratic Party button called...the Monica story. Mr. Obama is "imitating Ken Starr" by speaking of Mrs. Clinton's record, said Howard Wolfson. But Ken Starr documented malfeasance. Mr. Obama can't even mention it.

* * *

Back to Verdun. There a bitter officer corps debated a strategy of pointless carnage—so many deaths, so little seized terrain, all of it barren. In a bark-stripping piece of reportage in the Washington Post, Peter Baker and Anne Kornblut captured "a combustible environment" in Hillary Headquarters. They cannot agree on what to do, or even what has been done in the past. And the dialogue. *Blank you. Blank you! No blank you, you blank. Blank all of you.* It's like David Mamet rewritten by Joe Pesci.

These are the things that make life worth living.

As for the Clinton surrogates, they are unappealing when winning. My favorite is named Kiki. When Hillary is losing, Kiki is valiant and persevering on the talk shows, and in a way that appeals to one's sympathies. "Go, Kiki!" I want to say as she parries with Tucker. But when Hillary is winning they're all awful, including Kiki. By memory, from Tucker, this week: *Q: Why won't Hillary release her tax returns? A: It's February. Taxes are due April 15, are your taxes done? Q: No, no, we're talking past years, returns that have already been prepared. A: Are your taxes done? Mine aren't.*

Wicked Kiki! This is my great fear, in a second Clinton era: four, eight years of wicked Kiki.

I end with a deadly, deadpan prediction from Christopher Hitchens. Hillary is the next president, he told radio's Hugh Hewitt, because, "there's something horrible and undefeatable about people who have no life except the worship of power…people who don't want the meeting to end, the people who just are unstoppable, who only have one focus, no humanity, no character, nothing but the worship of money and power. They win in the end."

It was like Claude Rains summing up the meaning of everything in the film "Lawrence of Arabia": "One of them's mad and the other is wholly unscrupulous." It's the moment when you realize you just heard the truth, the meaning underlying all the drama. "They win in the end." Gave me a shudder.

Pity Party

The Wall Street Journal: May 16, 2008

Big picture, May 2008

The Democrats aren't the ones falling apart, the Republicans are. The Democrats can see daylight ahead. For all their fractious fighting, they're finally resolving their central drama. Hillary Clinton will leave, and Barack Obama will deliver a stirring acceptance speech. Then hand-to-hand in the general, where they see their guy triumphing. You see it when you talk to them: They're busy being born.

The Republicans? Busy dying. The brightest of them see no immediate light. They're frozen, not like a deer in the headlights but a deer in the darkness, his ears stiff at the sound. *Crunch. Twig. Hunting party.*

The headline Wednesday on Drudge, from Politico, said, "Republicans Stunned by Loss in Mississippi." It was about the eight-point drubbing the Democrat gave the Republican in the special House election. My first thought was: You have to be stupid to be stunned by that. Second thought: Most party leaders in Washington *are* stupid—detached, played out, stuck in the wisdom they learned when they were coming up, in '78 or '82 or '94. Whatever they learned then, they think pertains now. In politics especially, the first lesson sticks. For Richard Nixon, everything came back to Alger Hiss.

They are also—Hill leaders, lobbyists, party speakers—successful, well connected, busy and rich. They never guessed, back in '86, how government would pay off! They didn't know they'd stay! They came to make a difference and wound up with their butts in the butter. But affluence detaches, and in time skews thinking. It gives you the illusion you're safe, and that everyone else is. A party can lose its gut this way.

Many are ambivalent, deep inside, about the decisions made the past seven years in the White House. But they've publicly supported it so long they think they...support it. They get confused. Late at night they toss and turn in the antique mahogany sleigh bed in the carpeted house in McLean and try to remember what it is they really do think, and what those thoughts imply.

And those are the bright ones. The rest are in Perpetual 1980: We have the country, the troops will rally in the fall.

"This was a real wakeup call for us," someone named Robert M. Duncan, who is chairman of the Republican National Committee, told the New York Times. This was after Mississippi. "We can't let the Democrats take our issues." And those issues would be? "We can't let them pretend to be conservatives," he continued. Why not? Republicans pretend to be conservative every day.

The Bush White House, faced with the series of losses from 2005 through '08, has long claimed the problem is Republicans on the Hill and running for office. They have scandals, bad personalities, don't stand for anything. That's why Republicans are losing: because they're losers.

All true enough!

But this week a House Republican said publicly what many say privately, that there is another truth. "Members and pundits...fail to understand the deep-seated antipathy toward the president, the war, gas prices, the economy, foreclosures," said Rep. Tom Davis of Virginia in a 20-page memo to House GOP leaders.

The party, Mr. Davis told me, is "an airplane flying right into a mountain." Analyses of its predicament reflect an "investment in the Bush presidency," but "the public has just moved so far past that." "Our leaders go up to the second floor of the White House and they get a case of White House-itis." Mr. Bush has left the party at a disadvantage in terms of communications: "He can't articulate. The only asset we have now is the big microphone, and he swallowed it." The party, said Mr. Davis, must admit its predicament, act independently of the White House and force Democrats to define themselves. "They should have some ownership for what's going on. They control the budget. They pay no price...Obama has all happy talk, but it's from 30,000 feet. Energy, immigration, what is he gonna do?"

*   *   *

Could the party pivot from the president? I spoke this week to Clarke Reed of Mississippi, one of the great architects of resurgent Republicanism in the South. When he started out, in the 1950s, there were no Republicans in his state. The solid South was solidly Democratic, and Sen. James O. Eastland was thumping the breast pocket of his suit, vowing that civil rights legislation would never leave it. "We're going to build a two-party system in the South," Mr. Reed said. He helped create "the illusion of Southern power," as a friend put it, with the creation of the Southern Republican Chairman's Association. "If you build it they will come." They did.

There are always "lots of excuses," Mr. Reed said of the special-election loss. Poor candidate, local factors. "Having said all that," he continued, "let's just face it: It's not a good time." He meant to be a Republican. "They brought Cheney in, and that was a mistake." He cited "a disenchantment with the generic Republican label, which we always thought was the Good Housekeeping seal."

What's behind it? "American people just won't take a long war. Just—name me a war, even in a pro-military state like this. It's overall disappointment. It's national. No leadership, adrift. Things haven't worked." The future lies in rebuilding locally, not being "distracted" by Washington.

Is the Republican solid South over?

"Yeah. Oh yeah." He said, "I eat lunch every day at Buck's Cafe. Obama's picture is all over the wall."

How to come back? "The basic old conservative principles haven't changed. We got distracted by Washington, we got distracted from having good county organizations."

Should the party attempt to break with Mr. Bush? Mr. Reed said he supports the president. And then he said, simply, "We're past that."

We're past that time.

Mr. Reed said he was "short-term pessimistic, long-term optimistic." He has seen a lot of history. "After Goldwater in '64 we said, 'Let's get practical.' So we got ol' Dick. We got through Watergate. Been through a lot. We've had success a long time."

Throughout the interview this was a Reed refrain: "We got through that." We got through Watergate and Vietnam and changes large and small.

He was holding high the flag, but his refrain implicitly compared the current moment to disaster.

What happens to the Republicans in 2008 will likely be dictated by what didn't happen in 2005, and '06 and '07. The moment when the party could have broken, on principle, with the administration— over the thinking behind and the carrying out of the war, over immigration, spending and the size of government—has passed. What two years ago would have been honorable and wise will now look craven. They're stuck.

Mr. Bush has squandered the hard-built paternity of 40 years. But so has the party, and so have its leaders. If they had pushed away for serious reasons, they could have separated the party's fortunes from the president's. This would have left a painfully broken party, but they wouldn't be left with a ruined "brand," as they all say, speaking the language of marketing. And they speak that language because they are marketers, not thinkers. Not serious about policy. Not serious about ideas. And not serious about leadership, only followership.

This is and will be the great challenge for John McCain: the Democratic argument, now being market tested by Obama Inc., that a McCain victory will yield nothing more or less than George Bush's third term.

That is going to be powerful, and it is going to get out the vote. And not for Republicans.

Sex and the Sissy

The Wall Street Journal: May 23, 2008

She was born in Russia, fled the pogroms with her family, was raised in Milwaukee and worked the counter at her father's general store when she was 8. In early adulthood she made aliyah to Palestine, where she worked on a kibbutz, picking almonds and chasing chickens. She rose in politics, was the first woman in the first Israeli cabinet, soldiered on through war and rumors of war, became the first and so far only woman to be prime minister of Israel. And she knew what it is to be a woman in the world. "At work, you think of the children you've left at home. At home, you think of the work you've left unfinished... Your heart is rent." This of course was Golda Meir.

Another: She was born in a family at war with itself and the reigning power outside. As a child she carried word from her important father to his fellow revolutionaries, smuggling the papers in her school bag. War and rumors of war, arrests, eight months in jail. A rise in politics—administering refugee camps, government minister. When war came, she refused to flee an insecure border area; her stubbornness helped rally a nation. Her rivals sometimes called her "Dumb Doll," and an American president is said to have referred to her in private as "the old witch." But the prime minister of India preferred grinding her foes to dust to complaining about gender bias. In the end, and in the way of things, she was ground up, too. Proud woman, Indira Gandhi.

And there is Margaret Hilda Roberts. A childhood in the besieged Britain of World War II—she told me once of listening to the wireless and being roused by Churchill. "Westward look, the land is bright," she quoted him; she knew every stanza of the old poem. Her father, too, was a shopkeeper, and she grew up in the apartment above the store near the tracks. She went to Oxford on scholarship, worked as a chemist, entered politics, rose, became another first and only, succeeding not only in a man's world but in a class system in which they knew how to take care of ambitious little grocer's daughters from Grantham. She was to a degree an outsider within her own party, so she remade it. She lived for ideas as her colleagues lived for comfort and complaint. The Tories those days managed loss. She wanted to stop it; she wanted gain. Just before she became prime minister, the Soviets, thinking they were deftly stigmatizing an upstart, labeled her the "Iron Lady." She seized the insult and wore it like a hat. This was Thatcher, stupendous Thatcher, now the baroness.

Great women, all different, but great in terms of size, of impact on the world and of struggles overcome. Struggle was not something they read about in a book. They did not use guilt to win election—it comes up zero if you Google "Thatcher" and "You're just picking on me because I'm a woman." Instead they used the appeals men used: stronger leadership, better ideas, a superior philosophy.

* * *

You know where I'm going, for you know where she went. Hillary Clinton complained again this week that sexism has been a major dynamic in her unsuccessful bid for political dominance. She is quoted by the Washington Post's Lois Romano decrying the "sexist" treatment she received during the campaign and the "incredible vitriol that has been engendered" by those who are "nothing but misogynists." The New York Times reported she told sympathetic bloggers in a conference call that she is saddened by the "mean-spiritedness and terrible insults" that have been thrown "at you, for supporting me, and at women in general."

Where to begin? One wants to be sympathetic to Mrs. Clinton at this point, if for no other reason than to show one's range. But her last weeks have been, and her next weeks will likely be, one long exercise in summoning further denunciations. It is something new in politics, the How Else Can I Offend You Tour. And I suppose it is aimed not at voters—you don't persuade anyone by complaining in this way, you only reinforce what your supporters already think— but at history, at the way history will tell the story of the reasons for her loss.

So, to address the charge that sexism did her in:

It is insulting, because it asserts that those who supported someone else this year were driven by low prejudice and mindless bias.

It is manipulative, because it asserts that if you want to be understood, both within the community and in the larger brotherhood of man, to be wholly without bias and prejudice, you must support Mrs. Clinton.

It is not true. Tough hill-country men voted for her, men so backward they'd give the lady a chair in the union hall. Tough Catholic men in the outer suburbs voted for her, men so backward they'd call a woman a lady. And all of them so naturally courteous that they'd realize, in offering the chair or addressing the lady, that they might have given offense, and awkwardly joke at themselves to take away the sting. These are great men. And Hillary got her share, more than her share, of their votes. She should be a guy and say thanks.

It is prissy. Mrs. Clinton's supporters are now complaining about the Hillary nutcrackers sold at every airport shop. Boo hoo. If Golda Meir, a woman of not only proclaimed but actual toughness, heard about Golda nutcrackers, she would have bought them by the case and given them away as party favors.

It is sissy. It is blame-gaming, whining, a way of not taking responsibility, of not seeing your flaws and addressing them. You want to say "Girl, butch up, you are playing in the leagues, they get bruised in the leagues, they break each other's bones, they like to hit you low and hear the crack, it's like that for the boys and for the girls."

And because the charge of sexism is all of the above, it is, ultimately, undermining of the position of women. Or rather it would be if its source were not someone broadly understood by friend and foe alike to be willing to say anything to gain advantage.

*   *   *

It is probably truer that being a woman helped Mrs. Clinton. She was the front-runner anyway and had all the money, power, Beltway backers. But the fact that she was a woman helped give her supporters the special oomph to be gotten from making history. They were by definition involved in something historic. And they were on the right side, connected to the one making the breakthrough, shattering the glass. They were going to be part of breaking it into a million little pieces that could rain down softly during the balloon drop at the historic convention, each of them catching the glow of the lights. Some network reporter was going to say "They look like pieces of the glass ceiling that has finally been shattered."

I know: Barf. But also: Fine. Politics should be fun.

Meir and Gandhi and Mrs. Thatcher suffered through the political downside of their sex and made the most of the upside. Fair enough. As for this week's Clinton complaints, I imagine Mrs. Thatcher would bop her on the head with her purse. Mrs. Gandhi would say "That is no way to play it." Mrs. Meir? "They said I was the only woman in the cabinet and the only one with—well, you know. I loved it."

McCain Represents the Way We Were, Obama What We Are Becoming

The Wall Street Journal: June 14, 2008

And so it begins, the campaign proper. You probably guessed that there would be no letup in this relentless year, no break between the primaries and the general election, that both candidates would stay on the screen. You were right. They will not leave, and go, and rest. They feel they can't, it's inch by inch, slow and steady wins the race. This robs them of the power of disappearance. You disappear and then come back and people say, "Hey, look at that guy." They listen anew after a break in the drone.

Not this time. And maybe never again.

For Barack Obama this week, a Beltway setback. He chose for a key position a D.C. insider who got fat working the system. This was a poor decision by the candidate of change. "Meet the new boss, same as the old boss." But Jim Johnson was removed with dispatch, and the country didn't notice. Beltway bottom line: Mr. Obama the cool customer had a problem, removed the problem, has no problem.

John McCain had a worse time, with the famously awkward speech in front of the background whose color was variously compared to snot, puke and lime Jell-O. He was scored for not being adept with a teleprompter. The press knocked him, essentially, for not being smooth and manipulative enough. But if he were good at the teleprompter, they'd complain that he's too smooth and scripted.

The press will be nice to him again. When he's 17 points down.

It should not count against a man that he has not fully mastered the artifice of his profession. Then again, he should have nailed the prompter by now. Such things show a certain competence. Voters are slower to trust you with big things if they see a lack of skill in small things. In this vein, a suggestion. Podiums always seem to swallow Mr. McCain. He has limited mobility with his arms because of his torture in Vietnam. It restricts his ability to gesture. And he is not a big man. He often looks like he's flailing up there: *I'm not waving, I'm drowning!* His staff should build a podium for him, one that fits, and take it wherever he goes. For a seal, the great state of Arizona, which he has represented in the U.S. Senate for 22 years. Let him master the podium five months out. Other masteries will follow.

The lay of the land? Mr. Obama is ahead 47% to 41% in this week's Wall Street Journal/NBC poll, and no one is surprised. Everyone knows he's ahead. Everyone knows this is a Democratic year. But I think there are two particular subtexts this year, or per-haps I should say texts. One, obviously, is youth versus age. This theme is the clearest it's been since 1960, when the old general who'd planned the Normandy invasion found himself replaced by a young man who had commanded a rickety patrol torpedo boat in World War II. You know that on some level, at some moment, Dwight D. Eisenhower looked at John F. Kennedy and thought: *Punk.*

But 2008 will also prove in part to be a decisive political con-test between the Old America and the New America. Between the thing we were, and the thing we have been becoming for 40 years or so. (I'm not referring here to age. Some young Americans have Old America heads and souls; some old people are all for the New.)

Mr. McCain is the Old America, of course; Mr. Obama the New.

*   *   *

Roughly, broadly:

In the Old America, love of country was natural. You breathed it in. You either loved it or knew you should.

In the New America, love of country is a decision. It's one you make after weighing the pros and cons. What you breathe in is skepticism and a heightened appreciation of the global view.

Old America: Tradition is a guide in human affairs. New America: Tradition is a challenge, a barrier, a lovely antique.

The Old America had big families. You married and had children. Life happened to you. You didn't decide, it decided. Now it's all on you.

Old America, when life didn't work out: "Luck of the draw!" New America when life doesn't work: "I made bad choices!" Old America: "I had faith, and trust." New America: "You had limited autonomy!"

Old America: "We've been here three generations." New America: "You're still here?"

Old America: We have to have a government, but that doesn't mean I have to love it. New America: We have to have a government and I am desperate to love it.

Old America: Politics is a duty. New America: Politics is life.

The Old America: Religion is good. The New America: Religion is problematic. The Old: Smoke 'em if you got 'em. The New: I'll sue.

Mr. McCain is the old world of concepts like "personal honor," of a manliness that was a style of being, of an attachment to the fact of higher principles.

Mr. Obama is the new world, which is marked in part by doubt as to the excellence of the old. It prizes ambivalence as proof of thoughtfulness, as evidence of a textured seriousness.

Both Old and New America honor sacrifice, but in the Old America it was more essential, more needed for survival both personally (don't buy today, save for tomorrow) and in larger ways.

The Old and New define sacrifice differently. An Old America opinion: Abjuring a life as a corporate lawyer and choosing instead community organizing, a job that does not pay you in money but will, if you have political ambitions, provide a base and help you win office, is not precisely a sacrifice. Political office will pay you in power and fame, which will be followed in time by money (see Clinton, Bill). This has more to do with timing than sacrifice. In fact, it's less a sacrifice than a strategy.

A New America answer: He didn't become a rich lawyer like everyone else—and that was a sacrifice! Old America: Five years in a cage—*that's* a sacrifice!

In the Old America, high value was put on education, but character trumped it. That's how Lincoln got elected: Honest Abe had no formal schooling. In Mr. McCain's world, a Harvard Ph.D. is a very good thing, but it won't help you endure five years in Vietnam. It may be a comfort or an inspiration, but it won't see you through. Only character, and faith, can do that. And they are very Old America.

Old America: Candidates for office wear ties. New America: Not if they're women. Old America: There's a place for formality, even the Beatles wore jackets!

* * *

I weigh this in favor of the Old America. Hard not to, for I remember it, and its sterling virtues. Maybe if you are 25 years old, your sense of the Old and New is different. In the Old America, they were not enlightened about race and sex; they accepted grim factory lines and couldn't even begin to imagine the Internet. Fair enough. But I suspect the political playing out of a long-ongoing cultural and societal shift is part of the dynamic this year.

As to its implications for the race, we'll see. America is always looking forward, not back, it is always in search of the fresh and leaving the tried. That's how we started: We left tired old Europe and came to the new place, we settled the East and pushed west to the new place. We like new. It's in our genes. Hope we know where we're going, though.

The End of Placeness

The Washington Post: August 15, 2008

The end of placeness is one of the features of the campaign. I do not like it.

Pretend you are not a political sophisticate and regular watcher of the presidential race as it unfolds on all media platforms. Pretend, that is, that you are normal.

OK, quick, close your eyes. Where is Barack Obama from?

He's from Young. He's from the town of Smooth in the state of Well Educated. He's from TV.

John McCain? He's from Military. He's from Vietnam Township in the Sunbelt state.

Chicago? That's where Mr. Obama wound up. Modern but Midwestern: a perfect place to begin what might become a national career. Arizona? That's where Mr. McCain settled, a perfect place from which to launch a more or less conservative career in the 1980s.

Neither man has or gives a strong sense of place in the sense that American politicians almost always have, since Mr. Jefferson of Virginia, and Abe Lincoln of Illinois, and FDR of New York, and JFK of Massachusetts. Even Bill Clinton was from a town called Hope, in Arkansas, even if Hope was really Hot Springs. And in spite of his New England pedigree, George W. Bush was a Texan, as was, vividly, LBJ.

Messrs. Obama and McCain are not from a place, but from an experience. Mr. McCain of course was a Navy brat. He bounced around, as members of the families of our military must, and wound up for a time in the suburbs of Washington. Mr. Obama's mother was somewhat itinerant, in search of different climes. He was born in Hawaii, which Americans on the continent don't experience so much as a state as a destination, a place of physical beauty and singular culture. You go there to escape and enjoy. Then his great circling commenced: Indonesia, back to Hawaii, on to the western coast of America, then to the eastern coast, New York and Cambridge. He circled the continent, entering it, if you will, in Chicago, where he settled in his 30s.

The lack of placeness with both candidates contributes to a sense of their disjointedness, their floatingness. I was talking recently with a journalist who's a podcaster. I often watch him in conversation on the Internet. I told him I'm always struck that he seems to be speaking from No Place, with some background of beige wall that could exist anywhere. He leans in and out of focus. It gives a sense of weightlessness. He's like an astronaut floating without a helmet.

That's a little what both candidates are like to me.

Mr. Obama hails from Chicago, but no one would confuse him with Chicagoans like Richard Daley or Dan Rostenkowski, or Harold Washington. "There is something colorless and odorless about him," says a friend, "like an inert gas." And Mr. McCain, in his experience, history and genes, is definitely military, and could easily come from Indiana or South Carolina or California, and could easily speak of upholding the values of those places.

What are the political implications of candidates seeming unconnected to regional roots, or being shorn of them? I suppose the question first surfaced in 2000, when Al Gore won the national popular vote and lost Tennessee, his home state. But he hadn't ever really seemed of Tennessee. He was born and grew up in Washington, D.C., the son of a senator. That was his formative experience. They liked him better in New York and California than down South.

They like Mr. Obama in Illinois, but he hasn't locked up

neighboring Michigan, just as Mr. McCain has strong support in Arizona but still lags in Colorado and New Mexico.

On a policy level, the end of placeness may have implications. It may, for instance, lead a president to more easily oppose pork-barrel spending. If you're not quite from anywhere, you'll be slower to build a bridge to nowhere. If you don't feel the constant tug of Back Home—if it is your natural habit to think of the nation not first in specific and concrete terms but in abstract ones—then you might wind up less preoccupied by the needs and demands of the people Back Home. Mr. McCain is already a scourge of pork. Mr. Obama? Not clear. One doesn't sense any regional tug on his policy.

All this is part of a national story that wasn't new even a quarter century ago. Americans move. They like moving. Got a lot of problems? The answer may be geographical relocation. New problem in the new place? GTT. Gone to Texas.

It's in us. And yet.

I was at a gathering a few weeks ago for an aged Southern sage, a politico with an accent so thick you have to lean close and concentrate to understand every word, so thick, as they used to say, you could pour it on pancakes. Most of the people there were from the South, different ages and generations but Southerners—the men grounded and courteous in a certain way, the women sleeveless and sexy in a certain way. There was a lot of singing and toasting and drinking, and this was the thing: Even as an outsider, you knew them. They were Mississippi Delta people—Mizz-izz-DEHLT people—and the sense of placeness they brought into the room with them was sweet to me. It allowed you to know them, in the same way that at a gathering of, say, Irish Catholics from the suburbs of Boston, you would be able to know them, pick up who they are, with your American antennae. You grow up, move on, and bring the Delta with you, but as each generation passes, the Delta disappears, as in time the ward and the parish disappear.

I miss the old geographical vividness. But we are national now, and in a world so global that at the Olympics, when someone wins, wherever he is from, whatever nation or culture, he makes the same movements with his arms and face to mark his victory. South Korea's Park Tae-hwan moves just like Michael Phelps, with the "Yes!" and the arms shooting upward and the fists. This must be good. Why does it feel like a leveling? Like a squashing and squeezing down of the particular, local and authentic.

*   *   *

I end with a thought on the upcoming announcements of vice presidential picks. Major props to both campaigns for keeping it tight, who it's going to be, for by now they should know and have, please God, fully vetted him or her. On the Democrats, who are up first, I firmly announce I like every name floated so far, for different reasons (Joe Biden offers experience and growth; Evan Bayh seems by nature moderate; Sam Nunn is that rare thing, a serious man whom all see as a serious man.) But part of me tugs for Tim Kaine of Virginia, because he has a wonderful American Man haircut, not the cut of the man in first but the guy in coach who may be the air marshal. He looks like he goes once every 10 days to Jimmy Hoffa's barber and says, "Gimme a full Detroit."

Detroit: that's a place.

Obama and the Runaway Train

The Wall Street Journal: October 30, 2008

The case for Barack Obama, in broad strokes:

He has within him the possibility to change the direction and tone of American foreign policy, which need changing; his rise will serve as a practical rebuke to the past five years, which need rebuking; his victory would provide a fresh start in a nation in which a fresh start would come as a national relief. He climbed steep stairs, born off the continent with no father to guide, a dreamy, abandoning mother, mixed race, no connections. He rose with guts and gifts. He is steady, calm, and, in terms of the execution of his political ascent, still the primary and almost only area in which his executive abilities can be discerned, he shows good judgment in terms of whom to hire and consult, what steps to take and moves to make. We witnessed from him this year something unique in American politics: He took down a political machine without raising his voice.

A great moment: When the press was hitting hard on the pregnancy of Sarah Palin's 17-year-old daughter, he did not respond with a politically shrewd "I have no comment," or "We shouldn't judge." Instead he said, "My mother had me when she was 18," which shamed the press and others into silence. He showed grace when he didn't have to.

There is something else. On Feb. 5, Super Tuesday, Mr. Obama won the Alabama primary with 56% to Hillary Clinton's 42%. That evening, a friend watched the victory speech on TV in his suburban den. His 10-year-old daughter walked in, saw on the screen "Obama

Wins" and "Alabama." She said, "Daddy, we saw a documentary on Martin Luther King Day in school." She said, "That's where they used the hoses." Suddenly my friend saw it new. Birmingham, 1963, and the water hoses used against the civil rights demonstrators. And now look, the black man thanking Alabama for his victory.

This means nothing? This means a great deal.

John McCain's story is not of rise so much as endurance, not only in Vietnam, which was spectacular enough, but throughout a rough and rugged political career of 26 years. He is passionate, obstreperous, independent, sees existential fables within history. His self-confessed role model for many years was Robert Jordan in Ernest Hemingway's novel of the Spanish Civil War, "For Whom the Bell Tolls." Mr. McCain, in his last memoir: "He was and remains to my mind a hero for the twentieth century . . . an idealistic freedom fighter" who had "a beautiful fatalism" and who sacrificed "for something else, something greater." Actually Jordan fought on the side of the communists and died pointlessly, but never mind. He joined his personality to a great purpose and found meaning in his maverickness. In his campaign, Mr. McCain rarely got down to the meaning of things; he mostly stated stands. But separate and seemingly unconnected stands do not coherence make.

However: It was a night during the Republican Convention in September, and two former U.S. senators, who had served with Mr. McCain for a combined 16 years, were having drinks in a hotel dining room. I told them I collected stories of senators who'd been cursed out by John McCain, and they laughed and told me of times they'd been the target of his wrath on the Senate floor.

The talk turned to presidents they had known, and why they had wanted the job. This one wanted it as the last item on his resume, that one wanted it out of an inflated sense of personal destiny. Is that why Mr. McCain wants it? "No," said one, reflectively. "He wants to help the country." The other added, with almost an air of wonder,

"He wants to make America stronger, he really does." And then they spoke, these two men who'd been bruised by him, of John McCain's honest patriotism.

Those who have historically been sympathetic to the Republican Party or conservatism, and who support Barack Obama—Colin Powell, William Weld and Charles Fried, among others—and whose arguments have not passed muster with some muster-passers, go undamned here. Their objections include: The McCain campaign has been inadequate and some of his major decisions embarrassing. All too true.

But conservatives must honor prudence, and ask if the circumstances accompanying an Obama victory will encourage the helpful moderation and nonpartisan spirit these supporters attempt, in their endorsements, to demonstrate.

There is for instance, in the words of Minnesota's Gov. Tim Pawlenty, "the runaway train." The size and dimension of the likely Democratic victory seem clear. A Democratic House with a bigger, more fervent Democratic majority; a Democratic Senate with the same, and possibly with a filibuster-breaking 60 seats; a new and popular Democratic president, elected by a few points or more; a Democratic base whose anger and hunger have built for eight years; Democratic activists and operatives hungry for business and action. What will this mix produce? A runaway train with no one to put on the brakes, to claim a mandate for slowing, no one to cry "Crossing ahead"? Democrats in Congress will move for innovation when much of the country hopes only for stability. Who will tell Congress of that rest of the nation? Mr. Obama will be overwhelmed trying to placate the innovators.

America enjoyed divided government most successfully recently from 1994 to 2000, with Bill Clinton in the White House and Newt Gingrich in effect running Congress. It wasn't so bad. In fact, it yielded a great deal, including sweeping reform of the welfare system, and balanced budgets.

Whoever is elected Tuesday, his freedom in office will be limited. Mr. Obama is out of money and Mr. McCain is out of army, so what might be assumed to be the worst impulses of each—big spender, big scrapper—will be circumscribed by reality. In Mr. Obama's case, energy will likely be diverted to other issues. He will raise taxes, of course, but he may also feel forced to bow to a clamorous base with the nonspending items they favor: the rewriting of union law to force greater unionization of smaller shops, for instance, and a return to a "fairness doctrine" that would limit free speech on the air.

And there is this. The past few months as the campaign unfolded, I listened for Mr. Obama to speak thoughtfully about the life issues, including abortion. Our last Democratic president knew what that issue was, and knew by nature how to speak of it. Bill Clinton famously said, over and over, that abortion should be "safe, legal and rare." The "rare" mattered. It set a tone, as presidents do, and made an important concession: You only want a medical practice to be rare when it isn't good. For Mr. Obama, whose mind tends, as intellectuals' minds do, toward the abstract, it all seems so...abstract. And cold. And rather suggestive of radical departures. "That's above my pay grade." Friend, that is your pay grade, that's where the presidency lives, in issues like that.

But let's be frank. Something new is happening in America. It is the imminent arrival of a new liberal moment. History happens, it makes its turns, you hold on for dear life. Life moves.

A fitting end for a harem-scarem, rock-'em-sock-'em shakeup of a year—one of tumbling inevitabilities, torn coalitions, striking new personalities.

Eras end, and begin. "God is in charge of history." And so my beautiful election ends.

CHAPTER 13

The Loneliest President since Nixon

These pieces chart Barack Obama's decline from a figure of hope. When I think of him now I think of the comment of a smart acquaintance, a leftist Democrat who is a great Obama supporter and has worked and works closely with him.

Politics aside, I said, what is Obama's biggest flaw?

His answer was immediate. "He doesn't listen."

You mean, I said, that his mind has already been made up, and when he listens he's just going through the motions?

"No," he said. "He likes to talk. He talks a lot. He's not hearing you because he's telling you."

That is a bad flaw in a political leader.

* * *

The Special Assistant for Reality

The Wall Street Journal: November 26, 2010

A reporter covering the president's trip to Indiana this week said Mr. Obama was visiting the heartland in part to get out of the presidential bubble. I'm sure this was true. Presidents always get to the point where they want to escape Washington, and their lives, and their jobs. But they never can. Because when you're president and you go to Indiana, you take the bubble with you. Your bubble meets Indiana; your bubble witnesses Indianans. But you don't get out of the bubble in Indiana. Once you're in the bubble—once you're in the midst of a huge apparatus, once you have the cars and the aides and the security and the staffers—there is no getting out of it.

You cannot shake the bubble. Wherever you go, there it is. And the worst part is that the army of staff, security and aides that exists to be a barrier between a president and danger, or a president and inconvenience, winds up being a barrier between a president and reality.

You lose touch with America and Americans in the bubble, no matter who you are, or what party. This accounts for some of the spectacular blunders presidents make.

Because of the bubble, successful presidents have to walk into the presidency with an extremely strong sense of the reality of their country. In time, with the wear and tear of things, this sense of How Things Really Are may dissipate, disappear or remain stable, but it won't get stronger. It never gets stronger. High political office is like great affluence: It detaches you. It separates you from normal life.

Once you're president, you're not going to be able to change the features on your famous face; you're not going to be able to escape security, grab a fishing rod, and go sit on the side of a river waiting for normal Americans to walk by, settle in, fish with you, and say normal American things, from which you will garner insights into what normal Americans think.

What a president should ideally have, and what I think we all agree Mr. Obama badly needs, is an assistant whose sole job it is to explain and interpret the American people to him. Presidents already have special assistants for domestic policy, for congressional relations and national security. Why not a special assistant for reality? Someone to translate the views of the people, and explain how they think. An advocate for the average, a representative for the normal, to the extent America does normal.

If Mr. Obama had a special assistant for reality this week, this is how their dialogue might have gone over the anti-TSA uprising.

> **President:** This thing is all ginned up, isn't it? Right-wing Web sites fanned it. Then the mainstream media jumped in to display their phony populist street cred. Right?
>
> **Special Assistant for Reality:** No, Mr. President, it was more spontaneous. Web sites can't fan fires that aren't there. This is like the town hall uprisings of summer 2009. In the past month, citizens took videos at airports the same way town hall protesters made videos there, and put them on YouTube. The more pictures of pat-downs people saw, the more they opposed them.
>
> **President:** What's the essence of the opposition?
>
> **SAR:** Sir, Americans don't like it when strangers touch their

private parts. Especially when the strangers are in government uniforms and say they're here to help.

President: Is it that we didn't roll it out right? We made a mistake in not telling people in advance we were changing the procedure.

SAR: Um, no, Mr. President. If you'd told them in advance, they would have rebelled sooner.

President: We should have pointed out not everyone goes through the new machines, and only a minority get patted down.

SAR: Mr. President, if you'd told people, "Hello, there's only 1 chance in 3 you'll be molested at the airport today" most people wouldn't think, "Oh good, I like those odds."

President: But the polls are with me. People support the screenings.

SAR: At the moment, according to some. But most Americans don't fly frequently, and the protocols are new. As time passes, support will go steadily down.

President: I've noted with sensitivity that I'm aware all this is a real inconvenience.

SAR: It's not an inconvenience, it's a humiliation. In the new machine, and in the pat-downs, citizens are told to spread their feet and put their hands in the air. It's an attitude of submission—the same one the cops make the perps assume on "America's Most Wanted." Then, while you stand there in public in the attitude of submission, strangers touch intimate areas of your body. It's a violation of privacy. It leaves people feeling reduced. It's like society has decided you're a meat sack and not a soul. Humans have a natural, untaught understanding of the apartness of their bodies, and they don't like it when their space is violated. They recoil, and protest.

President: But you can have the pat-downs done in private.

SAR: Mr. President, you don't know this, but when you ask for that, a lot of TSA people get pretty passive-aggressive. They get Bureaucratic Dead Face and start barking, "I need a supervisor! Private pat-down!" And everyone looks, and the line slows down, and you start to feel like you're putting everyone out. You wait and wait, and finally they get another TSA person, and they take you into the little room and it's embarrassing, and you start to realize you're going to miss your plane. It's then that you realize: all this is how they discourage private pat-downs.

President: I've wondered if this general feeling of discomfort might be related to a certain Puritan strain within American thinking—a kind of horror at the body that, melded with, say, old Catholic teaching, not to be pejorative, might make for a pretty combustible cultural cocktail. This heightened consciousness of the body might suggest an element of physical shame we hadn't taken into account.

SAR: Mr. President, the rebellion isn't shame-based, it's John Wayne-based.

President: I don't follow.

SAR: John Wayne removes his boots and hat and puts his six-shooter on the belt, he gets through the scanner, and now he's standing there and sees what's being done to other people. A TSA guy is walking toward him, snapping his rubber gloves. Guy gets up close to Wayne, starts feeling his waist and hips. Wayne says, "Touch the jewels, Pilgrim, and I'll knock you into tomorrow."

President: John Wayne is dead.

SAR: No, he's not. You've got to understand that. Everyone's got an Inner Duke, even grandma.

President: What should I do?

SAR: Back off. Say you spent a day watching YouTube. You're not giving in to pressure, you're conceding to common sense. "Free men and women have a right not to be trifled with. We'll find a better way."

President: If I don't?

SAR: Well, every businessman in America already thinks you've been grabbing his gonads. You'll continue that general symbolism.

President: Janet Napolitano won't like it. Drudge is always after her. He'll get all "Big Sis Bows Now." She might quit.

SAR: Oh God, yes. A twofer!

President: I'd look like I got rolled.

SAR: Then look strong. Fire her. She's been a disaster from day one. Now she's the face of the debacle.

President: Won't they think I'm weak?

SAR: No. They'll think you returned to Planet Earth. They'll think ground control broke through to Major Tom. They'll think you took a step outside the bubble.

The Loneliest President since Nixon

The Wall Street Journal: November 24, 2014

Seven years ago I was talking to a longtime Democratic operative on Capitol Hill about a politician who was in trouble. The pol was likely finished, he said. I was surprised. Can't he change things and dig himself out? No. "People do what they know how to do." Politicians don't have a vast repertoire. When they get in a jam they just do what they've always done, even if it's not working anymore.

This came to mind when contemplating President Obama. After a devastating election, he is presenting himself as if he won. The people were not saying no to his policies, he explained, they would in fact like it if Republicans do what he tells them.

You don't begin a new relationship with a threat, but that is what he gave Congress: Get me an immigration bill I like or I'll change U.S. immigration law on my own.

Mr. Obama is doing what he knows how to do—stare them down and face them off. But his circumstances have changed. He used to be a conquering hero, now he's not. On the other hand, he used to have to worry about public support. Now, with no more elections before him, he has the special power of the man who doesn't care.

I have never seen a president in exactly the position Mr. Obama is, which is essentially alone. He's got no one with him now. The Republicans don't like him, for reasons both usual and particular: They have had no good experiences with him. The Democrats don't like him, for their own reasons plus the election loss. Before his post-election lunch with congressional leaders, he told the press that he will judiciously consider any legislation, whoever sends it to him, Republicans or Democrats. His words implied that in this he was less partisan and more public-spirited than the hacks arrayed around him. It is for these grace notes that he is loved. No one at the table looked at him with colder, beadier eyes than outgoing Senate Majority Leader Harry Reid, who clearly doesn't like him at all.

The press doesn't especially like the president; in conversation they evince no residual warmth. This week at the Beijing summit there was no sign the leaders of the world had any particular regard for him. They can read election returns. They respect power and see it leaking out of him. If Mr. Obama had won the election they would have faked respect and affection.

Vladimir Putin delivered the unkindest cut, patting Mr. Obama's shoulder reassuringly. Normally that's Mr. Obama's move, putting his hand on your back or shoulder as if to bestow gracious encouragement, needy little shrimp that you are. It's a dominance move. He's been doing it six years. This time it was Mr. Putin doing it to him. The president didn't like it.

From Reuters: "'It's beautiful, isn't it?' Putin was overheard saying in English in Obama's general direction, referring to the ornate conference room. 'Yes,' Obama replied, coldly, according to journalists who witnessed the scene."

The last time we saw a president so alone it was Richard Nixon, at the end of his presidency, when the Democrats had turned on him, the press hated him and the Republicans were fleeing. It was Sen. Barry Goldwater, the GOP's standard-bearer in 1964, and House Minority Leader John Rhodes, also of Arizona, who went to the White House to tell Nixon his support in Congress had collapsed, they would vote to impeach. Years later Goldwater called Nixon "the world's biggest liar."

But Nixon had one advantage Obama does not: the high regard

of the world's leaders, who found his downfall tragic (such ruin over such a trifling matter) and befuddling (he didn't keep political prisoners chained up in dungeons, as they did. Why such a fuss?).

Nixon's isolation didn't end well.

Last Sunday Mr. Obama, in an interview with CBS's Bob Schieffer, spoke of his motivation, how he's always for the little guy. "I love just being with the American people... You know how passionate I am about trying to help them." He said what is important is "a guy who's lost his job or lost his home or... is trying to send a kid to college." When he talks like that, as he does a lot, you get the impression his romantic vision of himself is Tom Joad in the movie version of "The Grapes of Wrath." "I'll be all around... wherever there's a fight so hungry people can eat, I'll be there."

I mentioned last week that the president has taken to filibustering, to long, rambling answers in planned sit-down settings—no questions on the fly walking from here to there, as other presidents have always faced. The press generally allows him to ramble on, rarely fighting back as they did with Nixon. But I have noticed Mr. Obama uses a lot of words as padding. He always has, but now he does it more. There's a sense of indirection and obfuscation. You can say, "I love you," or you can say, "You know, feelings will develop, that happens among humans and it's good it happens, and I have always said, and I said it again just last week, that you are a good friend, I care about you, and it's fair to say in terms of emotional responses that mine has escalated or increased somewhat, and 'love' would not be a wholly inappropriate word to use to describe where I'm coming from."

When politicians do this they're trying to mush words up so nothing breaks through. They're leaving you dazed and trying to make it harder for you to understand what's truly being said.

It is possible the president is responding to changed circumstances with a certain rigidity because no one ever stood in his way before. Most of his adult life has been a smooth glide. He had family challenges and an unusual childhood, but as an adult and a professional he never faced fierce, concentrated resistance. He was always magic. Life never came in and gave it to him hard on the jaw. So he really doesn't know how to get up from the mat. He doesn't know how to struggle to his feet and regain his balance. He only knows how to throw punches. But you can't punch from the mat.

He only knows how to do what he's doing.

In the meantime he is killing his party. Gallup this week found that the Republicans for the first time in three years beat the Democrats on favorability, and also that respondents would rather have Congress lead the White House than the White House lead Congress.

A few weeks ago a conservative intellectual asked me: "How are we going to get through the next two years?" It was a rhetorical question; he was just sharing his anxiety. We have a president who actually can't work with Congress, operating in a capital in which he is resented and disliked and a world increasingly unimpressed by him, and so increasingly predatory.

Anyway, for those who are young and not sure if what they are seeing is wholly unusual: Yes, it is wholly unusual.

Lafayette, We Are Not Here

The Wall Street Journal: January 12, 2015

It was not a missed public relations opportunity. PR is the showbiz of life, and that is not what this is.

Here are the reasons the president of the United States, or at very least the vice president, should have gone yesterday to the Paris march and walked shoulder to shoulder with the leaders of the world:

To show through his presence that the American people fully understand the import of what happened in the Charlie Hebdo murders, which is that Islamist extremists took the lives of free men and women who represented American and Western political freedoms, including freedom of speech;

To show through his presence that America and the West, and whatever nations choose to proclaim adherence to their democratic values, will stand together in rejecting and resisting extremist Islamist intolerance and violence;

To demonstrate the shared understanding that the massacre may amount to a tipping point, whereby those who protect and put forward Western political values will insist upon them in their sphere and ask their Muslim fellow citizens to walk side by side with them in shared public commitment;

To formally acknowledge the deep sympathy we feel that France, our oldest ally, suffered in the Charlie Hebdo murders a psychic shock akin to what America felt and suffered on 9/11/01. The day after our tragedy, the great French newspaper "Le Monde" ran an unforgettable cover with an editorial of affection and love titled

"Nous sommes tous Américains": "We are all Americans." That was an echo of what our American doughboys, who went to France in 1917 to save it, famously said as they landed: "Lafayette, we are here." Gen. Lafayette had been our first foreign friend and fought alongside Washington when we needed friends, in 1776. Is it sentimental to note this? Great nations run in part on sentiment.

For these reasons and more, Mr. President, Paris was worth a march.

It matters when, through absence and through bland statements, the leaders of America say: "Lafayette, we are not here." For all the ups and downs of the Franco-American relationship, the French are our friends. You march with your friends. It is civilizational: Sheer numbers and the importance of those marching show the world what unity, strength and shared commitment look like. Even Putin sent a top official.

The absence of the American president shows, too, what America would never in the past have conceded or acknowledged, and it was there in the photos of the order of the march. There in the center of the world leaders was Angela Merkel, leader of the West. I wrote a piece suggesting she had become that last spring. I was disturbed and saddened—actually I was mortified as I watched the entire march on TV in New York—to see that fact played out on every screen in the world.

Mr. Obama is wholly out of sync with U.S. thinking and sentiment.

Well, we sent the U.S. ambassador to France, Jane Hartley, down the street from the embassy to the march, say the administration's defenders. An Obama bundler, Hartley is widely acquainted with New York's journalists, who looked for her in the pictures of the crowd. I scanned dozens of pictures and could not find her. The French know a snub when they see one, and the French know how to snub back. I'm sure the organizers put her somewhere among the millions and perhaps through the obscurity of the position showed what they thought of the governmental status and standing of the person America "sent." Memo to this, past and future White Houses: just because you send fund-raisers to represent our country in high diplomatic posts does not mean those countries will pretend they were sent Chip Bohlen. The French, of all peoples, won't.

Were security concerns the reason for the president's absence? Life is a security concern, you must do what's right. Would massive U.S. security have inconvenienced others? Then make the security around the president less massive, less an imposition. There is no law that says it must be as Caesarian, and alienating, as it is. The president was too busy? He had an empty schedule. So did the vice president. The march was, at bottom, a preening and only symbolic show? When has this White House ever shown an aversion to preening and symbolic shows?

This was not caring enough.

Politico yesterday noted the president's reaction from day one of the Charlie Hebdo story has been "muted." He sat in an armchair in his office and pronounced the shootings "cowardly." He also said something that struck me at the time, that the murders violated "a universal belief in the freedom of expression." But there is no universal belief of free expression. Where it exists it has to be defended, in unity and with guts. That is the point.

Before I put up this post I searched the phrase "Lafayette, we are not here" to see if anyone had said it yet. It is already appearing on blogs and comment threads. Good. And it would be good to send our friends in France, again through social media, the sentence "Lafayette we are here, still, and with you, even if our leaders were not. The American people."

What a Disaster Looks Like

The Wall Street Journal: March 4, 2010

It is now exactly a year since President Obama unveiled his health-care push and his decision to devote his inaugural year to it—his branding year, his first, vivid year.

What a disaster it has been.

At best it was a waste of history's time, a struggle that will not in the end yield something big and helpful but will in fact make future progress more difficult. At worst it may prove to have fatally undermined a new presidency at a time when America desperately needs a successful one.

In terms of policy, his essential mistake was to choose health-care expansion over health-care reform. This at the exact moment voters were growing more anxious about the cost and reach of government. The practical mistake was that he did not include or envelop congressional Republicans from the outset, but handed the bill's creation over to a Democratic Congress that was becoming a runaway train. This at the exact moment Americans were coming to be concerned that Washington was broken, incapable of progress, frozen in partisanship.

His political mistakes were myriad and perhaps can be reduced to this:

There are all sorts of harm a new president can do to his presidency. Right now, part of the job of a new president in a hyper-mediaized environment is harm avoidance. This sounds defensive, and is at odds with the wisdom that presidents in times of crisis must boldly go forth and break through. But it all depends on what you're being bold about. Why, in 2009, create a new crisis over an important but secondary issue when we already have the Great Recession and two wars? Prudence and soundness of judgment are more greatly needed at the moment.

New presidents should never, ever, court any problem that isn't already banging at the door. They should never summon trouble. Mr. Obama did, boldly, perhaps even madly. And this is perhaps the oddest thing about No Drama Obama: In his first year as president he created unneeded political drama, and wound up seen by many Americans not as the hero but the villain.

In Washington among sympathetic political hands (actually, most of them sound formerly sympathetic) you hear the word "intervention," as in: "So-and-so tried an intervention with the president and it didn't work." So-and-so tried to tell him he's in trouble with the public and must moderate, recalibrate, back off from health care. The end of the story is always that so-and-so got nowhere. David Gergen a few weeks ago told the Financial Times the administration puts him in mind of the old joke: "How many psychiatrists does it take to change a lightbulb? Only one. But the lightbulb must want to change. I don't think President Obama wants to make any changes."

Sometimes when I look at the past three chief executives, I wonder if we were witnessing not three presidencies but three psychodramas played out on an intensely public stage.

What accounts for Mr. Obama's confidence and certainty?

Well, if you were a young progressive who'd won the presidency by a comfortable margin in a center-right country, you just might think you were a genius. You might not be surprised to find yourself surrounded by a cultish admiration: "They see him as a fabled figure," said a frequent White House visitor of some on the president's staff.

You might think the great strength you demonstrated during

the campaign—an ability to stay in the game you're playing and not the game someone else is playing, an ability to proceed undistracted by the crises or the machinations of your opponents, but to just keep playing your slow and steady game—is a strength suitable to your presidency. If you choose to play health care, that's the game you play, straight through, no jeers from the crowd distracting you.

If you were a young progressive who'd won the presidency against the odds, you probably wouldn't see yourself as someone who lucked out, with the stars perfectly aligned for a liberal victory. And you might forget we are more or less and functionally a 50–50 country and that you have to keep your finger very much on the pulse of the people if you're to survive and prosper.

And now here are two growing problems for Mr. Obama.

The first hasn't become apparent yet, but I suspect will be presenting itself, and soon. In order to sharpen the air of crisis he seems to think he needed to get his health-care legislation passed, in order to continue the air of crisis that might justify expanding government and sustaining its costs, and in order, always, to remind voters of George W. Bush, Mr. Obama has harped on what a horror the economy is. How great our challenges, how wicked our businessmen, how dim our future.

This is a delicate business. You can't be all rosy glow, you have to be candid. But attitude and mood matter. America has reached the point, a year and a half into the crisis, when frankly it needs some cheerleading. It can't always be mourning in America. We need some inspiration from the top, need someone who can speak with authority of what is working and can be made to work, of what is good and cause for pride. We are still employing 130 million people, and America is still competitive in the world, with innovative business leaders and practices.

The president can't be a hope purveyor while he's a doom merchant, and he appears to believe he has to be a doom merchant to justify ramming through his legislation. This particular legislation is not worth that particular price.

All this contributes to a second problem, which is a growing credibility gap. In his speech Wednesday, demanding an "up or down" vote, the president seemed convinced and committed—but nothing he said sounded true. His bill will "bring down the cost of health care for millions," it is "fully paid for," it will lower the long-term deficit by a trillion dollars.

Does anyone believe this? Does anyone who knows the ways of government, the compulsions of Congress, and how history has played out in the past, believe this? Even a little? Rep. Bart Stupak said Thursday that he and several of his fellow Democrats won't vote for the Senate version of the bill because it says right there on page 2,069 that the federal government would directly subsidize abortions. The bill's proponents say this isn't so. It would be a relief to have a president who could weigh in believably and make clear what his own bill says. But he seems to devote more words to obscuring than clarifying.

The only thing that might make his assertions sound believable now is if a group of congressional Republicans were standing next to him on the podium and putting forward a bill right along with him. Which, obviously, won't happen, for three reasons. First, they enjoy his discomfort. Second, they believe the bill is not worth saving, that at this point no matter what it contains—and at this point most people can no longer retain in their heads what it contains—it has been fatally tainted by the past year of mistakes and inadequacies.

And the third reason is that the past decade has taught them what a disaster looks like, and they've lost their taste for standing next to one.

CHAPTER 14

A Republic, If We Can Keep It

I saw the crash of '08 coming. In the years before you could feel it in the vibrations of New York, from jittery downtown to the fat, dumb Hamptons. Two things I will never forget.

I lived at the time at the busy, dangerous cross street of 96th Street and Park Avenue. It's a route across town, and to the FDR, and to the Triboro Bridge, and is always busy and full of fast-going cars. This is what I remember from the first weeks after the crash, in the fall of 2008: the constant sounds of cars suddenly hitting the brakes, screeching, the sound of honking, quick stops and distress. Everyone was distracted, everyone speeding around. Everything was frantic.

The second thing. I was visiting a friend in a pretty building on Lexington Avenue in the 90s. Waiting for the elevator was a young mother with two children. Next to her was a nanny or babysitter, a woman from the Caribbean. The mother was having some anxious conversation on the phone, her voice was high—money, accounts, the IRA. The babysitter silently watched with a look in her eye and the look said something cold and sad. "Welcome to my world."

* * *

We Live in an Age of Great Wealth— and Lousy Manners

The Wall Street Journal: October 27, 2007

So we are agreed. We are living in the second great Gilded Age, a time of startling personal wealth. In the West, the mansion after mansion with broad and rolling grounds; in the East, the apartments with foyers in which bowling teams could play. Or, on another level, the week's vacation in Disneyland or Dublin with the entire family—this in a nation in which, well within human memory, people with a week off stayed home and fixed things in the garage, or drove to the beach for a day and sat on a blanket from one of the kid's beds and thought: *This is the life.*

The Dow Jones Industrial Average has hit 14,000. The wealthy live better than kings. There isn't a billionaire in East Hampton who wouldn't look down on tatty old Windsor Castle. We have a potential presidential candidate who noted to a friend that if he won the presidency, the quality of his life would go down, not up.

The gap between rich and poor is great, and there is plenty of want, and also confusion. What the superrich do for a living now often seems utterly incomprehensible, and has for at least a generation. There is no word for it, only an image. There's a big pile of coins on a table. The rich shove their hands in, raise them, and as the coins sift through their fingers it makes...a bigger pile of coins. Then they sift through it again and the pile gets bigger again.

A general rule: If you are told what someone does for a living and it makes sense to you—orthodontist, store owner, professor—that means he's not rich. But if it's a man in a suit who does something

that takes him five sentences to explain and still you walk away confused, and castigating yourself as to why you couldn't understand
the central facts of the acquisition of wealth in the age you live in—
well, chances are you just talked to a billionaire.

* * *

There are good things and bad in the Gilded Age, pluses and
minuses. I write here of a minus. It has to do with our manners, the
ones we show each other on the street. I think riches, or the pursuit of riches, has made us ruder. You'd think broad comfort would
assuage certain hungers. It has not. It has sharpened them.

Here's a moment in the pushiness of the Gilded Age. I walk into
a shop on Madison Avenue daydreaming, trying to remember what
it was I thought last week I should pick up, what was it...

"Hi! Let me help you find what you're looking for!" She is a
saleswoman, cracking gum with intensity, about 25 years old, and
she has made a beeline to her mark. That would be me.

"Mmmm, actually—"

"We have summer sweaters on sale. What size are you?!" Her
style is aggressive friendliness.

In another shop, as soon as I walk in the door, "How are you
today? How can I help you?" Those dread words.

"Oh, I'm sort of just looking."

"I like your bag!"

"Um, thanks." What they are forcing you to do is engage. If you
engage—"Um, thanks"—you have a relationship. If you have a relationship, it's easier for them to turn you upside down and shake the
coins from your pockets.

It is like this in all the shops I go in now, except for the big stores
(Macy's, Duane Reade drugstore), where they ignore you.

There are strategies. You can do the full Garbo: "Leave me alone."

But they'll think you're a shoplifter and watch you. Or the strong lady with boundaries: "Thank you, if I need help I'll ask." But your reverie is broken. Or the acquiescent person: "Take me under your leadership, oh aggressively friendly salesperson." But this is bowing to the pushiness of the Gilded Age.

* * *

You leave the floor for the street and meet the woman with the clipboard. "Do you have two seconds for the environment?" Again, not a soft question but a challenge. Her question is phrased so that if you don't stop and hear her spiel, you are admitting you won't give two seconds for the environment, or two cents for it, either. You give the half-smile-nod, shake your head, walk on. She looks at you as if you're the reason the Earth is going to hell.

Do they know they're being manipulative? If they have a brain they do. Their trainers certainly know. Do they know it's also why no one quite trusts them? Do they care? Why would they? They're the manipulators on the street.

Or: I'm in a local restaurant with a friend. We sat down 40 seconds ago and are starting to catch up when: "What do you want to drink?" An interruption, but so what? We order, talk, my friend is getting to the punch line of the story when: "We have specials this evening." Not "Let me know when you're ready to hear the specials." We stop talking, listen. The waiter stands there, pad in hand. "You ready?" If you ask for a minute, he'll nod and be back in exactly one minute. "Do you know yet?" Again, this is not a request. One is being told to snap to it. Get 'em in, get 'em out. Move 'em.

It's funny. In a time of recession, you'd think salespeople would be more aggressive, because so much might hinge on the sale—a commission, a job. In a time of relative wealth, you'd think they might be less aggressive. But the opposite seems true.

* * *

Technology has not helped in this area. Cellphones are wonderful, but they empower the obnoxious and amplify the ignorant. Once they kept their thoughts to themselves. They had no choice. Now they have cellphones, into which they bark, "I'm on line at Duane Reade. Yeah. Ex-Lax." Oh, thank you for sharing. How much less my life would be if I didn't know.

BlackBerrys empower the obsessed. We wouldn't have them if the economy weren't high and we weren't pretty well off. Once, a political figure in New York invited me to a private dinner. I was seated next to him, and as the table conversation took off he leaned back, quietly took out his BlackBerry, and began to scroll. It occurred to me that if I said something live in person, it would not be as interesting to him as if I'd BlackBerryed him. It occurred to me that if I wanted to talk to him I'd have to BlackBerry him and say, "Please talk to me." And then he'd get the message.

It is possible that we are on the cellphone because we are lonely and hunger for connection, even of the shallowest kind; that we BlackBerry because we hope for a sense of control in a chaotic world; that we are frightened of stillness and must interrupt conversations; that we are desperate to make the sale in the highly competitive environment of the Banana Republic on 86th Street and must aggressively pursue customers.

It's also possible we have grown more boorish. I think it's that one. Many things thrive in the age of everything, including bad manners.

The Rise of the White-Collar Big-Money Psychopath

The Wall Street Journal: June 28, 2002

Three scenes.

It is a spring day in the early 1990s and I am talking with the head of a mighty American corporation. We're in his window-lined office, high in midtown Manhattan, the view—silver skyscrapers stacked one against another, dense, fine-lined, sparkling in the sun—so perfect, so theatrical it's like a scrim, like a fake backdrop for a 1930s movie about people in tuxes and tails. Edward Everett Horton could shake his cocktail shaker here; Fred and Ginger could banter on the phone.

The CEO tells me it is "annual report" time, and he is looking forward to reading the reports of his competitors.

Why? I asked him. I wondered what specifically he looks for when he reads the reports of the competition.

He said he always flipped to the back to see what the other CEOs got as part of their deal—corporate jets, private helicopters, whatever. "We all do that," he said. "We all want to see who has what."

Second scene: It is the mid-'90s, a soft summer day, and I am crossing a broad Manhattan avenue, I think it was Third or Lexington. I am doing errands. I cross the avenue with the light but halfway across I see the switch to yellow. I pick up my pace. From the corner of my eye I see, then hear, the car. Bright black Mercedes, high gloss, brand new. The man at the wheel, dark haired, in his 30s, is gunning the motor. *Vroom vroom!* He drums his fingers on the steering wheel impatiently. The light turns. He vrooms forward. I sprint the last few steps toward the sidewalk. He speeds by so close the wind makes my cotton skirt move. I realize: If I hadn't sprinted that guy would have hit me. I think: *Young Wall Street titan. Bonus bum.*

Third scene, just the other night. I am talking to a shrewd and celebrated veteran of Wall Street and Big Business. The WorldCom story has just broken; he tells me of it. He has a look I see more and more, a kind of face-lift look only it doesn't involve a face-lift. It's like this: The face goes blanched and blank and the eyes go up slightly as if the hairline had been yanked back. He looked scalped by history.

For years, he said, he had given speeches in Europe on why they should invest in America. We have the great unrigged game, he'd tell them, we have oversight and regulation, we're the stable democracy with reliable responsible capitalism. "I can't give that speech anymore," he said.

*   *   *

Something is wrong with—what shall we call it? Wall Street, Big Business. We'll call it Big Money. Something has been wrong with it for a long time, at least a decade, maybe more. Probably more. I don't fully understand it. I can't imagine that it's this simple: A new generation of moral and ethical zeroes rose to run Big Money over the past decade, and nobody quite noticed but they were genuinely bad people who were running the system into the ground. I am not sure it's this simple, either: A friend tells me it all stems from the easy money of the '90s, piles and piles of funny money that Wall Street learned to play with. That would be a description of the scandal, perhaps, but not the reason for it.

At any rate it no longer seems like a scandal. "Scandal" seems quaint. It is starting to feel like a tragedy. Not for Wall Street and for corporations—it's a setback for them—but for our country. For a way of living and being.

Those who invested in and placed faith in Global Crossing, Enron, Tyco or WorldCom have been cheated and fooled by individuals whose selfishness seems so outsized, so huge, that it seems less human and flawed than weird and puzzling. Did they think they would get away with accounting scams forever? Did they think they'd never get caught? Do they think they're operating in the end times and they better grab what they can now and go hide? What were they thinking?

We should study who these men are—they are still all men, and still being turned in by women—and try to learn how they rationalized their actions, how they excused their decisions or ignored the consequences, how they thought about the people they were cheating. I mention this because I've been wondering if we are witnessing the emergence of a new pathology: White-Collar Big-Money Psychopath.

* * *

I have been reading Michael Novak, the philosopher and social thinker and, to my mind, great man. Twenty years ago this summer he published what may be his masterpiece, "The Spirit of Democratic Capitalism." It was a stunning book marked by great clarity of expression and originality of thought. He spoke movingly of the meaning and morality of capitalism. He asked why capitalism is good, and answered that there is one great reason: Of all the systems devised by man it is the one most likely to lift the poor out of poverty.

But, he asserted unassailably, capitalism cannot exist in a void. Capitalism requires an underlying moral edifice. Without it nothing works; with it all is possible. That edifice includes people who have an appreciation for and understanding of the human person; it requires a knowledge that business can contribute to community and family; it requires "a sense of sin," a sense of right and wrong, and an appreciation that the unexpected happens, that things take surprising turns in life.

Mr. Novak was speaking, he knew, to an international intellectual community that felt toward capitalism a generalized contempt. Capitalism was selfish, exploitative, unequal, imperialistic, warlike. He himself had been a socialist and knew the critiques. But he had come to see capitalism in a new way.

Capitalism, like nature, wants to increase itself, wants to grow and create, and as it does it produces more: more goods, more services, more "liberation," more creativity, more opportunity, more possibilities, more unanticipated ferment, movement, action.

So capitalism was to Mr. Novak a public good, and he addressed its subtler critics. What of "the corruption of affluence," the idea that while it is moral discipline that builds and creates success, success itself tends to corrupt and corrode moral discipline? Dad made money with his guts, you spend it at your leisure. The result, an ethos of self-indulgence, greed and narcissism. The system works, goes this argument, but too well, and in the end it corrodes.

Mr. Novak answered by quoting the philosopher Jacques Maritain, who once observed that affluence in fact inspires us to look beyond the material for meaning in our lives. "It's exactly because people have bread that they realize you can't live by bread alone." In a paradoxical way, said Mr. Novak, the more materially comfortable a society becomes, the more spiritual it is likely to become, "its hungers more markedly transcendent."

Right now Mr. Novak certainly seems right about American society. We have not become worse people with the affluence of the past 20 years, and have arguably in some interesting ways become better. (Forty years ago men in the New York City borough of Queens ignored the screams of a waitress named Kitty Genovese as she was stabbed to death in an apartment building parking lot.

Today men of Queens are famous for strapping 60 pounds of gear on their back and charging into the Towers.)

But it appears that the leaders of business, of Wall Street, of big accounting have, many of them, become worse with affluence. Or maybe it's just worse with time. I think of a man of celebrated rectitude who, if he returned to the Wall Street of his youth, would no doubt be welcomed back with cheers and derided behind his back as a sissy. He wouldn't dream of cooking the books. He wouldn't dream of calling costs profits. He would never fit in.

* * *

Mr. Novak famously sees business as a vocation, and a deeply serious one. Business to him is a stage, a platform on which men and women can each day take actions that are either moral or immoral, helpful or not. When their actions are marked by high moral principle, they heighten their calling—they are suddenly not just "in business" but part of a noble endeavor that adds to the sum total of human joy and progress. The work they do builds things—makes connections between people, forges community, spreads wealth, sets example, creates a template, offers inspiration. The work they do changes the world. And in doing this work they strengthen the ground on which democracy and economic freedom stand.

They are, that is, patriots.

"The calling of business is to support the reality and reputation of capitalism," says Mr. Novak, "and not undermine [it]."

But undermining it is precisely what the men of WorldCom et al. have done. It is their single most destructive act.

* * *

Edward Younkins of the Acton Institute distills Mr. Novak's philosophy into "Seven Great Responsibilities for Corporations": satisfy customers with good services of real value; make a reasonable return to investors; create new wealth; create new jobs; defeat cynicism and envy by demonstrating internally that talent and hard work will and can be rewarded; promote inventiveness, ingenuity and creativity; diversify the interests of the republic.

As for business leaders, their responsibility is to shape a corporate culture that fosters virtue; to exemplify respect for the rule of law; to act in practical ways to improve society; to communicate often and openly with investors, pensioners, customers and employees; to contribute toward improved civil society; and to protect—lovely phrase coming—"the moral ecology of freedom."

*   *   *

To look at the current Big Money crisis armed with Mr. Novak's views on and love of capitalism is to understand the crisis more deeply.

Businessmen are not just businessmen. They are not just money-makers. Businessmen and -women are representatives of, leaders of, exemplars of an ethos and a way of life. They are the face and daily reality of free-market capitalism.

And when they undermine it with their actions they damage more than their reputations, more than the portfolios of investors. They damage and deal a great blow to our country. They make a great and decent edifice look dishonest and low because they are dishonest and low.

When we call them "thieves" or "con men" we are not, with these tough words, quite capturing the essence of the damage they do and have done.

It would be good if some great man or woman of business in America would rise and speak of that damage, and its meaning, and how to heal it. It would be good if the Securities and Exchange Commission held open hearings in New York on what has been done and why and by whom, and how they got away with it until they didn't anymore. It would be good if the business leaders of our country shunned those businessmen who did such damage to the very freedoms they used to make themselves wealthy. And it just might be good if some companies, on the next casual Friday, gave everyone in their employ the day off, with just one assignment: Go read a book in the park. They could start with "The Spirit of Democratic Capitalism," and go from there.

On Privacy...

These two pieces are about the lost world of privacy. I still grieve it. When you have lost a sense of privacy you have lost something intimate to yourself, something innate and personal. Think of your own most private thoughts. Think of their being broadcast to the world. Think of how you would experience that, as a gross violation of your personhood.

* * *

We All Know Too Much about One Another

The Wall Street Journal: May 21, 2010

This column is about privacy, a common enough topic but one to which I don't think we're paying enough attention. As a culture we may be losing it at a greater clip than we're noticing, and that loss will have implications both political and, I think, spiritual. People don't like it when they can't keep their own information, or their sense of dignified apartness. They feel violated when it's taken from them. This adds to the general fraying of things.

Privacy in America didn't fall like the Berlin Wall, with a cloud of cement dust and cheers. It didn't happen over a few days but a few decades, and it didn't fall exactly, but is falling. If you're not worried about that, or not feeling some nostalgia for the older, more contained and more private America, then you're just not paying attention.

We are all regularly warned about the primary threat of identity theft, in which technologically adept criminals break into databases to find and use your private financial information. But other things, not as threatening, leave many of us uneasy. When there is a terrorist incident or a big crime, we are inundated on TV with all the video-tape from all the surveillance cameras. "We think that's the terrorist there, taking off his red shirt." There are cameras all over. No terror-ist can escape them, but none of the rest of us can either. If you call 911, your breathless plea for help may be on tonight's evening news, even though a panicked call to the police is a pretty intimate thing.

Do you want anyone who can get your address on the Inter-net to be able to call up a photo of your house? If you don't, that's unfortunate, because it's all there on Google Street View, like it or not. Facebook has apparently taken to changing its default settings so that your information—the personal news you thought you were sharing only with friends—is available to strangers and mined for commercial data. And young people will say anything on network-ing sites because they're young, because no one has taught them not to, because they're being raised in a culture that has grown more exhibitionistic.

In the "Oxford English Dictionary" the first definition of pri-vacy is: "The state or condition of being alone, undisturbed, or free from public attention, as a matter of choice or right; seclusion; free-dom from interference or intrusion." The third definition casts some light on how our culture is evolving: "Absence or avoidance of pub-licity or display; secrecy, concealment, discretion; protection from public knowledge or availability. Now rare, or merging with sense 1." You said it, OED.

We increasingly know things about each other (or think we do) that we should not know, have no right to know, and have a right, actually, not to know. And of course technology is not the only force at work. An exhibitionist culture will develop brutish ways. And so candidates and nominees for public office (and TV stars) are now asked—forced is a closer word—to make public declarations about aspects of their lives that are, actually, personal, and private. "Rep. Smith, 45 and unmarried, has refused to answer persistent questions on whether he is gay. But bloggers have revealed that he owns antiques and has played badminton." Those who demand that everything be declared see themselves as street fighters for the freedom in men's souls. But they're not. They're bullies without boundaries.

"The private life is dead in the new Russia," said a Red Army officer in the film of Boris Pasternak's "Dr. Zhivago." There were many scarifying things in that great movie, but that was the scariest, the dry proclamation that the intimate experience of being alive would now be subordinate to the state. An odd thing is that when privacy is done away with, people don't become more authentic, they become less so. What replaces what used not to be said is something that must be said and is usually a lie.

When we lose our privacy, we lose some of our humanity; we lose things that are particular to us, that make us separate and distinctive as souls, as, actually, children of God. We also lose trust, not only in each other but in our institutions, which we come to fear. People who now have no faith in the security of their medical and financial records, for instance, will have even less faith in their government. If progressives were sensitive to this, they'd have more power. They always think the answer is a new Internet Privacy Act. But everyone else thinks that's just a new system to hack.

At technology conferences now they say, "Get over it." Privacy is gone, get with the new world. But I'm not sure technologically focused people can be sensitive to the implications of their instructions.

We all think of technology as expanding our horizons, and in many ways of course it does. How could we not be thrilled and moved that the instant transmission of an MRI from New York to Mumbai can result in the correct diagnosis that saves a child's life? But technology is also constricting. It can restrain movement and possibility.

Here is a fanciful example that is meant to have a larger point. If you, complicated little pirate that you are, find yourself caught in the middle of a big messy scandal in America right now, you can't go to another continent to hide out or ride out the storm. Earlier generations did exactly that, but you can't, because you've been on the front page of every Web site, the lead on every newscast. You'll be spotted in South Africa and Googled in Gdansk. Two hundred years ago, or even 100, when you got yourself in a big fat bit of trouble in Paris, you could run to the docks and take the first ship to America, arrive unknown and start over. You changed your name, or didn't even bother. It would be years before anyone caught up with you.

And this is part of how America was born. Gamblers, bounders, ne'er-do-wells, third sons in primogeniture cultures—most of us came here to escape something! Our people came here not only for a new chance but to disappear, hide out, tend their wounds and summon the energy, in time, to impress the dopes back home. America has many anthems, but one of them is "I'll show 'em!"

There is still something of that in all Americans, which means as a people we're not really suited to the age of surveillance, the age of no privacy. There is no hiding place now, not here, and this strikes me as something of huge and existential import. It's like the closing of yet another frontier, a final one we didn't even know was there.

A few weeks ago the latest right-track-wrong-track numbers came out, and the wrong-track numbers won, as they have since 2003. About 70% of respondents said they thought the country was on the wrong track. This was generally seen as "a commentary on the economy," and no doubt this is part of it. But Americans are more interesting and complicated people than that, and maybe they're also thinking, "Remember Jeremiah Johnson? The guy who went off by himself in the mountains and lived on his own? I'd like to do that. But they'd find me on Google Earth."

What We Lose if We Give Up Privacy

The Wall Street Journal: August 16, 2013

What is privacy? Why should we want to hold on to it? Why is it important, necessary, precious?

Is it just some prissy relic of the pretechnological past?

We talk about this now because of Edward Snowden, the National Security Agency revelations and new fears that we are operating, all of us, within what has become or is becoming a massive surveillance state. They log your calls here, they can listen in, they can read your emails. They keep the data in mammoth machines that contain a huge collection of information about you and yours. This of course is in pursuit of a laudable goal, security in the age of terror.

Is it excessive? It certainly appears to be. Does that matter? Yes. Among other reasons: The end of the expectation that citizens' communications are and will remain private will probably change us as a people, and a country.

* * *

Among the pertinent definitions of privacy from the "Oxford English Dictionary": "freedom from disturbance or intrusion," "intended only for the use of a particular person or persons," belonging to "the property of a particular person." Also: "confidential, not to be disclosed to others." Among others, the OED quotes the playwright Arthur Miller, describing the McCarthy era: "Conscience was no longer a private matter but one of state administration."

Privacy is connected to personhood. It has to do with intimate things—the innards of your head and heart, the workings of your mind—and the boundary between those things and the world outside.

A loss of the expectation of privacy in communications is a loss of something personal and intimate, and it will have broader implications. That is the view of Nat Hentoff, the great journalist and civil libertarian. He is 88 now and on fire on the issue of privacy.

"The media has awakened," he told me. "Congress has awakened, to some extent." Both are beginning to realize "that there are particular constitutional liberty rights that [Americans] have that distinguish them from all other people, and one of them is privacy."

Mr. Hentoff sees excessive government surveillance as violative of the Fourth Amendment, which protects "the right of the people to be secure in their persons, houses, papers, and effects, against unreasonable searches and seizures" and requires that warrants be issued only "upon probable cause... particularly describing the place to be searched, and the persons or things to be seized."

But Mr. Hentoff sees the surveillance state as a threat to free speech, too. About a year ago he went up to Harvard to speak to a class. He asked, he recalled: "How many of you realize the connection between what's happening with the Fourth Amendment with the First Amendment?" He told the students that if citizens don't have basic privacies—firm protections against the search and seizure of your private communications, for instance—they will be left feeling "threatened." This will make citizens increasingly concerned "about what they say, and they do, and they think." It will have the effect of constricting freedom of expression. Americans will become careful about what they say that can be misunderstood or misinterpreted, and then too careful about what they say that can be understood. The inevitable end of surveillance is self-censorship.

All of a sudden, the room became quiet. "These were bright kids, interested, concerned, but they hadn't made an obvious connection about who we are as a people." We are "free citizens in a self-governing republic."

Mr. Hentoff once asked Justice William Brennan "a schoolboy's question": What is the most important amendment to the Constitution? "Brennan said the First Amendment, because all the other ones come from that. If you don't have free speech you have to be afraid, you lack a vital part of what it is to be a human being who is free to be who you want to be." Your own growth as a person will in time be constricted, because we come to know ourselves by our thoughts.

He wonders if Americans know who they are compared to what the Constitution says they are.

Mr. Hentoff's second point: An entrenched surveillance state will change and distort the balance that allows free government to function successfully. Broad and intrusive surveillance will, definitively, put government in charge. But a republic only works, Mr. Hentoff notes, if public officials know that they—and the government itself—answer to the citizens. It doesn't work, and is distorted, if the citizens must answer to the government. And that will happen more and more if the government knows—and you know—that the government has something, or some things, on you. "The bad thing is you no longer have the one thing we're supposed to have as Americans living in a self-governing republic," Mr. Hentoff said. "The people we elect are not your bosses, they are responsible to us." They must answer to us. But if they increasingly control our privacy, "suddenly they're in charge if they know what you're thinking."

This is a shift in the democratic dynamic. "If we don't have free speech then what can we do if the people who govern us have no respect for us, may indeed make life difficult for us, and in fact belittle us?"

If massive surveillance continues and grows, could it change the national character? "Yes, because it will change free speech."

What of those who say "I have nothing to fear, I don't do anything wrong"? Mr. Hentoff suggests that's a false sense of security. "When you have this amount of privacy invasion put into these huge data banks, who knows what will come out?" Or can be made to come out through misunderstanding the data, or finagling, or mischief of one sort or another. "People say, 'Well, I've done nothing wrong so why should I worry?' But that's too easy a way to get out of what is in our history—constant attempts to try to change who we are as Americans." Asked about those attempts, he mentions the Alien and Sedition Acts of 1798, the Red Scare of the 1920s and the McCarthy era. Those times and incidents, he says, were more than specific scandals or news stories, they were attempts to change our nature as a people.

What of those who say they don't care what the federal government does as long as it keeps us safe? The threat of terrorism is real, Mr. Hentoff acknowledges. Al Qaeda is still here, its networks are growing. But you have to be careful about who's running U.S. intelligence and U.S. security, and they have to be fully versed in and obey constitutional guarantees. "There has to be somebody supervising them who knows what's right... Terrorism is not going to go away. But we need someone in charge of the whole apparatus who has read the Constitution."

Advances in technology constantly up the ability of what government can do. Its technological expertise will only become deeper and broader. "They think they're getting to how you think. The technology is such that with the masses of databases, then privacy will get even weaker."

Mr. Hentoff notes that J. Edgar Hoover didn't have all this technology. "He would be so envious of what NSA can do."

The MSM Is Suffering from Freedom Envy

The Wall Street Journal: February 17, 2005

"Salivating morons." "Scalp hunters." "Moon howlers." "Trophy hunters." "Sons of Sen. McCarthy." "Rabid." "Blogswarm." "These pseudo-journalist lynch mob people."

This is excellent invective. It must come from bloggers. But wait, it is the mainstream media and their maidservants in the elite journalism reviews, and they are talking about bloggers!

Those MSMers have gone wild, I tell you! The tendentious language, the low insults. It's the Wild Wild West out there. We may have to consider legislation.

When you hear name-calling like what we've been hearing from the elite media this week, you know someone must be doing something right. The hysterical edge makes you wonder if writers for newspapers and magazines and professors in J-schools don't have a serious case of freedom envy.

The bloggers have that freedom. They have the still pent-up energy of a liberated citizenry, too. The MSM doesn't. It has lost its old monopoly on information. It is angry.

But MSM criticism of the blogosphere misses the point, or rather points.

Blogging changes how business is done in American journalism. The MSM isn't over. It just can no longer pose as if it is the Guardian of Established Truth. The MSM is just another player now. A big one, but a player.

The blogosphere isn't some mindless eruption of wild opinion. That isn't their power. This is their power:

1. They use the tools of journalists (computer, keyboard, a spirit of inquiry, a willingness to ask the question) and of the Internet (Google, LexisNexis) to look for and find facts that have been overlooked, ignored or hidden. They look for the telling quote, the ignored statistic, the data that has been submerged. What they are looking for is information that is true. When they get it they post it and include it in the debate. This is a public service.

2. Bloggers, unlike reporters at elite newspapers and magazines, are independent operators. They are not, and do not have to be, governed by mainstream thinking. Nor do they have to accept the directives of an editor pushing an ideology or a publisher protecting his friends. Bloggers have the freedom to decide on their own when a story stops being a story. They get to decide when the search for facts is over. They also decide on their own when the search for facts begins. It was a blogger at the World Economic Forum, as we all know, who first reported the Eason Jordan story. It was bloggers, as we all know, who pursued it. Matt Drudge runs a news site and is not a blogger, but what was true of him at his beginning (the Monica Lewinsky story, he decided, is a story) is true of bloggers: It's a story if they say it is. This is a public service.

3. Bloggers have an institutional advantage in terms of technology and form. They can post immediately. The items they post can be as long or short as they judge necessary. Breaking news can be one sentence long: "Malkin gets Barney Frank earwitness report." In newspapers you have to go to the editor, explain to him why the paper should have another piece on the Eason Jordan affair, spend a day reporting it, only to find that all that's new today is that reporter Michelle Malkin got an interview with Barney Frank. That's not enough to merit 10 inches of newspaper space, so the Times doesn't carry what the blogosphere had 24 hours ago. In the old days a lot of

interesting information fell off the editing desk in this way. Now it doesn't. This is a public service.

4. Bloggers are also selling the smartest take on a story. They're selling an original insight, a new area of inquiry. Mickey Kaus of Kausfiles has his bright take, Andrew Sullivan has his, InstaPundit has his. They're all selling their shrewdness, experience, depth. This too is a public service.

5. And they're doing it free. That is, the Times costs me a dollar and so does the Journal, but Kausfiles doesn't cost a dime. This too is a public service. Some blogs get their money from yearly fundraising, some from advertisers, some from a combination, some from a salary provided by Slate or National Review. Most are labors of love. Some bloggers—a lot, I think—are addicted to digging, posting, coming up with the bright phrase. OK with me. Some get burned out. But new ones are always coming up, so many that I can't keep track of them and neither can anyone else.

But when I read blogs, when I wake up in the morning and go to About Last Night and Lucianne and Lileks, I remember what the late great Christopher Reeve said on "The Tonight Show" 20 years ago. He was the second guest, after Rodney Dangerfield. Dangerfield did his act and he was hot as a pistol. Then after Reeve sat down Dangerfield continued to be riotous. Reeve looked at him, gestured toward him, looked at the audience and said with grace and delight, "Do you believe this is free?" The audience cheered. That's how I feel on their best days when I read blogs.

That you get it free doesn't mean commerce isn't involved, for it is. It is intellectual commerce. Bloggers give you information and point of view. In return you give them your attention and intellectual energy. They gain influence by drawing your eyes; you gain information by lending your eyes. They become well known and influential; you become entertained or informed. They get something from it and so do you.

6. It is not true that there are no controls. It is not true that the blogosphere is the Wild West. What governs members of the blogosphere is what governs, to some degree, members of the MSM, and that is the desire for status and respect. In the blogosphere you lose both if you put forward as fact information that is incorrect, specious or cooked. You lose status and respect if your take on a story is patently stupid. You lose status and respect if you are unprofessional or deliberately misleading. And once you've lost a sufficient amount of status and respect, none of the other bloggers link to you anymore or raise your name in their arguments. And you're over. The great correcting mechanism for people on the Web is people on the Web.

There are blogs that carry political and ideological agendas. But everyone is on to them and it's mostly not obnoxious because their agendas are mostly declared.

7. I don't know if the blogosphere is rougher in the ferocity of its personal attacks than, say, Drew Pearson. Or the rough boys and girls of the great American editorial pages of the 1930s and '40s. Bloggers are certainly not as rough as the splenetic pamphleteers of the 18th and 19th centuries, who amused themselves accusing Thomas Jefferson of sexual perfidy and Andrew Jackson of having married a whore. I don't know how Walter Lippmann or Scotty Reston would have seen the blogosphere; it might have frightened them if they'd lived to see it. They might have been impressed by the sheer digging that goes on there. I have seen friends savaged by blogs and winced for them—but, well, too bad. I've been attacked. Too bad. If you can't take it, you shouldn't be thinking aloud for a living. The blogosphere is tough. But are personal attacks worth it if what we get in return is a whole new media form that can add to the true-information flow while correcting the biases and lapses of the mainstream media? Yes. Of course.

I conclude with a few predictions.

Some brilliant rising young reporter with a growing reputation at the Times or Newsweek or Post is going to quit, go into the blogging business, start The Daily Joe, get someone to give him a guaranteed ad for two years and become a journalistic force. His motive will be influence, and the use of his gifts along the lines of excellence. His blog will further legitimize blogging.

Most of the blogstorms of the past few years have resulted in outcomes that left and right admit or bray were legitimate. Dan Rather fell because his big story was based on a fabrication, Trent Lott said things that it could be proved he said. But coming down the pike is a blogstorm in which the bloggers turn out to be wrong. Good news: They'll probably be caught and exposed by bloggers. Bad news: It will show that blogging isn't nirvana, and its stars aren't foolproof. But then we already know that, don't we?

Some publisher is going to decide that if you can't fight blogs, you can join them. He'll think like this: *We're already on the Internet. That's how bloggers get and review our reporting. Why don't we get our own bloggers to challenge our work? Why don't we invite bloggers who already exist into the tent? Why not take the best things said on blogs each day and print them on a Daily Blog page? We'd be enhancing our rep as an honest news organization, and it will further our branding!*

Someone is going to address the "bloggers are untrained journalists" question by looking at exactly what "training," what education in the art/science/craft/profession of journalism the reporters and editors of the MSM have had in the past 60 years or so. It has seemed to me the best of them never went to J-school but bumped into journalism along the way—walked into a radio station or newspaper one day and found their calling. Bloggers signify a welcome return to that old style. In journalism you learn by doing, which is what a lot of bloggers are doing.

Finally, someday in America the next big bad thing is going to happen, and lines are going to go down, and darkness is going to descend, and the instant communication we now enjoy is going to be compromised. People in one part of the country are going to wonder how people in another part are doing. Little by little lines are going to come up, and people are going to log on, and they're going to get the best, most comprehensive, and ultimately, just because it's there, most heartening information from...some lone blogger out there. And then another. They're going to do some big work down the road.

Campaigns Have Always Been Negative but They Haven't Always Been Ubiquitous

The Wall Street Journal: February 8, 2012

A man's voice, urgent:

"America is in crisis. It feels like we're coming apart."

Shots from a hand-held camera—blurry, indistinct. Angry citizens, protests. Close-up on a bearded young man, his face distorted by rage.

"We face unprecedented challenges."

Cuts of lonely farms, small houses with for-sale signs. A little girl with pleading eyes.

"Is this any time for inexperience?"

A tattered flag blows in the wind.

"One candidate has silky words, but what do they mean? What do we really know of him?"

Video shot from behind a candidate who stands at a podium. We see his back, the jerky movement of his arms. We see faces in the crowd—confused, shaking their heads. Are they being gulled?

"His backwoods chatter can't hide the facts. He's never had a college education—or any education at all. He claims he read the classics at night, by candlelight. But that's not really what the frontier was about."

Cut to a raucous bonfire—frantic dancing, men and women, drinking. A hysterical laugh pierces the outer darkness.

"He says he's for the little guy. Why is he hiding the fact that he's a big-time lawyer who sold himself to the highest bidder?"

Archival film shot: a saloon table, a wad of bills gathered up by a fat man's hand. Gleaming cuff links, ruby ring. In the background, a woman's chuckle. Somehow we know her name is Belle.

"He served just one term in the House—one. And wasn't re-elected."

Blurry photo of a man. We're not sure who it is. Slowly it begins to come into focus—stark face, rude cheekbones, slick black hair. Now cut to close-up: his irregular eyes. One pupil is more dilated than the other. He's cockeyed.

"He ran for the Senate, and failed."

Video of torches being extinguished. A slump-shouldered voter walks away, alone.

"They said they loved his speeches, but what were they beyond words? His wife? Imperious. His address? Impeccable. As for the family he came from, he left them in the backwoods when he went to the big city."

Shot of sad, impoverished family in an empty field.

Then quick shots: An honest American worker in front of a tool shed. Yearning families on farms and in cities. A little girl holding a flag, which droops wanly on her shoulder.

"This is a time of crisis—and he's telling jokes."

Screen goes black.

"They call him 'Honest Abe.' But he's just another Springfield insider."

Another man's voice:

"I'm Stephen A. Douglas, and I approved this message."

So that's my Abe Lincoln attack ad. It can claim to be factual, or at least arguable, and the parts that are too mean would ensure it got plenty of free play on "Hardball," "Special Report" and "Morning Joe," where we'd all deplore it. Then the Douglas campaign would pull it after complaining they have no control over their stupid, independent Super PAC, Americans for Sort of More Slavery at Least for a While.

I wish someone would make this ad and show it across the country and say at the end: "Cheer up, have faith, greatness is possible, sometimes it's there but you only see it in retrospect. Not everyone's a bum."

Attack ads are the dreck of democracy. There are too many of them and there will be more. In the next 8½ months we will be engulfed. The Republican presidential primary is in full swing so we've already seen Bain Capital Took Your Job and Newt Is a Hypocritical Big Government Hack. Senate and House candidates will launch this spring and summer, so it's going to get a lot more negative.

Why are attack ads bad? Because at the end of the day they are damaging to our country and its processes, and they are most damaging to the degree their messages enter our children's heads.

Someone once said that if you want to know the source of a person's political views, go back to the newspaper headlines when he was 20. See what the country was talking about, and how it was talking about it, when he first started thinking of himself as a citizen, a stakeholder, a member of America.

But imagine you are today 8 or 10 or 12. You watch TV, you hear the radio in the car, you go on the computer, you see the ads. They inundate you. And they make, in the aggregate, an indelible impression: "They are all bad."

If your child is a happy little psychopath, he will be encouraged: "Good, I'll fit right in when I grow up." But assuming your children are not psychopaths, and in spite of their daily behavior that tends to be true, they will be discouraged. They would never want to take part in public life some day. They would never even want to pay attention to it. Because they want to grow up and be admirable.

We are poisoning their minds. I used to say liberalism was more damaged by this because liberals are inclined to think the answer to public ills resides in governmental action. Negative ads imply the people who run government are bad, so government must be, too. Why trust it? But conservatism is undercut just as much, certainly

now, because to make the changes they want, they need big numbers, big margins. Numbers come from passion. Passion is dimin-
ished by sourness, by "they're all bums."

Many say our politics are no more negative than they used to be,
and they have a point: It's always been a brute sport. We all know
the drill, from "Ma, Ma, where's my Pa?" to the presidential election
of 1800. Thomas Jefferson had one of his henchmen—excuse me,
surrogates—accuse John Adams, in a series of newspaper essays, of
being a "hideous hermaphroditical character," a "strange compound
of ignorance and ferocity, of deceit and weakness," a "repulsive ped-
ant." That's worse than what Mitt said about Newt. By the end,
Adams was so beside himself he lost his temper and called Alexander
Hamilton "a man devoid of every moral principle, a bastard…a for-
eigner." That's worse than what Newt said about Mitt.

The man in front of whom Adams lost his temper made sure to
get the word out, through letters, the press and word of mouth. And
that of course is what's different now. They didn't have mass media
to blanket everyone's minds. You used to have to be sort of sophisticated to know Alexander Hamilton hated Adams. You had to read
long newspaper accounts to find out why, and you had to go to the
city to find the newspapers. You could find it if you wanted to, but if
you didn't, there was less chance it would find you.

And now there's no place to hide. All screens are on.

What remedies might ease this situation will have no impact on
2012. What about self-policing?

You there, political consultant, genius ad cutter, sitting at your
laptop reviewing the images and the script. Are you making a brutal
ad to take the enemy down? Are you thinking of anything but your
status as an effective guru and your pay? Are you thinking at all of
the net effects of your dark work?

No? Then a curse upon you as you hit "save" and "send." May
your hand be palsied. May it lose its power.

On Immigration…

I care about immigration so much because I came from immigrants, feel and am close to their lived experience, and care about America. Who we are and how we operate matters.

And I'll tell you now what I'd do about immigration if magical powers were suddenly granted to me.

I would first find every profession that needs more members in the United States, and I would see to an increase in legal immigration for those professions. A sovereign nation has a right to decide what it needs.

I would, for reasons of national security and also fairness to those here, clamp down on our southern border and stop illegal immigration. I would do what it takes—a wall of bricks or a wall of soldiers, whatever will work. I would set federal agencies to find and expatriate those from other countries who have illegally overstayed their visas.

Having controlled the border and the visa situation, there would be less of an air of crisis about the entire issue. Everyone would spend the next five years settling in to the new reality. I would try to figure out what the U.S. saved by stanching the flow of illegal immigrants, take that money and dedicate it to the teaching, assisting and encouraging of America's long-term unemployed and underemployed.

After five years, with the crisis abated and the clamor quieted, I would announce a one-time-only amnesty for every illegal immigrant living within the United States. There would be certain regulations accompanying that—no criminal record, learn English, etc. And America, seeing that the crisis was over and understanding the utility of bringing everyone out of the shadows and into the system, would accept or support such amnesty, after a few grouchy arguments.

It would not be bad for any *political party to be the party that stopped the hemorrhaging at the border and later gave amnesty to all within it.*

This of course is fanciful.

But this is not: The only president who will get, in the future, a comprehensive immigration reform bill through Congress will be a man or woman who strongly opposed illegal immigration and took real steps to stop it. That person will be allowed to be generous.

* * *

What Does It Mean That Your First Act on Entering a Country Is Breaking Its Law?

The Wall Street Journal: December 8, 2005

As Congress considers the Bush administration's guest-worker plan, as Republicans try to figure out what their immigration philosophy is and as political observers parse the implications of yesterday's California House race, here are some small and human questions on immigration to the United States.

I recently found out through one of her daughters that my grandmother spent her first night in America on a park bench in downtown Manhattan. She had made her way from Ireland to Ellis Island, and a cousin was to meet the ship. It was about 1920. The cousin didn't show. So Mary Dorian, age roughly 20, all alone, with no connections and no relatives interested enough to remember her arrival in the New World, spent her first night in America alone on a bench, in the dark, in a strange country. Later she found her way to Brooklyn and became a bathroom attendant at the big Abraham & Straus department store on Fulton Street. (It's now a Macy's. I buy Christmas gifts there.)

Two generations after my grandmother arrived, I was in the Oval Office of the American president saying "I think you oughta." And amazingly enough he was listening.

In two generations. *Two.*

What a country.

* * *

Am I proud of this? Sure. It's the American way to point out that your people went from zero to 60, or will or can. It's the American way to acknowledge, too, that someone made the car you jumped into. There was an assembly line. My grandparents were ahead of me in that line, and the Founders were ahead of them. Every time an American brags about where he came from and where he wound up, he's really complimenting the guys on the line.

In my case before there was the car there was a ship. I do not know the name of the ship that took Mary Dorian to America, and yet it gave me my future. I know she wore an inspection card attached to her clothing. I have such a card, encased in plastic, on a table in my home. It is the card worn by Mary Dorian's future husband's sister, who came over at roughly the same time.

It says at the top: "To assist Inspection in New York Harbour." It notes dates, departure points, "Name of Immigrant." On the side there's a row of numbers that mark each day of what appears to have been a 10-day trip. Each day was stamped by the ship's surgeon at daily inspection. You got the stamp if you appeared to be free of disease.

You know how the card looks? Thin. An old piece of paper that looks vulnerable. I guess that's why I encased it in plastic, to keep it safe, because it's precious.

*   *   *

Here is what is true of my immigrants and of the immigrants of America's past: They fought for citizenship. They earned it. They waited in line. They passed the tests. They had to get permission to come. They got money that was hard-earned and bought a ticket. They had to get through Ellis Island or the port of Boston or Philadelphia, get questioned and eyeballed by a bureaucrat with a badge, and get the nod to take their first step on American soil. Then they had to find the A&S.

They knew citizenship was not something cheaply held but something bestowed by a great nation.

Did the fact that they had to earn it make joining America even more precious?

Yes. Of course.

We all know it is so often so different now. Perhaps a million illegal immigrants come into the United States each year, joining the 10 million or 20 million already here—nobody seems to know the number. Our borders are less borders than lines you cross if you want to. When you watch videotape of some of the illegal border crossings on a show like Lou Dobbs's—who is not a senator or congressman but a media star and probably the premier anti-illegal-immigration voice in the country—what you absorb is a sense of anarchy, an utter collapse of authority.

It's not good. It does not bode well.

*   *   *

The questions I bring to the subject are not about the flow of capital, the imminence of globalism or the implications of uncontrolled immigration on the size and cost of the welfare state. They just have to do with what it is to be human. What does it mean that your first act on entering a country—your first act on that soil—is the breaking of that country's laws? What does it suggest to you when that country does nothing about your lawbreaking because it cannot, or chooses not to? What does that tell you? Will that make you a better future citizen, or worse? More respecting of the rule of law in your new home, or less?

If you assume or come to believe that that nation will not enforce its own laws for reasons that are essentially cynical, that have to do with the needs of big business or the needs of politicians, will that assumption or belief make you more or less likely to be moved by that country, proud of that country, eager to ally yourself with it emotionally, psychologically and spiritually?

When you don't earn something or suffer to get it, do you value it less highly? If you value it less highly, will you bother to know it, understand it, study it? Will you bother truly to become part of it? When you are allowed to join a nation for free, as it were, and without the commitment of years of aboveboard effort, do you experience your joining that country as a blessing or as a successful con? If the latter, what was the first lesson America taught you?

These are questions that I think are behind a lot of the more passionate opposition to illegal immigration.

* * *

There are people who want to return to the old ways and rescue some of the old attitudes. There are groups that seek to restore border integrity. But they are denigrated by many, even the president, who has called them vigilantes. The New Yorker this week carries a mildly snotty piece by a writer named Daniel Kurtz-Phelan in which he interviews members of a group of would-be Minutemen who seek to watch our borders with Mexico and Canada. They are "running freelance patrols"; they are xenophobic; they dismiss critics as "communists" and "child molesters." How nice to be patronized by young men whose place is so secure they have two last names. How nice to be looked down on for caring.

And they do care, that's the thing. And pay a price for caring. They worry in part that what is happening on our borders can damage our country by eroding the sense of won citizenship that leads to the mutual investment and mutual respect—the togetherness, if that isn't too corny—that all nations need to operate in the world and that our nation will especially need in the coming world.

This is what I fear about our elites in government and media, who will decide our immigration policy. It is that they will ignore the human questions and focus instead, as they have in the past, only on economic questions (we need the workers) and political ones (we need the Latino vote). They think that's the big picture. It's not. What goes on in the human heart is the big picture.

Again: What does it mean when your first act is to break the laws of your new country? What does it mean when you know you are implicitly supported in lawbreaking by that nation's ruling elite? What does it mean when you know your new country doesn't even enforce its own laws? What does it mean when you don't even have to become an American once you join America?

* * *

Our elites are lucky people. They were born in a suburb, went to Yale and run the world from a desk. Which means this great question, immigration, is going to be decided by people who don't know what it is to sleep on a bench. Who don't know what it is to earn your space, your place. Who don't know what it is to grieve the old country and embrace the new country. Who don't know what it is to feel you're a little on the outside and have to earn your way in to the inside. Who think it was without a cost, because it was without cost for them.

The problem with our elites as they make our immigration policy is not that they have compassion and open-mindedness. It is that they are unknowing and empty-headed. They don't know, most of them, what others had to earn, and how much they, and their descendents, prize it and want to protect it.

Slow Down and Absorb

Open borders? Mass deportations? How about some common sense instead?

The Wall Street Journal: May 25, 2007

Why do people want to come here? Same reasons as 100 years ago. For a job. For opportunity. To rise. To be in a place where one generation you can be a bathroom attendant at a Brooklyn store and the next your boy can be the star of "Ted Mack's Amateur Hour," with everyone in the neighborhood listening on the radio, or, today, "American Idol," with everyone watching and a million-dollar contract in the wings. To be in a place of weird magic where the lightning strikes. Boom: You got the job in the restaurant. Crack: Now you're the manager. Boom: You've got a mortgage, you have a home.

"Never confuse movement with action," said Ernest Hemingway. But America gives you both. What an awake place. And what a tortured and self-torturing one. Your own family will be embarrassed by you if you don't rise, if you fall, if you fail. And the country itself is never perfect enough for its countrymen; we're on a constant Puritan self-healing mission, a constant search-and-destroy-mission for our nation's blemishes—racism, sexism, ethnocentrism—out damn spots.

I asked myself a question this week and realized the answer is "Only one." The question is: Have I ever known an immigrant to America who was lazy? I have lived on the East Coast all my life, mostly in New York, and immigrants both legal and illegal have been and are part of my daily life, from my childhood when they surrounded me to an adulthood in which they, well, surround me. And the only lazy one I knew was a young woman, 20, European, not mature enough to be fully herself, who actually wanted to be a good worker but found nightlife too alluring and hangovers too debilitating.

But she was the only one. And I think she went home.

Everyone else who comes here works hard, grindingly hard, and I admire them. But it's more than that, I love them and I'm rooting for them. When I see them in church (it is Filipino women who taught me the right posture for prayer; Central Americans helped teach me the Bible) I want to kiss their hands. I want to say "Thank you." They have enriched my life, and our country's.

Naturally I hope the new immigration bill fails. It is less a bill than a big dirty ball of mischief, malfeasance and mendacity, with a touch of class malice, and it's being pushed by a White House that is at once cynical and inept. The bill's Capitol Hill supporters have a great vain popinjay's pride in their own higher compassion. They are inclusive and you're not, you cur, you gun-totin' truckdriver's-hat-wearin' yahoo. *It's all so complex, and you'd understand this if you weren't sort of dumb.*

But it's not so complex. The past quarter century an unprecedented wave of illegal immigrants has crossed our borders. The flood is so great that no one—no one—can see or fully imagine all the many implications, all the country-changing facts of it. No one knows exactly what uncontrolled immigration is doing and will do to our country.

So what should we do?

* * *

We should stop, slow down and absorb. We should sit and settle. We should do what you do after eating an eight-course meal. We should digest what we've eaten.

We should close our borders. We should do whatever it takes to close them tight and solid. Will that take the Army? Then send the Army. Does it mean building a wall? Then build a wall, but the wall must have doors, which can be opened a little or a lot down the road once we know where we are. Should all legal immigration stop? No. We should make a list of what our nation needs, such as engineers and nurses, and then admit a lot of engineers and nurses. We should take in what we need to survive and flourish.

As we end illegal immigration, we should set ourselves to the Americanization of the immigrants we have. They haven't only joined a place of riches, it's a place of meaning. We must teach them what it is they've joined and why it is good and what is expected of them and what is owed. We stopped Americanizing ourselves 40 years ago. We've got to start telling the story of our country again.

As to the eight or 10 or 12 or 14 million illegals who are here—how interesting that our government doesn't know the number—we should do nothing dramatic or fraught or unlike us. We should debate what to do, at length. Debate isn't bad. There's a lot to say. We can all join in. We should do nothing extreme, only things that are commonsensical.

Here is the truth: America has never deported millions of people, and America will never deport millions of people. It's not what we do. It's not who we are. It's not who we want to be. The American people would never accept evening news pictures of sobbing immigrants being torn from their homes and put on a bus. We wouldn't accept it because we have hearts, and as much as we try to see history in the abstract, we know history comes down to the particular, to the sobbing child in the bus. We don't round up and remove. Nor should we, tomorrow, on one of our whims, grant full legal status and a Cadillac car. We take it a day at a time. We wait and see what's happening. We do the small discrete things a nation can do to make the overall situation better. For instance: "You commit a violent crime? You are so out of here." And, "Here, let me help you learn English."

*   *   *

Let's take time and find out if the immigrants who are here see their wages click up and new benefits kick in as the endless pool stops expanding. It would be good to see them gain. Let's find out if it's true that Americans won't stoop to any of the jobs illegals do. I don't think it is. Years ago I worked in a florist shop removing the thorns from roses. It was painful work and I was happy to do it, and I am very American. I was a badly paid waitress in the Holiday Inn on Route 3 in New Jersey.

The young will do a great deal, and not only the young. The dislike for Americans evinced by the Americans-won't-do-hard-work crowd is, simply, astonishing, and shameful. It says more about the soft and ignorant lives they lived in Kennebunkport and Greenwich than it does about the American people.

Digest, absorb, teach. Settle in, settle down, protect our country. Happy Memorial Day.

We Need to Talk

America can't afford to lose its common language.

The Wall Street Journal: July 6, 2007

It is late afternoon in Manhattan on the Fourth of July, and I'm walking along on Lexington and 59th, in front of Bloomingdale's. Suddenly in my sight there's a young woman standing on a street grate. She is short, about 5 feet tall, and stocky, with a broad brown face. She is, I think, Latin American, maybe of Indian blood. She has a big pile of advertisements in her hand, and puts one toward me. "MENS SUITS NEW YORK—40% to 60% Off Sale!— Armani, Canali, Hugo Boss, DKNY, Zegna. TAILOR ON PREM- ISES. EXCELLENT SERVICE LARGE SELECTION." Then the address and phone number.

You might have seen this person before. She's one of a small army of advertisement giver-outers in New York. Which means her life right now consists of standing in whatever weather and trying to give passersby a thing most of them don't want. If this is her regu- lar job, she spends most of her time being rebuffed or ignored by busy people blurring by. You should always take an advertisement, or 10, from the advertisement giver-outers, just to give them a break, because once they give out all the ads, they can go back and get paid. So I took the ad and thanked her and walked on.

And then, half a block later, I turned around. I thought of a woman I'd met recently who had gone through various reverses in life and now had a new job, as a clerk in the back room of a store. She was happy to have it, a new beginning. But there was this thing:

They didn't want to pay for air conditioning, so she sweltered all day. This made her want to weep, just talking about it. Ever since that conversation, I have been so grateful for my air conditioning. I had forgotten long ago to be grateful for it.

Anyway, I look back at the woman on the street grate. It's summer and she's in heavy jeans and a black sweatshirt with a hood. On top of that, literally, she's wearing a sandwich board—MENS SUITS NEW YORK. Her hair is long and heavy, her ponytail limp on her shoulders. She's out here on a day when everybody else, as she well knows—the streets are not crowded—is at a ballgame or the beach. Everyone else is off.

So I turned around and went back. I wanted to say something— I don't know what, find out where she was from, encourage her. I said hello, and she looked at me and I patted her arm and said, "Happy Fourth of July, my friend." She was startled and then shy, and she smiled and made a sound, and I realized: She doesn't speak English. "God bless you," I said, because a little while in America and you know the word "God" just as 10 minutes in Mexico and you learn the word "Dios." And we both smiled and nodded and I left.

I went into Bloomingdale's and wrote these words: "We must speak the same language so we can hearten each other."

*   *   *

The question of whether America should have an "official language," of whether English should be formally declared our "national language," is bubbling, and will be back, in Congress, the next few sessions.

When you look at papers outlining the facts of the debate, things break down into dryness very quickly. Should "issues of language diversity" be resolved by imposing "linguistic uniformity"? This is like asking if the robots should speak logarithmically or algorithmically. There are few things you can rely on in this turbulent world, but one is the tendency of academics to use language poorly, even when discussing language.

But there's something odd about the English question. It feels old-fashioned. Because we all know America has an official language, and a national language, and that it is English. In France they speak French, and in China they speak Chinese. In Canada they have two national languages, but that's one reason Canada often seems silly. They don't even know what language they dream in.

The real question, ultimately, is whether America wants to go that route. Should we allow America to devolve into a nation of two official languages—in this case, following recent demographic trends and realities, English and Spanish?

We've never done that in more than 200 years. It would be radical, and destructive, to do it now.

We speak English here. It's a great language, luckily, a rich one. It's how we do government and business. It's the language of the official life, the outer life, in America. As for the inner life of America, the language of the family, it would be just as odd to change longtime tradition there, which has always been: Anything goes. You speak what you came over speaking, and you learn the new language. Italian immigrants knew two languages, English and Italian. They enriched the first with the second—this was a great gift to all of us—and wound up with greater opportunities for personal communication to boot. Talk about win-win. And so with every group, from every place.

But in a deeper sense, we should never consider devolving from one national language down into two, or three, because if we do we won't understand each other. And we're confused enough as it is.

In the future, with the terrible problems we face, we are going to need to understand each other more and more, better and better. We're going to need to know how to say "This way" and "Let me help" and "stop" and "here." We're going to have to negotiate our way through a lot of challenges, some dramatic, some immediate, and it will make it all the harder, all the more impossible-seeming, if we can't even take each other's meaning, and be understood.

*   *   *

The only other debate I suppose we should really be having on languages is how to help our future generations learn more of them. (Mexican immigrants who speak Spanish and English have a leg up here, and will benefit from it.) We live in the world, and we want that world to understand us better. We want to understand it better, too. Europe is lucky: All those different cultures and languages are bundled up all close to each other and next to each other. They learn each other's languages with ease. We have oceans to the left and right, and vastness. For us, or at least the older of us, learning another language is still a leap. As a nation we probably should leap more.

But on English as the language in which we live our shared national life, and share our culture, and our dreams, we should stay where we are. Which hasn't, for 231 years now and counting, been a bad place to be.

CHAPTER 15

State of the Union

A subtext of all these pieces is the growing distance between Washington and the public it dominates. This has only grown worse in my lifetime. You can hear it in the language Washington uses—dodgy, roundabout, bureaucratic—and in its subject matter. They never talk about what the people are half desperate to hear.

* * *

A Time to Get Serious

Thoughts on George H. W. Bush and his 1992 GOP acceptance speech.

Newsweek Magazine: August 24, 1992

MEMO TO: The President

FROM: Noonan

RE: Your acceptance speech

Mr. President, remember the scene in that movie you liked, "Moonstruck," in which Cher slugs very fine and decent but also dispirited Nicolas Cage and says, "Snap out of it!"? That is our text for today.

You are George Herbert Walker Bush and you have been serving your country and keeping high its ideals since the day you were born. You went out to defend it with your life when you were an 18-year-old boy.

You chucked security, got in the car, dug the oil, created a business, gave people jobs, got an ulcer worrying about the payroll, met it every week, kept trucking, went to Congress, went to China, protected the CIA in its toughest days, served a great man named Reagan with quiet, dogged loyalty, became a landslide president of the United States, went to victorious war against a nut with nukes, helped transform the Soviet Union—and kept, all this time, all these years, the honest, yearning love of your children and your wife.

You have lived a *life*. And now this—this Elvis impersonator, this boomer on a bus, this guy who calls his climb up the greasy pole "answering the call of public service," as if he were sacrificing ambition for good works, as if politics were a nunnery and not a whore. Well.

And his friends, the newspaper poets! Back there tap-tap-tapping in the back of the plane, and every time they see Clinton their eyes shine because what they're really seeing is...*the house in McLean and the phone call in the night, the journal entry: "The president called again tonight, I knew why he was up, alone. Sarajevo. Again."*

Buttheads with laptops! Going for the Bradlee Cup! That's what you think of them in your less charitable moods. Well, stay less charitable for a minute.

Mr. President, Clinton says you're washed up. He says you're through, you're yesterday, and a new generation tempered by zip and disciplined by zero is going to run the country. And he will—right into the ground! You going to let him? Or are you going to teach him a little lesson in respect?

(Phew. It's not easy doing a Roger Ailes impersonation.)

Four years ago today you were working on what we all thought was the most important speech of your career. We were wrong. This is. It's also the most challenging. A lot has changed in the last four years. Last time you were up against a man caught somewhere between inept and inert. This time you're up against a savvy young pol.

Both the Democrats and the Republicans think that you're in trouble because of the economy. But it's more. People are angry about the costs and demands of government, angry that no one has the courage to cut spending. They are uneasy about our culture, about its increasing coarseness, vulgarity, violence. If people had seen the past three years that you were led by discernible principle, if they had been able to see that you were thinking long term, long range, they'd have stuck with you from boom to bust. But they didn't, so they haven't.

A hunch: You know what a lot of voters feel, deep in their hearts, with a certitude that finds no expression in focus groups? They think this election is a white-guy fistfight over power. Stephanopoulos does, Teeter does, Carville does, Rich Bond. Bush, Clinton. People hate it. It makes them think that none of you are serious.

The Democrats ceded seriousness to sentiment at their convention. But seriousness is your salvation. It means that if you win, you win with meaning, if you lose, you lose with class. The first gives you a mandate, the second adds heft to your historical reputation. Here are some ideas:

Put the contest in context: The '92 campaign is a fight, on the one hand, between a solid Republican Party that has in your lifetime done an amazing thing: it has *changed history for the better;* it is the party that helped change an evil empire into a benign cluster of democracies; that unleashed a historic economic boom and that spoke, again, for our country and the world, of the rightness of freedom.

On the other side, an evolving Democratic Party that has not evolved enough to lead. Their policies are new ideas wrapped in old entanglements, with the obvious left quiet now, but poised to move in a Clinton administration. Nothing will change the Democrats but more history; their evolution is incomplete.

You think this. But you'll say it better.

Your biggest problem? "Read my mind": Four years ago you said: *The Congress will push me to raise taxes, and I'll say no, and they'll push again. And I'll say to them: Read my lips. No new taxes.*

Once FDR made a campaign pledge in a speech in Philadelphia. Later he broke it. When his image handlers wondered what to do, he merrily instructed them to deny he was in Philadelphia. My advice: Don't deny you were in New Orleans, tell people why you did what you did.

You said you'd fight the congressional Democrats' desire to raise taxes by pushing back and refusing. Instead you compromised, trading taxes for spending controls.

Everyone has his reasons, and you had yours. But you never told them to the people. All they saw was a guy jogging by the cameras, saying "Read my hips." Your worst public moment as president.

Explain it. You knew you had to get the deficit under control, and the deficit is a spending problem. You felt facing the Democrats off to a standstill would get you nowhere, produce nothing but a daily argument, like a bad marriage. "[The people] did not send us here to bicker," you said in your Inaugural, and you meant it.

So you held back from a war with Congress that had to be fought. You put your personal credibility on the line, you broke your word—but only in hopes it would break Congress's habits. It didn't. They're still spending, the deficit is growing, but you learned something: never again. (This, as Henry Kissinger used to say, had the added benefit of being true. You *will* never do it again.)

A mistake stays a scandal until you explain it. And this is a mistake to be turned to your advantage. It was the Democrats, Bill Clinton's party, who insisted on the tax raise. Now they condemn you for giving them what they begged for. What will Clinton do when a Democratic Congress tells him to raise taxes even more than he intends?

Say what you did right. There's plenty. But this year the Republicans have had trouble going positive—about themselves. One reason: Good news that is old news is not news. How do you make it interesting that Republicans arrested inflation when inflation hasn't mugged anyone lately? One way is to be terse, true—and funny. Give people something they can get a smile or a laugh with when they quote it to the neighbors. People want to fight on your side—a good line is ammunition.

They're ba-a-ck: "Clinton says he'll take back America and he will—to the Carter years." That's how Jim Pinkerton speaks of the Democratic ticket. Pinkerton, Mary Matalin, all the young, smart ones on your staff: They say to remind people the Democrats aren't the answer, they're the problem. You said it yourself: They're not the fireman, they're the arsonist. Drive it home.

War talk: In private you speak of Desert Storm with humility and quiet pride. On the stump your references take on a kind of agitated boastfulness.

Your normal approach to things is low key, modest, often wry.

But your advisers tell you to show how you "feel" when you make a speech, so you "act" how you feel, and sometimes it doesn't work because—you're not an actor. (As a former adviser I feel free to say: Kill the advisers.)

You could use the war to make two points. (1) Tell about building the coalition against Saddam Hussein. You gathered together the civilized world. It was masterful. Underscore the fact that Clinton has nothing like your quarter century experience in foreign affairs. (2) The war was fought with minimum loss of life because of state-of-the-art hardware that was only developed because Republicans led the nation the past 12 years. (Imagine people who two years ago had VISUALIZE PEACE on their bumper stickers in charge of the Pentagon budget!)

My only lobbying: Mr. President, we need a defense to protect our continent from a madman with a well-aimed missile. A week ago the Democratic Senate voted all of SDI down. You care about it. Fight for it in this speech.

The Democrats, the media, hate it. Do you know what regular people on the street know that the elites don't? It is not possible for so many men to have so many nuclear arms and no one will ever use one. It's going to save lives someday.

No more tears: Some will say: Show your heart. They'll mean: Be personal and autobiographical and talk about the pain in this thing called life. You'll refuse. On behalf of the American people, thank you.

When Al Gore was talking about his son at the Democratic convention I saw a television producer watching with tears in his eyes. At the end she turned to me and said, "That was so manipulative." I said, "You were moved." She shrugged. "I'm a mother, I got a cheap cry." Everyone's on to everything. Cheap tears win no votes.

Watch out: Democrats keep saying it will be a mean campaign and here's a reason why: They still think they lost '88 because of Willie Horton, and they still don't understand that voters viewed

Dukakis's actions (refusing to meet with Horton's victims, etc.) as . . . liberal arrogance.

The Democrats think it was all an ugly racist trick. The good news: This means they're still confused about why people vote against them. The bad news: People who think you've been evil to them usually do evil in return.

And don't forget the merry pranksters in the press. They are so hungry for ugly, in my view, that the smallest thing you do will be turned into a big thing. And they'll goad you into the small thing. You'll be walking through the plane to say hello to reporters and someone will ask, "How did you like the dress Mrs. Clinton wore on 'Arsenio' last night?" And you, wanting to be diplomatic but also not wanting to look like a weenie who's afraid to have fun, will say, "Oh, the dress, well, not my favorite color, but . . ." That's all they'll need. He's even attacking her clothing!

Mr. President, if a prankster baits you, wag your finger and give 'em a little Ward Cleaver. "Now, Beaver, it's good to try and make life fun, but it isn't nice to start trouble. Wally, I'd like you to talk to your brother about taking democracy seriously."

The importance of belief: Some of your staff used to walk around calling the Reagan years "the pre-Bush era." There are many names for such people; "historical idiot" is one. You know and feel that Ronald Reagan was, is, a great man. When your delegates hear his voice Monday night they will erupt in joy. They will shake their heads and say, "I miss his voice." They'll mean: I miss belief.

You have a chance to tell people, again, what you believe, what you intend, how you will achieve it. If you meet the challenge, voters will give you a second look.

People like to forgive. When a friend says, "I'm sorry if I let you down. But I know what went wrong and it won't happen again and I'm asking for another chance," you'd have to be ungenerous to turn the guy down. And you will be talking to the most generous people on earth.

George H. W. Bush's Defeat

New York Times: November 5, 1992

Having rebuffed a fine man whose presidency failed, about half the country, I suspect, will have the rueful blues this weekend. George Bush was our last president from the great generation that held fast through a bitter depression and fought gallantly in war for a country they never doubted for a second deserved their love. Their stewardship, begun when John F. Kennedy brought the junior officers of World War II to power (Theodore White's phrase), somehow deserves better than this sodden end.

The old order passeth, a new generation riseth.

All day I've been thinking of a dream my brother-in-law Joe had a few years ago. His late father came to him to tell him, in the dream, the birth of his first child, expected in a matter of weeks, was imminent. The old man stood in his work clothes in a driveway in New Jersey, squinting in the sun. Joe put his hand on his father's shoulder. "Thanks, Pop," he said, "You done good." When he awoke, he took his wife to the hospital, where later that day their son was born.

Joe's words—"Thanks, Pop"—seem appropriate as a tough old generation that protected, for us, a world, softly retreats.

* * *

In a way, the election was always a choice between depression and anxiety. When voters imagined picking up the paper Wednesday morning and seeing a headline that said "Bush Wins in Close Race," their hearts sank. When they imagined "President Clinton!" their hearts raced. Forced to choose between melancholy and nervousness, they took the latter; it seemed the more awake, and so the more hopeful choice. But such thoughts only characterize the election for me; they don't explain it.

Mr. Bush's fortunes in '92 were hurt, like his presidency, by a misunderstanding of what voters did four years before. He thought the American people voted for him in 1988. They didn't. They voted for the continuation of basic Reaganesque policies, which is what George Bush said he stood for.

He vowed in '88 to keep the size of government down. He let it grow. He said he would not raise taxes. He raised them. He said he'd resist the heavy weight of government. He allowed more regulation.

The voters who created the Reagan coalition abandoned Mr. Bush in '92 because they were never loyal to him; they were loyal to the beliefs he espoused from 1981 through 1989.

Some will say Mr. Bush was done in by a bad convention and a bad campaign. But if both had gone better the outcome would have been the same. And I don't think it all came down to the economy, either. It's true George Bush didn't have a good one, true he was late to see it and speak of it. But Ronald Reagan, who had a worse recession in '82, won by a landslide in '84.

That was because he had clear beliefs based on what voters saw as commonsense principles; when things didn't work right away, they cut him some slack and gave him some time. President Bush sometimes seemed as if he had few beliefs that were not subjects to shifts in wind, ground and circumstance. At the end, voters thought he wasn't serious.

Serious people in public life stand for things and fight for them; the ensuing struggle is meant to yield progress and improvement. Mr. Bush seemed embarrassed to believe. It left those who felt sympathy for him embarrassed to support him.

His economic wound was, to a significant extent, self-inflicted.

It wasn't external forces that created the crisis, no mullah half a world away who took our people hostage. The 1990 budget deal did what Mr. Bush said Michael Dukakis would do—impede growth and damage the economy.

The president's aides were not sufficiently alive to history, which was bad, because history was against them. The modern Republican Party stood triumphant on two pillars. The first was sober and effective anti-communism, the second was a principled small-government policy. History took the first from Mr. Bush; he took the second from himself. Without the pillars, he fell.

The president's great moment, the war against Iraq—and it was a great moment, with masterly diplomacy—made his problems fatal by obscuring them. Desert Storm gave the White House a false sense of security and encouraged carelessness. The staff was too dazed by the polls to see.

As president, Mr. Bush reverted to his behavior as vice president: He stopped seeing the connection between words and action. He did not communicate. I used to wonder if, traumatized by what he saw as the Reagan White House's too great attention to the public part of the presidency, to the Rose Garden backdrops and the commemorative events, Mr. Bush concluded the public part was all show and not worthy of a sincere and honest man.

But the public part of the presidency, the persuading-in-the-pulpit part, is central to leadership. The worst thing is to lie to the people, but the second worst is to ignore them and not tell what you are doing and why.

In domestic affairs, the president leaned on yesterday's men. The aides and cabinet members who represented the new conservatism and the future of the party—Jack Kemp, William Bennett, Vin Weber—were given access and then ignored. The president listened to those—Richard Darman, Nicholas Brady—who represented the "realistic" and "sophisticated" thinking of Republicans who came of age during Watergate. They thought they were on the losing side of history; they thought their job was not to win but to limit inevitable loss. The president's choice here revived the old party divisions Mr. Reagan had healed and further sundered the Republican coalition.

After 12 years in power, the most talented Republicans were the most exhausted. They had lost touch with the grass roots when they used to be the grass roots. Years ago, Henry Kissinger said the government is all intellectual outgo, that you never have time for inflow, for reading and thinking. (The conservatives around Mr. Bush who make good use of their time off and become reacquainted with their country will come back strong in '96 or 2000.)

Bill Clinton ran a creative campaign. Buses, Elvis, answering each attack with more and bigger verbal warheads. A lot of people find it hard not to daydream during his speeches—for me it's like watching a soap opera; I can never quite follow the narrative—but he made no major rhetorical mistakes. His people were smart and hungry, and they had the press. The media were partial to Bill Clinton not only because they lean toward liberalism and many are baby boomers but because they want a new story, a new headline, new news. They love their country; they want change; they're sick unto death of Republicans. (Note to the Clinton staff: Your new friends have built you up for a steep fall.)

Finally, on the Republican side, the myth of the great campaign tacticians was revealed. A lot of them were jockeys who won because the horse they rode was fast. Ronald Reagan carried them across the line, they didn't carry him. When they rode George Bush, they failed, because he couldn't win for them.

Those are the reasons for George Bush's defeat, as I see it.

Back in '88, the Democrats around Michael Dukakis sized up Mr. Bush and history and said, "If we can't win this one we might as well find another country." That was not true then but was true this time. The good news for Republicans is if you know what went wrong you can correct it. More good news: Every defeat carries within it the seeds of victory, and every victory carries within it the seeds of defeat.

Someone said that to me once—I think Lee Atwater. He may be another reason the theme of this article is not victory.

The Risk of Catastrophic Victory

Obama is in the midst of one. Can the GOP avert one of their own?

The Wall Street Journal: January 7, 2010

Passage of the health-care bill will be, for the administration, a catastrophic victory. If it is voted through in time for the State of the Union Address, as President Obama hopes, half the chamber will rise to their feet and cheer. They will be cheering their own demise.

If health care does not pass, it will also be a disaster, but only for the administration, not the country. Critics will say, "You didn't even waste our time successfully."

What a blunder this thing has been, win or lose, what a miscalculation on the part of the president. The administration misjudged the mood and the moment. Mr. Obama ran, won, was sworn in and began his work under the spirit of 2008—expansive, part dreamy and part hubristic. But as soon as he was inaugurated, the president ran into the spirit of 2009—more dug in, more anxious, more bottom line—and didn't notice.

At the exact moment the public was announcing it worried about jobs first and debt and deficits second, the administration decided to devote its first year to health care, which no one was talking about. The great recession changed everything, but not right away.

In a way Mr. Obama made the same mistake President Bush did on immigration, producing a big, mammoth, comprehensive bill when the public mood was for small, discrete steps in what might reasonably seem in the right direction.

The public in 2009 would have been happy to see a simple bill that mandated insurance companies offer coverage without respect to previous medical conditions. The administration could have had that—and the victory of it—last winter.

Instead, they were greedy for glory.

It was not worth it—not worth the town-hall uprisings and the bleeding of centrist support, not worth the rebranding of the president from center-left leader to leftist leader, not worth the proof it provided that the public's concerns and the administration's are not the same, not worth a wasted first year that should have been given to two things and two things only: economic matters and national security.

Those were not only the two topics on the public's mind the past 10 months, they were precisely the issues that presented themselves in screaming headlines at the end of the year: unemployment and the national security breakdowns that led to the Christmas bomb plot and, earlier, the Fort Hood massacre. "That's two strikes," said the president's national security adviser, James Jones, to USA Today's Susan Page. Left unsaid: Three and you're out.

Just as bad, or worse, the president's focus on health care allowed the public to infer that his mind was not focused on our security. He'd frittered his attention on issues that were secondary and tertiary—climate change, health care—while al Qaeda moved, and the system stuttered. A lack of focus breeds bureaucratic complacency, complacency gives rise to slovenliness, slovenliness results in what was said in the report issued Thursday: that, faced with clear evidence of coming danger, the government failed, as they're saying on TV, to "connect the dots." Dots? They were boulders.

* * *

I am wondering if the Obama administration thinks it vaguely dishonorable to be popular. If you mention to Obama staffers that they really have to be concerned about the polls, they look at you with a certain...not disdain but patience, as if you don't understand the purpose of politics. That purpose, they believe, is to move the governed toward greater justice. Just so, but in democracy you do this by garnering and galvanizing public support. But they think it's weasely to be well thought of.

In politics you must tend to the garden. The garden is the constituency, in Mr. Obama's case the country. No great endeavor is possible without its backing. In a modern presidency especially you have to know this, because there will be times when history throws you a crisis, and to address it you may have to do an unpopular thing. A president in those circumstances must use all the goodwill he's built up over the months and years to get through that moment and survive doing what he thinks is right. Mr. Obama acts as if he doesn't know this. He hasn't built up popularity to use on a rainy day. If he had, he'd be getting through the Christmas plot drama better than he is.

The Obama people have taken to pointing out how their guy doesn't govern by the polls. This is all too believable. The Bush people, too, used to bang away about how he didn't govern by the polls. They both added unneeded stress to the past 10 years, and it is understandable if many of us now think, "Oh for a president who'd govern by the polls."

If Mr. Obama is extremely lucky—and we're not sure he's a lucky man anymore—he will get a Republican Congress in 2010, and they will do for him what Newt Gingrich did for Bill Clinton: right his ship, give him a foil, guide him while allowing him to look as if he's resisting, bend him while allowing him to look strong.

*   *   *

Which gets us to the Republicans. The question isn't whether they'll win seats in the House and Senate this year, and the question isn't even how many. The question is whether the party will be worthy of victory, whether it learned from its losses in 2006 and '08, whether it deserves leadership. Whether Republicans are a worthy alternative. Whether, in short, they are serious.

I spoke a few weeks ago with a respected Republican congressman who told me with some excitement of a bill he's put forward to address the growth of entitlements and long-term government spending. We only have three or four years to get it right, he said. He made a strong case. I asked if his party was doing anything to get behind the bill, and he got the blanched look people get when they're trying to keep their faces from betraying anything. Not really, he said. Then he shrugged. "They're waiting for the Democrats to destroy themselves."

This isn't news, really, but it was startling to hear a successful Republican political practitioner say it.

Republican political professionals in Washington assume a coming victory. They do not see that 2010 could be a catastrophic victory for them. If they seize back power without clear purpose, if they are not serious, if they do the lazy and cynical thing by just sitting back and letting the Democrats lose, three bad things will happen. They will contribute to the air of cynicism in which our citizens marinate. Their lack of seriousness will be discerned by the Republican base, whose enthusiasm and generosity will be blunted. And the Republicans themselves will be left unable to lead when their time comes, because operating cynically will allow the public to view them cynically, which will lessen the chance they will be able to do anything constructive.

In this sense, the cynical view—we can sit back and wait—is naive. The idealistic view—we must stand for things and move on them now—is shrewder.

Political professionals are pugilistic, and often see politics in terms of fight movies: "Rocky," "Raging Bull." They should be thinking now of a different one, of Tom Hanks at the end of "Saving Private Ryan." "Earn this," he said to the man whose life he'd helped save.

Earn this. Be worthy of it. Be serious.

Meanwhile, Back in America...

The growing distance between Washington and the public it dominates.

The Wall Street Journal: January 31, 2014

The State of the Union was a spectacle of delusion and self-congratulation in which a Congress nobody likes rose to cheer a president nobody really likes. It marked the continued degeneration of a great and useful tradition. Viewership was down, to the lowest level since 2000. This year's innovation was the Parade of Hacks. It used to be the networks only showed the president walking down the aisle after his presence was dramatically announced. Now every cabinet-level officeholder marches in, shaking hands and high-fiving with breathless congressmen. And why not? No matter how bland and banal they may look, they do have the power to destroy your life—to declare the house you just built as in violation of EPA wetland regulations, to pull your kid's school placement, to define your medical coverage out of existence. So by all means attention must be paid and faces seen.

I watched at home and thought: They hate it. They being the people, whom we're now supposed to refer to as the folks. But you look at the polls at how people view Washington—one, in October, had almost 9 in 10 disapproving—and you watch a kabuki-like event like this and you know the distance, the psychic, emotional and experiential distance, between Washington and America, between the people and their federal government, is not only real but, actually, carries dangers. History will make more of the distance than we do. Someday in the future we will see it most vividly when a truly bad thing happens and the people suddenly need to trust what Washington says, and will not, to everyone's loss.

In the country, the president's popularity is underwater. In the District of Columbia itself, as Gallup notes, it's at 81%. The Washington area is now the wealthiest in the nation. No matter how bad the hinterlands do, it's good for government and those who live off it. The country is well aware. It is no accident that in the national imagination Washington is the shallow and corrupt capital in "The Hunger Games," the celebrity-clogged White House Correspondents' Dinner, "Scandal" and the green room at MSNBC. It is the chattering capital of a nation it less represents than dominates. Supposedly people feel great rage about this, and I imagine many do. But the other night I wondered if what they're feeling isn't something else.

* * *

As the president made his jaunty claims and the senators and congressmen responded semirapturously I kept thinking of four words: *Meanwhile, back in America...*

Meanwhile, back in America, the Little Sisters of the Poor were preparing their legal briefs. The Roman Catholic order of nuns first came to America in 1868 and were welcomed in every city they entered. They now run about 30 homes for the needy across the country. They have, quite cruelly, been told they must comply with the ObamaCare mandate that all insurance coverage include contraceptives, sterilization procedures, morning-after pills. If they don't— and of course they can't, being Catholic, and nuns—they will face ruinous fines. The Supreme Court kindly granted them a temporary stay, but their case soon goes to court. The Justice Department brief, which reads like it was written by someone who just saw "Philomena," suggests the nuns are being ignorant and balky, all they have to do is sign a little, meaningless form and the problem will go away. The sisters don't see the form as meaningless; they know it's not. And so they fight, in a suit along with almost 500 Catholic nonprofit groups.

Everyone who says that would never have happened in the past is correct. It never, ever would have under normal American political leadership, Republican or Democratic. No one would've defied religious liberty like this. The president has taken to saying he isn't ideological, but this mandate—his mandate—is purely ideological.

It also is a violation of traditional civic courtesy, sympathy and spaciousness. The state doesn't tell serious religious groups to do it their way or they'll be ruined. You don't make the Little Sisters bow down to you.

This is the great political failure of progressivism: They always go too far. They always try to rub your face in it.

Meanwhile, back in America, disadvantaged parents in Louisiana— people who could never afford to live in places like McLean, Va., or Chevy Chase, Md.—continue to wait to see what will happen with the state's successful school voucher program. It lets poor kids get out of failed public schools and go to private schools on state scholarships. What a great thing. But the Obama Justice Department filed suit in August: The voucher system might violate civil rights law by worsening racial imbalance in the public schools. Gov. Bobby Jindal, and the parents, said nonsense, the scholarship students are predominately black, they have civil rights too. Is it possible the Justice Department has taken its action because a major benefactor of the president's party is the teachers' unions, which do not like vouchers because their existence suggests real failures in the public schools they run?

Meanwhile, back in America, conservatives targeted and harassed by the Internal Revenue Service still await answers on their years-long requests for tax-exempt status. When news of the IRS targeting broke last spring, agency officials lied about it, and one took the Fifth. The president said he was outraged, had no idea, read about it in the papers, boy was he going to get to the bottom of it. An investigation was announced but somehow never quite materialized. Victims of the targeting waited to be contacted by the FBI to be asked about their experience. Now the Justice Department has made clear its investigation won't be spearheaded by the FBI but by a department lawyer who is a campaign contributor to the president and the Democratic Party. Sometimes you feel they are just laughing at you, and going too far.

In the past five years many Americans have come to understand that an agency that maintained a pretty impressive record for a very long time has been turned, at least in part, into a political operation. Now the IRS has proposed new and tougher rules for grassroots groups. Cleta Mitchell, longtime attorney for many who've been targeted, says the IRS is no longer used in line with its mission: "They're supposed to be collecting revenues, not snooping and trampling on the First Amendment rights of the citizens. We are not subjects of a king, we are permitted to engage in First Amendment activities without reporting those activities to the IRS."

All these things—the pushing around of nuns, the limiting of freedoms that were helping kids get a start in life, the targeting of conservative groups—all these have the effect of breaking bonds of trust between government and the people. They make citizens see Washington as an alien and hostile power.

*   *   *

Washington sees the disaffection. They read the polls, they know.

They call it rage. But if feels more like grief. Like the loss of something you never thought you'd lose, your sense of your country and your place in it, your rights in it.

A Separate Peace

America is in trouble—and our elites are merely resigned.

The Wall Street Journal: October 27, 2005

It is not so hard and can be a pleasure to tell people what you see. It's harder to speak of what you *think* you see, what you think is going on and can't prove or defend with data or numbers. That can get tricky. It involves hunches. But here goes.

I think there is an unspoken subtext in our national political culture right now. In fact I think that a lot of people are carrying around in their heads, unarticulated and even in some cases unnoticed, a sense that the wheels are coming off the trolley and the trolley off the tracks. That in some deep and fundamental way things have broken down and can't be fixed, or won't be fixed any time soon. That our pollsters are preoccupied with "right track" and "wrong track" but missing the number of people who think the answer to "How are things going in America?" is "Off the tracks and hurtling forward, toward an unknown destination."

I'm not talking about "Plamegate." As I write no indictments have come up. I'm not talking about "Miers." I mean...the whole ball of wax. Everything. Cloning, nuts with nukes, epidemics; the growing knowledge that there's no such thing as homeland security; the fact that we're leaving our kids with a bill no one can pay. A sense of unreality in our courts so deep that they think they can seize grandma's house to build a strip mall; our media institutions imploding—the spectacle of a great American newspaper, the New York Times, hurtling off its own tracks, as did CBS. The fear of parents that their children will wind up disturbed, and their souls actually imperiled, by the popular culture in which we are raising them. Senators who seem owned by someone, actually owned, by an interest group or a financial entity. Great churches that have lost all sense of mission, and all authority. Do you have confidence in the CIA? The FBI? I didn't think so.

But this recounting doesn't quite get me to what I mean. I mean I believe there's a general and amorphous sense that things are broken and tough history is coming.

* * *

Let me focus for a minute on the presidency, another institution in trouble. In the past I have been impatient with the idea that it's impossible now to be president, that it is impossible to run the government of the United States successfully or even competently. I always thought that was an excuse of losers. I'd seen a successful presidency up close. It can be done. But since 9/11, in the four years after that catastrophe, I have wondered if it hasn't all gotten too big, too complicated, too crucial, too many-fronted, too…impossible.

I refer to the sheer scope, speed and urgency of the issues that go to a president's desk, to the impossibility of bureaucracy, to the array of impeding and antagonistic forces (the 50-50 nation, the mass media, the senators owned by the groups), to the need to have a fully informed understanding of and stand on the most exotic issues, from avian flu to the domestic realities of Zimbabwe.

The special prosecutors, the scandals, the spin for the scandals, nuclear proliferation, wars and natural disasters, Iraq, stem cells, earthquakes, the background of the Supreme Court backup pick, how best to handle the security problems at the port of Newark, how to increase production of vaccines, tort reform, did Justice bungle the anthrax case, how is Cipro production going, did you see this morning's Raw Threat File? Our public schools don't work, and there's little refuge to be had in private schools, however pricey, in part because teachers there are embarrassed not to be working in the slums and make up for it by putting pictures of Frida Kahlo where Abe Lincoln used to be. Where is Osama? What's up with trademark infringement and intellectual capital? We need an answer on an amendment on homosexual marriage! We face a revolt on immigration.

The range, depth and complexity of these problems, the crucial nature of each of them, the speed with which they bombard the Oval Office, and the psychic and practical impossibility of meeting and answering even the most urgent of them, is overwhelming. And that doesn't even get us to Korea. And Russia. And China, and the Mideast. You say we don't understand Africa? We don't even understand Canada!

Roiling history, daily dangers, big demands; a government that is itself too big and rolling in too much money and ever needing more to do the latest important, necessary, crucial thing.

It's beyond "The president is overwhelmed." The *presidency* is overwhelmed. The whole government is. And people sense when an institution is overwhelmed. Citizens know. If we had a major terrorist event tomorrow half the country—more than half—would not trust the federal government to do what it has to do, would not trust it to tell the truth, would not trust it, period.

It should be noted that all modern presidents face a slew of issues, and none of them have felt in control of events but have instead felt controlled by them. JFK in one week faced the Soviets, civil rights, the Berlin Wall, the southern Democratic mandarins of the U.S. Senate. He had to face Cuba, only 90 miles away, importing Russian missiles. But the difference now, 45 years later, is that there are a million little Cubas, a new Cuba every week. It's all so much more so. And all increasingly crucial. And it will be for the next president, too.

*   *   *

A few weeks ago I was chatting with friends about the sheer number of things parents now buy for teenage girls—bags and earrings and shoes. When I was young we didn't wear earrings, but if we had, everyone would have had a pair or two. I know a 12-year-old with dozens of pairs. They're thrown all over her desk and bureau. She's not rich, and they're inexpensive, but her parents buy her more when she wants them. Someone said, "It's affluence," and someone else nodded, but I said, "Yeah, but it's also the fear parents have that we're at the end of something, and they want their kids to have good memories. They're buying them good memories, in this case the joy a kid feels right down to her stomach when the earrings are taken out of the case." This, as you can imagine, stopped the flow of conversation for a moment. Then it resumed, as delightful and free flowing as ever. Human beings are resilient. Or at least my friends are, and have to be.

Let me veer back to the president. One of the reasons some of us have felt discomfort regarding President Bush's leadership the past year or so is that he makes more than the usual number of decisions that seem to be looking for trouble. He makes startling choices, as in the Miers case. But you don't have to look for trouble in life, it will find you, especially when you're president. It knows your address. A White House is a castle surrounded by a moat, and the moat is called trouble, and the rain will come and the moat will rise. You should buy some boots, do your work, hope for the best.

* * *

Do people fear the wheels are coming off the trolley? Is this fear widespread? A few weeks ago I was reading Christopher Lawford's lovely, candid and affectionate remembrance of growing up in a particular time and place with a particular family, the Kennedys, circa roughly 1950–2000. It's called "Symptoms of Withdrawal." At the end he quotes his Uncle Teddy. Christopher, Ted Kennedy and a few family members had gathered one night and were having a drink in Mr. Lawford's mother's apartment in Manhattan. Teddy was expansive. If he hadn't gone into politics he would have been an opera singer, he told them, and visited small Italian villages and had pasta every day for lunch. "Singing at la Scala in front of three thousand people throwing flowers at you. Then going out for dinner and having more pasta." Everyone was laughing. Then, writes Mr. Lawford, Teddy "took a long, slow gulp of his vodka and tonic, thought for a moment, and changed tack. 'I'm glad I'm not going to be around when you guys are my age.' I asked him why, and he said, 'Because when you guys are my age, the whole thing is going to fall apart.'" Mr. Lawford continued, "The statement hung there, suspended in the realm of 'maybe we shouldn't go there.' Nobody wanted to touch it. After a few moments of heavy silence, my uncle moved on."

Lawford thought his uncle might be referring to their family—that it might "fall apart." But reading, one gets the strong impression Teddy Kennedy was not talking about his family but about... the whole ball of wax, the impossible nature of everything, the realities so daunting it seems the very system is off the tracks.

And—forgive me—I thought: *If even Teddy knows...*

*   *   *

If I am right that trolley thoughts are out there, and even prevalent, how are people dealing with it on a daily basis?

I think those who haven't noticed we're living in a troubling time continue to operate each day with classic and constitutional American optimism intact. I think some of those who have a sense we're in trouble are going through the motions, dealing with their own daily challenges.

And some—well, I will mention and end with America's elites. Our recent debate about elites has had to do with whether opposition to Harriet Miers is elitist, but I don't think that's our elites' problem.

This is. Our elites, our educated and successful professionals, are the ones who are supposed to dig us out and lead us. I refer specifically to the elites of journalism and politics, the elites of the Hill and at Foggy Bottom and the agencies, the elites of our state capitals, the rich and accomplished and successful of Washington and elsewhere. I have a nagging sense, and think I have accurately observed, that many of these people have made a separate peace. That they're living their lives and taking their pleasures and pursuing their agendas; that they're going forward each day with the knowledge, which they hold more securely and with greater reason than nonelites, that the wheels are off the trolley and the trolley's off the tracks, and with a conviction, a certainty, that there is nothing they can do about it.

I suspect that history, including great historical novelists of the future, will look back and see that many of our elites simply decided to enjoy their lives while they waited for the next chapter of trouble. And that they consciously, or unconsciously, took grim comfort in this thought: I got mine. Which is what the separate peace comes down to: "I got mine, you get yours."

You're a lobbyist or a senator or a cabinet chief, you're an editor at a paper or a green-room schmoozer, you're a doctor or lawyer or Indian chief, and you're making your life a little fortress. That's what I think a lot of the elites are up to.

Not all of course. There are a lot of people—I know them and so do you—trying to do work that helps, that will turn it around, that can make it better, that can save lives. They're trying to keep the boat afloat. Or, I should say, get the trolley back on tracks.

That's what I think is going on with our elites. There are two groups. One has made a separate peace, and one is trying to keep the boat afloat. I suspect those in the latter group privately, in a place so private they don't even express it to themselves, wonder if they'll go down with the ship. Or into bad territory with the trolley.

Politics in the Modest Age

Is a humble postpresidency imaginable today?

The Wall Street Journal: July 17, 2014

"I'm just plain Mr. Truman now, a private citizen." So said an overwhelmed Harry S. Truman to a boisterous, affectionate crowd that surprised him as he ventured to a private home in Washington for a farewell lunch soon after his successor, Dwight Eisenhower, was sworn in as president of the United States. It was January 20, 1953.

Later, a regular Baltimore & Ohio train with a special car attached would take Truman and his wife, Bess, from Union Station westward, to their home in Independence, Mo. Thousands saw them off at the station. "So long, Harry!" they cried, as if they knew him. "At 6:30, with the crowd singing 'Auld Lang Syne,' the train began pulling slowly out of the station, until it was beyond the lighted platform. It had been a long road from Independence to the White House, and now Truman was going home." (This is from David McCullough's magisterial 1992 biography, "Truman.")

And he really did go home. He had, for almost eight years since the death of Franklin D. Roosevelt, been the most powerful man on earth, the wager and completer of wars and saver of Europe. In his diary Truman wrote of Cincinnatus, the Roman farmer who led in his country's hour of need and then, work done, returned to his plow. It is what George Washington did. Heck, it's what Calvin Coolidge, like Truman from modest means, did.

Truman would go back to being "just anybody again." But there was something people didn't know. He was—amazingly, this wasn't a lie—pretty much dead broke.

Mr. McCullough: "He had traveled home from Washington unprotected by Secret Service agents and there were to be none watching over him. He had come home without salary or pension. He had no income or support of any kind from the federal government other than his army pension of $112.56 a month." He had saved a little from his salary but put it in government bonds. In his final weeks as president he took out a loan from a Washington bank to tide him over.

He wasn't sure how he would make a living. His great concern was not to do anything that might exploit or "commercialize" the office he'd just left. He was offered small fortunes to associate himself with real estate companies and other corporations but he turned them down. Mr. McCullough: "His name was not for sale. He would take no fees for commercial endorsements or for lobbying or writing letters or making phone calls. He would accept no 'consulting fees.'" Offered a new Toyota as a demonstration of harmonious relations between the U.S. and Japan, he refused: It might look like a product endorsement. Anyway, he believed in American cars.

His transition was hard. He had become used to the pressures of the office and felt lost without them. He missed the people he worked with, especially Dean Acheson, his secretary of state and closest friend. And he missed "those bright lights."

But he worked it out. He rented office space in Kansas City, where on the day he arrived thousands of letters were already waiting for him. (The letters never abated, which I know because a dozen years later, as a teenager, I would write one, expressing my admiration and requesting his autograph. "Harry Truman, State of Missouri," I wrote on the envelope. That was all that was needed. He promptly and sweetly wrote back.)

The former president had to relearn things—how and whom to tip in restaurants, how to call a cab—that presidents don't have to do. For this unassuming man there were humbling moments. One day he walked by a road project and asked the man in charge if he didn't need a good straw boss. The man looked at him, looked at the workers, looked back at Truman and smiled: "You are out of a job, aren't you?"

Truman took part in the planning of his presidential library, trekking to possible sites, drawing what he thought it should look like—his grandfather's house. The federal government contributed nothing, Truman did the fund-raising himself.

He agreed to write his memoirs and signed a big contract—$600,000. But it was to be paid over five years, and the first payment came on delivery of a manuscript, so he had to hustle. It was a struggle. "I'm not a writer," he wailed, not as a complaint but an assertion of his predicament. He got help and didn't hide it. On notes toward a first draft he scrawled, "Good God, what crap!"

He and Bess took a break to visit friends back in Washington; Truman drove all the way. That was challenging because cops stopped him to warn about speeding but really to get autographs, and patrons of diners surrounded him to watch him eat.

When the book came out it sold fine and earned respectful reviews. But friends thought Harry's pungent, blunt manner of expression had been squashed down and evened out by collaborators, or perhaps by self-consciousness. A bigger disappointment was money. With the cost of staff, researchers and office rent, his net profit, he figured, was only $37,000 over five years. He was shocked he had to pay 67% federal and state income taxes. Truman had supported high tax rates for broad government services pretty much all his political life. There was a sense in his letters this was the first time he personally felt the cost of the policies he'd professed. He called the taxes "crushing." He pushed for a bill in Washington for office money for former presidents, and—rightly, fairly—got it.

Truman wasn't financially secure until five years after he left the White House, when he sold family farmland whose fields he had worked as a boy. It made him sad: He liked thinking of himself as a farmer. But if he hadn't sold, he said, "I would practically be on relief."

He died the day after Christmas 1972, age 88, and his death was not only marked but mourned. A friend had described to the New York Times Magazine how he had achieved happiness: "Harry feels that he's square with the world, that he gave it his best, and got its best in return."

God bless him, he did.

* * *

Why are we talking about Harry Truman? You know.

We live in a time when politicians relentlessly enrich themselves. We are awed and horrified by the wealth they accumulate, by their use of connections, of money lines built on past and future power. It's an operation to them. They are worth hundreds of millions. They have houses so fancy the houses have names. They make speeches to banks and universities for a quarter million dollars and call their fees contributions to their foundations. They are their foundations.

They grab and grub. They never leave. They never go home. They don't have a "home": They were born in a place, found a launching pad and shot themselves into glamour and wealth. They are operators—entitled, assuming. They "stand for the people." They stand for themselves.

So I just wanted to note how it used to be, when leaders thought they had to be respectable. When they were respectable.

"Harry Truman, not a money-grubbing slob." Who, years ago, imagined that would come to be remarkable?

CHAPTER 16

The Moment It Hits You

Socialism Gets a Second Life

The Wall Street Journal: January 29, 2016

I was watching Bernie Sanders speak last week at a town hall in Bedford when an early intuition became a conviction: *Take Mr. Sanders seriously.* He is not just another antic presence in Crazy Year 2016. His rise signifies a major shift within the Democratic Party.

The big room was full, 700 to 800 people, good for 5 p.m. on a Friday. The audience wasn't raucous or full of cheers as at his big rallies, but thinking and nodding. They were young and middle-aged, with not many white-haired heads. There was a working-class feel to them, though Bedford is relatively affluent.

"Let me disabuse you," Mr. Sanders says to those who think he cannot win. He quotes New Hampshire polls, where he's way ahead. He can defeat Donald Trump, he says. Chris Arnade, a photographer whose travels and pictures reveal an America that is battered but standing, a society that is atomized but holding on.

In July, South Carolina Sen. Tim Scott told me this was an "unpollable" election. He was spot on.

Trump, unlike Romney, understands that ideology isn't enough to provide the unity America needs.

Then the meat. He described America as a place of broad suffering—"student debt," "two-job families" with strained marriages and insufficient child care, "the old on fixed incomes."

We can turn it around if we make clear to "the billionaire class" that income inequality "is not moral." The economy is "rigged." Real unemployment is not 5% but twice that. "Youth unemployment is off the charts." He wants job-training programs for the young. The minimum wage is "a starvation wage." Raise it to "a living wage—15 bucks an hour."

The audience is attentive, supportive. "Yeah!" some shout.

He speaks of Goldman Sachs, of "banksters" and of a Republican Party owned by "the oil industry, coal industry."

"Health care is a right of all people, not a privilege." He asks if any in the audience have high-insurance deductibles. They start to call out: "$4,000," "5,000," "6,000!" Someone yells: "Nothing's covered!"

No one mentions Obamacare, but it seems clear it hasn't worked here.

Mr. Sanders says people don't go to the doctor when they're sick because of the deductibles. "Same with mental-health care!" a woman calls out. "Mental-health care must be considered part of health care," he responds, to applause. He is for "a Medicare-for-all, single-payer system."

How to pay for it all? "Impose a tax on Wall Street speculation," he says, briefly. He does not elaborate and is not pressed to.

Mr. Sanders's essential message was somber, grim, even dark. It's all stark—good guys and bad guys, angels and devils. But it's also clear and easy to understand: We are in terrible trouble because our entire system is rigged, the billionaires did it, they are the beneficiaries of the biggest income transfer from the poor to the rich in the history of man, and we are going to stop it. How? Through "a political revolution." But a soft one that will take place in voting booths. We will vote to go left.

As the audience left, they seemed not pumped or excited, but satisfied.

I listen to Mr. Sanders a lot, and what he says marks a departure from the ways the Democratic Party has been operating for at least a generation now.

Formally, since 1992, the Democratic Party has been Clintonian in its economics—moderate, showing the influence of the Democratic Leadership Council. Free-market capitalism is something you live with and accept; the wealth it produces can be directed toward public programs and endeavors. The Clinton administration didn't hate Wall Street, it hired Wall Street. Big government, big Wall Street—it all worked. It was the Great Accommodation, and it was a break with more-socialist approaches of the past.

All this began to shatter in the crash of 2008, not that anyone noticed—it got lost in the Obama hoopla. In March 2009, when Mr. Obama told Wall Street bankers at the White House that his administration was the only thing standing between them and "the pitchforks," he was wittingly or unwittingly acknowledging the Great Accommodation.

The rise of Bernie Sanders means that accommodation is ending, and something new will take its place.

Surely it means something that Mr. Obama spent eight years insisting he was not a socialist, and Bernie Sanders is rising while saying he is one.

It has left Hillary Clinton scrambling, unsteady. She thought she and her husband had cracked the code and made peace with big wealth. But her party is undoing it—without her permission and without her leading the way. She is meekly following.

It is my guess that Mr. Sanders will win in Iowa and New Hampshire. But the tendency he represents—whether it succeeds this time or simply settles in and grows—is, I suspect, here to stay.

A conservative of a certain age might say: "No, he's a fad. Socialism is yesterday! Marx is dead, the American economic behemoth rolled over and flattened him. Socialism is an antique idea that rocks with age. America is about the future, not the past."

I disagree. It's back because it's new again.

For so many, 2008 shattered faith in the system—in its fairness, usefulness and efficacy, even in its ability to endure.

As for the young, let's say you're 20 or 30, meaning you'll be voting for a long time. What in your formative years would have taught you about the excellence of free markets, low taxes, "a friendly business climate"? A teacher in public high school? Maybe one—the faculty-lounge eccentric who boycotted the union meetings. And who in our colleges teaches the virtues of capitalism?

If you are 20 or 30, you probably see capitalism in terms of two dramatic themes. The first was the crash of '08, in which heedless, irresponsible operators in business and government kited the system and scrammed. The second is income inequality. Why are some people richer than the richest kings and so many poor as serfs? Is that what capitalism gives you? Then maybe we should rethink this!

And Mr. Sanders makes it sound so easy. We're rich, he says; we can do this with a few taxes. It is soft Marxism. And it's not socialism now, it's "democratic socialism" like they have in Europe. You've been to Europe. Aside from its refugee crisis and some EU problems, it's a great place—a big welfare state that's wealthy! The French take three-hour lunches.

Socialism is an old idea to you if you're over 50 but a nice new idea if you're 25.

Do you know what's old if you're 25? The free-market capitalist system that drove us into a ditch.

Polls show the generation gap. Mr. Sanders does poorly among the old. They remember socialism. He does well among the young, who've just discovered it and have little to no knowledge of its effects. A nationwide Marist poll in November showed Mr. Sanders already leading Mrs. Clinton, 58% to 35%, among voters under 30. She led him among all other age groups, and 69% to 21% among those 60 and older. By this month a CBS/New York Times poll had Mr. Sanders up 60% to 31% among voters *under 45*.

Bernie Sanders is an indicator of the Democratic future. He is telling you where that party's going. In time some Democrats will leave over it, and look for other homes.

It's all part of the great scrambling that is happening this political year—the most dramatic, and perhaps most consequential, of our lifetimes.

Trump and the Rise of the Unprotected

The Wall Street Journal: February 25, 2016

We're in a funny moment. Those who do politics for a living, some of them quite brilliant, are struggling to comprehend the central fact of the Republican primary race, while regular people have already absorbed what has happened and is happening. Journalists and politicos have been sharing schemes for how Marco parlays a victory out of winning nowhere, or Ted roars back, or Kasich has to finish second in Ohio. But in my experience any nonpolitical person on the street, when asked who will win, not only knows but gets a look as if you're teasing him. Trump, they say.

I had such a conversation again Tuesday with a friend who repairs shoes in a shop on Lexington Avenue. Jimmy asked me, conversationally, what was going to happen. I deflected and asked who he thinks is going to win. "*Troomp!*" He's a very nice man, an elderly, old-school Italian-American, but I saw impatience flick across his face: *Aren't you supposed to know these things?*

In America now only normal people are capable of seeing the obvious.

But actually that's been true for a while, and is how we got in the position we're in.

Last October I wrote of the five stages of Trump, based on the Kübler-Ross stages of grief: denial, anger, bargaining, depression and acceptance. Most of the professionals I know are stuck somewhere between four and five.

But I keep thinking of how Donald Trump got to be the very

likely Republican nominee. There are many answers and reasons, but my thoughts keep revolving around the idea of protection. It is a theme that has been something of a preoccupation in this space over the years, but I think I am seeing it now grow into an overall political dynamic throughout the West.

There are the protected and the unprotected. The protected make public policy. The unprotected live in it. The unprotected are starting to push back, powerfully.

The protected are the accomplished, the secure, the successful—those who have power or access to it. They are protected from much of the roughness of the world. More to the point, they are protected *from the world they have created.* Again, they make public policy and have for some time.

I want to call them the elite to load the rhetorical dice, but let's stick with the protected.

They are figures in government, politics and media. They live in nice neighborhoods, safe ones. Their families function, their kids go to good schools, they've got some money. All of these things tend to isolate them, or provide buffers. Some of them—in Washington it is important officials in the executive branch or on the Hill; in Brussels, significant figures in the European Union—literally have their own security details.

Because they are protected, they feel they can do pretty much anything, impose any reality. They're insulated from many of the effects of their own decisions.

One issue obviously roiling the U.S. and Western Europe is immigration. It is the issue of the moment, a real and concrete one but also a symbolic one: It stands for all the distance between governments and their citizens.

It is of course the issue that made Donald Trump.

Britain will probably leave the European Union over it. In truth immigration is one front in that battle, but it is the most salient

because of the European refugee crisis and the failure of the protected class to address it realistically and in a way that offers safety to
the unprotected.

If you are an unprotected American—one with limited resources
and negligible access to power—you have absorbed some lessons
from the past 20 years' experience of illegal immigration. You know
the Democrats won't protect you and the Republicans won't help
you. Both parties refused to control the border. The Republicans
were afraid of being called illiberal, racist, of losing a demographic
for a generation. The Democrats wanted to keep the issue alive to use
it as a wedge against the Republicans and to establish themselves as
owners of the Hispanic vote.

Many Americans suffered from illegal immigration—its impact on
labor markets, financial costs, crime, the sense that the rule of law was
collapsing. But the protected did fine—more workers at lower wages.
No effect of illegal immigration was likely to hurt them personally.

It was good for the protected. But the unprotected watched and
saw. They realized the protected were not looking out for them, and
they inferred that they were not looking out for the country, either.

The unprotected came to think they owed the establishment—
another word for the protected—nothing, no particular loyalty, no
old allegiance.

Mr. Trump came from that.

Similarly in Europe, citizens on the ground in member nations came
to see the EU apparatus as a racket—an elite that operated in splendid
isolation, looking after its own while looking down on the people.

In Germany the incident that tipped public opinion against
Chancellor Angela Merkel's liberal refugee policy happened on New
Year's Eve in the public square of Cologne. Packs of men said to be
recent migrants groped and molested groups of young women. It
was called a clash of cultures, and it was that, but it was also wholly
predictable if any policy maker had cared to think about it. And it

was not the protected who were the victims—not a daughter of EU officials or members of the Bundestag. It was middle- and working-class girls—the unprotected, who didn't even immediately protest what had happened to them. They must have understood that in the general scheme of things they're nobodies.

What marks this political moment, in Europe and the U.S., is the rise of the unprotected. It is the rise of people who don't have all that much against those who've been given many blessings and seem to believe they have them not because they're fortunate but because they're better.

You see the dynamic in many spheres. In Hollywood, as we still call it, where they make our rough culture, they are careful to protect their own children from its ill effects. In places with failing schools, they choose not to help them through the school liberation movement—charter schools, choice, etc.—because they fear to go up against the most reactionary professional group in America, the teachers unions. They let the public schools flounder. But their children go to the best private schools.

This is a terrible feature of our age—that we are governed by protected people who don't seem to care that much about their unprotected fellow citizens.

And a country really can't continue this way.

In wise governments the top is attentive to the realities of the lives of normal people, and careful about their anxieties. That's more or less how America used to be. There didn't seem to be so much distance between the top and the bottom.

Now it seems the attitude of the top half is: You're on your own. Get with the program, little racist.

Social philosophers are always saying the underclass must re-moralize. Maybe it is the overclass that must re-moralize.

I don't know if the protected see how serious this moment is, or their role in it.

The Republican Party Is Shattering

The Wall Street Journal: March 3, 2016

I'm interested in where we are. I think we are seeing a great political party shatter before our eyes. I'm not sure I see a way around or through. I said so on TV the other night and got a lot of responses on social media. They said: Good. They said, "They are corrupt," and "I am through." Good riddance to bad rubbish. Next.

I am not experiencing it that way. For me the Republican Party was always the vehicle of a philosophy, conservative political thought—no more, no less. I have the past 10 years been its critic on wars and immigration, on the establishment's self-seeking and failures of imagination. And yet at the prospect of the party's shattering I feel somewhat shattered, too. So many lives, so much effort went into its making. "I am more faithful than I intended to be."

I knew Tuesday night I was witnessing something grave, something bigger than 1976, that traumatic year when a Republican insurgent almost toppled the incumbent Republican president. Bigger, too, than 1964, when Goldwater conservatism swept the primaries and convention and lost the country. What is happening now is bigger and less remediable in part because the battles in the past were over conservatism, an actual political philosophy.

And I find myself receiving with some anger, even though I understand, those—especially on the top of the party—who are so blithely declaring the end of things. Do they understand what they're ending? *Did they ever?* It started in 1860. Its first great figure was a man called Lincoln. *We'll start a new party and call it Fred,* they tweet. *We'll be the party in exile.* Implicitly: *And I and my friends will run it.* Like little boys knocking over building blocks. And they say Donald Trump is careless.

But we are witnessing history. Something important is ending. It is hard to believe what replaces it will be better.

No one knows where this goes. The top of the party and the bottom have split. They disagree on the essentials.

Donald Trump won big Tuesday night, carrying seven states. As others have noted, if it were someone else, he'd be called unassailable, the victor—"time to get in line."

If trends continue—and political trends tend to—Mr. Trump will win or come very close to winning by the convention in July. If party forces succeed in finagling him out of the nomination, his supporters will bolt, which will break the party. And it's hard to see what kind of special sauce, what enduring loyalty, would make them come back in the future.

If, on the other hand, Mr. Trump is given the crown in Cleveland, party political figures, operatives, loyalists, journalists and intellectuals, not to mention sophisticated suburbanites and, God knows, donors will themselves bolt. That is a smaller but not insignificant group. And again it's hard to imagine the special sauce—the shared interests, the basic worldview—that would allow them to reconcile with Trump supporters down the road.

It's no longer clear what shared principles endure. Everything got stretched to the breaking point the past 15 years.

Party leaders and thinkers should take note: It's easier for a base to hire or develop a flashy new establishment than it is for an establishment to find itself a new base.

Even if the party stays together with a Trump win, what will it be? It will have been reconstituted. Yes, it will be a formal and proactive foe of illegal immigration, and it will rethink its approach to entitlements, but it will also be other things. What?

We are in uncharted territory. But the point is fissures and tensions simmering and growing for 15 years burst through, erupted.

The establishment was slow to see what was happening, slow to see Mr. Trump coming, in full denial as he continued to win. Their denial is self-indicting. They couldn't see his appeal because they had no idea how their own people were experiencing America. I have been thinking a lot about establishments and elites. A central purpose of both, a prime responsibility, is to understand those who are *not* establishment and elite and look out for them, take care of them. Not in a government-from-on-high way, not with an air of noblesse oblige, but in a way that is respectfully attentive to the facts of their lives. You have a responsibility when you lead not to offend needlessly, not to impose realities you yourself can buy your way out of. You don't privately make fun of people as knuckle-draggers, victims of teachers-union educations, low-information voters.

We had a low-information elite.

This column has been pretty devoted the past nine months to everything that gave rise to this moment, to Mr. Trump. His supporters disrespect the system—fair enough, it's earned disrespect. They see Washington dysfunction and want to break through it—fair enough. In a world of thugs, they say, he will be our thug. Politics is a freak show? He's our freak. They know they're lowering standards by giving the top political job in America to a man who never held office. But they feel Washington lowered all standards first. They hate political correctness—there is no one in the country the past quarter-century who has not been embarrassed or humiliated for using the wrong word or concept or having the wrong thought—and see his rudeness as proof he hates PC, too.

"He can think outside the box." Can he ever.

He is a one-man wrecking crew of all political comportment, and a carrier of that virus. Yet his appeal is not only his outrageousness.

He is a divider of the Republican Party and yet an enlarger of the tent. His candidacy is contributing to record turnouts in primary after primary, and surely bringing in Democrats and independents. But it should concern his supporters that his brain appears to be a grab bag of impulses, and although he has many views and opinions, he doesn't seem to know anything about public policy or the way the White House or the government actually works.

He is unpredictable, which his supporters see as an advantage. But in a harrowing, hair-trigger world it matters that the leaders of other nations be able to calculate with some reasonable certainty what another leader would do under a given set of circumstances.

"He goes with his gut." Yes. But George W. Bush was a gut player, too, and it wasn't pretty when his gut began to fail.

The GOP elite is about to spend a lot of money and hire a lot of talent, quickly, to try to kill Trump off the next two weeks. There will be speeches, ads—an onslaught. It will no doubt do Mr. Trump some damage, but not much.

It will prove to Trump supporters that what they think is true— their guy is the only one who will stand up to the establishment, so naturally the establishment is trying to kill him. And Trump supporters don't seem to have that many illusions about various aspects of his essential character. One of them told me he's "a junkyard dog."

They think his character is equal to the moment.

That Moment When 2016 Hits You

The Wall Street Journal: April 21, 2016

Have you had your 2016 Moment? I think you probably have, or will.

The Moment is that sliver of time in which you fully realize something epochal is happening in politics, that there has never been a presidential year like 2016, and suddenly you are aware of it in a new, true and personal way. It tends to involve a poignant sense of dislocation, a knowledge that our politics have changed and won't be going back.

We've had a lot to absorb—the breaking of a party, the rise of an outlandish outsider; a lurch to the left in the other party, the popular rise of a socialist. Alongside that, the enduring power of a candidate even her most ardent supporters accept as corrupt. Add the lowering of standards, the feeling of no options, the coarsening, and all the new estrangements.

The Moment is when it got to you, or when it fully came through.

My friend Lloyd, a Manhattan lawyer and GOP campaign veteran, had two Moments. The first came when he took his 12-year-old on a father-son trip to New Hampshire to see the primary. They saw Ted Cruz speak at a restaurant, and Bernie Sanders in a boisterous rally. "It was great and wonderful," Lloyd said.

Then it happened. "The Monday night before the voting we were at a Donald Trump rally. A woman in the audience screamed out the P-word to refer to a rival candidate. Trump repeated it from the podium, and my kid heard it and looked at me." Lloyd was mortified. Welcome to the splendor of democracy, son. "I thought, 'So we have come to this.' "

It didn't end there. Lloyd's second Moment came a month later, the morning after the raucous GOP debate that featured references to hand size. Lloyd was in the car with his son, listening to the original Broadway cast recording of "Hamilton." "I blurted out, 'How exactly has America managed to travel from *that* to *this*?' " American history is fiercely imperfect and made by humans. "Yet in the rear-view mirror it appears ennobling and grand. And now it feels jagged, and the fabric is worn."

A friend I'll call Bill, a political veteran from the 1980s and '90s, also had his Moment with his child, a 14-year-old daughter who is a budding history buff. He had never taken her to the Reagan Library, so last month they went. As she stood watching a video of Reagan speaking, he thought of Reagan and FDR, of JFK and Martin Luther King. His daughter, he realized, would probably never see political leaders of such stature and grace, though she deserved to. Her first, indelible political memories were of lower, grubbier folk. "Leaders with Reaganesque potential no longer go into politics— and why would they, with all the posturing and plasticity that it requires?"

He added: "I felt a wave of sadness."

Another political veteran, my friend John, also had his Moment during the New Hampshire primary. Out door-knocking for Jeb Bush, "I was struck as I walked along a neighborhood using the app that described the voters in each house. So many multigenerational families of odd collections of ages in houses with missing roof shingles or shutters askew or paint peeling. Cars needing repair."

What was the story inside those houses? Unemployment, he thought, elder care, divorce, custody battles. "It was easy to see a collective loss of hope in a once-thriving town." He sensed "years of neglect and sadness. Something is brewing."

My Moment came a month ago. I'd recently told a friend my emotions felt too close to the surface—for months history had been going through me and I felt like a vibrating fork. I had not been laughing at the splintering of a great political party but mourning it. Something of me had gone into it. Party elites seemed to have no idea why it was shattering, which meant they wouldn't be able to repair it, whatever happens with Mr. Trump.

I was offended that those curiously quick to write essays about who broke the party were usually those who'd backed the policies that broke it. Lately conservative thinkers and journalists had taken to making clear their disdain for the white working class. I had actually not known they looked down on them. I deeply resented it and it pained me. If you're a writer lucky enough to have thoughts and be paid to express them and there are Americans on the ground struggling, suffering—some of them making mistakes, some unlucky—you don't owe them your airy, well-put contempt, you owe them your loyalty. They, too, have given a portion of their love to this great project, and they are in trouble.

A few nights earlier, I'd moderated a panel in New York, on, yes, the ironic soundtrack of election year 2016, "Hamilton." At one point I quoted a line. It is when Eliza sings, just as war has come and things are bleak: "How lucky we are to be alive right now." As I quoted it, my voice caught. I asked a friend later if he'd noticed. Yes, he said, quizzically, comfortingly, we did.

The following day I spoke at a school in Florida, awoke the next morning spent, got coffee, fired up the iPad, put on cable news. I read an email thread from a group of conservative women—very bright, all ages, all decorous and dignified. But tempers were high, and they were courteously tearing each other apart over Mr. Trump and the GOP.

Then to my own email, full of notes from people pro- and anti-Trump, but all seemed marked by some kind of grieving. I looked up and saw Hillary Clinton yelling on TV and switched channels. Breaking news, said the crawl. A caravan of Trump supporters driving to an outdoor rally in Fountain Hills, Ariz., had been blocked by demonstrators. The helicopter shot showed a highway backed up for miles. No one seemed to be in charge, as is often the case in America. It was like an unmovable force against an unmovable object.

I watched dumbly, tiredly. Then for no reason—this is true, it just doesn't sound it—I thought of an old Paul Simon song that had been crossing my mind, "The Boy in the Bubble." I muted the TV, found the song on YouTube, and listened as I stared at the soundless mile of cars and the soundless demonstrators. As the lyrics came— "...Don't cry baby / Don't cry"—my eyes filled with tears. And a sob welled up and I literally put my hands to my face and sobbed, silently, for I suppose a minute.

Because my country is in trouble.

Because I felt anguish at all the estrangements.

Because some things that shouldn't have changed have changed.

Because too much is being lost. Because the great choice in a nation of 320 million may come down to Crazy Man versus Criminal.

And yes, I know this is all personal, and not column-ish.

But that was my Moment.

You'll feel better the next day, I promise, but you won't be able to tell yourself that this is history as usual anymore. This is big, what we're living through.

Trump Was a Spark, Not the Fire

The Wall Street Journal: May 5, 2016

God bless our beloved country as it again undergoes one of its quiet upheavals.

Donald Trump will receive the Republican nomination for the presidency and nothing will be the same. How we do politics in America is changed and will not be going back. The usual standards and expectations have been turned on their head, and more than one establishment has been routed.

A decent interval should be set aside for sheer astonishment.

We face six months of what will be a historically hellacious campaign. Yes, we picked the wrong time to stop taking opioids.

Before I go to larger issues I mention how everyone, especially the media, is blaming the media for Donald Trump's rise. I hate to get in the way of their self-flagellation but that's not how I see it. From the time he announced, they gave Mr. Trump unprecedented free media in long, live interviews, many by phone, some possibly from his bathtub. We'll never know. It was a great boon to him and amounted, by one estimate, to nearly $2 billion worth of airtime.

But the media did not make Donald Trump's allure, his allure made for big ratings. Mr. Trump was a draw from the beginning. If anyone had wanted to listen to Jeb Bush, cable networks would have been happy to show his rallies, too.

When Mr. Trump was on, ratings jumped, but it wasn't only ratings, it was something else. It was the freak show at its zenith, it was great TV—you didn't know what he was going to say next! He didn't know! It was better than everyone else's boring, prefabricated, airless, weightless, relentless word-saying—better than Ted Cruz, who seemed like someone who practiced sincere hand gestures in the mirror at night, better than Marco the moist robot, better than Hillary's grim and horrifying attempts to chuckle like a person who chuckles.

And it was something else. TV producers were all sure he'd die on their show. They weren't for Mr. Trump. By showing him they were revealing him: Look at this fatuous dope, see through him! They knew he'd quickly enough say something unforgivable, and if he said it on their air, he died on their show! They took him down with the question! It was only after a solid six months of his not dying that they came to have qualms. They now understood they were helping him. Nothing he says is unforgivable to his supporters! Or, another way to put it, his fans would forgive anything so long as he promised to be what they want him to be, a human bomb that will explode by timer under a bench in Lafayette Park and take out all the people but leave the monuments standing.

In this regard today's television producers remind me of the producers of 1969 who heard one day that Spiro Agnew, the idiotic new Republican vice president, was going to make a big speech lambasting the media for its liberal bias. They knew Agnew was about to make a fool of himself. Who would believe him? So they covered that speech all over the place, hyped it like you wouldn't believe—no one in America didn't hear about it. It made Agnew a sensation. The American people—"the silent majority"—saw it as Agnew did. "Nattering nabobs of negativism," from the witty, alliterative pen of William Safire, entered the language.

The producers had projected their own loathing. They found out they and America loathed different things.

That's a little like what happened this year with TV and Mr. Trump.

My, that wasn't much of a defense, was it?

The Trump phenomenon itself would normally be big enough for any political cycle, but another story of equal size isn't being sufficiently noticed and deserves mention. The Democratic base has become more liberal—we all know this part—but in a way the Republican base has, too. Or rather it is certainly busy updating what conservative means. The past few months, in state after state, one thing kept jumping out at me in primary exit polls. Democrats consistently characterize themselves as more liberal than in 2008, a big liberal year. This week in Indiana, 68% of Democratic voters called themselves liberal or very liberal. In 2008 that number was 39%. That's a huge increase.

In South Carolina this year, 53% of Democrats called themselves very or somewhat liberal. Eight years ago that number was 44%—again, a significant jump. In Pennsylvania, 66% of respondents called themselves very or somewhat liberal. That number eight years ago was 50%.

The dynamic is repeated in other states. The Democratic Party is going left.

But look at the Republican side. However they characterize themselves, a majority of GOP voters now are supporting the candidate who has been to the left of the party's established thinking on a host of issues—entitlement spending, trade, foreign policy. Mr. Trump's colorfully emphatic stands on immigration have been portrayed as so wackily rightist that the nonrightist nature of his other, equally consequential positions has been obscured.

In my observation it is a mistake to think Mr. Trump's supporters are so thick they don't know his stands. They do.

It does not show an understanding of the moment to say Donald Trump by himself has changed the Republican Party. It is closer to the mark to say the base of the party is changing and Mr. Trump's electric arrival on the scene made obvious what was already happening.

For this reason among others, I do not understand the impulse of the NeverTrump people to anathametize and shun those Republicans who will not vow to oppose Mr. Trump and commit to defeating him. They have been warned that if they don't do these things, they will not be allowed to help rebuild the party after Mr. Trump destroys it. Conservatives love to throw conservatives out of conservatism; it's like an ancestral tic. But great political movements should not be run like private clubs. And have the anathemitizers noticed they aren't in charge anymore? That in the great antiestablishment disruption of 2016 they have been upended, too?

We don't know what's coming in 2016, or what happens to the GOP if Mr. Trump wins or loses. If there is a rebuilding of the party, as opposed to an ongoing reinvention, we don't know when that will commence. If it is a rebuilding, on what grounds do the Never-Trump forces think it will be rebuilt? As a neoconservative, functionally open-borders, slash-the-entitlements party?

I am not sure, whatever happens in 2016, that there will ever again be a market for that product. All this cycle I've been thinking of what Lee Atwater said when he wanted to communicate to a politician that a policy was not popular: "The dawgs don't like the dawg food."

Centers of gravity are shifting. The new Republican Party will not be rebuilt and re-formed in McLean, it will be rebuilt or re-formed in Massapequa.

Finally, can Mr. Trump win? Of course. Uphill but possible. If this year has taught us anything, it is what Harrison Salisbury said he'd learned from a lifetime in journalism: "Expect the unexpected."

A Wounded Boy's Silence, and the Candidates

The Wall Street Journal: August 25, 2016

With the campaign proper about to begin, on Labor Day, a last August thought, a very simple one: War is terrible. It is my impression our candidates for president don't really know this. They never say it, not in formal speeches or in thinking aloud, in reveries in friendly interviews. I would say of most of America's political class that they have their heads all screwed up about war, that they approach the subject coolly, as a political and geopolitical matter, and that they see it through prisms of personal political need and ideological gain. They are missing the central fact of it—that it is terrible. Before the election is over, it would be good if someone said it.

The thought arises most recently from the harrowing photo and videotape of the 5-year-old boy in Aleppo, Syria. You have seen one or both. His name is Omran Daqneesh and he lived with his parents and three siblings in the rebel-held Qaterji neighborhood, which late Wednesday night last week either Russian or Syrian forces targeted in a brutal airstrike. Omran was pulled from the rubble. He was placed on a seat in the back of an ambulance.

The left side of his head was covered in blood. His thick dark hair was stiff from smoke and dust. His legs were marked by soot and what looked like bruises. One report said he'd been in the rubble an hour before they dug him out.

They wouldn't let the ambulance go until it was full. There was room for more children, and they came. But Omran is the one you can't stop watching. He stares mutely, like a shocked old man. Photojournalists make flashes of light as they take his picture. No one has—or takes—a moment to call any comfort to him, to the 5-year-old boy as he stares ahead.

He can't fully see out of his left eye, which seems damaged. Tentatively, calling no attention to himself, he brings his left hand up to his head and touches around for the wound. He seems to find it, then puts his hand down on his legs, as if not to call attention to his wounds.

Watching the videotape, posted on YouTube by an anti-Assad group, you see what is most harrowing. It isn't only his youth, his aloneness, the blood—it's that he isn't crying.

Children, by nature and instinct, cry when they are infants. But as they grow older, 3 and 4 and 5, crying is sometimes more of a decision. Children who know they're cared for cry in the expectation that someone will comfort them. If by 3 or 4 you haven't had that, or haven't had that enough—if circumstances were harsh enough that you couldn't rely on help or comfort—then you might not cry. Because it won't bring the help you need, or may in fact bring negative responses.

For all 5 years of his life, Omran Daqneesh lived in a country wracked by civil war, surrounded by the tension, fear and hardship war brings.

Anyway, he didn't cry. He was taken to a local underground hospital called M10, treated for head wounds and released. There are reports his older brother has since died.

War is terrible. It abuses the innocent and takes their lives, it wastes all kinds of treasure, it kills generations and whole cultures. It strikes me as rather mad that our candidates for commander in chief of the most powerful armed forces in the world don't ever simply think aloud about this.

About 18 months ago I asked a potential Republican presidential candidate, in conversation, if he hated war. He got the dart-eyed look politicians get when they sense a trick question. This startled me. How do you not know the answer? After a few seconds I said, "This is not a trick question." I explained I was thinking of Franklin D. Roosevelt, who said, "I hate war," roughly five years before prosecuting one with unambivalent vigor.

The potential candidate then stuttered that of course he doesn't like war, but sometimes it's necessary. Well, yes, sometimes it is. But why would you fear stating that war is hell, and hell ain't where we want to be?

Afterward, and again this week, I went back to FDR's famous speech, delivered at Chautauqua, N.Y., Aug. 14, 1936—80 years ago this month. He was "less cheerful," he admitted, about world events than domestic ones—this at the depth of the Depression. What happens in the world may have an impact on the United States, but we can serve the cause of peace by "setting an example" and following the policy of the good neighbor—"the neighbor who resolutely respects himself and, because he does so, respects the rights of others." Because of this practice "the whole world now knows that the United States cherishes no predatory ambitions. We are strong; but less powerful nations know that they need not fear our strength."

He observed that "the noblest monument to peace... in all the world is not a monument... but the boundary which unites the United States and Canada—3,000 miles of friendship." Still, so long as war exists there is danger of being "drawn into" one. That grieves him, he said, because "I have seen war. I have seen war on land and sea... I have seen cities destroyed... I hate war."

It's quite a speech, a deep and persuasive exposing of thoughts on the most essential of human and governmental subjects. But what really surprised me on rereading it was that I don't think a Republican or Democratic candidate would feel free to speak like that anymore. They'd fear being called soft. That isn't good, or even practical.

FDR after all was pretty good at waging war. It only made him more powerful, made his decisions more convincing, that he'd laid down the predicate that he'd never wanted it and in fact hated it.

Unless I'm missing something, neither candidate for president appears to have an informed or deeply felt sense of the tragedy of war. Hillary Clinton was subjected, in the primaries, to sharp criticism from the left that she was too bellicose, was wrong to go all in on Iraq, wrong to support regime change in Libya, wrong to be so temperamentally activist in this area. When Moammar Gadhafi was killed in the field after the fall of his government, she laughed with a reporter: "We came, we saw, he died."

As for Donald Trump, he is usually equally aggressive in speaking of potential U.S. military actions, though it's clear he hates war at least for himself. He did not serve and famously told Howard Stern that dodging incoming STDs was his personal Vietnam.

Our leaders are shallow on the subject of war. No, worse than shallow—they're silent. Which is one reason they will likely not be fully trusted should they make rough decisions down the road on Syria, or Iran, or elsewhere.

War is terrible. That should be said over and over, not because it's a box you ought to check on the way to the presidency but because you're human and have a brain.

You should hate war. A 5-year-old knows that.

Remembering a Hero, 15 Years After 9/11

The Wall Street Journal: September 9, 2016

What do I think about when I think about that day? The firemen who climbed "the stairway to Heaven" with 50, 60 pounds of gear. The people who called from Windows on the World and said: "I just want you to know I love you." The men on the plane who tried to take the cockpit of Flight 93 before it went down in a Pennsylvania field: "Let's roll."

And I think about Welles Crowther, the man in the red bandanna.

He was 24, from Nyack, N.Y. He played lacrosse at Boston College, graduated and got an internship at Sandler O'Neill, the investment bank. In two years he was a junior associate on the trading desk. He worked in the south tower of the World Trade Center, on the 104th floor.

When United Flight 175 hit that tower at 9:03 a.m., it came in at a tilt, ripping through floors 78 through 84. Many of those who never got out were on those floors, or the ones above. Welles Crowther had already called his mother, Alison, and left a voicemail: "I want you to know that I'm OK." Only one stairwell was clear. He found it. Most people would have run for their lives, but he started running for everyone else's.

Welles was beloved—bright, joyous, grounded. Family was everything to him. He idolized his father, Jefferson, a banker and volunteer fireman. They went to the firehouse together when Welles was a child. Welles would clean the trucks, getting in close where no one else could fit. One Sunday when Welles was 7 or 8 his mother dressed him for church in his first suit. His father had a white handkerchief in his breast pocket. Could he have one? Jefferson put one in Welles's front pocket and then took a colored one and put it in Welles's back pocket. One's for show, he said, the other's for blow.

"Welles kept it with him, a connection to his father," said Alison Crowther this week by phone. "He carried a red bandanna all his life." It was a talisman but practical, too. It could clean up a mess. When he'd take it from his pocket at Sandler O'Neill, they'd tease him. What are you, a farmer? That is from Tom Rinaldi's lovely book "The Red Bandanna," which came out this week. He'd tease back: "With this bandanna I'm gonna change the world."

As Welles went down the stairwell he saw what happened on the 78th floor sky lobby. People trying to escape had been waiting for elevators when the plane hit. It was carnage—fire, smoke, bodies everywhere. A woman named Ling Young, a worker for the state tax department, sat on the floor, badly burned and in shock. From out of the murk she heard a man's voice: "I found the stairs. Follow me."

"There was something she heard in the voice, an authority, compelling her to follow," Mr. Rinaldi writes. Ms. Young stood, and followed. She saw that the man was carrying a woman. Eighteen floors down the air began to clear. He gently placed the woman down and told them both to continue walking down. Then he turned and went back upstairs to help others.

Judy Wein of Aon Corporation had also been in the 78th floor. She, too, was badly injured and she, too, heard the voice: "Everyone who can stand now, stand now. If you can help others, do so." He guided her and others to the stairwell.

Apparently Welles kept leading people down from the top floors to the lower ones, where they could make their way out. Then he'd go up to find more. No one knows how many. The fire department credits him with five saved lives.

He never made it home. His family hoped, grieved, filled out
forms. On the Friday after 9/11 Alison stood up from her desk and
suddenly she knew Welles was there, right behind her. She could feel
his energy, his force; it was him. She didn't turn. She just said: Thank
you. She knew he was saying he was OK. After that she didn't dare
hope he'd be found alive because she knew he wouldn't.

They found him six months later, in the lobby of the south tower.
He'd made it all the way down. He was found in an area with many
firefighters' remains. It had been the FDNY command post. It was
where assistant fire chief Donald Burns was found. He and his men
had probably helped evacuate thousands. Welles could have left and
saved his own life—they all could have. But they'd all stayed. "He
was helping," said Alison.

The Crowthers never knew what he'd done until Memorial Day
weekend 2002. *The New York Times* carried a minute-by-minute
report of what happened in the towers after the planes hit. Near the
end it said: "A mysterious man appeared at one point, his mouth and
nose covered with a red handkerchief." It mentioned Ms. Young and
Ms. Wein. The Crowthers sent them pictures of Welles.

That was him, they said. Ms. Wein had seen his face when he
took the bandanna from his face as the air cleared on the lower
floors. Ms. Young said: "He saved my life."

As a child, Welles Crowther had wanted to be a fireman. Few
knew he'd decided to apply for the FDNY while he was still at
Sandler. After his father found his application the department did
something it had done only once in the 141 years since its founding.
It made Welles an honorary member.

His father sometimes felt guilt—maybe taking him to the fire
department so much when he was a kid was why Welles died. Alison
said no: "That gave him the tools to be the fullest person he was that
day."

She thinks now of something else. The family spent the Labor

Day before 9/11 together, at the house in Nyack. All weekend, said Alison, Welles was subdued—"quiet, introspective." Normally he'd be charging around, playing basketball. At one point he sat with his mother in the living room. "He said, 'You know, Mom, I don't know what it is but I know I'm meant to be part of something really big.' I didn't get it. Who would get it? But he definitely sensed something was coming."

I asked Alison Crowther a hard question, embarrassing for a parent to answer: How do you make a hero? She paused. "We tried to instill honesty," she said. "The fearlessness he came with—my husband said he came with that hardware installed. He was this good-hearted little guy, very protective from an early age. Honesty was a big thing with us, and taking responsibility."

It wasn't us, she was saying, it was him. It was Welles.

The way I see it, courage comes from love. There's a big unseen current of love that hums through the world, and some plug into it more than others, more deeply and surely, and they get more power from it. And it fills them with courage. It makes everything possible.

People see the fallen, beat-up world around them and ask: What can I do? Maybe: Be like Welles Crowther. Take your bandanna, change the world.

The Year of the Reticent Voter

The Wall Street Journal: September 22, 2016

The signature sentence of this election begins with the words "In a country of 320 million..." I hear it everywhere. It ends with "how'd it come down to these two?" or "why'd we get *them*?"

Another sentence is a now a common greeting among Republicans who haven't seen each other in a while: "What are we gonna do?"

The most arresting sentence of the week came from a sophisticated Manhattan man friendly with all sides. I asked if he knows what he'll do in November. "I know exactly," he said with some spirit. "I will be one of the 40 million who will deny, the day after the election, that they voted for him. But I will."

A high elected official, a Republican, got a faraway look when I asked what he thought was going to happen. "This is the unpollable election," he said. People don't want to tell you who they're for. A lot aren't sure. A lot don't want to be pressed.

That's exactly what I've seen the past few weeks in North Carolina, New Jersey, Tennessee and Minnesota.

Every four years I ask people if they'll vote, and if they have a sense of how. Every four years they tell me—assertively or shyly, confidently or tentatively. This year is different. I've never seen people so nervous to answer. It's so unlike America, this reticence, even defensiveness. It's as if there's a feeling that to declare who you're for is to invite others to inspect your soul.

"I feel like this is the most controversial election ever," said a food-court worker at La Guardia Airport. She works a full shift,

4 a.m. to noon, five days a week, then goes full-time to a nearby college. We'd been chatting awhile, and when I asked the question she told me, carefully, that she hasn't decided how she'll vote, and neither have her family members. I said a lot of people seem nervous to say. She said: "Especially Trump people. They're afraid you'll think they're stupid."

Which is how I knew she was going to vote for Donald Trump.

It's true: Trump voters especially don't want to be categorized, judged, thought stupid—racist, sexist, Islamophobic, you name it. When most of them know, actually, that they're not.

Voters who talk about 2016 are very careful to damn both sides, air their disappointment, note that they've been following the election closely. They know each candidate's history.

In Tennessee I asked a smart businessman who he's for. He carefully and at length outlined his criticisms and concerns regarding both candidates. Then, as I started to leave, he threw in, from nowhere: "So I think Trump."

When I talk to strangers—which I do a lot, and like it—I sometimes say dour, mordant things, to get them going by establishing that anything can be said. I say if Hillary Clinton is elected there will be at least one special prosecutor, maybe two, within 18 months, because her character will not be reborn on crossing the threshold of the White House; the well-worn grooves of her essential nature will kick in. If Mr. Trump is elected there will be a constitutional crisis within 18 months because he doesn't really know what a president does, doesn't respect traditional boundaries, doesn't reflect on implications and effects. I always expect pushback. I am not getting it! I get nods, laughs and, in two recent cases, admissions that whoever wins they'd been wondering how soon impeachment proceedings would begin.

Oh, my pained and crazy country.

A final observation, underlying all. Under the smiles and beyond the reticence it is clear how seriously Americans are taking their decision, how gravely. As if it's not Tweedledum and Tweedledee but an actual choice between two vastly different dramas, two different worlds of outcome and meaning. The cynic or the screwball? Shall we go to the bad place or the crazy place?

I returned knowing I was wrong about something. I thought everyone has been watching the election more than a year, everyone knows their opinion of Mrs. Clinton and Mr. Trump, this thing is pretty much settled. No, it's fluid. This cake is not baked.

I talked to Peter D. Hart, the veteran Democratic pollster. Are things as much in play as I think? Yes and no, he said. People do have a firm opinion of the two candidates, the clichés are set: "Hillary competent and cold, Trump an incompetent loose cannon." But "the part that is evolving is a sense of what we need to do and where we need to go." Everyone wants change, but people are deciding, "constructive change or radical change?"

Pollster Glen Bolger of Public Opinion Strategies says nothing is settled. "Voters are angry at Clinton because she can't tell the truth and they're scared of Trump because they're afraid he's gonna start a war. There are times her un-truthiness outweighs their concern about him overreacting and starting a war. It goes back and forth."

He disagrees with the "unpollable" premise: "It's pollable. But if anyone says their results are cast in concrete, that's a mistake. There's a lot of fluidity."

The veteran pollster Kellyanne Conway, now Trump campaign manager, says: "This thing is fluid in a way we don't understand." She is a close student of Barack Obama's 2008 campaign in all its aspects. Like Mr. Obama, she says, Mr. Trump is "a candidate built for the 21st century...The most fundamental truth of politics is there's no substitute for a great, magnetic, compelling candidate."

She speaks of "undercover" Trump voters. "To call them hidden is a mistake. They're undercover because they've gotten to the point they're tired of arguing... Some have been voting Democratic all their life, they voted for Obama, they're tired of defending and explaining themselves" to family and coworkers. "They don't want to proselytize."

Mr. Hart said the debates are unusually important this year. "Trump is the central character—it's his last opportunity to get a fresh look from voters. A debate is an open window. Voters suspend opinions and look afresh. Attitudes toward Trump have not changed—temperament questions, can he do the job?" This is a chance for him to "establish credibility at this stage of the game." By contrast, "Hillary's problems are not professional but personal—can I like her, does she understand me... It's an opportunity for her to get voters saying, 'You know something, she's not a bad egg.' "

Ms. Conway, too, says the debates are key. "People like a clash of the titans. They like a contest. These debates are the ultimate reality show—the stakes have never been higher." After the Democratic convention the Clinton campaign, in a major miscalculation, "lowered the bar" for Trump, "calling him unfit, unpresidential." That turned him into the underdog. "Americans love an underdog."

Ms. Conway remembered what happened in 2008 when John McCain referred to his long experience. "Obama said if experience means you got us into this mess overseas and tanked the economy, maybe experience is overrated. We are turning this around on Clinton now."

Mr. Trump's advantage? "Americans love to say they think outside the box. Trump lives outside the box. Hillary *is* the box."

No More Business as Usual, Mr. Trump

The Wall Street Journal: November 24, 2016

The other day I experienced a flash of alarm. There was a claim from an Argentine journalist that when the president of Argentina, Mauricio Macri, phoned Donald Trump to congratulate him on his election victory, the talk turned to permits for the building of a Trump skyscraper in Buenos Aires. Mr. Macri's press officer quickly and sharply denied the report: "They didn't talk about the tower at all. It's absolutely untrue." So did the Trump transition office. The journalist apparently offered no proof. The story more or less ended there.

But what alarmed me was this question: Does Donald Trump *know* he can't ever have a conversation like this? Does he fully understand that a president can never use the office, its power and influence, for his own financial enrichment? That he can't, however offhandedly, both do business and be president? That future and credible reports that he had engaged in such a conflict of interest would doom his presidency? And that solving the question of his businesses and their relation to his presidency is urgent?

This week, in an interview with the *New York Times*, Mr. Trump was not reassuring. When pressed on how, exactly, he means to distance himself from his business interests, he couldn't stop himself from promoting a few of them: "We just opened a beautiful hotel on Pennsylvania Avenue," he said. "The brand is certainly a hotter brand."

"In theory, I can be president of the United States and run my business 100%," he said, adding that he is "phasing that out now."

"In theory I don't have to do anything. But I would like to do something. I would like to try and formalize something, because I don't care about my business."

He said, "I've greatly reduced meetings with contractors, meetings with different people." Thank goodness for that. He's the president-elect.

He noted that presidents are exempt from conflict-of-interest laws, but "I understand why the president can't have a conflict of interest now because everything a president does in some ways is like a conflict of interest, but I have—I've built a very great company and it's a big company and it's all over the world. People are starting to see, when they look at all these different jobs, like in India and other things, No. 1, a job like that builds great relationships with the people of India, so it's all good." Business partners come in, they want a picture, "I think it's wonderful to take a picture."

Might he sell his businesses? "That's a very hard thing to do, you know what, because I have real estate." Selling real estate isn't like selling a stock. "I don't care about my company. I mean, if a partner comes in from India or if a partner comes in from Canada, where we did a beautiful big building that just opened, and they want to take a picture and come into my office, and my kids come in and I originally made the deal with these people, I mean what am I going to say? 'I'm not going to talk to you,' 'I'm not going to take pictures'?"

Yes, that's exactly what you say! *I'm not going to pose with you because I will soon be president of the United States and the prestige of that office precludes taking the picture you'll soon use in your brochure.*

In the interview Mr. Trump was not defensive—he was garrulous, forthcoming as to his thought processes, and yet he seemed curiously unaware as to the urgency of the subject.

If he is not aware it is crucial, the reason may come down to five words: the habits of a lifetime.

For half a century Donald Trump has devoted all his professional energies to money, profit, the deal. That is how he thinks: It's his deepest neural pathway. He's a free-market capitalist who started with a lot and turned it into more. He created jobs, employs many. Good! But that's his mind: money, profit, the deal. He has brought up his children to enter his business. Whatever else they do, they have surely absorbed the family ethos.

And now, for the first time in his life, money, profit, the deal is not his job.

He will be president of the United States. He can't help the family business as president. He can't help his children make a living as president.

He has to be *losing* money as president and putting personal profit motives behind him. Which means putting the ways and habits of a lifetime behind him.

Because he's entered something much bigger: the presidency. History. The welfare of the republic.

That's his job now, and it requires sacrifice.

I don't know if there's anyone around him who can convince him that the attitude with which he's operated for 50 years must end, and something wholly new and different begin.

But whoever does must be aware of this:

The press, which wants to kill him, is going to zero in on his biggest weak spot: money, profit, the deal. Democrats, too, will watch like hawks. And this is understandable! Presidents shouldn't ever give the impression things aren't on the up and up. And Mr. Trump campaigned saying he'd dismantle the rigged system, drain the swamp, fight the racket.

The press does not believe, not for a second, and Democrats do not believe, not for a second, that Mr. Trump will be able to change the habits of a lifetime. They are relying on it.

Mr. Trump shocked them by winning. He should shock them now with rectitude.

Financial sophisticates know and explain how complicated all this is. Mr. Trump can't establish a blind trust because blind trusts normally consist of stocks, bonds—liquid assets. Mr. Trump's wealth is in famous entities, in his brand. He knows where his buildings are, his past and current deals are.

He said when campaigning that if elected he'd turn the business over to his children. But that would require never talking to them about matters touching on the central family ethos: money, profit, the deal.

The editorial page of this newspaper offered a sound though difficult route: Mr. Trump should liquidate his stake in his company and put the proceeds in a true blind trust, in which the Trump children keep the assets in their name. He can "transfer more to them as long as he pays a hefty gift tax." A fire sale on real estate would no doubt be seized upon by buyers like Donald Trump—people looking for the greatest asset at the lowest price. But it's hard to see how any other plan would help Mr. Trump avoid endless accusations that he is enriching himself as president, that he is, in fact, a dopey kleptocrat who can't help doing what he does.

It would be a painful act, selling the business he loves and around which he has ordered his life. But there would be comfort in this: In doing the right thing, in denying his opponents a sword, in enhancing his stature and demonstrating that yes, he will sacrifice for his country.

That's pretty great comfort.

You've made your money. Now go be a patriot.

In Celebration of Modest Christmases Past

The Wall Street Journal: December 24, 2016

A long time ago in a country far, far away, America had less of everything and holidays were easier and more modest.

Only 50 and 60 years ago, well within human memory, Christmas was a plainer, simpler affair. Everyone—even the rich, but certainly the poor and in-between—had less. Because America had less. You'd get a sweater and socks instead of five toys, or five toys instead of 10. Technology was something that existed at places like NASA. No one's wish list had a hoverboard, an iPad, or a brightly wrapped drone. There were more big families, whose children understood that even Santa couldn't cover them all.

You could *make* gifts. Or you could buy one after saving up, and the recipient could guess the sacrifice involved. And because there were fewer gifts, the one you got made a big impression.

And so a nod to the more modest Christmases of years past. These memories came with a declared or implied, "We didn't have much, but..." And this was said not with resentment or self-pity but a kind of pride and wistfulness.

For the New York businessman Vin Pica, one Christmas stands out. "All I wanted was a wooden Daniel Boone 'musket,' " he says, like the one Fess Parker slung over his shoulder as he walked through the woods. "I mentioned it at dinner Christmas Eve, and my father mysteriously disappeared, and magically, the next morning, on Dec. 25, 1959, it was under the tree..."

Here is a friend of mine, from a large Irish Catholic family in New Jersey—seven kids, no money. She is in her 60s now, but still shy about revisiting those days. She doesn't recall any specific gifts she received—"It wasn't like we were going to get a smartphone, it wasn't like that"—but she remembers the time the baby of the family, Cathy, age 5, let everyone know Santa was going to give her something very special.

But Cathy wouldn't tell anyone what it was. On Christmas Eve, her resourceful mother finally told her to write Santa a thank-you note and put it under the tree. She did, and later her mother peeked at the note: Cathy thanked Santa for the "bride doll" that he had hidden for her in the bookcase. But it was Christmas Eve—the stores were closed. After Cathy went to bed, one of my friend's other sisters remembered a pile of old dolls down in the basement. "We found a doll, cleaned it, found a dress, washed and ironed," my friend recalls. "We combed the hair, we gave it earrings and jewelry." At dawn, Cathy ran down the stairs and found in the back of the bookcase the beautiful doll she knew would be there.

Susan Woodbury and I were best friends in Massapequa, N.Y., when we were 12. All she wanted when she was 10 or 11 was a wooden guitar. In the weeks before Christmas, she ransacked the house, looking under beds, steeling herself for disappointment. "My mother rarely gave me what I wanted, but what she thought I should have," Susan says. Then she found it, in the back of her parents' closet: "It was a blond-wood guitar with this great knotty finish on the back, and simple strings." Christmas morning it was under the tree, covered by a towel. Susan enacted surprise. "I should have won an Academy Award."

The New York attorney Lloyd Green was a kid in the 1970s in Borough Park, Brooklyn. "My favorite Hanukkah memory was my folks gave me Strat-O-Matic Baseball as a gift, a stats-filled board game. Come Shabbat afternoon, my friends and I would play it for hours, until we had to attend afternoon worship. The game gave me a lifelong appreciation for baseball, and for numbers telling a story...Mom, Dad, and Hanukkah, thank you."

Kathy Enright and I were in high school together. Her father was in the Navy and often away. "When I was 8 years old in Hacketstown, N.J.," Kathy recalls, "there was a Pink Lady bike by Schwinn in the window of a store. I wanted it so badly and my mother said, 'We can't afford it, we can't afford it.' Mostly I got shoes and socks and underwear, things that we needed that were practical." And yet that Christmas Eve, "I walked into the living room and my Pink Lady bike was in front of the Christmas tree. I rode it until I graduated high school."

The stories got me thinking this week of the little book that has the best Christmas scene since Charles Dickens, *A Tree Grows in Brooklyn*, by Betty Smith. Francie and her brother, Neeley, are in grade school. Their family can't afford a Christmas tree, but then a chance arises. The guy who sells Christmas trees down the block always has a few scrawny ones left by midnight Christmas Eve, and to get rid of them he has an annual Christmas Tree Throw. Poor kids and poor fathers gather on the street every year, and the salesman heaves a tree up in the air—if you can catch it and don't fall, it's yours. Francie and Neeley stand on the cold, snowy pavement, steady themselves, catch a tree...and keep their footing. It's theirs. They march it triumphantly upstairs to their tenement apartment, and on the way the neighbors, hearing the commotion, poke their heads out their doors, saying, "Congratulations!" and "Merry Christmas!" And Francie's family stood the tree in a big tin bucket. There were no ornaments, "but the big tree standing there was enough."

My favorite gift of childhood was so surprising and moving and big. I was 9 or 10 and badly wanted a desk. I needed a desk because I had been selling neighborhood subscriptions to a local weekly newspaper called, as I remember it, the *Massapequa Post*. My success convinced me that I would someday be a great newspaper executive. I noticed in the old movies that played on channel 9 that what were then called career women—Rosalind Russell and Katharine Hepburn played those parts—often had a long, triangular nameplate on their desks. I made one for myself out of cardboard at school. Now all I needed was the desk. But such a piece of furniture was too expensive, too much to ask for in a family of nine.

I was in a religious phase, however, and prayed. And on Christmas morning, there beside the tree was a rough, oblong piece of beige plywood stapled or nailed to two pieces of plywood supporting it on either side. And if you looked at it with imagination, it looked exactly like...a desk. I was in heaven. I got a kitchen chair, sat at the desk and closed my eyes and thanked God. Then, suddenly, with my eyes closed, in my imagination, I saw it. Everything. There was a manger in the darkness and a man and a woman, and it was cold and there were stars in the sky, and hills, and wise men came with staffs and gazed in wonder. I saw it all, as if on film in a newsreel. It hit me like an electric bolt. I thought: "It's all true. It really happened. I just saw it."

I never forgot it, of course, and in later years, teaching catechism classes, I'd say at the end, "All you have to do is remember: It's all true. It really happened. Just keep that in your mind."

To be given a moment like that and take it through your life— that was some kind of gift.

Acknowledgments

Many to thank:

At the *Wall Street Journal* the redoubtable James Taranto, my editor of fifteen years; the chief of the editorial page, Paul Gigot; editorial features editor Mark Lasswell, and his predecessors, Tunku Varadarajan and Max Boot; deputy editorial features editor Howard Dickman; and Rupert Murdoch. Thanks too to the production editor Angela Morris, arts/graphics editor Kate LaVoie, and the artists whose work has given such a lift to mine, including Martin Kozlowski and Chad Crowe. At *Forbes* I thank my friend of many years Steve Forbes, and the memory of Jim Michaels. At CBS, my thanks to David Rhodes.

At Twelve, a group of professionals do what they do brilliantly, with judgment, creativity and dispatch. I don't think I've ever seen a book come together so seamlessly, and as such a coordinated group effort. My gratitude to my editor, Sean Desmond, who's both old school (he reads the manuscript then reads it again, pursues the vision, keeps it all going) and new (a marked appreciation for the lay of the technological land). He is a great professional operating within a great calling. Thanks also to Twelve's publisher, Deb Futter, as charming as she is committed, and to my friends Brian McLendon, Paul Samuelson, Libby Burton, the trained poet, Bailey Donoghue, Catherine Casalino, Yasmin Mathew, Antoinette Marotta, and Thomas Whatley. I thank Jamie Raab, the president of Grand

Central Publishing, and Michael Pietsch, the CEO of Hachette Book Group, for employing all of them and joining so enthusiastically in this venture.

Dana Perino, former press secretary to president George W. Bush, is so beautiful and funny people are sometimes startled at how wise she is, how piercing her intelligence. She helped shepherd this book along with Bob Barnett, a peerless guide and advisor who doesn't necessarily mean to become your good friend and does. He cares about how the project goes and sticks with it beginning to end.

I have for 25 years been thanking the same group of friends for their encouragement, affection and generosity. They're still here. I thank them again.

Index

About the Author

Peggy Noonan is the bestselling author of nine books and a weekly columnist for the *Wall Street Journal*. She lives in New York City.